CORPORATE INNOVATION

Effectiveness is the underlying theme for this introduction to disruptive innovation. The book tells the manager, or student, what they need to know in transforming the thinking in an organization to an innovative mindset in the twenty-first century.

Corporate Innovation explains the four stages of the innovation process, and demonstrates how to improve skills in the innovation process, and unleash personal innovative abilities. This book also presents ways to assess the organization's attitudes toward innovation, providing insights into how to diagnose creative and innovative performance problems in the organization. Beginning with an overview of concepts involved with an innovative organization today, this book explores the fundamental aspects of the individual, the organization and the implementation. An I-Organization is a combination of:

- I-Skills developed within individuals
- I-Design thinking functions needed to shape innovation
- I-Teams that emerge from the HR perspective of structuring the appropriate climate
- I-Solution needed to provide a foundation for implementing any innovative ideas.

Essential reading for students of corporate innovation, corporate ventures, corporate strategy, or human resources, this book also speaks to the specific needs of active managers charged with the expectation of enhancing the innovative prowess of their organization.

Instructors' outlines, lecture slides, and a test bank round out the ancillary online resources for this title.

Donald F. Kuratko is the Jack M. Gill Distinguished Chair and Professor of Entrepreneurship at Indiana University-Bloomington, USA.

Michael G. Goldsby is the Chief Entrepreneurship Officer and Stoops Distinguished Professor of Entrepreneurship at Ball State University, USA.

Jeffrey S. Hornsby is the Henry W. Bloch/Missouri Endowed Chair of Entrepreneurship at University of Missouri-Kansas City, USA.

CORPORATE INNOVATION

Disruptive Thinking in Organizations

Donald F. Kuratko, Michael G. Goldsby, and Jeffrey S. Hornsby

Routledge
Taylor & Francis Group

NEW YORK AND LONDON

First published 2019
by Routledge
52 Vanderbilt Avenue, New York, NY 10017

and by Routledge
2 Park Square, Milton Park, Abingdon, Oxon, OX14 4RN

Routledge is an imprint of the Taylor & Francis Group, an informa business

Library of Congress Cataloging in Publication Data
A catalog record has been requested for this book.

ISBN: 978-1-138-59404-3 (hbk)
ISBN: 978-1-138-59405-0 (pbk)
ISBN: 978-0-429-48914-3 (ebk)

Typeset in Bembo
by Swales & Willis Ltd, Exeter, Devon, UK

Visit the eResource: www.routledge.com/9781138594050

To my wife Debbie and my daughters Christina and Kellie, who have been the light of my life and the inspiration for all my career accomplishments.

—Donald F. Kuratko

To my grandparents, Ivis and Mary Ann McNeely and Nora Ellen Goldsby, who provided support and encouragement at every stage of my life and career.

—Michael G. Goldsby

With loving thanks to my wife Peg and children Dan, Brigid, and Michael. Your love and support are major reasons for my accomplishments.

—Jeffrey S. Hornsby

CONTENTS

PREFACE

Disruptive Innovation in Organizations

Whether you want to become a successful innovator within your organization or develop an environment that spawns an innovative mindset, this book can be helpful to you. Accomplished entrepreneurs create successful new ventures and implement them successfully. To do this consistently takes a blend of entrepreneurship, creativity, innovation and knowing how to make teams work effectively. The concepts behind corporate innovation mirror many of these same principles.

This book will help you develop an understanding of an innovative organization, the specific processes involved in corporate innovation, and how to assess your organization's readiness for entrepreneurial activity and innovation. It will help you learn how to get more ideas successfully to market and how to write effective innovation plans for the implementation of innovative ideas. As opposed to simply entrepreneurship or technology entrepreneurship, the principal focus of this book will be new product and service innovations. What distinguishes structures for innovation from the processes for innovation will be explored. The corporate innovation process chapter will examine the various stage gate and other non-linear models in the new product development literature. Finally, since it is about "disruption" in today's industries, we explore the outcomes that are being accelerated and specify the kinds of metrics that are involved.

Innovation has long been associated with entrepreneurship and now it is an imperative for organizations to grasp. This book helps you to understand innovation by explaining the four stages of the innovation process, how to improve your skills in the innovation process, and unleash your personal innovative abilities. In addition, you will find ways to assess the organization's attitudes toward innovation, giving you insights into how to diagnose creative and innovative performance problems in the organization.

For specific areas of interest, we present a quick guide for subtopics within the book.

If your area of interest is to . . .	*Read Chapter(s)*
• get a basic understanding of an innovative organization (I-Organization)	Preface, 1, 2
• understand the process of corporate innovation and innovative design	2, 5, 6
• learn about individual ideation and innovation (I-Skills)	3, 4
• develop excellent innovation teams (I-Teams)	8, 9
• increase the innovative performance in an organization	3, 4, 5, 6, 7
• get more new ideas successfully to market	7, 10, 12
• learn analytics to measure innovative readiness	
• write effective innovation plans	11

Objectives of the Book

Corporate Innovation provides an introduction to transforming an organization from the "old" way of thinking to the newer "innovative" ways of thinking and acting. The basic fundamentals of integrating and managing an innovative climate within the organization are explored. This book was developed based on the concepts needed for handling disruptive innovation confronting any organization. Transforming into an innovative organization requires a combination of the needed innovative skills that must be developed. Beginning with the general understanding of concepts involved with an innovative organization today, this book then explores the fundamental aspects of the individual, the organization and the implementation. An *I-Organization* is a combination of *I-Skills* developed within individuals, the *I-Design* thinking functions needed to shape innovation, the *I-Teams* that emerge from the HR perspective of structuring the appropriate climate, and the *I-Solution* needed to provide a foundation for implementing any innovative ideas. The book is designed for collegiate or executive education markets. This text is designed for courses in corporate innovation, corporate ventures, corporate strategy, or human resources that involve three distinct but related constituencies. First, the textbook is designed to be useful to professors who related the latest research to each topic as they teach the course. Second, the textbook has been written for students to *read*. The subject matter is presented in an interesting, easy-to-understand style. Finally, the specific needs of active managers charged with the expectation of enhancing the innovative prowess of their organization have been considered. The book's coverage of the key aspects of developing and implementing innovation from the employees' perspective will help them to improve their management effectiveness on the job. Thus, the chapters ahead provide deeper insights into the ways in which twenty-first-century organizations can handle disruptive innovation by transforming their thinking towards continual innovative performance.

Distinguishing Features

A number of distinguishing features make this book informative, up to date, and useful.

Comprehensive Organization

The book has four distinct parts. Each part has a unique subtitle to indicate to the student or practicing manager what is really involved in the chapters ahead.

Part 1 includes an introduction that provides an examination of the challenges of disruptive innovations that are plaguing today's organizations. We use the term *I-Challenge* to signify the new challenges awaiting managers. Part 1 then discusses the various ways individuals find innovative opportunities in organizations through the basic concepts of entrepreneurial thinking. The overall process of corporate innovation and entrepreneurship is discussed from the standpoint of new product and service innovations. We have called this entire part the *I-Organization* in order to characterize the overall nature of the chapters.

Part 2 presents the ideation and innovation techniques from an individual perspective. Individual creativity and innovative skills are highlighted in these chapters. We have called this part *I-Skills*, which describes the emphasis placed on the development of skills. How these skills transfer to the process of innovation is a focus of this part.

Part 3 outlines the elements of design thinking that are needed for innovation. The design thinking process stages of *define, research, ideate, prototype, choose, implement*, and *learn* are covered. This *I-Design* part focuses on how to shape and model the innovative idea into tangible form for customer development and lean start-up.

Part 4 explains the elements needed from an organizational or corporate environment perspective. The climate, structure and HR challenges are all examined in this part. The basic structures used for new product and new process innovations are also examined. We call this part *I-Teams* to signify the focus on development of the right personnel in the right form in order to advance innovation.

Part 5 deals with the implementation of innovative ideas. This part focuses on understanding some key analytics that can be used to measure innovative readiness as well as how ideas move from initial stages to commercialization (or market). "Accelerating" innovation will be explored from the outcomes perspective with specific metrics presented. Developing effective innovative venture plans is presented in order to have a final tool that can be used for eventual implementation. This indicates the level of emphasis placed on the planning approach in the implementation of innovation.

In addition this part focuses on the challenge of maintaining the momentum in an organization once innovation begins. Attention is directed to unique challenges confronting managers from a human resource perspective as well as a strategic perspective. We call this part *I-Solution* to represent the final conclusion of this book.

The subject matter of the book moves from consideration of innovative organizations in general to the very specific needs of individual managers charged with this challenge. The underlying theme is effectiveness; that is, the book tells the manager what they need to know in transforming the thinking in an organization to an innovative mindset in the twenty-first century.

Pedagogical Aids

Illustrations

Numerous tables, charts, and exhibits present data, summarize information, and reinforce important concepts.

Italicized Terms

Key terms and concepts are highlighted with italics when they are introduced and explained.

Chapter Summaries

Every chapter concludes with a concise, point-by-point summary of key topics.

Review and Discussion Questions

Relevant questions address the major chapter concepts at the end of each chapter.

Suggestions for Further Reading

Numerous notes refer readers to primary sources of information—most of them journal articles. These readings can be used to supplement the book material and as sources of information for writing projects.

Index

A comprehensive index helps students locate information and specific names efficiently.

PowerPoint Slide Deck (available online)

A complete set of PowerPoint slides to assist instructors cover the critical elements of each chapter.

Instructor's Manual

A set of lecture outlines and complete test bank will accompany this book.

Interest-Based Features

Innovation-in-Action

To stimulate the thinking of innovation within organizations, the story of a successful innovative company is featured in each chapter. Many of these boxed inserts have been adapted from key innovative companies featured in *Fortune*, *Business Week*, *FSB*, and *Fast Company* magazines or websites.

A List of Suggested Innovation Cases

At the end of the book in the Appendix is a list of suggested case studies with information for how to obtain them. The problems posed in these cases are comprehensive and they call for the application of all the material in the chapters as well as the student's experience and prior education.

A Complete Innovation Plan

A complete innovative venture plan (GSK in Africa) is provided at the end of the textbook. This is provided as a guide for the manager searching for the exact look and style of a successful plan.

ACKNOWLEDGMENTS

We are grateful to a number of individuals in the development of this book. First, our deepest appreciation goes to our families, from whom we took away so much time to pursue this project. Our wives, Debbie, Peg, and Beth, have our love and gratitude for their support and motivation for all of our publishing endeavors. Second, our respective centers, the Johnson Center for Entrepreneurship & Innovation at Indiana University's Kelley School of Business, the John H. Schnatter Institute for Entrepreneurship and Free Enterprise at Ball State University, and the Regnier Institute for Entrepreneurship & Innovation at the UMKC's Henry W. Bloch School of Management, for their continued support of our entrepreneurial endeavors. Third, specific individuals that provided invaluable contributions and deserve special recognition would include: Sandy Martin and Mandy Priest from the Johnson Center for Entrepreneurship & Innovation at Indiana University's Kelley School of Business; Dr. Rob Mathews and Margo Allen from the John H. Schnatter Institute for Entrepreneurship and Free Enterprise; and the Student Ambassadors from the Regnier Institute for Entrepreneurship & Innovation at the UMKC's Henry W. Bloch School of Management. Finally, the professional editing team at Routledge/Taylor & Francis Group including: Meredith Norwich, Senior Editor; Erin Arata, Editorial Assistant; and Cathy Hurren, Senior Production Editor. Our deepest gratitude to all of these professionals who helped turn this book into a reality. Finally we express our gratitude to our Deans at Indiana University (Idie F. Kesner), Ball State University (Jennifer P. Bott), and University of Missouri-Kansas City (Brian Klaas), who have supported our innovative efforts.

Dr. Donald F. Kuratko
Indiana University
Dr. Michael G. Goldsby
Ball State University
Dr. Jeffrey S. Hornsby
University of Missouri-Kansas City

ABOUT THE AUTHORS

Dr. Donald F. Kuratko (known as Dr. K) is the Jack M. Gill Distinguished Chair of Entrepreneurship; Professor of Entrepreneurship; Executive & Academic Director, Johnson Center for Entrepreneurship & Innovation, The Kelley School of Business, Indiana University–Bloomington. Dr. Kuratko is considered a prominent scholar and national leader in the field of entrepreneurship. He has published over 200 articles on aspects of entrepreneurship, new venture development, and corporate entrepreneurship. His work has been published in journals such as *Strategic Management Journal, Academy of Management Executive, Journal of Business Venturing, Entrepreneurship Theory & Practice, Journal of Operations Management, Journal of Product Innovation Management, Small Business Economics, Journal of Small Business Management, Family Business Review,* and the *Journal of Business Ethics.* Professor Kuratko has authored 30 books, including one of the leading entrepreneurship books in universities today, *Entrepreneurship: Theory, Process, Practice,* 10th ed. (Cengage/SouthWestern Publishers, 2017), as well as *New Venture Management,* 2nd ed. (Routledge, 2018), *Corporate Entrepreneurship & Innovation,* 3rd ed. (South-Western/Thomson Publishers, 2011), *Innovation Acceleration* (Pearson/Prentice Hall Publishers, 2012), and *Entrepreneurial Leadership* (Edward Elgar Publishers, 2013). In addition, Dr. Kuratko has been consultant on corporate innovation and entrepreneurial strategies to a number of major corporations. Dr. Kuratko was also the co-founder and served as Executive Director of the Global Consortium of Entrepreneurship Centers (GCEC), an organization comprising over 300 top university entrepreneurship centers throughout the world. Under Professor Kuratko's leadership and with one of the most prolific entrepreneurship faculties in the world, Indiana University's Entrepreneurship Program has consistently been ranked as the number 1 university for entrepreneurship research by the *Global Entrepreneurship Productivity Rankings;* number 1 university for Global Entrepreneurship Research in a *Journal of Small Business Management 12 year analysis for entrepreneurship research productivity;* the number 1 University Entrepreneurship Program in the United States (public universities) by *Fortune;* as well as the number 1 Graduate Business School and the number 1 Undergraduate Business School for Entrepreneurship (Public Institutions) by *U.S. News & World Report*. In addition, Indiana University was awarded the National Model MBA Program in Entrepreneurship for the MBA Program in Entrepreneurship & Innovation. Professor Kuratko's honors include the George Washington Medal of Honor; the Leavey Foundation Award for Excellence in Private Enterprise; the NFIB Entrepreneurship Excellence Award; and the National Model Innovative Pedagogy Award for Entrepreneurship. In addition, he was named the National Outstanding Entrepreneurship Educator by the U.S. Association for Small Business and Entrepreneurship; selected as a USASBE/Justin Longenecker Fellow; named one of the Top Entrepreneurship Professors in the United States by *Fortune*; and named a 21st Century Entrepreneurship Research Fellow by the Global Consortium of Entrepreneurship Centers. Dr. Kuratko was honored by his peers in *Entrepreneur* magazine as one of the Top Entrepreneurship Program Directors in the nation for three consecutive years, including the number 1 Entrepreneurship Program Director in the nation. The U.S. Association for Small Business & Entrepreneurship honored him with the John E. Hughes Entrepreneurial Advocacy Award for his career achievements in entrepreneurship and the National Academy of Management honored Dr. Kuratko with the Entrepreneurship Advocate Award for his career contributions to the development and advancement of the discipline of entrepreneurship. Professor Kuratko has been named one of the Top 25 Entrepreneurship Scholars in the world and was the recipient of the Riata Distinguished Entrepreneurship Scholar Award. He was the inaugural recipient of the Karl Vesper Entrepreneurship Pioneer Award for his career dedication to developing the field of entrepreneurship and in 2014 he was honored by the National Academy of Management with the Entrepreneurship Mentor Award for his exemplary mentorship to the next generation of entrepreneurship

Dr. Michael G. Goldsby is the Chief Entrepreneurship Officer, Executive Director of the John H. Schnatter Institute for Entrepreneurship and Free Enterprise, the Stoops Distinguished Professor of Entrepreneurship, Professor of Management, and Director Emeritus of the Entrepreneurship Center and Program at Ball State University. He teaches creativity, innovation, and design in the university's nationally ranked undergraduate and graduate programs in entrepreneurship. Ball State University's Entrepreneurship Program and Center earned national rankings under his leadership, including: top 20 in *Business Week*, *Success*, and *Entrepreneur* magazines; and top 10 in *U.S. News & World Report*'s elite ranking. Professor Goldsby has produced 35 refereed journal articles. He is also the co-author of *Innovation Acceleration* (Prentice Hall) and *Design-Centered Entrepreneurship* (Routledge). His research has been reported in many international media outlets, such as ABC, NBC, CBS, MSNBC, CNN, and the Associated Press. His study on entrepreneurship and fitness was covered by *Runner's World*, *Prevention Magazine*, *Muscle and Fitness*, and *Health Magazine*, among others. His video series *The Entrepreneur's Toolkit* was released by the Great Courses, and is available on DVD, CD, and digital download. The Great Courses is a professionally produced series of lectures featuring the top 1 percent of professors in the country in their area of expertise.

Dr. Goldsby attained his undergraduate degree in business economics and public policy from the Kelley School of Business at Indiana University, his master's degree in economics from Indiana State University, and his doctorate in strategic management and business ethics from the Pamplin College of Business at Virginia Tech. While at Virginia Tech, he was awarded the Jack Hoover Award for Teaching Excellence. Professor Goldsby is a certified Professional Innovation Advisor, holding Level IV certification with Basadur Applied Creativity. He is a member of many management professional organizations, and has served as vice president and a member of the board of directors for the United States Association of Small Business and Entrepreneurship (USASBE), of which he has received a distinguished service award. He also serves on the advisory board of the Ball State Innovation Corporation. He has been a co-principal investigator of three major research grants: The Ball State/U.S. State Department Entrepreneurship Project for Afghanistan, the U.S. Navy/Department of Defense Military 2 Market Technology Transfer Program, and the Launch Indiana Initiative with the Indiana Office of Small Business and Entrepreneurship and Office of the Lieutenant Governor. He is also the founding executive director of the John H. Schnatter Institute for Entrepreneurship and Free Enterprise.

Dr. Goldsby's current research interests focus on design, innovation, and applied creativity. In his spare time, Professor Goldsby enjoys athletic pursuits, such as running, triathlon, weightlifting, rock climbing, golfing, hiking, skiing, swimming, and cycling. He has completed 25 marathons, including eight Boston Marathons, and enjoys training and competing in Ironman triathlons.

Dr. Jeffrey S. Hornsby is the Executive Director of the Regnier Institute for Entrepreneurship and Innovation and Chair of the Department of Global Entrepreneurship and Innovation at the University of Missouri–Kansas City. He also holds the Henry Bloch/Missouri Endowed Chair of Entrepreneurship. He has authored or co-authored 75 refereed journal articles and 87 proceedings articles. His work has appeared in the top journals in entrepreneurship and management including *Strategic Management Journal, Journal of Applied Psychology, Journal of Business Venturing, Entrepreneurship Theory and Practice,* and *Journal of Operations Management.* His research has earned five conference "best paper awards." Recently, Dr. Hornsby and his co-authors were recipient of the *Journal of Operations Management* Ambassador Award for the best cross-discipline article in the past five years. It was awarded at the 2016 Academy of Management Meetings. In addition to this current book, Dr. Hornsby has co-authored six books, entitled: *New Venture Management, Innovation Acceleration: Transforming Organizational Thinking, New Venture Management: The Entrepreneur's Roadmap, The Human Resource Function in Emerging Enterprises, Frontline HR: A Handbook for the Emerging Manager,* and *Training Systems Management.* He is co-editor of the *Journal of Small Business Management.* Dr. Hornsby is currently on the board of the Global Consortium of Entrepreneurship Centers and the Collegiate Entrepreneurs Organization. He recently served as 2016 Conference Chair for the 2016 USASBE Conference in San Diego. He has consulted with entrepreneurial start-ups to Fortune 500 companies in the areas of business planning, leadership, human resources, high performance work systems, corporate entrepreneurship, creativity, and innovation. Dr. Hornsby received is bachelor's degree from Miami University, M.S. from Western Kentucky University and PhD from Auburn University.

Dr. Hornsby's awards and honors include: named the Entrepreneurship Educator of the Year for the University of Missouri System; recipient of the 2016 John E. Hughes Award for Entrepreneurial Advocacy by the United States Association of Small Business and Entrepreneurship; named a United States Association of Small Business and Entrepreneurship Longenecker Fellow; named Henry W. Bloch/Missouri Endowed Chair in Entrepreneurship and Innovation at UMKC 2013; named Jack Vanier Chair of Innovation and Entrepreneurship, Kansas State University 2008; founded the Center for the Advancement of Entrepreneurship at Kansas State University 2008; selected as the 2004 University Outstanding Faculty Member for Ball State University; Ball State University Graduation Commencement Speaker Summer 2005; and named Ball Distinguished Professor of Management, Ball State University 2004.

PART 1

The Innovative Organization (*I-Organization*)

1

UNDERSTANDING THE INNOVATIVE MINDSET

Wealth in the new regime flows directly from innovation, not optimization; that is, wealth is not gained by perfecting the known, but by imperfectly seizing the unknown.

~Kevin Kelly[1]

Introduction: The "I-Challenge"

We are all confronting a global innovation challenge. The development, application, and enhancement of new technologies are occurring at a breathtaking pace and innovation is determining the way business is being conducted. As the number of new ventures, products, technologies, and patents literally explodes worldwide, established companies can either become victims of this innovation challenge or they can answer the call. The world is in the midst of a new wave of disruption in every industry, with entrepreneurship and innovation as the catalysts.

The nature of business has been transformed in this fast-paced, highly threatening, and increasingly global environment. Dramatic and ongoing changes are forcing leaders of organizations to re-examine their basic purpose and to become much more innovative with their approach to multiple stakeholders. Organizations today must continually redefine their markets, restructure their operations, and disrupt their business models. Effective companies in the twenty-first century have made the fundamental discovery that innovation drives success.[2] The ability to continually innovate (to engage in an ongoing process of entrepreneurial actions) has become the source of competitive advantage.

While innovative actions are a phenomenon that have captivated the interest of executives in many corporate boardrooms, there is a danger that managers can get too caught up in the excitement of a particular innovation or inspiring stories of individual corporate innovators. It is easy to become enamored with the idea of innovation, but the true value of innovation lies in the extent to which it becomes a corporate strategy to create sustainable competitive advantage.[3] The early twenty-first century has been a time when innovative (or entrepreneurial) actions have been recognized widely as the path to competitive advantage and success in organizations of all types and sizes.[4] Moreover, a lack of innovative (or entrepreneurial) actions in today's global economy could be a recipe for failure.

In today's competitive landscape, the opportunities and threats happen swiftly and are relentless in their frequency, affecting virtually all parts of an organization simultaneously. The business environment is filled with ambiguity and discontinuity, and the rules of the game are subject to constant revision. The job of management effectively becomes one of continual experimentation—experimenting with new structures, new reward systems, new technologies, new methods, new products, new markets, and much more. The quest remains the same: sustainable competitive advantage. Innovation and entrepreneurial actions represent the guiding light and the motivating force for organizations as they attempt to find their way down this path.

Achieving innovation (and entrepreneurial actions) is not something that you as a manager can simply decide to do. Corporate innovation must be understood by each individual and there must be a realization that it does not produce instant success. It requires considerable training, time, and investment, and there must be continual reinforcement. By their nature, organizations impose constraints on innovative behavior. To be sustainable, innovative thinking must be integrated into the mission, goals, strategies, structure, processes, and values of the organization. The managerial mindset must become an opportunity-driven mindset, where actions are never constrained by resources currently controlled.[5] We call this the "innovative mindset."

Although some earlier researchers concluded that innovation (entrepreneurship) and bureaucracies were mutually exclusive and could not coexist,[6] today we find many researchers examining innovation within the enterprise framework.[7] Leading strategic thinkers are moving beyond the traditional product and service innovations to pioneering innovation in processes, value chains, business models, and all functions of management.[8] Thus, innovative attitudes and behaviors are necessary for firms of all sizes to prosper and flourish in competitive environments.

Developing a corporate innovative philosophy provides a number of advantages. One is that this type of atmosphere often leads to the development of new products and services and helps the organization expand and grow. A second is it creates a workforce that can help the enterprise maintain its competitive posture. A third is it promotes a climate conducive to high achievers and helps the enterprise motivate and keep its best people.

This new millennium has been characterized as an age of instant information, ever-increasing development and application of technology, disruptive changes, revolutionary processes, and global competition. It is now an age filled with turbulence and paradox. The key descriptive words used about this new "innovation challenge" of the twenty-first century are: *dreaming, creating, exploring, inventing, pioneering,* and *imagining!* We believe this is a point in time when the gap between what can be imagined and what can be accomplished has never been smaller. It is a time requiring innovative vision, courage, calculated risk-taking, and strong leadership. It is simply answering *"the innovative challenge of the twenty-first century."* Thus, the "I-Challenge" confronts all organizations today.

Innovative Thinking

The constantly changing economic environment provides a continuous flow of potential opportunities *if* an individual can recognize a profitable idea amid the chaos and cynicism that also permeates such an environment. Thousands of alternatives exist since every individual creates and develops ideas with a unique frame of reference. Thus, *innovative thinking* has become a critical skill for the twenty-first century. During the last two decades, the entrepreneurial flame has caught on throughout the world, with the world's economies searching for the free enterprise solution through innovative development.

However, *innovative thinking* goes beyond the mere creation of business. The characteristics of seeking opportunities, taking risks beyond security, and having the tenacity to push an idea through to reality combine into a special perspective that permeates innovative individuals. Innovative thinking can be developed in individuals. This mindset can be exhibited inside or outside an organization, in profit or not-for-profit enterprises, and in business or non-business activities for the purpose of bringing forth creative ideas. As one author stated, "Ideas come from people. Innovation is a capability of the many. That capability is utilized when people give commitment to the mission and life of the enterprise and have the power to do something with their capabilities."[9]

Thus, innovative thinking is an integrated mindset that permeates individuals and organizations in an effective manner. Let's examine exactly what innovation is and how this mindset can be nurtured in individuals.

The Concept of Innovation

Innovation, Creativity, and Entrepreneurship

The terms *entrepreneurship, creativity,* and *innovation* are sometimes used interchangeably, and while that is understandable, it can be misleading. Creativity and innovation are very similar concepts, but there are some differences. Creativity is typically described as the process of generating new ideas, while innovation takes creativity a step further by being a process that turns those ideas into reality. Innovation is often the basis on which entrepreneurship is built because of the competitive advantage it provides. Innovation is a key function in the entrepreneurial process. Researchers and authors in the field of innovation and entrepreneurship are, for the most part, in agreement with renowned consultant and author Peter F. Drucker about the concept of innovation:

> *Innovation is the specific function of entrepreneurship. . . . It is the means by which the entrepreneur either creates new wealth-producing resources or endows existing resources with enhanced potential for creating wealth.*[10]

Thus, innovation is the process by which entrepreneurs convert opportunities (ideas) into marketable solutions. Innovation is a process that transforms ideas into outputs. It is the means by which entrepreneurs become catalysts for change.[11] The emerging perspective by researchers in the field of innovation is to define innovation in the broadest context possible, as in this specific example:

> *Innovation is the process of making changes, large and small, radical and incremental, to products, processes, and services that results in the introduction of something new for the organization that adds value to customers and contributes to the knowledge store of the organization.*[12]

There are numerous alternative definitions of *innovation*. One popular alternative is to present innovation as an invention that has been exploited commercially.[13] Innovation can also be viewed as the systematic approach to creating an environment based on creative discovery, invention, and commercial exploitation of ideas that meet unmet needs. However, there are millions of innovations that are often much smaller in scale, do not involve an invention, or are not necessarily exploited in the same commercial sense. Therefore, one simplified alternative definition might be:

> *Innovation = Creativity + Exploitation*

In this sense innovation becomes the composition of creative thoughts and the determination to implement those ideas into a marketable concept. Since there are numerous ways in which individuals apply creative thoughts into exploitation of opportunities, there also are numerous ways to categorize innovation.

Categorizing Innovation

Types

The term *innovation* can be associated with physical products, processes that make products, services that deliver products, and services that provide intangible products. Thus, the basic types of innovation relate to products, processes, and services.

Product innovation is about making beneficial changes to physical products.

Process innovation is about making beneficial changes to the processes that produce products or services.

Service innovation is about making beneficial changes to services that customers use.

Methods

Whether it is product, process, or service, there are four basic methods that describe the ways that innovation will take place. These extend from new inventions to modifications of existing products or services. In order of originality, these are the four methods:

- *Invention:* the creation of a new product, service, or process, often one that is novel or untried. Such concepts tend to be "revolutionary."
- *Extension:* the expansion of a product, service, or process already in existence. Such concepts make a different application of a current idea.
- *Duplication:* the replication of an already existing product, service, or process. The duplication effort, however, is not simply copying but adding the entrepreneur's own creative touch to enhance or improve the concept to beat the competition.
- *Synthesis:* the combination of existing concepts and factors into a new formulation. This involves taking a number of ideas or items already invented and finding a way so together they form a new application.[14]

Trajectories

The final way to categorize innovation is through the trajectory that the innovation takes. In this manner there are three major trajectories for innovation: radical, incremental, and disruptive.

Radical innovation is the launching of inaugural breakthroughs such as personal computers and overnight mail delivery. These innovations take experimentation and determined vision, which are not necessarily managed but *must* be recognized and nurtured. These are considered changes at a significant magnitude. The term *radical* often refers to the level of contribution made to the efficiency or revenue of the organization.[15] Radical innovation can transform the industry itself by changing the existing market and developing the next industry wave.[16] Undertaking radical innovation can bring dramatic benefits for an organization in terms of increased sales and profits, but it also carries intensive resource requirements as well as greater risk. Consider pharmaceutical companies that can invest more than $1 billion in drug development with no guarantee that it will ever make it to the marketplace. However, one major drug breakthrough could be worth billions of dollars every year once it makes the marketplace.

Incremental innovation refers to the systematic evolution of a product or service into newer or larger markets. Examples include the typical improvements and advances in current products and services. Many times the incremental innovation will take over after a radical innovation introduces a breakthrough. The structure, marketing, financing, and formal systems of a corporation can help implement incremental innovation. Although radical innovations often make headlines, most organizations spread the risk associated with innovation by also looking for incremental innovations to their products, processes, and services. Incremental innovation is less ambitious in its scope and offers less potential for financial gains to the organization, but consequently the associated risks are reduced. Incremental innovations consist of smaller initiatives, making them easier to manage than their radical counterparts. However, organizations may have to undertake numerous incremental innovations to achieve the necessary growth.

Disruptive innovation goes beyond radical innovation and transforms business practice to rewrite the rules of an industry. In other words, the business practice of an entire industrial sector could be changed radically. Disruptive innovation often occurs because new sciences and technology are introduced or applied to a new market that offers the potential to exceed the existing limits of technology.[17] (The largest modern disruptive technology to emerge has been the Internet.) Research laboratories and universities are usually a good source of disruptive technologies. Many companies work in cooperation with universities in order to develop the latest disruptive technologies, which can take many years to develop, wait for the outcome of this type of technology, and choose the potential successes that demonstrate market adoption. Organizations must be careful in pursuing the correct disruptive innovations to pursue because the wrong technology can waste scarce resources and place the organization in a position of significant competitive disadvantage. Researchers note that organizations often struggle to achieve a successful balance between developing radical and disruptive innovations while still protecting their traditional business operations.[18]

Misconceptions of Innovation

The entire concept of innovation conjures up many thoughts and misconceptions. It seems everyone has an opinion as to what innovation entails. We present some of the commonly accepted innovation misconceptions, along with reasons why these are misconceptions and not facts:[19]

- *Innovation is planned and predictable.* This statement is based on the old concept that innovation should be left to the research and development (R&D) department under a planned format. In truth, innovation is unpredictable and may be introduced by anyone.
- *Technical specifications must be thoroughly prepared.* This statement comes from the engineering arena, which drafts complete plans before moving on. Thorough preparation is good, but it can sometimes take too long. Quite often it is more important to use a try/test/revise approach.
- *Big projects will develop better innovations than smaller ones.* This statement has been proven false time and time again. Larger firms are now encouraging their people to work in smaller groups, where it often is easier to generate creative ideas.
- *Technology is the driving force of innovation success.* Technology is certainly one source for innovation, but it is not the only one. There are numerous sources for innovative ideas, and while technology is certainly a driving factor in many innovations, it is not the only success factor. Moreover, the customer or market is the driving force behind any innovation. Market-driven or customer-based innovations have the highest probability of success.

Innovation and Learning

Innovation is a process that needs to be managed within an organization. This includes activities such as encouraging ideas, defining goals, prioritizing projects, improving communications, and motivating teams. For organizations to sustain their mission, they must continuously innovate and replace existing products, processes, and services with more effective ones. Focusing on innovation as a continuous process acknowledges the effect that learning has on knowledge creation within the organization. Learning how to innovate effectively entails managing knowledge within the organization and offers the potential to enhance the way the organization innovates.

In addition, entrepreneurs must "learn" from their experiences as well. An organization that can continuously learn and adapt its behavior to external stimuli does so by continuously adding to its collective knowledge store. Researcher Andrew C. Corbett has identified the importance of acquiring and transforming the information and knowledge through the learning process. His research was able to lend credence to the theories about the cognitive ability of individuals to transform information into recognizable opportunities.[20] So, how an organization acquires, processes, and learns from the prior knowledge that it has gained is critical to the complete innovation process.

The Innovative Mindset In Individuals

In recognizing the importance of the evolution of innovative thinking into the twenty-first century, one integrated definition of entrepreneurship acknowledges the critical factors needed for this phenomenon:

> *Entrepreneurship is a dynamic process of vision, change, and innovation. It requires an application of energy and passion towards the creation and implementation of new ideas and creative solutions. Essential ingredients include the willingness to take calculated risks—in terms of time, equity, or career; the ability to formulate an effective venture team; the creative skill to marshal needed resources; the fundamental skill of building a solid business plan; and, finally, the vision to recognize opportunity where others see chaos, contradiction, and confusion.*[21]

This definition demonstrates that innovative ability is a process that each and every individual could choose to pursue. Today's current generation of the twenty-first century may become known as "Generation E" because they are becoming the most entrepreneurial and innovative generation since the Industrial Revolution. Every person has the potential to pursue their ideas and become an innovator. Exactly what motivates individuals to make a choice for innovative thinking has not been identified, at least not as one single event, characteristic, or trait. However, there has been some research associated with specific skills and characteristics.

In the simplest of theoretical forms for studying innovation, innovators cause innovation. That is, $I = f(i)$ states that innovation is a function of the innovator. Thus, an examination of known entrepreneurial or innovative characteristics does help in the evolving understanding of innovative thinking. Below are some of the most commonly cited characteristics.

Determination and perseverance: more than any other factor, a total dedication to success as an innovator can overcome obstacles and setbacks. Sheer determination and an unwavering commitment to succeed often win out against odds that many people would consider insurmountable. They can also compensate for personal shortcomings.

Achievement drive: innovators are self-starters who appear to others to be internally driven by a strong desire to compete, to excel against self-imposed standards, and to pursue and attain challenging goals. This need to achieve has been well documented, beginning with David McClelland's pioneering work on motivation in the 1950s and 1960s.[22] High achievers tend to be moderate risk takers. They examine a situation, determine how to increase the odds of winning, and then push ahead. As a result, high-risk decisions for the average businessperson often are moderate risks for the well-prepared high achiever.

Goal orientation: one clear pattern among innovators is their focus on opportunity rather than on resources, structure, or strategy. They start with the opportunity and let their understanding of it guide other important issues. They are goal oriented in their pursuit of opportunities. Setting high but attainable goals enables them to focus their energies, to selectively sort out opportunities, and to know when to say "no." Their goal orientation also helps them to define priorities and provides them with measures of how well they are performing.

Internal locus of control: successful innovators do not believe the success or failure of their idea will be governed by fate, luck, or similar forces. They believe their accomplishments and setbacks are within their own control and influence and they can affect the outcome of their actions. This attribute is consistent with a high-achievement motivational drive, the desire to take personal responsibility, and self-confidence.

Tolerance for ambiguity: innovators face uncertainty compounded by constant changes that introduce ambiguity and stress into every aspect of the innovation. Setbacks and surprises are inevitable; lack of organization, structure, and order is a way of life. Yet successful innovators thrive on the fluidity and excitement of such an ambiguous existence.

Calculated risk taking: as discussed in the "myths" section below, successful innovators are not high-rolling gamblers. When they decide to explore an idea, they do so in a very calculated, carefully thought-out manner. They do everything possible to get the odds in their favor, and they often avoid taking unnecessary risks. These strategies include getting others to share inherent financial and business risks with them.

Tolerance for failure: innovators use failure as a learning experience. The iterative, trial-and-error nature of becoming a successful innovator makes serious setbacks and disappointments an integral part of the learning process. The most effective innovators are realistic enough to expect such difficulties. Furthermore, they do not become disappointed, discouraged, or depressed by a setback or failure. Many of them believe they learn more from their early failures than from their early successes.

High energy level: the extraordinary workloads and the stressful demands innovators may face place a premium on energy. Many innovators fine-tune their energy levels by carefully monitoring what they eat and drink, establishing exercise routines, and knowing when to get away for relaxation.

Creativity: creativity was once regarded as an exclusively inherited trait. Judging by the level of creativity and innovation in the United States compared with that of equally sophisticated but less creative and innovative cultures, it appears unlikely this trait is solely genetic. An expanding school of thought believes creativity can be learned. Innovations often have a collective creativity that emerges from the joint efforts of teams of individuals.

Vision: innovators need to have a vision or concept of what their idea can be. Not all innovators have predetermined visions for their innovations. In many cases this vision develops over time as the individual begins to realize what the firm is and what it can become.

Researchers have continued to examine the psychological and cognitive aspects of entrepreneurs which have helped to expand our understanding of the innovative mindset.[23] New characteristics are continually being added to this ever-growing list. At this point, however, let us examine some of the most often cited entrepreneurial characteristics. Although this list admittedly is incomplete, it does provide important insights into the innovative mindset.[24]

The Motivation for Innovation

Although innovation can be characterized as the interaction of the skills that we listed in the previous section, it is the "motivation" towards innovative behavior that is most important.

The quest for innovative thinking as well as the willingness to *sustain* that thinking is directly related to an individual's *entrepreneurial motivation*. In that vein, one research approach examines the motivational process an entrepreneur experiences.[25] Examining the motivation to sustain entrepreneurial behavior is an effective analogy to the process of innovative behavior. Figure 1.1 illustrates the key elements of this approach.

The decision to behave entrepreneurially (or innovatively) is the result of the interaction of several factors. One set of factors includes the individual's personal characteristics, the individual's personal environment, the relevant business environment, the individual's personal goal set, and the existence of a viable business idea.[26] In addition, the individual compares their perception of the probable outcomes with the personal expectations they have in mind. Next, an individual looks at the relationship between the entrepreneurial (or innovative) behavior they would implement and the expected outcomes.

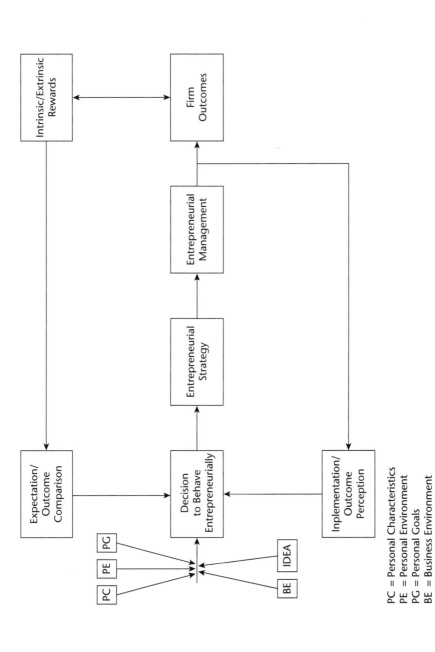

PC = Personal Characteristics
PE = Personal Environment
PG = Personal Goals
BE = Business Environment

FIGURE 1.1 A Model of Entrepreneurial Motivation.

According to the model, the entrepreneur's expectations are finally compared with the actual or perceived firm outcomes. Future entrepreneurial (innovative) behavior is based on the results of all of these comparisons. When outcomes meet or exceed expectations, the entrepreneurial (innovative) behavior is positively reinforced, and the individual is motivated to continue to behave entrepreneurially (innovatively), either within the current venture or possibly through the initiation of additional ventures, depending on the existing entrepreneurial goal. When outcomes fail to meet expectations, the entrepreneur's motivation will be lower and will have a corresponding impact on the decision to continue to act entrepreneurially (innovatively). These perceptions also affect succeeding strategies, strategy implementation, and management of the firm.[27]

Once again we see the importance of the individual in the entrepreneurial (or innovative) process. It is only through individuals that innovation can be initiated and sustained.

An Experiential View

The prevalent view in the literature is that entrepreneurs and innovators create ventures. While that is a true statement, it misses the complete process of entrepreneurship and innovation because of its narrow framing. This narrow perspective misses much of the reality regarding how ventures and entrepreneurs/innovators come into being. Researchers point out that as with a painting that emerges based on the individual interacting with, feeling, and agonizing over their creation, an entrepreneur does not simply produce a venture. Entrepreneurs do not pre-exist— they emerge as a function of the novel, idiosyncratic, and experiential nature of the venture creation process. Venture creation is a lived experience that, as it unfolds, forms the entrepreneur. In fact, the creation of a sustainable enterprise involves three parallel, interactive phenomena: emergence of the opportunity, emergence of the venture, and emergence of the entrepreneur. None are predetermined or fixed—they define and are defined by one another.[28] Thus, the perspective of the entrepreneurial or innovative experience has gained new momentum in the research of the twenty-first century.

This experiential view of the entrepreneur captures the emergent and temporal nature of entrepreneurship. It moves us past a more static "snapshot" approach and encourages consideration of a dynamic, socially-situated process involving numerous actors and events. It allows for the fact that the many activities addressed as a venture unfolds are experienced by different actors in different ways.[29] Moreover, it acknowledges that venture creation transcends rational thought processes to include emotions, impulses, and physiological responses as individuals react to a diverse, multifaceted, and imposing array of activities, events, and developments. This perspective is consistent with some of the research interested in a situated view of entrepreneurial and innovative action.[30]

Drivers (Sources) of Innovation

So, where do innovators seek out sources for the ideas and concepts that result in innovation? Most innovations result from a conscious, purposeful search for new opportunities. This process begins with the analysis of the sources of new opportunities. Renowned business consultant and author Peter Drucker noted that because innovation is both conceptual and perceptual, would-be innovators must go out and look, ask, and listen. Successful innovators use both the right and left sides of their brains. They look at figures. They look at people. They analytically work out what the innovation has to be to satisfy the opportunity. Then they go out and look at potential product users to study their expectations, values, and needs.[31] The following presents some of the most effective sources for the recognition of opportunities.

Trends: trends signal shifts in the current paradigm (or thinking) of the major population. Observing trends closely will allow an entrepreneur the ability to recognize a potential opportunity. Trends need to be observed in society, technology, economy, and government.

Unexpected occurrences: these are successes or failures that, because they were unanticipated or unplanned, often end up proving to be a major innovative surprise to everyone.

Incongruities: these occur whenever a gap or difference exists between expectations and reality.

Process needs: these exist whenever a demand arises for an answer to a particular need. Venture capitalists often refer to this as the "pain" that exists in the marketplace and the entrepreneur must recognize an innovative solution or "painkiller."

Industry and market changes: continual shifts in the marketplace occur, caused by developments such as consumer attitudes, advancements in technology, and industry growth. Industries and markets are always undergoing changes in structure, design, or definition.

Demographic changes: as mentioned above with the trends, these arise from trend changes in population, age, education, occupations, geographic locations, and similar factors. Demographic shifts are important and often provide new entrepreneurial opportunities.

Perceptual changes: these changes occur in people's interpretation of facts and concepts. They are intangible yet meaningful. Perception can cause major shifts in ideas to take place.

Knowledge-based concepts: these are the basis for the creation or development of something brand new. Inventions are knowledge-based; they are the product of new thinking, new methods, and new knowledge. Such innovations often require the longest time period between initiation and market implementation because of the need for testing and modification.

Mythology Associated with Innovators

In order to better understand "innovative thinking" we must first examine some of the damaging myths that have prevailed for years due to the lack of understanding surrounding this concept. It should be recognized that some executives and managers reject the "entrepreneurial" concept because of certain longstanding beliefs about entrepreneurship and innovation. These myths have developed through the years and are the result of a slow emergence of research in entrepreneurship and individual innovation. As many researchers in the field have noted, the study of entrepreneurship and innovation is still emerging, and thus "folklore" will tend to prevail until it is dispelled with contemporary research findings. Listed below are five of the most notable myths with an explanation to dispel each myth.[32]

"Individuals Are Born to Innovate"

The prevailing idea that innovation cannot be taught or learned, that there are innate traits with which one must be born, has a long history. These traits include aggressiveness, initiative, drive, a willingness to take risks, creative ability, and perseverance. While these traits may certainly have an effect on an individual, they do not dictate nor predict whether one is predisposed to innovative thinking. The recognition of entrepreneurship and innovation as a discipline in universities today has helped to dispel this myth.

"Innovators Must Be Inventors"

The idea that innovators are always inventors is a result of misunderstanding and tunnel vision. While many inventors are also entrepreneurs, there are numerous entrepreneurs who encompass all sorts of innovative activity. For example, Steve Jobs did not invent the computer, but his innovative ideas have made Apple one of the leading technology enterprises in the world. A contemporary understanding of innovative thinking covers more than just invention. There must be a complete understanding of innovative behavior in all forms.

"Fitting the Innovator's Profile"

Many books and articles have presented checklists of characteristics of the successful entrepreneurs and innovators. These lists were neither validated nor complete; they were based on case studies and on research findings among achievement-oriented people. Today we realize that a standard entrepreneurial profile is hard to compile. The environment, the idea itself, and the individual have interactive effects, which result in many different types of profiles. Contemporary studies being conducted at universities across the world will, in the future, provide more accurate insights into the various profiles of successful innovators. It is more likely that successful innovators benefit from "entrepreneurial experiences" and innovative education where they can learn rather than conform to a particular profile.

"Innovation Is Being Lucky"

Being at "the right place at the right time" is always an advantage. But "luck happens when preparation meets opportunity" is an equally appropriate adage.

Prepared innovators who seize the opportunity when it arises often appear to be "lucky." They are, in fact, simply better prepared to deal with situations and turn them into successes. What appears to be luck is actually the result of preparation, determination, desire, knowledge, and innovativeness.

"Innovators Are Gamblers"

The concept of risk is a major element in the innovation process. However, the public's perception of the risk assumed by most innovators is distorted. While it may appear that an innovator is "gambling" on a wild chance, the fact is that they are usually working on a moderate or "calculated" risk. Most successful innovators work hard through planning and preparation to minimize the risk involved, in order to better control the destiny of their vision.

We present these myths to provide a background for current thinking on innovators. By sidestepping the "folklore," we can build a foundation for critically understanding the processes of innovative thinking.

However, understanding the characteristics, motivations, experiences, and myths associated with innovation is not a shield from the stress that the pursuit of innovation can produce. We must always be aware that the process of innovation may also present a "stressful" experience to individuals.

Innovation and Stress . . . Beware!

Research studies of entrepreneurs and innovators show that those who achieve goals often pay a high price.[33] As an example, in one study a majority of entrepreneurs surveyed had back problems, indigestion, insomnia, or headaches. To achieve their goals, however, these entrepreneurs (innovators) were willing to tolerate these effects of stress.

In general, stress can be viewed as a function of discrepancies between a person's expectations and ability to meet demands, as well as discrepancies between the individual's expectations and personality. If a person is unable to fulfill role demands, stress occurs. To the extent innovators' work demands and expectations exceed their abilities to perform as idea initiators, they are likely to experience stress. Innovative roles and operating environments can lead to stress.

Many times innovators must bear the cost of their mistakes while playing a multitude of roles, such as salesperson, recruiter, spokesperson, and negotiator. These simultaneous demands can lead to role overload. The innovative mindset requires a large commitment of time and energy, often at the expense of family and social activities.[34]

Sources of Stress

Researchers have identified some of the key causes of entrepreneurial stress that can be applied to the innovation process as well.[35] They include:

Insulation: long hours at work prevent them from seeking the comfort and counsel of friends and family members. Because of this insulation from others they tend not to participate in social activities unless they provide a business benefit.

Addiction to the innovation: one of the ironies of innovation is that successful innovators can become married to their ideas. They work long hours, leaving little time for civic organizations, recreation, or further education.

Perfectionist syndrome: most innovators experience frustration, disappointment, and aggravation with partners, fellow employees, customers, and investors. Successful innovators are to some extent perfectionists and know how they want things done; often they spend a lot of time trying to get other, more lackadaisical, employees to meet their performance standards. And, frequently, because of irreconcilable conflict, many partnerships are dissolved.

Achievement orientation: the innovator is never satisfied with their work, no matter how well it was done. They seem to recognize the dangers of unbridled ambition, but they have a difficult time tempering their achievement need. They seem to believe that if they stop or slow down, some competitor is going to come from behind, and everything they have built will fall apart.

Managing the Stress

It is important to point out that not all stress is bad. Certainly, if stress becomes overbearing and unrelenting in a person's life, it wears down the body's physical abilities. However, if stress can be kept within constructive bounds, it could increase a person's efficiency and improve performance.

One research study presented stress reduction techniques.[36] Although classic stress reduction techniques such as meditation, biofeedback, muscle relaxation, and regular exercise help reduce stress, there are a few techniques that can help relieve stress Presented here are six specific ways innovators can cope with stress.

Network: one way to relieve the insulation of the innovator's mindset is to share experiences by networking with other innovators. The objectivity gained from hearing about the triumphs and errors of others is itself therapeutic.

Refresh yourself: the best antidote to immersion in an innovation may be a holiday. If vacation days or weeks are limited by valid business constraints, short breaks still may be possible. Such interludes allow a measure of self-renewal.

The personal touch: innovators are in close contact with fellow employees and can readily assess the concerns of their staff. The personal touches such as company-wide outings, flexible hours, and congratulatory celebrations are many times very useful in helping other employees be not only more productive but also experience much less stress.

Gain new perspectives: countering the obsessive need to achieve can be difficult because the innovator's personality is inextricably bound in the fabric of the innovation. Innovators need to get away from their ideas occasionally and become more passionate about life itself. In other words, they need to gain some new perspectives.

Delegate: implementation of coping mechanisms requires implementation time. To gain this time, the innovator has to learn to delegate tasks. Innovators can find delegation difficult because they think they have to be involved in every aspect of the innovation. But if time is to be gained for alleviation of stress, appropriate delegation must be used.

Exercise: exercise can often be an excellent method of reducing stress for individuals. As an example, researchers Michael G. Goldsby, Donald F. Kuratko, and James W. Bishop examined the relationship between exercise and the attainment of personal and professional goals for entrepreneurs.[37] The study addressed the issue by examining the exercise regimens of 366 entrepreneurs and the relationship of exercise frequency with the company's sales and the entrepreneur's personal goals. Specifically, the study examined the relationship that two types of exercise—running and weightlifting—had with sales volume, extrinsic rewards, and intrinsic rewards. The results indicated that running is positively related to all three outcome variables, while weightlifting is positively related to extrinsic and intrinsic rewards. This study demonstrates the value of exercise regimens on relieving the stress associated with entrepreneurs and innovators.

Managing Innovative Individuals

In order to maintain this "innovative mindset," managers must assume certain ongoing responsibilities.[38] The first responsibility involves *framing the challenge.* In other words, there needs to be a clear definition of the specified challenges that everyone involved with innovative projects should address. It is important to think in terms of, and regularly reiterate, the challenge. Second, leaders have the responsibility to *absorb the uncertainty* that is perceived by team members. Innovative leaders make uncertainty less daunting. The idea is to create the self-confidence that lets others act on opportunities without seeking managerial permission. Employees must not be overwhelmed by the complexity inherent in many innovative situations. A third responsibility is to *define gravity*—that is, what must be accepted and what cannot be accepted. The term *gravity* is used to capture limiting conditions. For example, there is gravity on Earth, but that does not mean it must limit our lives. If freed from the psychological cage of believing that gravity makes flying impossible, creativity can permit us to invent an airplane or spaceship. This is what the innovative mindset is all about—seeing opportunities where others see barriers and limits. A fourth managerial responsibility involves *clearing obstacles* that arise as a result of internal competition for resources. This can be a problem especially when the innovation is beginning to undergo significant growth. An expanding and sometimes popular new concept will often find itself pitted squarely against other (often established) aspects of the firm in a fierce internal competition for funds and staff. Creative tactics, political skills, and an ability to regroup, reorganize, and attack from another angle become invaluable. A final responsibility for leaders is to keep their finger on the pulse of the innovative projects. This involves constructive monitoring and control of the developing opportunity.

Sustained efforts with innovation are contingent upon individual members continuing to undertake innovative activities and upon positive perceptions of the activity by the organization's executive management, which will in turn support the further allocation of necessary organizational antecedents.

The dynamic innovative organizations of this twenty-first century will be ones that are capable of merging strategic action with innovative action on an ongoing basis.[39] This type of innovative organization could be conceptualized in the "new thinking" that is needed by today's leaders. As has been shown in much of the recent literature, the strategic mindset must lean towards the more innovative concepts in leading organizations today. It is our belief that the basis for any organization pursuing innovation as their strategy needs to understand the concept of "innovative thinking." It is the techniques and principles of this emerging discipline that will drive the innovative organization in the twenty-first century.

Innovation-in-Action

Hiring for Creativity

According to *Inc. Magazine* there are some specific strategies that can be utilized to find creative and innovative people to work in your organization.

1. Decide Which Kind of Creativity Counts

How much creativity do you want to tolerate? You need to distinguish between "breadth creativity," which is the ability to see the big picture and draw connections or spot trends, and "depth creativity," which is creativity within a specific knowledge or skill area (such as a specific job). The type of desired creativity should be based on the creative culture of the organization. An organization may not necessarily need or want to tolerate many individuals with "breadth creativity." If not, they should focus on identifying individuals who demonstrate ingenuity in problem-solving for a specific job.

2. Attract the Brightest Lights

Market your company to prospective employees. You need to examine how your company's web pages, career pages, and other materials convey your goals and values (which should include creativity). What creative tools do you use to get the interest of creative types? Some examples cited include employee testimonials on YouTube, Facebook pages, and job descriptions that emphasize more passionate and conversational calls for talent. You should also focus on skills and experiences that demonstrate adaptability versus rigidity. Employees with varied life and job experiences are likely to act more creatively. Also, recruit from nontraditional sources. Ask your most creative employees for referrals. And consider looking outside your industry. Expertise can be acquired; creativity generally can't.

3. Put Candidates to the Test

In order to assess creative skills, utilize behavioral interviewing that requires candidates to describe on-the-job experiences that involved the skills and abilities the prospective job requires. To assess creative skill, you could ask questions such as: "Describe a recent new problem you have had to deal with in your current job and describe what you did to solve it." If the candidate has too little previous work experiences, you may also use hypothetical questions that provide possible work-related problems and ask them how they would solve them. Either way, you get job-related insights on the extent to which an applicant can apply creative problem-solving skills.

(Adapted from: www.inc.com/magazine/20101001/guidebook-how-to-hire-for-creativity.html. Originally published October 1, 2010.)

Key Terms

corporate innovation

disruptive innovation

duplication

entrepreneurial actions

entrepreneurial motivation

extension

gravity

I-Challenge

incongruities

incremental innovation

innovation trajectories

innovative stress

internal locus

process innovation

radical innovation

risk taker-gambler

tolerance for ambiguity

unexpected occurrences

Discussion Questions

1. What is innovation and how does it differ from entrepreneurship?
2. Identify the three types of innovation.
3. Describe the four methods of innovation—invention, extension, duplication, and synthesis.
4. Explain the different trajectories of innovation.
5. Identify three misconceptions about innovation.
6. Some of the characteristics attributed to innovators include internal locus of control, tolerance for ambiguity, and calculated risk taking. Discuss how these relate to the innovative mindset.
7. Explain the motivation of innovation.
8. What are the major drivers of innovative ideas? Explain and give an example of each.
9. What are the key myths associated with innovation? Debunk each.
10. What are four causes of stress among innovators? How can stress be managed?

Notes

1 Kelly, K. 1999. *New Rules for the New Economy*, New York: Penguin Books.
2 "Announcing the 2017 World's Most Innovative Companies", *Fast Company*. Accessed August 1, 2017 from: www.fastcompany.com/3067756/announcing-the-2017-worlds-50-most-innovative-companies; and "The World's Most InnovativeCompanies" *Forbes*, 2017. Accessed August 1, 2017 from: www.forbes.com/innovative-companies/list.
3 Vanhaverbeke, W. & Peeters, N. 2005. Embracing innovation as strategy: corporate venturing, competence building, and corporate strategy making. *Creativity and Innovation Management*, 14(3): 246–257; and Ireland, R.D., Covin, J.G. & Kuratko, D.F. 2009. Conceptualizing corporate entrepreneurship strategy. *Entrepreneurship Theory Practice*, 33: 19–46.
4 Covin, J.G., Slevin, D.P. & Heeley, M.B. 2000. Pioneers and followers: competitive tactics, environment, and firm growth. *Journal of Business Venturing*, 15: 175–210; and Hornsby, J.S., Kuratko, D.F., Shepherd, D.A. & Bott, J.P. 2009. Managers' corporate entrepreneurial actions: examining perception and position. *Journal of Business Venturing*, 24(3): 236–247.
5 Morris, M.H., Kuratko, D.F. & Covin, J.G. 2011. *Corporate Entrepreneurship and Innovation*, 3rd ed., Mason, OH: Cengage/South-Western Publishers.
6 Morse, C.W. 1986. The delusion of intrapreneurship. *Long Range Planning*, 19(2): 92–95; and Duncan, W.J., Ginter, P.M., Rucks, A.C. & Jacobs, T.D. 1988. Intrapreneuring and the reinvention of the corporation. *Business Horizons*, 31(3): 16–21.
7 Kuratko, D.F, Ireland, R.D. & Hornsby, J.S. 2001. The power of entrepreneurial outcomes: insights from Acordia, Inc. *Academy of Management Executive*, 15(4): 60–71; Kuratko, D.F., Ireland, R.D., Covin, J.G. & Hornsby, J.S. 2005. A model of middle level managers' entrepreneurial behavior. *Entrepreneurship Theory and Practice*, 29(6): 699–716; Miles, M.P. & Covin, J.G. 2002. Exploring the practice of corporate venturing: some common forms and their organizational implications. *Entrepreneurship Theory and Practice*, 26(3): 21–40; and Kuratko, D.F., Hornsby, J.S. & Covin, J.G. 2014. Diagnosing a firm's internal environment for corporate entrepreneurship. *Business Horizons*, 57(1): 37–47.
8 Govindarajan, V. & Trimble, C. 2005. Building breakthrough businesses within established organizations. *Harvard Business Review*, 83(5): 58–68.

9   Brandt, S.C. 1986. *Entrepreneuring in Established Companies*, Homewood, IL: Dow-Jones-Irwin, p. 54.
10 Drucker, P.F. 1985. *Innovation and Entrepreneurship*, New York: Harper & Row, p. 20.
11 Schroeder, D.M. 1990. A dynamic perspective on the impact of process innovation upon competitive strategies. *Strategic Management Journal*, 11: 25–41.
12 O'Sullivan, D. & Dooley, L. 2009. *Applying Innovation*, Thousand Oaks, CA: Sage Publications.
13 Martin, M.J.C. 2004. *Managing Innovation and Entrepreneurship in Technology Based Firms*, New York: Wiley.
14 Adapted from: Hodgetts, R.M. & Kuratko, D.F. 2001. *Effective Small Business Management*, 7th ed., Fort Worth, TX: Harcourt College Publishers, pp. 21–23.
15 MacLaughlin, I. 1999. *Creative Technological Change: The Shaping of Technology and Organizations*, London: Routledge.
16 Christensen, C.M. 1997. *The Innovator's Dilemma*, Boston: Harvard Business School Press; Utterback, J.M. 1996. *Mastering the Dynamics of Innovation*, Boston: Harvard Business School Press.
17 Christensen, C.M. 1997. *The Innovator's Dilemma*, Boston: Harvard Business School Press.
18 O'Reilly III, C.A. & Tushman, M.L. 2004. The ambidextrous organization. *Harvard Business Review*, 82(4): 74–81.
19 Adapted from: Drucker, P.F. 1985. The discipline of innovation. *Harvard Business Review*, (May/June): 67–72.
20 Corbett, A.C. 2005. Experiential learning within the process of opportunity identification and exploitation. *Entrepreneurship Theory and Practice*, 29(4): 473–491; and Corbett, A.C. 2007. Learning asymmetries and the discovery of entrepreneurial opportunities, *Journal of Business Venturing*, 22(1): 97–118.
21 Kuratko, D.F. 2017. *Entrepreneurship: Theory, Process, and Practice*, 10th ed., Boston: Cengage/South-Western Publishing.
22 McClelland, D.C. 1961. *The Achieving Society*, New York: Van Nostrand; and Business drive and national achievement, *Harvard Business Review*, (July/August 1962): 99–112.
23 Mitchell, R.K., Busenitz, L., Lant, T., McDougall, P.P., Morse, E.A. & Smith, J.B. 2004. The distinctive and inclusive domain of entrepreneurial cognition research. *Entrepreneurship Theory and Practice*, 28(6): 505–518; and Grégoire, D.A., Corbett, A.C. & McMullen, J.S. 2011. The cognitive perspective in entrepreneurship: an agenda for future research. *Journal of Management Studies*, 48(6): 1443–1477.
24 For some articles on entrepreneurial characteristics, see Kickul, J. & Gundry, L.K. 2002. Prospecting for strategic advantage: the proactive entrepreneurial personality and small firm innovation. *Journal of Small Business Management*, 40(2): 85–97; and Brigham, K.H., DeCastro, J.O. & Shepherd, D.A. 2007. A person-organization fit model of owners-managers' cognitive style and organization demands. *Entrepreneurship Theory and Practice*, 31(1): 29–51.
25 Naffziger, D.W., Hornsby, J.S. & Kuratko, D.F. 1994. A proposed research model of entrepreneurial motivation. *Entrepreneurship Theory and Practice*, 18(3): 29–42.
26 Reuber, A.R. & Fischer, E. 1999. Understanding the consequences of founders' experience. *Journal of Small Business Management*, (February): 30–45.
27 Kuratko, D.F., Hornsby, J.S. & Naffziger, D.W. 1997. An examination of owner's goals in sustaining entrepreneurship. *Journal of Small Business Management*, (January): 24–33.
28 See: Morris, M.H., Allen, J.A., Kuratko, D.F. & Brannon, D. 2010. Experiencing family business creation: differences between founders, non-family managers, and founders of non-family firms. *Entrepreneurship Theory and Practice*, 34(6): 1057–1084; and Morris, M.H., Kuratko, D.F. & Schindehutte, M. 2011. Framing the entrepreneurial experience. *Entrepreneurship Theory and Practice*, 36(1): 11–40.
29 Politis, D. 2005. The process of entrepreneurial learning: a conceptual framework. *Entrepreneurship Theory and Practice*, 29(4): 399–424.
30 Davidsson, P. 2004. A general theory of entrepreneurship: the individual-opportunity nexus. *International Small Business Journal*, 22(2): 206–219; and Berglund, H. 2007. Entrepreneurship

and phenomenology: researching entrepreneurship as lived experience, in J. Ulhoi and H. Neergaard (eds.), *Handbook of Qualitative Research Methods in Entrepreneurship*, London: Edward Elgar, pp. 75–96.

31 Adapted from: Taylor, W. 1990. The business of innovation. *Harvard Business Review*, (March/April): 97–106; and George, G. & Bock, A.J. 2009. *Inventing Entrepreneurs: Technology Innovators and Their Entrepreneurial Journey*, Upper Saddle River, NJ: Pearson/Prentice Hall.

32 Kuratko, D.F. 2017. *Entrepreneurship: Theory, Process, and Practice*, 10th ed., Boston: Cengage/South-Western Publishing.

33 Akande, A. 1992. Coping with entrepreneurial stress. *Leadership and Organization Development Journal*, 13(2): 27–32; and Buttner, E.H. 1992. Entrepreneurial stress: is it hazardous to your health? *Journal of Managerial Issues*, (summer): 223–240.

34 Buttner, "Entrepreneurial stress"; see also Rabin, M.A. 1996. Stress, strain, and their moderators: an empirical comparison of entrepreneurs and managers. *Journal of Small Business Management*, (January): 46–58.

35 Boyd, D.P. & Gumpert, D.E. 1983. Coping with entrepreneurial stress. *Harvard Business Review*, (March/April): 46–56.

36 Boyd & Gumpert, "Coping with entrepreneurial stress."

37 Goldsby, M.G., Kuratko, D.F. & Bishop, J.W. 2005. Entrepreneurship and fitness: an examination of rigorous exercise and goal attainment among small business owners. *Journal of Small Business Management*, 43(1) (January): 78–92; see also: Levesque, M. & Minniti, M. 2006. The effect of aging on entrepreneurial behavior. *Journal of Business Venturing*, 21(2): 177–194.

38 McGrath, R.G. & MacMillan, I. 2000. *The Entrepreneurial Mindset*, Boston: Harvard Business Press; and Kuratko, D.F. 2009. The entrepreneurial imperative. *Business Horizons*, 52(5): 421–428.

39 Ketchen, D.J., Ireland, R.D. & Snow, C.C. 2008. Strategic entrepreneurship, collaborative innovation, and wealth creation. *Strategic Entrepreneurship Journal*, 1(3–4): 371–385; and Kuratko, D.F. & Audretsch, D.B. 2009. Strategic entrepreneurship: exploring different perspectives of an emerging concept. *Entrepreneurship Theory and Practice*, 33(1): 1–17.

2

THE PROCESS OF CORPORATE INNOVATION

As corporations seek out innovation as the key competitive advantage, corporate entrepreneur-
ial leaders must be critical contributors to economic growth through their innovations, research
and development effectiveness, job creation, competitiveness, productivity, and formation of
new industry.

~Donald F. Kuratko[1]

Introduction

As we discussed in the Preface, companies cannot be static—they must continually adjust, adapt, or redefine themselves. The twenty-first century is seeing corporate strategies focused heavily on innovation. The contemporary thrust of innovative thinking has become the major force *inside* enterprises.[2] Successful corporate innovation has been used in many different companies and today a wealth of popular business literature previously described a new "corporate revolution" taking place thanks to the infusion of innovative thinking into large bureaucratic structures.[3] Today, this revolution or infusion is referred to as *corporate entrepreneurship, corporate innovation*, or *intrapreneurship*, and represents innovative activity inside of the organization where individuals (innovators) will "champion" new ideas from development to complete reality. Corporations enhance the innovative abilities of their employees, and increase corporate success through the creation of new products, markets, or methods. Successfully applying the innovative process within larger, established organizations requires that the manager appreciate the unique nature of corporate entrepreneurship or corporate innovation.[4]

However, corporate innovative activity can be difficult since it involves radically changing traditional forms of internal corporate behavior and structural patterns. Yet, the desire to pursue corporate innovation (entrepreneurship) has arisen from a variety of pressing problems, including: (1) increased global competition; (2) continual downsizing of organizations seeking greater efficiency; (3) dramatic changes, innovations, and improvements in the marketplace; (4) perceived weaknesses in the traditional methods of organizational management; and (5) the exodus of innovative-minded employees who are disenchanted with bureaucratic organizations.

However, the pursuit of corporate innovation as a strategy to counter these problems creates a newer and potentially more complex set of challenges on both a practical and theoretical level. On a practical level, organizations need some guidelines to direct or redirect resources towards establishing effective innovative strategies. They also need to continually reassess the components or dimensions which predict, explain, and shape the environment in which corporate innovation flourishes. There have been only a limited number of studies focusing on various factors contributing to, or enhancing the establishment of, corporate innovation. This chapter presents an overview of the concept of corporate innovation from an organizational perspective by outlining recommended steps for a strategy in corporate innovation and entrepreneurship based upon the critical factors that enhance the development of innovative-minded employees.

Obstacles to Corporate Innovation

A number of researchers have attempted to examine particular factors which are associated with success in corporate innovation. For example, issues such as financial factors, incentive and control systems, market and entry approaches and market-driven vs. technology-driven demand have all been examined as possible causal factors in the success or failure of corporate innovative activity.[5]

However, a number of researchers have explained the process of innovation from the perspective of obstacles. They have identified a large set of obstacles that reflect aspects of organizational culture that prevent innovation from occurring. Today, many corporations are viewed to have obsolete ideas about cooperative cultures, management techniques, and values of management and employees. Organizations have to stimulate, support, and protect innovative individuals.

The entrepreneurial/innovative process does not conform to standard operating procedures, as innovation represents the antithesis of standard operating procedures. Innovation requires individuals willing to challenge "business as usual." Michael H. Morris, Donald F. Kuratko, and Jeffrey G. Covin[6] presented critical obstacles in the corporate innovation process, including: lack of time, lack of rewards, lack of resources, turfism, and lack of a sponsor. Let's examine each of these.

No Time

Because of increased global competition and the birth of the information age, business professionals are extremely busy keeping up with a wealth of available information and changes in technology. There just isn't a lot of time during the work day to engage in innovation. A few companies encourage their employees to spend a portion of their time on ideas outside their normal course of duties. However, this lack of time should not prevent an innovative individual who has a passion for an idea from putting together a team, writing a business plan, harnessing the necessary internal resources, and making the innovation a reality.

Poor Rewards

Traditionally, corporations do not necessarily reward (financially or otherwise) employees for being innovative. Many companies have recently implemented reward systems for cost-saving suggestions or ideas presented through structured suggestion programs. But, with few exceptions, rewards for innovative thinking and behavior are not built into organizational performance systems.

Underfunded

Without financing, a corporate innovator's idea will remain only a vision. For this reason, the successful innovator must either develop knowledge about financial projections and calculations, or recruit a member of their team who has this knowledge and is willing and able to develop this portion of the venture plan. Executives are not going to invest money in a new venture unless the entrepreneur can demonstrate the potential for a return on the investment that the company needs to achieve. As with any organization, funds are limited, and support of new products and services is determined by extensive market research, detailed financial projections, and contingency plans in case the sales projections are overestimated.

Job Domain

Trying to be innovative in an established company, an individual may find that departments are more concerned with protecting their "domain" than they are with developing new ideas that will benefit the organization. Frequently, the corporate innovator will run into "power plays" and battles for control over decision-making occurring between vice presidents and/or their respective areas. The successful innovator needs to avoid these power plays if at all possible, and be willing to work beyond the traditional boundaries of a particular job.

No Allies

To help them in their assessment of these political wars, the corporate innovator needs an ally higher in the organization who oversees the progress of the corporate venture. These allies also act as buffers guarding innovators against unnecessary organizational bureaucratic interference. This allows the corporate entrepreneur to concentrate on their venture. Sponsors can also act as coaches for corporate innovators. They are most effective if they have personally championed an idea earlier in their career. In the latter case, they also serve as role models who can offer empathy and optimism through a critical but trusting attitude.

Fellow Employees

The greatest of all the obstacles may actually be with fellow employees. Management may be able to fix the structure and remove bureaucratic rules and procedures, but the challenges involved in getting employees to embrace innovative thinking, change the way they do things, collaborate on projects involving new ideas, and give up resources to support innovative initiatives can be especially challenging. Innovative ideas can represent tremendous opportunity to the firm but they can also threaten individuals inside the firm. For many employees, innovative ideas could mean that current products will be eliminated, budgets will be re-allocated, or processes will be modified. As a result, many new ideas are blocked by:

- making premature and uninformed judgments;
- neophobia—the dread of anything new or novel, fear of the unknown; sense of embarrassment or humiliation that accompanies the admission that existing products or procedures are inferior to new proposals;
- caution—it's safer to have "the me-too-later" attitude;
- politics—new ideas frequently pose a threat to the corporate stature and vested interests of managers who are anxious to maintain the existing hierarchical structure.

These obstacles share a common element—namely, they represent situations in which, to meet the needs of a new project, the corporate innovator must attempt to convince someone or some unit to change current behavior patterns from what the person or unit might otherwise prefer to do. Therefore, two methods for handling some of the obstacles are building social capital and acquiring resources.

Building Social Capital

Corporate entrepreneurs must rely on their ingenuity and persistence to build influence. They need to build "social capital," which is defined as an inventory of trust, gratitude, or obligations that can be "cashed in" when the new project is in demand (Blau, 1964). Building this capital can be accomplished in a number of ways, including:

- sharing information;
- creating opportunities for people to demonstrate their skills and competence;
- building and using influence networks.[7]

Resource Acquisition

The major method of securing the necessary resources is through co-optation or leveraging of the resources currently underutilized by the firm. Starr and MacMillan identified four distinct strategies for co-optation:

- *Borrowing:* borrowing strategies are employed to temporarily or periodically secure the use of assets or other resources, on the premise that they will eventually be returned.
- *Begging:* begging strategies are employed to secure resources by appealing to the owner's goodwill. In this way, venture managers gain the use of the resources without needing to return them, despite the fact that the owner recognizes the value of the assets. In her research, Kanter (1985)[8] identifies many cases of "tincupping," in which venture managers begged or scrounged resources from the rest of the firm.
- *Scavenging:* scavenging strategies extract usage from goods that others do not intend to use or that they might actually welcome an appropriate opportunity to divest themselves of. This approach involves learning about unused or underused resources (e.g., obsolete inventory, idle equipment, or underutilized personnel).
- *Amplifying:* amplification is the capacity to lever far more value out of an asset than is perceived by the original owner of the asset.[9]

These ideas may help the innovator to secure resources that would otherwise have to be secured by economic exchange at a much greater cost. There are three critical benefits of relying on these methods of resource acquisition: by appropriating underutilized resources, venture managers reduce the cost of start-up, they reduce the risk of start-up by dramatically bringing down the initial investment, and they increase the return on assets of the venture.

Corporate Innovation as a Strategy

Operational definitions of corporate innovation have evolved over the last 30 years. For example, one researcher[10] noted that corporate innovation is a very broad concept that includes the generation, development, and implementation of new ideas or behaviors. An innovation can be a new product or service, an administrative system, or a new plan or program pertaining to organizational members. Another researcher[11] observed that corporate innovation may be formal or informal activities aimed at creating new businesses in established companies through product and process innovations and market developments. These activities may take place at the corporate, division (business), functional, or project levels. Sharma and Chrisman[12] established one of the most cited definitions of corporate entrepreneurship when they described it as a process whereby an individual or a group of individuals, in association with an existing organization, creates a new organization or instigates renewal or innovation within the organization. Under this definition, strategic renewal, innovation, and corporate venturing are all important and legitimate parts of the corporate innovation process.

Morris, Kuratko, and Covin[13] cited two phenomena as constituting the domain of corporate entrepreneurship—namely, corporate venturing and strategic entrepreneurship. *Corporate venturing* approaches have as their commonality the adding of new businesses (or portions of new businesses via equity investments) to the corporation. This can be accomplished through three implementation modes—internal corporate venturing, cooperative corporate venturing, and external corporate venturing. By contrast, *strategic entrepreneurship* approaches have as their commonality the exhibition of large-scale or otherwise highly consequential innovations that are adopted in the firm's pursuit of competitive advantage. These innovations may or may not result in new businesses for the corporation. With strategic entrepreneurship approaches, innovation can be in any of five areas—the firm's strategy, product offerings, served markets, internal organization (i.e., structure, processes, and capabilities), or business model.[14]

As the field has further evolved, the concept of corporate innovation as a strategy began to develop. Ireland, Covin, and Kuratko define a corporate entrepreneurial (innovative) strategy as "a vision-directed, organization-wide reliance on entrepreneurial behavior that purposefully and continuously rejuvenates the organization and shapes the scope of its operations through the recognition and exploitation of entrepreneurial opportunity."[15] Today we see a number of companies that have adopted this innovative perspective. Apple, Google, Intel, Samsung, and Amazon are companies that continually appear on the lists of the "most innovative companies." This type of achievement can only come through an organization-wide commitment to a corporate innovative strategy.

For corporate entrepreneurship/innovation to operate as a strategy, it must "run deep" within organizations. Eisenhardt, Brown, and Neck[16] perhaps best captured where firms' strategies lie along the "innovation" continuum in their observations that firms with entrepreneurial strategies remain close to the "edge of time," judiciously balancing the exploitation of current entrepreneurial opportunities with the search for future entrepreneurial opportunities. Top managers are increasingly recognizing the need to respond to the entrepreneurial imperatives created by their competitive landscapes. Minimal responses to these entrepreneurial imperatives, reflecting superficial commitments to corporate innovation strategy, are bound to fail. Moreover, while top management can instigate the strategy, top management cannot dictate it. Those at the middle and lower ranks of an organization have a tremendous effect on and significant roles within entrepreneurial and strategic processes.[17] Without sustained and strong commitment from all levels of the organization, innovative behavior will never be a defining characteristic of the organization.

An innovative strategy is hard to create and, perhaps, even harder to perpetuate in organizations. The presence of certain external environmental conditions may be sufficient to prompt an organization's leaders into exploring the possibility of adopting such a strategy. However, the commitment of individuals throughout the organization to making an innovative strategy work and the realization of personal and organizational innovative outcomes that reinforce this commitment will be necessary to ensure that innovative strategy becomes a defining aspect of the organization. Alignments must be created in evaluation and reward systems such that congruence is achieved in the innovative behaviors induced at the individual and organizational levels. Thus, while external conditions may be increasingly conducive to the adoption of a corporate innovative strategy, managers should harbor no illusions that the effective implementation of these strategies will be easily accomplished.

The Critical Elements

Many companies that have made systematic efforts to learn how to conduct effective corporate innovation programs have found them to be viable and effective. They have proved that an effective innovative process can be developed. However, what elements are involved in such programs? Since a corporate innovation strategy is sometimes difficult to grasp, let alone develop, five critical elements have been suggested in the implementation of any innovative strategy: vision, innovation, environment, managers, and teams.[18] In this section, we examine these five elements in order to identify what it takes to establish a successful program. These elements become the critical steps for any executive seeking to establish the foundation for an innovative strategy within the organization.

Clarifying the Vision

The first step in planning a corporate innovation strategy for the enterprise is clarifying the vision of innovation that the corporate leaders wish to achieve.[19] The vision must be clearly articulated by the organization's leaders, as that is the key to the value proposition of the corporate innovation. Indeed, research is now showing that the value proposition of a corporate venture will evolve from the original vision over time and that will be directly related to the performance of the corporate venture. Although, the value proposition evolution–performance relationship was moderated by the parent corporation's familiarity with the venture's target market.[20] However, the specific objectives are then developed by the managers and employees of the organization. Because it is suggested that corporate innovation results from the creative talents of people within the organization, employees need to know about and understand this vision and its value proposition. Shared vision is a critical element for a strategy that seeks innovative pursuits of the managers and employees. This shared vision requires identification of specific objectives for corporate innovative strategies and of the programs needed to achieve those objectives.

Encouraging Innovative Thinking

The second step is encouraging innovation as the specific tool of the corporate entrepreneur. Corporations must understand and develop innovation as the key element in their strategy. Numerous researchers have examined the importance of innovation within the corporate environment.[21] Described as chaotic and unplanned by some authors,[22] other researchers insist it is a systematic discipline.[23] Both of these positions can be true depending on the nature of the innovation. As we explained in Chapter 1, one way to understand the concept of innovation is to focus on two different trajectories of innovation: radical and incremental.

Radical innovation is the launching of inaugural breakthroughs that take experimentation and determined vision (such as personal computers, Post-it Notes,
disposable diapers, and overnight mail delivery). Whereas, *incremental innovation*
refers to the systematic evolution of a product or service into newer or larger
markets (examples include microwave popcorn or popcorn used for packaging to
replace Styrofoam). The structure, marketing, financing, and formal systems of a
corporation can all contribute to incremental innovation. Both radical and incremental innovations require vision and support. This support takes different steps
for effective development. For example, it has been widely recognized that innovative activity needs a champion—the person with a vision and the ability to share
it. In addition, both types of innovation require an effort by top management to
develop and educate employees concerning innovation and entrepreneurship.

Encouraging innovation requires a willingness to not only tolerate failure but also
to learn from it. As an example, one of the early founders of 3M, Francis G. Oakie,
had an idea to replace razor blades with sandpaper. He believed that men could rub
sandpaper on their face rather than use a sharp razor. He was wrong and the idea
failed. But, his ideas continued until he developed waterproof sandpaper for the auto
industry—a blockbuster success! In the process, 3M's philosophy was born.

Innovation is often a numbers game; the more ideas a company has, the better the
chances for a successful innovation. This philosophy has paid off for 3M. Antistatic
videotape, translucent dental braces, synthetic ligaments for knee surgery, heavy-duty
reflective sheeting for construction signs, and of course, Post-it Notes, are just some
of the great innovations developed at 3M. Overall, the company has a catalogue of
60,000 products that contributed to over $10.6 billion in sales. Today, 3M follows a set
of innovative rules that encourage employees to the foster ideas.[24] Two key rules are:

> *Don't Kill a Project:* If an idea can't find a home in one of 3M's divisions, a
> staffer can devote 15 percent of his or her time to prove it is workable. For
> those who need seed money, as many as 90 Genesis grants of $50,000 are
> awarded each year.

> *Tolerate Failure:* By encouraging plenty of experimentation and risk taking,
> there are more chances for a new product hit. The goal: divisions must derive
> 25 percent of sales from products introduced in the past five years. The target
> may be boosted to 30 percent.

Establish an Innovative Environment

The third step and possibly the most critical element is establishing an innovative
environment. In establishing the drive to innovate in today's corporations, there
must be a commitment to invest heavily in *innovative* activities that allow new
ideas to flourish in an innovative environment. This concept, when coupled with
the other specific elements of a strategy for innovation, enhances the potential for
employees to become innovation developers. In fact, in developing employees as
a source of innovations for corporations, researchers have found that companies

need to provide more nurturing and information-sharing activities. In addition to establishing innovative ways and nurturing innovators, there is a need to develop a climate that will help innovative-minded people reach their full potential. The perception of an innovative climate is critical for stressing the importance of management's commitment to not only the organization's people but also to the innovative projects. The importance of establishing the proper organizational climate is made clear by Morse when he questioned the ability of organizational bureaucracies to foster innovation:

> *It seems clear to me that in the absence of a company-wide culture specifically designed to encourage entrepreneurial activity, large firms are well advised to consider other means to stimulate innovation. Large companies with bureaucratic systems cannot hope to provide either the expectation of reward, or the entrepreneurial people. Entrepreneurship does not hold out hope of success in these companies because the reward structure will not permit compensation in line with the expectations of entrepreneurs, the locus of control in the organization does not allow for sufficient personal autonomy, and the corporate climate in bureaucratically organized firms promotes stability which often runs counter to the needs of innovative processes.*[25]

Specific organizational antecedents of an organization's innovative actions have been identified in the literature—top management support, work discretion, rewards/reinforcement, time availability, organizational boundaries.[26] Employee perception of these factors for an innovative environment is critical for stressing the importance of management's commitment.[27] Thus it is not enough to simply believe these factors are in place; they must be perceived by the employees as strong.

Develop Innovative Managers

The fourth step is to develop individual managers for corporate innovative leadership. As a way for organizations to develop key managers for innovative leadership, a corporate innovation training program (Corporate Innovation Program) often induces the change needed in the work atmosphere. It is not my intent to elaborate completely on the content of a training program here, but a brief summary of an actual program is presented to provide a general understanding of how such a program is designed to introduce an innovative environment in a company. This award-winning training program was intended to create an awareness of innovative opportunities in organizations.[28] The Corporate Innovation Program consists of seven modules, each designed to train participants to support corporate innovation in their own work area. The modules and a brief summary of their contents follow:

1. *The Innovative Experience.* An enthusiastic overview of the Innovative Experience in which participants are challenged to think innovatively with an emphasis on the need for innovative strategies in today's organizations.
2. *Innovative Thinking.* The process of thinking innovatively is foreign to most traditional managers. The misconceptions about thinking innovatively are

reviewed, and a discussion of the most common inhibitors is presented. After completing an innovation inventory, managers engage in several exercises designed to facilitate their own innovative thinking.

3. *Idea Acceleration Process.* Managers generate a set of specific ideas on which they would like to work. The process includes examining a number of aspects of the corporation including structural barriers and facilitators. Additionally, managers determine resources needed to accomplish their projects.

4. *Barriers and Facilitators to Innovative Thinking.* The most common barriers to innovative behavior are reviewed and discussed. Managers complete several exercises that will help them deal with barriers in the workplace. In addition, video case histories are shown that depict actual corporate innovators that have been successful in dealing with corporate barriers.

5. *Sustaining Innovative Teams.* Managers work together to form teams based on the ideas that have been circulating among the entire group. Team dynamics is reviewed for each group to understand.

6. *The Innovation Plan.* After managers examine several aspects of facilitators and barriers to behaving innovatively in their organization, groups are asked to begin the process of completing a plan. The plan includes setting goals, establishing a work team, assessing current conditions, developing a step-by-step timetable for project completion, and project evaluation.

7. *Assessing the Innovative Culture.* A survey instrument is provided and described which assesses the level of innovative culture within the organization. Participants complete the survey as a post-training phase and results will be fed back to all participants. Areas for improvement are then addressed.

Corporate innovation training that is viewed as a one-time activity cannot succeed. The more widespread the understanding of corporate innovation, the more likely it is that real culture changes will occur in the organization. The organizations that have utilized the training understand that. They all have attempted to repeat the program for as broad an audience as possible.

To validate the training program's effectiveness, an instrument entitled the "Corporate Entrepreneurship Assessment Instrument" (CEAI) was developed to provide for a psychometrically sound instrument that measured key innovative climate factors. The responses to the CEAI were statistically analyzed and resulted in five identified factors. The CEAI was originally developed as an "intrapreneurial" instrument to measure the perceptions of managers on the critical factors necessary for an innovative environment to exist.[29] The CEAI has been further refined by Holt, Rutherford, and Clohessy (2007)[30] and Rutherford and Holt (2007).[31] In essence, Ireland, Kuratko, and Morris (2006)[32] have argued that the CEAI provides a sound basis for managers to effectively manage, facilitate, and improve corporate innovative activities.

Thus, several studies have tried to isolate the organizational factors that promote corporate innovation. Specifically, Hornsby et al. (2002),[33] Kuratko et al. (2005),[34] and Ireland et al. (2006a; 2006b)[35] have taken steps toward answering this question by attempting to empirically and theoretically identify a parsimonious set of factors that influence corporate innovation. The results suggested that there are five stable organizational antecedents of middle-level managers' innovative behavior. These antecedents are: (1) *management support* (the willingness of top-level managers to facilitate and promote innovative behavior, including the championing of innovative ideas and providing the resources people require to take innovative actions); (2) *work discretion/autonomy* (top-level managers' commitment to tolerate failure, provide decision-making latitude and freedom from excessive oversight and to delegate authority and responsibility to middle-level managers); (3) *rewards/reinforcement* (developing and using systems that reward based on performance, highlight significant achievements and encourage pursuit of challenging work); (4) *time availability* (evaluating workloads to ensure that individuals and groups have the time needed to pursue innovations and that their jobs are structured in ways that support efforts to achieve short- and long-term organizational goals); and (5) *organizational boundaries* (precise explanations of outcomes expected from organizational work and development of mechanisms for evaluating, selecting, and using innovations). In interpreting their results, Hornsby et al. (2002)[36] highlighted the importance of middle-level managers receiving information from top-level managers regarding their position relative to the five antecedents and then effectively communicating that information to operating-level managers. In Chapter 7 we cover the instrument and its applications in greater depth.

Commit to Innovation Teams

The fifth step is to encourage the creation and use of innovation teams, as they hold the potential for producing innovative results and productivity breakthroughs. Companies that have committed to an innovation team approach often label the change they have undergone a "transformation." This new breed of work team is a powerful strategy for many firms. They have been referred to as self-directing, self-managing, high-performing, and empowering; although in reality an innovation team includes all of those descriptions (Francis and Sandberg, 2002).[37] In Chapter 9 we develop the concept of teams in further detail.

In examining many of the successful innovative developments within established corporations, innovative activity is not the sole province of the company's founder or top managers. Rather, it is diffused throughout the firm where experimentation and development go on all the time, as the company searches for new ways to build on knowledge accumulated by its workers. It has been referred to as "collective entrepreneurship," where individual skills are integrated into a group and their collective capacity to innovate becomes greater than the sum of its parts. Over time, as group members work through various problems and approaches, they learn about each other's abilities. Specifically, they learn how they can help one another perform better, what each can contribute to a particular project, and how they can best take advantage of one another's experience. Each participant is constantly on the lookout for small adjustments that will speed and smooth the evolution of the whole.

The net result of many such small-scale adaptations, affected throughout the organization, is to propel the enterprise forward. There are, in fact, specific key roles that must be filled on the venture team. In putting together the venture team, management must ensure that certain key roles are filled. The following roles are the most significant:

- *innovator:* the person who has made the major technical innovation;
- *venture manager:* the internal entrepreneur responsible for the overall progress of the project;
- *champion:* any individual who makes a decisive contribution to the project by promoting its progress through the critical early stages, particularly up to the point of implementation;
- *innovative CEO:* the individual who is in charge of the venture and controls the allocation of resources (e.g., a sub-CEO, a division manager, or a venture division manager);
- *sponsor:* the high-level person in the parent company who acts as buffer protector, and modifier of rules and policies and who helps the venture obtain the needed resources.

Sustaining Corporate Innovation

So, the question is, "how does an organization sustain the corporate innovative process?" The answer lies in the actions of senior managers. In order to maintain this innovative mindset in an organization, managers must assume certain ongoing responsibilities.[38] The first responsibility is to establish a clear definition of the specified challenges that everyone involved with innovative projects should address. Second, managers have the responsibility to make the uncertainty of pursuing innovative projects less daunting. Create the self-confidence within all employees that they can act on innovative opportunities without seeking managerial permission. Employees must not be overwhelmed by the complexity inherent in many innovative situations. Finally, managers need to clear out any obstacles that arise as a result of the innovative project progress. This can be a problem especially when the innovation begins to undergo significant growth. The ability to regroup and reorganize becomes invaluable. Organizational leaders must monitor and control the developing innovation.

From another perspective, it becomes apparent that change is inevitable in the organizational structure if innovative activity is going to exist and prosper. The change process consists of a series of emerging constructions of the people, the organizational goals, and the existing needs. In short, the organization will encourage innovation by relinquishing controls and changing the traditional bureaucratic structure.

One process model (Figure 2.1) adapted from a number of researchers illustrates the critical elements needed for sustained corporate innovative activity.[39] Specifically, the model integrates and extends previous models that have examined the organizational or individual components of innovative activity. The model provided additional theoretical foundation, emphasizing the importance of perceived implementation/output relationships at both the individual and organizational level. The perceived satisfaction of these relationships provides the basis for whether or not a corporate innovative activity will be sustained.

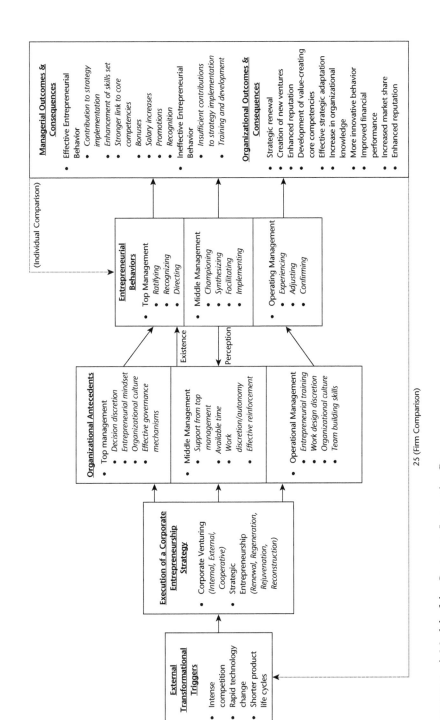

FIGURE 2.1 A Model of the Corporate Innovation Process.

(Individual Comparison)

Managerial Outcomes & Consequences
- Effective Entrepreneurial Behavior
  - *Contribution to strategy implementation*
  - *Enhancement of skills set*
  - *Stronger link to core competencies*
  - *Bonuses*
  - *Salary increases*
  - *Promotions*
  - *Recognition*
- Ineffective Entrepreneurial Behavior
  - *Insufficient contributions to strategy implementation*
  - *Training and development*

Organizational Outcomes & Consequences
- Strategic renewal
- Creation of new ventures
- Enhanced reputation
- Development of value-creating core competencies
- Effective strategic adaptation
- Increase in organizational knowledge
- More innovative behavior
- Improved financial performance
- Increased market share
- Enhanced reputation

Entrepreneurial Behaviors
- Top Management
  - *Ratifying*
  - *Recognizing*
  - *Directing*
- Middle Management
  - *Championing*
  - *Synthesizing*
  - *Facilitating*
  - *Implementing*
- Operating Management
  - *Experiencing*
  - *Adjusting*
  - *Confirming*

Existence

Perception

Organizational Antecedents
- Top management
  - *Decision discretion*
  - *Entrepreneurial mindset*
  - *Organizational culture*
  - *Effective governance mechanisms*
- Middle Management
  - *Support from top management*
  - *Available time*
  - *Work discretion/autonomy*
  - *Effective reinforcement*
- Operational Management
  - *Entrepreneurial training*
  - *Work design discretion*
  - *Organizational culture*
  - *Team building skills*

Execution of a Corporate Entrepreneurship Strategy
- Corporate Venturing (Internal, External, Cooperative)
- Strategic Entrepreneurship (Renewal, Regeneration, Rejuvenation, Reconstruction)

External Transformational Triggers
- Intense competition
- Rapid technology change
- Shorter product life cycles

25 (Firm Comparison)

The model in Figure 2.1 shows that change or transformational triggers cause organizations to pursue strategies for innovative activities and to institute certain internal organizational factors to ensure their implementation. As demonstrated in this model, it is the degree of ongoing innovative behavior of individuals and the perceptions of an organization's executive management toward innovative activities that need to be focused upon. This model provides insights for understanding the entire corporate innovation process from both the individual and organizational levels.

Researchers Michael H. Morris, Donald F. Kuratko, and Jeffrey G. Covin warn that corporate innovation does not produce instant success. It requires considerable time and investment, and there must be continual reinforcement. By their nature, organizations impose constraints on innovative behavior.

> *To be sustainable, entrepreneurial thinking must be integrated into the mission, goals, strategies, structure, processes, and values of the organization. Flexibility, speed, innovation, and entrepreneurial leadership are the cornerstones. The managerial mindset must become an opportunity-driven mindset, where actions are never constrained by resources currently controlled.*[40]

Innovation-in-Action

"Innovation for the Sake of Dominance"

When the landscape of technology is surveyed, there is little doubt that the two most powerful companies in the world are Microsoft and Google. Microsoft long ago claimed dominance over the desktop, and Google has been working diligently to stake its claim on online applications. So, it would seem that the two companies might be resigned to live happily alongside one another, each overseeing its own domain with little attention paid to the other. The problem lies in the fact that their two worlds are colliding and slowly merging into a single realm, where consumers glide from desktop to online without distinguishing between the two. As a result, the two companies have begun an epic battle to prove their dominance through innovation.

Beyond Microsoft's dominant position in operating systems with the ubiquitous Windows series, it has also controlled the market in office suites with Microsoft Office and Internet brewers with Internet Explorer. Google, on the other hand, has largely been restricted to its namesake search engine, which has approximately 70 percent of the search-advertising market. Thus, the stage is set for the two companies to discover ways in which each can intrude on the other's turf.

Google's approach has become evident with the introduction of its own internet browser Google Chrome. The company's plan is to integrate the browser with its existing Google Apps and Google search in order to offer a full-scale operating system as a service, which will be known as Google Chrome. Google is banking on consumers' movement towards smaller laptops, known as netbooks, which have less capacity and, thus, benefit from online applications that do not take up storage space or processing power.

Microsoft's approach is to wrangle the search-advertising market away from Google with its own search engine by taking its existing Live Search and rebranding it as Bing. Despite Microsoft's reputation as an archaic company which is too lethargic to compete with more innovative companies such as Google, the company has surprised industry experts by gaining market share since its launch, slowly edging in on Yahoo's second-place position. Given that Microsoft's search-advertising market share had been declining for more than two years, the shift in trajectory is notable. According to analysts, every percentage point of market share is equivalent to $100 million of revenue, so even small gains can mean big dollars.

The question is no longer what approach the companies will take in their efforts to steal market share from the other, but rather how successful they will be in their attempts. Despite Google's impressive track record, many analysts are skeptical of its ability to profit from Chrome. After all, out of all of the tools Google has developed, it has only managed to monetize the use of its search engine, resulting in the company being labeled as a one-trick pony. And, though Microsoft's gain in search-advertising market share has been impressive, analysts point to its $150 million PR effort as the only reason for the gain, leading them to speculate whether Microsoft's gain is merely a short-term by-product of its marketing push.

Moreover, the two companies did not ascend to supremacy blithely. Each took care to ensure that once they gained control of their respective markets that they would be able to retain it. Google's distribution deal with the popular Firefox browser has guaranteed that it will not be easily toppled from its market position, and Microsoft's first-mover advantage with its operating system, Internet browser and office suite will force Google to take on every business's biggest competition: the status quo. Users have grown accustomed to using Microsoft's software, and consumer behavior can be difficult, if not impossible, to change.

In the end, the possibility exists that neither company will be able to claim absolute victory, but competition breeds innovation, and innovation breeds new technology and, in turn, more choices for consumers. So, for the sake of the consumer, let the fighting commence.

(Adapted from: Goldman, D. 2009. Bing gaining on Google and Yahoo. *CNNMoney.com*. Retrieved July 25, 2009, from: http://money.cnn.com/2009/07/15/technology/bing_google_yahoo_search/index.htm; Goldman, D. 2009. Google Chrome: Microsoft killer? *CNNMoney.com*. Retrieved July 25, 2009, from: http://money.cnn.com/2009/07/08/technology/google_chrome_microsoft/index.htm; and Vogelstein, F. 2009. Why is Obama's top antitrust cop gunning for Google? *Wired*. Retrieved July 27, 2009, from: www.wired.com/print/techbiz/it/magazine/17-08/mf_googlopoly.)

Key Terms

amplifying

CEAI

champion

corporate innovation

corporate innovative strategy

corporate venturing

innovation teams

neophobia

social capital strategic entrepreneurship

sponsor

turfism

Discussion Questions

1. What are two reasons that such a strong desire to develop corporate innovators has arisen in recent years?
2. What are some of the corporate obstacles that must be overcome to establish a corporate innovative environment?
3. What are the two major domains that comprise corporate entrepreneurship?
4. Define a "corporate innovation strategy."
5. Identify the five key elements on which managers should concentrate to develop a corporate innovation strategy.
6. Explain the differences between radical and incremental innovation.
7. Identify the five specific innovative climate factors that organizations need to address in structuring their environment.
8. Why are innovation teams emerging as part of a new strategy for many corporations?
9. Identify the key roles that members of an innovation team could fulfill.
10. Describe the elements that are involved in sustaining corporate innovation.

Notes

1 Kuratko, Donald F. 2017. The challenge of corporate entrepreneurial leadership, in Harrison, Richard & Leitch, Claire M. (eds.), *Research Handbook on Entrepreneurship and Leadership*, Cheltenham, UK: Edward Elgar Publishing, pp. 219–220.
2 Morris, M.H., Kuratko, D.F. & Covin, J.G. 2011. *Corporate Entrepreneurship and Innovation*, Mason, OH: Cengage/SouthWestern Publishers.
3 Hamel, G. 2000. *Leading the Revolution*, Boston: Harvard Business School Press.
4 Kuratko, D.F., Ireland, R.D. & Hornsby, J.S. 2001. Improving firm performance through entrepreneurial actions: Acordia's corporate entrepreneurship strategy. *Academy of Management Executive*, 15(4): 60–71.
5 Sykes, H.B. & Block, Z. 1989. Corporate venturing obstacles: sources and solutions. *Journal of Business Venturing*, (winter): 159–167.
6 Morris, M.H., Kuratko, D.F. & Covin, J.G. 2011. *Corporate Entrepreneurship and Innovation*, Mason, OH: Cengage/SouthWestern Publishers.
7 Blau, P. 1964. *Exchange and Power in Social Life*, New York: John Wiley & Sons.

8 Kanter, R.M. 1985. Supporting innovation and venture development in established companies. *Journal of Business Venturing*, 1: 47–60.

9 Starr, J.A. & MacMillan, I.C. 1990. Resource co-optation via social contracting: resource acquisition strategies for new ventures. *Strategic Management Journal*, 11 (Summer): 79–92.

10 Damanpour, F. 1991. Organizational innovation: a meta-analysis of effects of determinant and moderators. *Academy of Management Journal*, 34: 355–390.

11 Zahra, S.A. 1991. Predictors and financial outcomes of corporate entrepreneurship: an exploratory study. *Journal of Business Venturing*, 6: 259–286.

12 Sharma, P. & Chrisman, J.J. 1999. Toward a reconciliation of the definitional issues in the field of corporate entrepreneurship. *Entrepreneurship Theory and Practice*, 23(3): 11–28.

13 Morris, M.H., Kuratko, D.F. & Covin, J.G. 2011. *Corporate Entrepreneurship and Innovation*, Mason, OH: Cengage/SouthWestern Publishers.

14 Ireland, R.D. & Webb, J.W. 2007. Strategic entrepreneurship: creating competitive advantage through streams of innovation. *Business Horizons*, 50(1): 49–59.

15 Ireland, R.D., Covin, J.G. & Kuratko, D.F. 2009. Conceptualizing corporate entrepreneurship strategy. *Entrepreneurship Theory and Practice*, 33(1): 19–46.

16 Eisenhardt, K.M., Brown, S.L. & Neck, H.M. 2000. Competing on the entrepreneurial edge, in Meyer, G.D. & Heppard, K.A. (eds.), *Entrepreneurship as Strategy*, Thousand Oaks, CA: Sage Publications, pp. 49–62.

17 Hornsby, Jeffrey S., Kuratko, Donald F., Shepherd, Dean A. & Bott, Jennifer P. 2009. Managers' corporate entrepreneurial actions: examining perception and position. *Journal of Business Venturing*, 24(3): 236–247.

18 Kuratko, D.F. 2017. *Entrepreneurship: Theory, Process, and Practice*, 10th ed., Mason, OH: Cengage/South-Western Publishing.

19 Collins, J.C. & Porras, J.I. 1996. Building your company's vision. *Harvard Business Review*, (September–October): 65–77.

20 Covin, J.G., Garrett, R.P., Kuratko, D.F. & Shepherd, D.A. 2015. Value proposition evolution and the performance of internal corporate ventures. *Journal of Business Venturing*, 30(5): 749–774.

21 Schroeder, D.M. 1990. A dynamic perspective on the impact of process innovation upon competitive strategies. *Strategic Management Journal*, 2: 25–41; and Fiol, C.M. 1995. Thought worlds colliding: the role of contradiction in corporate innovation processes. *Entrepreneurship Theory and Practice*, 20(3): 71–90.

22 Peters, T. 1990. Get innovative or get dead. *California Management Review*, 33: 18–26.

23 Drucker, P.F. 1985. The discipline of innovation. *Harvard Business Review*, (May/June): 67–72.

24 Von Hipple, E., Thomke, S. & Sonnack, M. 1999. Creating breakthroughs at 3M. *Harvard Business Review*, (September–October): 47–57.

25 Morse, C.W. 1986. The delusion of intrapreneurship. *Long Range Planning*, 19(2): 92–95.

26 Kuratko, D.F., Montagno, R.V. & Hornsby, J.S. 1990. Developing an entrepreneurial assessment instrument for an effective corporate entrepreneurial environment. *Strategic Management Journal*, 11(Special Issue): 49–58; Hornsby, J.S., Kuratko, D.F. & Montagno, R.V. 1999. Perception of internal factors for corporate entrepreneurship: a comparison of Canadian and U.S. managers. *Entrepreneurship Theory and Practice*, 24(2): 9–24; and Hornsby, J.S., Kuratko, D.F. & Zahra, S.A. 2002. Middle managers' perception of the internal environment for corporate entrepreneurship: assessing a measurement scale. *Journal of Business Venturing*, 17: 49–63.

27 Ireland, R.D., Kuratko, D.F. & Morris, M.H. 2006. A health audit for corporate entrepreneurship: innovation at all levels—part I. *Journal of Business Strategy*, 27(1): 10–17.

28 Kuratko, D.F., Covin, J.G. & Hornsby, J.S. 2014. Why implementing corporate innovation is so difficult. *Business Horizons*, 57(5): 647–655.

29 Kuratko, D.F., Montagno, R.V. & Hornsby, J.S. 1990. Developing an entrepreneurial assessment instrument for an effective corporate entrepreneurial environment. *Strategic Management Journal*, 11(Special Issue): 49–58; and Hornsby, J.S., Kuratko, D.F. & Montagno, R.V. 1999. Perception of internal factors for corporate entrepreneurship: a comparison of Canadian and U.S. Managers. *Entrepreneurship Theory and Practice*, 24(2): 9–24.

30 Holt, D.T., Rutherford, M.W. & Clohessy, G.R. 2007. Corporate entrepreneurship: an empirical look at individual characteristics, context, and process. *Journal of Leadership and Organizational Studies*, 13(4): 40–54.

31 Rutherford, M.W. & Holt, D.T. 2007. Corporate entrepreneurship: an empirical look at the innovativeness dimension and its antecedents. *Journal of Organizational Change Management*, 20(3): 429.

32 Ireland, R.D., Kuratko, D.F. & Morris, M.H. 2006. A health audit for corporate entrepreneurship: innovation at all levels—part I. *Journal of Business Strategy*, 27(1): 10–17.

33 Hornsby, J.S., Kuratko, D.F. & Zahra, S.A. 2002. Middle managers' perception of the internal environment for corporate entrepreneurship: assessing a measurement scale. *Journal of Business Venturing*, 17: 49–63.

34 Kuratko, D.F., Ireland, R.D., Covin, J.G. & Hornsby, J.S. 2005. A model of middle level managers' entrepreneurial behavior. *Entrepreneurship Theory and Practice*, 29(6): 699–716.

35 Ireland, R.D., Kuratko, D.F. & Morris, M.H. 2006a. A health audit for corporate entrepreneurship: innovation at all levels—part I. *Journal of Business Strategy*, 27(1): 10–17; Ireland, R.D., Kuratko, D.F. & Morris, M.H. 2006b. A health audit for corporate entrepreneurship: innovation at all levels—part II. *Journal of Business Strategy*, 27(2): 21–30.

36 Hornsby, J.S., Kuratko, D.F. & Zahra, S.A. 2002. Middle managers' perception of the internal environment for corporate entrepreneurship: assessing a measurement scale. *Journal of Business Venturing*, 17: 49–63.

37 Francis, D.H. & Sandberg, W.R. 2002. Friendship within entrepreneurial teams and its association with team and venture performance. *Entrepreneurship Theory and Practice*, 25(2): 5–25.

38 McGrath, R.G. & MacMillan, I. 2000. *The Entrepreneurial Mindset*, Boston: Harvard Business Press.

39 Adapted from: Ireland, R.D., Covin, J.G. & Kuratko, D.F. 2009. Conceptualizing corporate entrepreneurship strategy. *Entrepreneurship Theory and Practice*, 33(1): 19–46; Kuratko, D.F., Ireland, R.D., Covin, J.G. & Hornsby, J.S. 2005. A model of middle-level managers' entrepreneurial behavior. *Entrepreneurship Theory and Practice*, 29(6): 699–716; and Kuratko, D.F., Hornsby, J.S. & Goldsby, M.G. 2004. Sustaining corporate entrepreneurship: a proposed model of perceived implementation/outcome comparisons at the organizational and individual levels. *International Journal of Entrepreneurship and Innovation*, 5(2): 77–89.

40 Morris, M.H., Kuratko, D.F. & Covin, J.G. 2011. *Corporate Entrepreneurship and Innovation*, Mason, OH: Cengage/SouthWestern Publishers, p. 457.

PART 2
Individual Innovation Skills (*I-Skills*)

3

UNLEASHING INDIVIDUAL CREATIVITY

Ideas are like fish. If you want to catch fish, you can stay in the shallow water. But if you want to catch the big fish, you've got to go deeper. Down deep, the fish are more powerful and more pure. They're huge and abstract. And they're beautiful.

~David Lynch, director[1]

Introduction

Finding ideas for new products and services may be one of the hardest challenges a manager faces today; however, it's critically important that creativity and innovation become the backbone of a company's operations. Lower wages, easily accessible communication networks, and enhanced supply chain management allow competitors around the world to compete against more well-known companies. The deciding factor in today's hypercompetitive markets is creatively offering better products and services that serve customers in new ways.[2] Today's customers expect companies to surprise and delight them. Unfortunately, many managers have been educated and trained to increase the efficiency of doing what has been successful in the past. Additionally, education is often based on getting "the" right answer, instead of learning to work with the ambiguity and uncertainty found in innovative activities.

Clayton Christiansen of the Harvard Business School states that this mindset can lead to the demise of a company, as the organization continues to deliver what the customer expects without looking to new opportunities in the marketplace. When better products come out by entrepreneurial startups and more innovative competitors, the established company has difficulties meeting the new challenges.[3] A big reason for this lapse is the inertia found in established companies. Hit with deadlines and performance goals, managers often focus on generating recurrent revenues by meeting production standards at the expense of developing new markets. Thinking about new products and services becomes a sideline activity, but it's innovation that likely got the company started in the first place.[4] Thus, managers must regain their entrepreneurial edge by being more creative.

The entrepreneurial process inside an organization is guided by a manager or employee who has a unique idea and has the self-discipline and perseverance to commercialize it. A new opportunity or idea is the beginning of the entrepreneurship process, and creative thinking on the part of the individual births the idea.

In this chapter, we explain what creativity is and is not, the elements that support creative activity, the four phases of the creative process, and seven areas where people can focus their creativity. In the process, you will learn how your brain comes up with new ideas, and what steps you can take to develop your own and your employees' creativity. We begin by examining the concept of creativity.

The Nature of Creativity

Creativity is one of the most misunderstood topics in our society. It's prized and coveted while being feared and mistrusted at the same time. Most people see it as magical and incorrectly believe that only a genius can be creative. Most people also assume that some people are born creative and others aren't, or only the highly intelligent person is capable of generating creative ideas and insights. The authors of this book don't accept these views. Neither does Nancy C. Andreasen of the University of Iowa, who's done extensive studies of creativity in science, business, and art, and found that everyone's creative potential can be enhanced. As Andreasen states:

> We know that even prehistoric people possessed the gift of creativity—the capacity to see something new that others could not. Someone picked up a stone and saw a tool. Someone realized that it could be made sharp and pointed by chipping away at it. Someone recognized that a group of people could join together and hunt large food-rich animals, using their collective intellect and strength. Someone suspected that seeds could be planted and crops grown, thereby creating a more secure food supply. Someone figured out how to concentrate light or to chip flints together to create a fire and cook. Someone worked out that circular wheels could facilitate moving heavy objects. . . . We have so many amazing examples of human creativity from human prehistory and history—an ongoing progression of varied and enduring human creative achievements.[5]

Thus, *to be human is to be creative*, but as is the case with many domains like athletics and art, some people have more advanced abilities than others. This chapter explains how creativity is a skill set for looking at the world in new ways. And since creativity is a set of thinking skills, it can be developed. Therefore, anyone can become more creative by developing the habit of looking for new problems to solve and seizing opportunities to make things better for other people.

Creative workers and managers have a different mindset than their peers. They use alternative ways of looking at the world and overcome the limitations of conventional thinking. They amaze others around them in their company, because they are capable of thinking in new ways that are different from the rational, linear, analytical, and logical ways we are taught in school. Steve Jobs and Steve Woczniak, for example, amazed an entire generation when they saw the potential in everyone owning a computer. When they shared their bold vision with conventional companies, they were met with laughs and shrugs. In the 1970s, only large institutions like Fortune 500 firms and research universities used computers, but that would change with the personal computer revolution spearheaded by Apple. Every age has its pioneers. In the twenty-first century, even other worlds will provide new markets that an earlier generation of entrepreneurs and executives could only dream about entering. Leading the charge in developing the space business is Elon Musk, the founder of PayPal and Tesla, Inc. Musk's company SpaceX is pioneering reusable rockets and exploring how to man a mission to Mars. It's too early to know when he'll actually accomplish the feat, but Musk says, "SpaceX is in this for the long haul and, come hell or high water, we are going to make this work."[6] Like Musk and SpaceX, tomorrow's great successes will come from those managers in entrepreneurial companies that exploit opportunities where others only see crises or impossibilities. Yesterday's science fiction becomes today's business reality because of the creativity of entrepreneurial executives like Jobs and Musk. But the first question that needs to be answered in order to make this happen is, what is creativity?

Popular Misconceptions Surrounding Creativity

Sir Ken Robinson proclaims that creative capacities are the greatest resource available to an organization, but in order to maximize that potential people must first understand the real nature of creativity.[7] Creativity is a tricky concept to understand. Many people are interested, but few understand its true nature. One way we can better understand creativity is by understanding what it is *not*. Creativity is shrouded with misconceptions. If we pursue our goals by following these misconceptions, we'll miss our mark. By following commonly accepted wisdom instead of empirically verified principles, we return to making the same mistakes over and over again. Misconceptions mislead our thinking and keep us from developing skills. Therefore, it's imperative for us to rectify our misunderstanding, so that we can approach our creative pursuits with the right practices. Let's now examine why most people misunderstand creativity. Leading creativity scholar Keith Sawyer states that the following misconceptions are the leading culprits of preventing people from developing their creative potential.[8]

Misconception 1: Creativity comes totally from the subconscious.

While the subconscious plays a role in various stages of creative activity, conscious awareness and focused effort are also important. Without a certain degree of structure, breakthroughs aren't made. Sawyer has observed that "creativity rarely comes in a sudden burst of insight. Instead, scientists have discovered that creativity is mostly conscious, hard work."[9] This is because creative individuals have invested a lot of time and energy learning a domain. With the knowledge gained, they can then search for problems, knowledge gaps, and opportunities in the area of study. A newcomer rarely, if ever, makes a major breakthrough in a field.

Furthermore, stories of instant success are usually myths themselves. In *Outliers*, Malcolm Gladwell tells the real story behind "overnight sensations" such as Bill Gates. Long before Bill Gates was a billionaire he was learning computer programming in his middle school in 1968. Gates' mother, along with his other classmates' parents in the school, bought a mainframe computer for the students to use. He took advantage of this opportunity and began logging thousands of hours on the school's system. By the time Gates was 16 years old, he was one of the top 50 programmers in the world. It's no wonder he achieved a fortune based on software at a young age.[10] Warren Buffett has a similar story. His position as one of the world's richest people has its foundation in his studies as a young man. Buffett had a keen interest in business and finance as a boy, operating a pinball machine business in his hometown. When he went to Columbia University to learn finance, he studied under the legendary investor Benjamin Graham. Professor Graham gave his only A+ to Buffett. Buffett applied Graham's teachings to building his own investment company, and, after a slow start, Bershire Hathaway eventually became one of the most successful entrepreneurial ventures over the last 40 years.[11] Creative success is a long road paved by hard work and learning. Innovators pay their dues before hitting on their breakthroughs.

Misconception 2: Children are more creative than adults.

This is one of the most repeated misstatements in our society. Children are portrayed as being the most creative creatures on the planet, and it's thought that schools and society squash their creativity over time. Sawyer points out that this too is a myth. Children actually aren't very creative, and, in fact, school and society provide stimuli and knowledge that adults apply later in their creative pursuits. Experience and knowledge matter. In order to generate new ideas, a person needs a collection of concepts in their brains to reassemble into new combinations. While it's true that biases and paradigms can sometimes limit creativity, knowledge is the reservoir from which new ideas are drawn. In fact, Anders Ericsson, the leading authority on expertise, has proven Nobel Prize winner Herbert Simon's belief that great contributions in a field require a person to first partake in 10,000 hours, or roughly ten years, of hard, deliberate practice on a topic.[12] When skills and knowledge are gained, then a person can recognize what their field needs and values. So, while children clearly can be spontaneous and fun loving, they do not have the requisite training or knowledge to be truly impactful in society.

Misconception 3: Creativity is spontaneous inspiration.

Much of this myth is the result of nineteenth-century idealistic images of the creative genius. We still accept the romantic idea of the great artist shunning social conventions and traditions, working in isolation, rebuffing social critics, and rejecting the guidance of peers and teachers. Sawyer says that that vision of the art world could not be further from the truth. While the general public still believes that artists reject convention, in reality an increasing number of people are entering art school to be trained in the mechanics and methodologies of painting and sculpting. In fact, many of the world's great artists hold a master's in fine arts degree. Formal schooling does not squash an artist's creative contribution, but rather provides the training needed to develop advanced techniques through their career.

Within traditional business and technology fields there is an oft-cited myth that many successful entrepreneurs required no formal schooling, pointing to college dropouts like Bill Gates, Steve Jobs, and Mark Zuckerberg. But it should be noted that even this trio explored their original business ideas within the safe confines of a university setting where they could interact with fellow classmates and investigate classes that interested them. When their entrepreneurial concepts were ready for further development, they left the ivory tower, but they could always return if their ideas didn't pan out. And many of their entrepreneurial peers—like Elon Musk of Tesla, Larry Page and Sergey Brin of Google, and Jeff Bezos of Amazon—*did* complete their college degrees before building their legendary companies. Therefore, managers wanting to be more creative would be wise to pursue formal training to accelerate their learning on topics they would like to build new product lines around. Structured learning environments provide the opportunity to meet like-minded students and supportive professors. After all, much of our current economy was hatched around the college campuses near Silicon Valley and Cambridge, Massachusetts. Innovative managers place themselves in intellectual hotspots. As Louis Pasteur stated, "Chance favors the prepared mind."

Misconception 4: Many creative works go unrecognized and are only discovered decades later.

According to Sawyer, "One of our most stubborn creativity myths is that unrecognized genius is quite common."[13] In actuality, creative output of high quality normally *does* get recognized in a society. In order to generate quality work, an innovator is likely well networked in their field. Therefore, a built-in audience already exists for their discoveries and inventions. One often-cited example of overlooked genius is Gregor Mendel and his experiments on cross-breeding peas. Credited for being the pioneer of modern genetics, legend has it that it took 35 years for his work to be known. In fact, his work was well received during his lifetime. The main problem with the legend is that others from his era were also doing work that had an equal or larger impact on genetic research. Mendel didn't create the field from scratch, but his methodology for applying ratios to better understand genetics was very helpful to future generations of scientists. Another classic example of overlooked genius resides in the impressionist art movement in France. While it's true that the impressionists' works weren't displayed in the French academy, their art was still displayed in many galleries in Europe and the United States, actually resulting in fortunes for some of the artists. As these examples demonstrate, creativity is dependent to a certain degree on accepted quality as well as originality. Therefore, original, high-quality work, if properly promoted, will usually find an appreciative audience in society.

Misconception 5: Everyone is creative.

We sometimes assume that everyone's generating original work, but unfortunately this isn't always the case. Since what's deemed creative is largely dependent on societal acceptance, selection factors in a culture often don't recognize a lot of artistic, scholarly, scientific, and economic output. Evaluation criteria by members of a domain select what original work is accepted and what is forgotten. While it's true that everyone has *potential* to create original work, the hard work and training needed to shape an idea into acceptance isn't always done. Making an original contribution requires putting in many hours of structured work to learn what gaps in a field need to be addressed. Then, the person must work equally long hours to make the concept real. Most entrepreneurial successes have a rich, complex story that is often overly simplified in popular accounts and legends. The popular stories lead most people to think that they aren't capable of original contributions, when the truth is that with proper training and good work habits creative outcomes are possible. Breakthroughs are not the work of superhuman geniuses, but rather hardworking, real people with a desire and persistence to find solutions and answers.

Defining Creativity

Now that we know what creativity isn't, we're better prepared to learn what it is. The science of creativity is relatively new. It wasn't until J.P. Guilford's presidential address to the American Psychological Association in 1950 that the scientific community began to consider it worthy of study. Since then creativity has slowly begun to be studied more, but through its development there's been debate as to what its true nature is. The aforementioned myths illustrate that there are many different interpretations in society as to what it is. As E. Paul Torrance observed in 1988:

> *Creativity defies precise definition. This conclusion does not bother me at all. In fact, I am quite happy with it. Creativity is almost infinite. It involves every sense—sight, smell, hearing, feeling, taste, and even perhaps the extrasensory. Much of it is unseen, nonverbal, and unconscious. Therefore, even if we had a precise conception of creativity, I am certain we would have difficulty putting it into words. However, if we are to study it scientifically, we must have some approximate definition.*[14]

Since Torrance's statement, leading researchers have taken on the challenge of defining the elusive concept. A major advancement in psychology occurred when the social nature of creativity was identified as a key factor. Creativity was no longer seen as the process of a lone individual, but rather a socially constructed phenomenon. Robert Sternberg and colleagues, for example, defined creativity as the "ability to produce work that is novel (i.e., original, unexpected), high in quality, and appropriate (i.e., useful, meets task constraint)."[15] Thus, in order to generate impactful ideas, a person must ensure certain socially expected attributes are contained within it to gain acceptance. In *The Hit Makers*, Derek Thompson canvased popular designs in products ranging from music to daily appliances and discovered that the biggest commercial hits are combinations of the familiar, so that they're comforting and reassuring when used, and the novel, so that they're interesting when first experienced. We want something unique, but not so different that we're confused or frustrated when using it.[16]

Gaining acceptance for a new idea from a target market can be achieved by thoroughly understanding the domain where it resides. According to Howard Gardner:

> *A person isn't creative in general—you can't just say a person is "creative." You have to say a person is creative in X, whether it's writing, being a teacher, or running an organization. People are creative in something . . . People who are creative are always thinking about the domains in which they work. They're always tinkering. They're always saying, "What makes sense here, what doesn't make sense?" And if it doesn't make sense, "Can I do something about it?"*[17]

Or, as psychologist Mihaly Csikszentmihalyi has observed:

> *Creativity occurs when a person, using the systems of a given domain such as music, engineering, business, or mathematics, has a new idea or sees a new pattern, and when this novelty is selected by the appropriate field for inclusion into the relevant domain.*[18]

That is, ideas alone do not qualify as creative outputs. Rather, the ideas must also be of interest and use to others. After all, everyone gets ideas, but it's the uniqueness and usefulness, functionally and/or aesthetically, that determines if something is creative. This view serves entrepreneurial managers well since new products, regardless of how original and unique, must also be accepted by their company and the market in order to be successful. Therefore, in an organizational setting, we can say that creativity occurs when a manager has a new idea or sees an opportunity that's feasible and profitable for the company.

Now that we've debunked the misconceptions of creativity and gained a better understanding of the concept's true nature, we can now examine what elements can bring it about. By understanding what factors increase creative behavior, we can begin to inculcate creativity into our own lives.

The Three Elements of Creativity

If we want to increase our creative output, we must include three elements in our pursuit: domain skills, creative thinking skills, and intrinsic motivation. Teresa Amabile of the Harvard Business School believes mixing these elements is comparable to cooking a stew:

The essential ingredient, something like vegetables or the meat in a stew, is expertise in a specific area: domain skills. These skills represent your basic mastery of a field . . . Creative thinking skills are like spices and herbs you use to bring out the flavor of the basic ingredients in a stew. They make the flavors unique, help the basic ingredients to blend and bring out something different . . . Finally, the element that really cooks the creative stew is passion. Creativity begins to cook when people are motivated by the pure enjoyment of what they are doing.[19]

In the following sections, we examine these ingredients in more depth.

Domain Skills

Neuroscience has proven that creativity isn't supernatural. Ideas don't come out of thin air or from the whisper of a mysterious muse, but instead are a result of new combinations of old and new concepts stored in brains. As Steven Johnson explains in his study of scientific pioneers:

Ideas are built out of self-exciting networks of neurons, clusters of clusters, with each group associated with some shade of a thought or memory or emotion. When we think of a certain concept, or experience some new form of stimulus, a complex network of neuronal groups switches on in synchrony.[20]

The more clusters of information we can draw from, the more potential for new combinations we have. Figure 3.1 depicts this view and shows how our brains are complex networks of circuits, comprising skills and knowledge that interconnect and share information. Domain skills, also known as expertise, encompass the ability to perceive and handle the challenges and details that arise in new combinations.

The Best Way to Develop Expertise Is to Immerse Ourselves in a Domain

One form of immersion is *external*. To more fully understand a domain, we must first interact with topical experts to uncover what's passing for thought leadership and stirring excitement in a field. Immersing yourself in an entrepreneurial city helps, but it comes with a price. A market premium exists for gaining access to experts with needed talent and knowledge. Still, businesses are willing to invest in larger cities because they know the rewards from interactions with other talented people will be worth it.[21] As Geoffrey West, a Santa Fe Institute distinguished professor, observes:

The real essence of a city is its people—they provide its buzz, its soul, and its spirit, those indefinable characteristics we viscerally feel when we are participating in the life of a city. . . . It is all too forgotten that the whole point of a city is to bring people together, to facilitate interaction, and thereby to create ideas and wealth, to enhance innovative thinking and encourage entrepreneurship and cultural activity by taking advantage of the extraordinary opportunities that the diversity of a great city offers.[22]

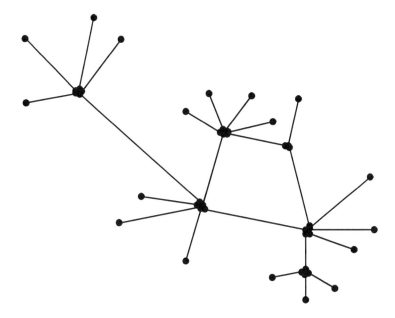

FIGURE 3.1 The Shape of an Idea Forming in the Brain.

Source: Adapted from Steven Johnson, *The Invention of Air*.
New York: Riverhead Books.

As mentioned previously, the archetype of a lone genius with a breakthrough idea is a myth. Michelangelo, for example, produced his masterpieces in Florence, Italy, where other greats like Donatello and Giotto were located. He didn't sculpt David in the small rural village of Caldine. Michelangelo was near the action in his field. However, where that spot of opportunity for you is depends on what field you're in. In *The Geography of Genius*, Eric Weiner chronicles the rise of innovative cities throughout history, and concludes that, "Certain places, at certain times, produced a crop of brilliant minds and good ideas."[23] He identifies ancient Athens as a bohemian port city in the Mediterranean Sea that had an "openness to foreign goods, odd people, and strange ideas."[24] Edinburgh during the Scottish Enlightenment was a place that celebrated practical advancement in medicine, agriculture, and industry rather than the arts, and although it wasn't blessed with a lot of natural resources or a hospitable climate, it thrived. Weiner notes that great achievements occurred there because the Scots celebrated inventors, and "what is honored in a country will be cultivated there."[25] On the other hand, while Edinburgh focused on practical triumphs, Vienna, Austria, in the nineteenth and twentieth centuries celebrated its arts and humanities. Legends in classical composing, like Haydn, Mozart, and Beethoven, and in psychology, like Freud and Jung, thrived in Austria, inspiring each other while also competing for the public's attention among themselves. As Weiner observes, "The essential characteristic of a highly civilized society is not that it is creative but that it is appreciative."[26]

Locating in a place with a dense network of diverse professionals, technologists, and artists can help you develop your ideas.

The second form of immersion in a domain is *internal*. As previously mentioned in the mythology section of this chapter, Anders Ericsson found that 10,000 hours, or roughly ten years, of studying and working in a domain is required to be an expert, and experts are more likely to make significant contributions to society. Again, revisiting Bill Gates' rise to entrepreneurial stardom exemplifies this well. In 1968, when most colleges didn't even own computers, young Gates practically lived in the computer room at his school. By his senior year, he was writing computer code for projects commissioned by the Bonneville Power Station in southern Washington state. By the time Gates dropped out of Harvard as a sophomore and started his own company, he had put in well past 10,000 hours of computer programming. While Gates may have been young when he made his fortune, he wasn't a newcomer to computers. The truth is, he was a seasoned programmer who happened to be young. Thus, if someone wants to make breakthroughs like Gates did, they must first gain knowledge in a domain. This is best done by locating near others in the domain and interacting with that group whenever possible. If a company doesn't have knowledge of a domain, it must hire experts from outside its walls if it's to make breakthroughs. This is why larger companies often buy smaller, innovative companies, and concurrently why this is often an exit strategy for entrepreneurs. It's easier and faster sometimes to acquire that knowledge than build it from scratch. Knowledge and asymmetric information bring a high price in the market.

Creative Thinking Skills

Knowledge and expertise on their own aren't enough for achieving creative outcomes. While sufficient domain expertise provides the foundation for generating advanced ideas in a field, it's creative thinking skills that enable managers to take full advantage of their acquired knowledge. They must be able to diverge on possibilities and converge on favorite options. Thus, there are times where divergence is called for and times when convergence is needed. Divergent and convergent thinking must be employed in a deliberate fashion to come up with a better quality and quantity of new ideas. Fortunately, since divergence and convergence are skills, they can be developed and honed.

Divergent thinking, also known as *ideation*, is perhaps the least developed thinking skill in business, but one that is critical to creativity. Divergent thinking is the process of generating many possible options. It's also a skill limited sometimes by expertise. If a manager has a lot of experience in a market, they may have certain expectations or biases that limit their exploratory nature about new products, services, or processes.[27] They navigate with a fixed cognitive map based on past successes and failures without an open awareness of what their market might become. However, an experienced manager has more opportunity for creative output if they can generate a larger quantity of ideas like children do. Domain knowledge mixed with divergent thinking creates a world of possibilities.

Perhaps no group is better known for generating new ideas and technologies in this way than the Imagineers of the Walt Disney Company. Imagineers are the creative arm of the Disney Parks and Resorts division. Their creations include the audio-animatronic characters in landmark rides such as the Pirates of the Caribbean and manmade mountains like the one that houses Expedition Everest. Imagineers achieve these breakthroughs by embracing a "blue sky" philosophy that supports ideation throughout their workshops. "blue sky" means that the sky's the limit. Anything is possible. Imagineers are given a general goal, such as: "design an authentic Hawaiian-themed resort on the island of Oahu that celebrates the customs and traditions of the local people." After a thorough immersion in Hawaiian culture, they go to work drawing a flurry of initial concepts. Constraints are absent during this stage of the creative process. In the words of the Imagineers, "Limitations only weigh on the wings of an idea as it soars wild and free on the updrafts of possibility. Creative freedom allows us to do anything imaginable, anything at all."[28] This divergent mindset is utilized in the early stages of every project, whether it's a new store design, new ride, or an entirely new park layout. Disney executives know that within these raw and unfiltered concepts lie a few gems that, with added attention and polish, can become hits with park guests for many years to come.

But you don't have to be an Imagineer to practice blue sky thinking. The approach that Disney follows as a part of its creative routines can be developed in any business. Professor Min Basadur and colleagues tested this premise in an experiment. Basadur had 65 engineers participate in a three-day (24-hour) training program on ideation. The first step included training participants on the concept of ideation. Trainees performed a series of exercises that helped them assess how well they diverge and were then given feedback on how to improve their ability to generate ideas. The divergence guidelines helped the participants produce greater quantities of ideas after each exercise. The second step included giving participants a case to read and asking them to generate solutions to the key problems found in it. They were then instructed to share their answers with their fellow workshop attendees. The variety of solutions generated by others in the session surprised them. The interaction helped the engineers discover that there are many different ways of looking at a problem and developing a solution.[29]

It's important for you to gain this perspective as well. Basadur provides seven guidelines in developing these critical thinking skills.[30] First, *withhold judging the quality of ideas while diverging*. The more ideas you have, the better. In order to accomplish this, it's important to remove inadvertent killer phrases like "that's impossible" when diverging. Table 3.1 lists the top ten idea "killers" used in daily business conversations. Although people may not realize they're shutting down others' thinking, these simple, negative phrases stop the flow of creative ideas in a workplace.[31] Second, *don't worry about being right*. There's a time for evaluating ideas later, but during divergence you want to open up your mind and the minds of others to possibilities. From these initial ideas, something better may come. Third, *be aware that the generation of a lot of ideas is the goal of this stage*. From quantity comes quality. Fourth, *don't interrupt a stream of thought*. Write everything down and capture it on paper. You can look back on your ideas later. In a frantic creative work session, ideas can be easily lost. Fifth, *reach for radical, impossible ideas*. Some of history's greatest ideas appeared to be a little foolish when first proposed, but with some follow-up work were shaped into acceptable form. Often in outlandish thoughts, there's a deep kernel of truth. Sixth, *draw your ideas on paper and search for possible connections*. Be open to what new connections come to you as you study the picture. Seventh, *build on others' ideas*. One idea can be a launching point for many other ideas. This is why it's important to never critique or analyze ideas during this stage. Utilizing these seven principles repetitively will generate divergent thinking skills and be a major step toward being a more creative person.

While it's important to generate a lot of ideas, there's also a time when selection of the best options is needed. This selection skill is known as *convergence*, in that we converge down to the best options. While critical people have trouble generating ideas, "big idea" people often struggle with picking something and moving forward. They stay in dream mode, and love every idea that crosses their mind. This habit is why some people procrastinate. They seek perfection and big hits, instead of focusing on progress. In almost any creative pursuit, however, we'll make mistakes and miscalculations. The missteps provide feedback that helps us to learn and correct our mistakes. As W.H. Murray, the Scottish adventurer and rock climber, once said:

> *Until one is committed, there is hesitancy, the chance to draw back, always ineffectiveness. Concerning all acts of initiative (and creation), there is one elementary truth the ignorance of which kills countless ideas and splendid plans: that the moment one definitely commits oneself, the providence moves too. A whole stream of events issues from the decision, raising in one's favor all manner of unforeseen incidents, meetings and material assistance, which no man could have dreamt would have come his way.*

TABLE 3.1 The Most Common Idea Killers

1.	"Naah."
2.	"Can't" (said with a shake of the head and an air of finality).
3.	"That's the dumbest thing I've ever heard."
4.	"Yeah, but if you did that. . ." (poses an extreme or unlikely disaster case).
5.	"We already tried that—years ago."
6.	"I don't see anything wrong with the way we're doing it now."
7.	"We've never done anything like that before."
8.	"We've got deadlines to meet—we don't have time to consider that."
9.	"It's not in the budget."
10.	"Where do you get these weird ideas?"

Source: Adapted from *The Creative Process*, ed. Angelo M. Biondi (Hadley, MA: The Creative Education Foundation, 1986).

I learned a deep respect for one of Goethe's couplets: "Whatever you can do or dream you can, begin it. Boldness has genius, power and magic in it!"[32]

Thus, there comes a point where we must move forward and start getting results. Walt Disney understood this. He often said, "Dream and do," and, "The way to get started is to quit talking and begin doing."[33] One of his most famous risk taking adventures was the creation of the world's first theme park. In 1953, he picked a site in Anaheim, California, to build Disneyland and gave his team only two years to design and build it. This project would be an apt example of Jim Collins' idea of a Big, Hairy, Audacious Goal (BHAG). There had never been anything built like Disneyland before. Critics called it "Disney's Folly" and predicted it would be a colossal failure, but in two short years he completed major construction on the park. Disneyland opened on July 17, 1955, on time as scheduled, but opening day was anything but smooth. Walt and his executives called it "Black Sunday." More people showed up to the park than expected on an unusually hot day, visitors passed out from heat exhaustion, food and beverage stands went empty, and many other mini-catastrophes occurred. But Disney didn't expect perfection right out of the gate. In time, he and his colleagues corrected the problems found on opening day, and within a few weeks the park was operating more smoothly. Today the Disneyland experience is a cherished standard for exemplary customer service in corporate America.

Had it not been for Disney making decisions, setting deadlines, and getting the team and resources together to move forward, Disneyland would never have been built. While Disney loved big ideas and encouraged his employees to stretch themselves, he also appreciated the convergent behavior of disciplined follow-through. As he once said, "Get a good idea, and stay with it. Dog it, and work at it until it's done, and done right."[34] The "blue sky" thinking got the projects started, but pragmatic implementation ensured the movies, parks, and hotels were produced. To be a good leader, you must be open to possibilities and not thwart ideas, but you also must be willing to make the tough calls and expect results.

So, how do we decide what ideas to move forward? First, we have to decide what's important to us. One place to start is our value system. *What do we value? What do we stand for? What are we selling? What's our mission as an organization?* For Disney, it was providing happiness to those that watched his movies and visited his park. If a park employee was grumpy to customers, they were told to cheer up or leave. In designing the parks, he tried to instill the same sense of aesthetics and values that the movies had. If a project strayed from those guidelines, it was modified or terminated.

The second thing to consider in choosing an idea is referring back to the original problem or issue you were trying to address and solve in the first place. Ask yourself, what are the critical success factors in addressing this issue? Then choose the solution that best appears to meet the criteria. For example, when Walt Disney was entertaining different ways to build a mountain in Disneyland, he originally thought he would build a place in the park where guests could take sled rides on real snow . . . in the middle of July in Anaheim, California! He gave this challenge to his Imagineers and waited for their designs and plans. They weren't particularly enthusiastic about the idea. Finally Disney accepted the Imagineers' advice that creating Snow Mountain would be too costly and that melting ice would cause problems with water runoff in the park. While he was aware of the outlandishness of his idea, he didn't let the concept of a mountain in Disneyland die. During a movie shoot in Switzerland in 1958, Walt could often be found looking for hours at a mountain in the distance called the Matterhorn. A few days later he sent a postcard of the mountain to his Imagineers in California with two words scribbled on it: "Build this!" Those marching orders led to the 1959 opening of the Matterhorn Sled Ride in Disneyland.[35] While the structure was made of concrete and steel rather than dirt and snow, Disney got his mountain. Because of his use of the skills of divergence and convergence, Disney was quite literally able to move mountains—he moved the Matterhorn from Switzerland to Anaheim. Like Disney and the Imagineers, we too can move mountains if we become good at using both divergence and convergence.

A third critical thinking skill is deferral of judgment, or being aware of the difference between divergence and convergence and understanding when to use each. Deferral of judgment requires the conscious separation of divergence and convergence. We must withhold judgment and generate many possibilities when diverging, and then make good decisions and move forward when converging. If we don't conscientiously work on these thinking skills, we limit our creative output.

Intrinsic Motivation

The final element of the creative stew is intrinsic motivation, commonly referred to as passion. While it's important to have expertise and good thinking, it's perhaps more important to be passionate about your work. A creative breakthrough requires a lot of effort and, without firm belief and commitment to an idea, it's much harder to see it through to completion. Fortunately, passion and exuberance can be channeled when a manager is engaged with a purpose in their work. As Louis Pasteur observed:

> *The Greeks understood the mysterious power of the hidden side of things. They bequeathed to us one of the most beautiful words in our language—the word "enthusiasm"—en theos—a god within. The grandeur of human actions is measured by the inspiration from which they spring. Happy is he who bears a god within, and who obeys it.*[36]

Or as Jesus says in the non-canonical Gospel of Thomas, "If you do not bring forth what is within you, what you do not bring forth will destroy you."

So it would make sense that we're better off pursuing ideas that inspire us, but can we really know where passion comes from? And is it possible to develop it in a person? The answer to both these questions is "yes." Some places are very adept at creating superstars in certain fields, and give us living labs for learning how to ignite passion in people. In his study of nine talent hotbeds around the world, Daniel Coyle found that future superstars became deeply committed to a pursuit when one or more of the following events occurred. The first, and perhaps most important, factor is that a tiny idea resonates deeply within a person. The same idea may be quickly forgotten by someone else, but for the inspired person a *spark* has been lit that builds into a roaring fire of curiosity and passion. The idea just feels "right," and the person feels compelled to work on the endeavor and makes a personal commitment to devote immense time and energy to become good at it. This factor plays a more important role than IQ and physical attributes in reaching stardom. A 5-year-old Albert Einstein, for example, became interested in physics when his father gave him a small, magnetic compass. Einstein spent hours studying how the needle always pointed to true north. Later in his life, he pointed to this moment as the spark that lit his curiosity about the underlying order of the physical world. Howard Gardner informs us that a spark like the one experienced by Einstein "essentially moves you to take steps to learn more about the thing that interests you, and to discover its complexities, its difficulties, its strengths and obscurities. From that initial love of doing something comes persistence."[37] And from persistence comes the development of knowledge and skills that makes breakthroughs possible.

The second factor Coyle pinpoints for igniting passion in a person is the role of a good mentor or teacher. A good teacher guides their pupil on what to examine and reveals the subtle intricacies of complex domains. Left on our own, we might wander aimlessly searching for knowledge, but a good teacher breaks a domain down into its critical elements and steers us to better performance. More efficient learning can save us years of frustration and put us on a path to better performance at a younger age. And better performance fosters a positive self-image within ourselves, which motivates us to continue our learning. Thus, self-belief is the fuel needed to develop abilities. Without it, we're less likely to endure shortcomings that occur during the early days of skill acquisition. Karen Connolly Armitage, a senior concept designer at Walt Disney Imagineering, shares a moment that set her on a path to her future career:

> My mom told a story in later years about an airy drawing of mine with a bold dash of blue under a magnificent swirl of pink. She would recall that I presented it proudly.
> "What is it, dear heart?" she asked as she turned it around and around. I stuck my four-year-old chin out and with all the indignation of a misunderstood genius, turned it the proper way and retorted, "It's an elephant getting out of the bathtub!" Soon it was framed, matted, under glass, and hung with pride in the hall, for all to see. My self-belief was started.[38]

While your employees may not be drawing elephants getting out of bathtubs, they may occasionally come up with ideas that leave you scratching your head. At that point, encourage the effort and offer support on where the idea can go. Start building belief in the person. Doing otherwise could shut the person down and prevent them from presenting an idea that might actually be a big hit one day.

The third factor that stimulates intrinsic motivation is finding *a role model* you can relate to. The role model shows you what's possible, and you'll find yourself thinking, "I want to be like them. If she can do it, why can't I?" Once this thought is embedded in your head, the next one is just as powerful: "Better get busy."

Coyle gives the example of Roger Bannister and the four-minute mile as proof of this phenomenon. Physiologists and athletes alike used to believe that it was physically impossible to run a mile in under four minutes. Bannister didn't agree with the commonly accepted wisdom and trained specifically to go sub-four by running quarter-mile repeats in 60 seconds in practice. He figured if he could string together three consecutive 60-second quarter miles in a race, he would only need to run the last one a second faster to go sub-four. The plan worked. Bannister's feat of running the mile in 3:59.4 in 1954 was deemed the greatest athletic accomplishment of the twentieth century by *Sports Illustrated*. Once Bannister ran sub-four, other milers around the world thought, "If a medical student in Britain can do it, I can too." And within three years, 17 other runners accomplished the once impossible feat. Bannister had provided a role model to the other runners that it could be done, and then they got busy and trained with that goal in mind.

Reading biographies of legends like Bannister can spur your motivation. When you learn the *real* story of how superstars attained their success, you'll see that it came from hard work. You too can go on to big accomplishments if you apply yourself to the task like they did. You'll engrain in your mind the important knowledge that great leaders and innovators used to achieve their breakthroughs. The backstory of their trials and errors in learning the intricacies of their craft will inspire you. Once you see that legends are also human, you'll learn that you too can make similar creative leaps.

Talent Hotbeds

Every field seems to have an epicenter of talent that produces its leading performers. Coyle found that taking people with an interest in a topic and placing them with great teachers and role models produces unusual numbers of exceptional performers in a field. What's most encouraging about his findings is that we don't have to be blessed with the best and latest technologies and facilities for this to occur. Brazilian youths, for example, learn soccer on dirt fields and in crowded streets, and yet produce 900 players who are signed every year by professional European clubs. The Spartak Tennis Club in Moscow produces some of the top men's and women's professional players in the world on one single indoor court led by a 77-year-old master teacher named Larisa Preobrazhenskaya. Coyle believes the key way these places ignite passion is by continually sending primal cues—people, images, and ideas—that tell a person that they too can achieve great things. Thus, state-of-the-art workplaces aren't necessary if you want to train your employees and yourself to be more creative. What *is* required is that when you see a spark in someone's eye, you support their idea and let them run with it. It doesn't mean that you have to fully accept it, but be open to where the person goes with the idea, because that spark may lead to a creative outburst that you've never recognized in that person before. Once it appears the person is serious about the idea, surround them with mentors who have championed others' ideas in the past. The mentors can then suggest practices that have been proven to work in your company in the past. With proper coaching and support, the employee will see that their vision can become a reality. They will never approach their work in the same way again.

It's impossible for every student of the Spartak Tennis Academy to win Wimbledon, but the players are appreciative of the opportunity to train with Coach Preobrazhenskaya and get their shot at the big time. Likewise, it is important to celebrate effort in your company, regardless of whether a project is eventually green-lighted or not. Employees of creative companies know they're part of a unique organization that provides them with the opportunity to develop their strengths. Not every project in your company can be implemented, but with enough people embracing a creative mindset, odds are favorable that some ideas will turn out to be a hit product or service one day. Companies with a creative culture win out in today's marketplace.

In summary, domain knowledge, creative thinking skills, and intrinsic motivation are the three key elements of creativity. If we have this combination, we greatly increase our odds of generating more creative output. However, we still need guidance on how to actually work with ideas and bring them into reality. In the following section, we examine the actual process people go through when they create new things.

The Creative Process

Creativity is a process that can be developed and improved.[39] This process comes easier for some because they've been raised and educated in an environment that encouraged them to develop their creativity. For others, the process is more difficult because they haven't been positively reinforced; if they're to be creative, they must learn how to implement the creative process.[40] The creative process has four commonly agreed-on phases or steps, although experts may refer to them by a variety of names.[41] Experts also agree that these phases do not always occur in the same order for every creative activity. We shall examine this four-step process using the most typical framework.

Phase 1: Background or Knowledge Accumulation

Investigation and information-gathering generally precede the development of a creative idea. Discovery activities include extensive reading, conversations with others working in the field, feedback from stakeholders like customers and suppliers, attendance at professional meetings and workshops, and a general absorption of information relative to the problem or issue under study. Additional investigation in unrelated fields is sometimes involved as well. Exploration provides a variety of perspectives on a problem.

A manager's existing knowledge base will help in identifying a new opportunity, as it serves as the basis for processing new experiences. This knowledge base could take the form of general industry knowledge, prior market knowledge, prior customer understanding, specific interest knowledge, or any previous knowledge that helps the manager to better identify opportunities. Every manager in a creative organization needs to use their own unique knowledge base to interpret the various sources of opportunities the company has. Thus, each individual's experiences are uniquely valuable to the company in generating new ideas for products, services, and processes.[42]

Managers can practice the creative search for background knowledge in a number of ways. Some of the most helpful are: (1) read in a variety of fields; (2) join professional groups and associations; (3) attend professional meetings and seminars; (4) travel to new places; (5) talk to anyone and everyone about your topic; (6) scan magazines, newspapers, and journals for articles related to the subject; (7) develop a subject library for future reference; (8) carry a small notebook and record useful information; (9) devote time to pursue natural curiosities; and (10) survey stakeholders.[43]

Phase 2: The Incubation Process

After we acquire knowledge on our subject, it's often good to get away from it for a while. Creative individuals allow their subconscious to mull over the tremendous amounts of information they gathered during the preparation phase. Neuroscience supports this approach with the computational theory of mind, which posits that the brain is essentially a pattern recognition machine. However, in order to assemble patterns, it needs time to store and process the large amounts of data it holds. During the incubation process, the brain clumps related information together into mental clusters, places new incoming data with similar pre-existing clusters, and reorganizes the clusters as we experience new events. Figure 3.2 illustrates this mental mechanism.[44] As noted cognitive scientist Steven Pinker states:

> *The mind owes its power to its synaptic, compositional, combinatorial abilities. Our complicated ideas are built out of simpler ones, and the meaning of the whole is determined by the meanings of the parts and the meanings of the relations that connect them.*[45]

Essentially, the brain is trying to make sense of its world by organizing and reorganizing knowledge and new data, and then predicting future possibilities related to your goals, desires, needs, and survival. Your brain then matches up input from the external world with mental models you've constructed, in order to determine what the best possible outcome will be among various options. When there's a disconnect between input and stored patterns, your brain makes adjustments for a wider range of possible scenarios in the future and selects the one that makes the most sense to you. Thus, we're capable of developing new business ideas by consciously gathering

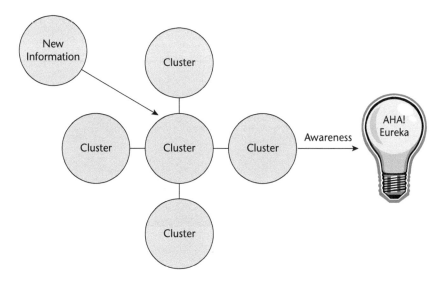

FIGURE 3.2   New Information Linking with Knowledge for Insight.

new information on a market or societal trend and letting our subconscious relate it to past experience and knowledge.[46]

Incubation spurs new idea formulation by giving our brains time to recombine information into new combinations, which essentially is what creativity is. We drop our evaluative frame of mind and relax our mental filters, and then the subconscious goes to work. From this perspective, we can imagine the mind resembling an iceberg, with a majority of cognition taking place below the surface of consciousness.[47] Figure 3.3 illustrates how this subconscious mechanism comprises hidden networks of neurons that share information with each other. As medical researcher Robert Burton explains:

> The hidden layer is a powerful metaphor for the brain's processing of information. It is in the hidden layer that all elements of biology (from genetic predispositions to neurotransmitter variations and fluctuations) and all past experience, whether remembered or long forgotten, affect the processing of incoming information. It is the interface between incoming sensory data and a final perception, the anatomic crossroad where nature and nurture intersect. It is why your red is not my red, your idea of beauty isn't mine, why eyewitnesses offer differing accounts of an accident, or why we don't all put our money on the same roulette number.[48]

It's also why one person may come up with a new business idea that's different from others who are looking at the same situation. The incubation phase brings forth new ideas by stirring the creative stew.

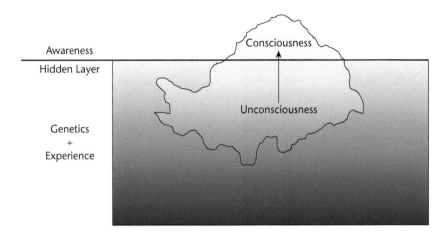

FIGURE 3.3 Iceberg Model of the Brain.

The incubation process often occurs while people are engaged in activities totally unrelated to the subject or problem. It happens even when they're sleeping. This accounts for the advice frequently given to a person who's frustrated by what seems to be an impossible challenge: "Why don't you sleep on it?" Getting away from a problem and letting the subconscious mind go to work allows creativity to spring forth. Some of the most helpful steps to induce incubation are to: (1) engage in routine, "mindless" activities (cutting the grass, painting the house); (2) exercise regularly; (3) play (sports, board games, puzzles); (4) think about the project or problem before falling asleep; (5) meditate; (6) sit back and relax on a regular basis; and (7) travel.[49]

Phase 3: The Idea Experience

Phase 3 of the creative process is often the most exciting, because it's when the idea or solution the individual is seeking is discovered. When the brain makes a connection that makes logical sense for that person, it's thrown into conscious awareness to be considered for action. The subconscious has made a connection that appears to solve a challenging puzzle, and your body has sent you a signal that tells you success is on the way. It's this powerful feeling that often brings us back to pursuing creative endeavors over and over again. It can almost be addictive.

Sometimes referred to as the "eureka moment," this phase is also the one the average person incorrectly perceives as the only component of creativity. While it's the phase most chronicled in popular accounts of breakthroughs, we must always remember the preparation, hard work, and time that go into attaining a powerful idea. Phase 3 rarely happens without Phases 1 and 2. Great discoveries require patience.

As with the incubation process, new ideas often emerge while the person is busy doing something unrelated to the problem (for example, taking a shower, driving on an interstate highway, or leafing through a newspaper). Sometimes the idea appears as a bolt out of the blue. In most cases, however, the answer comes in incremental fashion. Slowly but surely, the person begins to formulate the solution. Because it's often difficult to determine when the incubation process ends and the idea experience phase begins, many people are unaware of the transition from Phase 2 to Phase 3.

Following are ways to speed up the idea experience: (1) daydream and fantasize about your project; (2) practice your hobbies; (3) work in a leisurely environment (for example, at home instead of at the office); (4) put the problem on the back burner; (5) keep a notebook at bedside to record late-night or early-morning ideas; and (6) take breaks while working.[50]

The awareness of how the brain gets ideas will assist you in becoming more creative. You'll have a better understanding of how to gather information; you'll trust that your subconscious is working for you in the background; and you'll develop more patience and persistence, traits that are of supreme importance in creative pursuits. If you haven't found a good idea yet, you'll know that it's not because of a lack of ability on your part. You just need more information and time to solve the problem.

The creative process can be taxing sometimes. You're working hard, but the answer doesn't seem to be coming to you. Don't worry. Frustration and confusion are normal feelings during the creative process. Hang in there. When you come across pertinent information that might be helpful in solving a problem or creating a new product or service, your brain will let you know!

Phase 4: Evaluation and Implementation

This is the most difficult step of a creative endeavor and requires a great deal of courage, self-discipline, and perseverance. Successful managers don't give up when they run into temporary obstacles. They may even fail several times before their ideas are useful. In Phase 4, an idea may need to go in an entirely different direction than originally intended. Much of the reason for a change in course is because ideas that emerge from Phase 3 are often very rough. Modification and testing are needed for an idea to take practical shape. For these reasons, Phase 4 can be an exhausting time for a manager, so it's important to maintain your health and wellbeing as you navigate the obstacles associated with getting to market. Some of the most useful suggestions for carrying out this phase are to: (1) increase your energy level with proper exercise, diet, and rest; (2) further educate yourself on innovation and what steps are needed to make an idea a reality; (3) test your ideas with knowledgeable people; (4) take notice of your intuitive hunches and feelings; (5) educate yourself on how to collaborate with others on your idea; (6) examine organizational policies and practices on bringing ideas to market; (7) seek advice from others (friends, experts, etc.); and (8) view the problems you encounter as challenges that can better your skills and expertise.[51]

Figure 3.4 illustrates the four phases of the creative thinking process. If a person encounters a major problem while moving through the process, it's sometimes

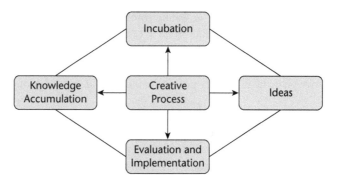

FIGURE 3.4 The Critical Thinking Process.

helpful to go back to a previous phase and try again. For example, if an individual is unable to formulate an idea or solution (Phase 3), a return to Phase 1 often helps. By immersing themselves in the data, the individual allows their unconscious mind to begin anew, processing the data, establishing cause–effect relationships, and formulating potential solutions.

Areas in which People Are Creative

Remember, everyone has the potential to be creative. Some are creative all the time while others stifle it, and most of us fall somewhere in between the two. The reality is that people often don't recognize when or how they're being creative. Furthermore, they fail to recognize the many opportunities for creativity that arise within their jobs on a daily basis. Creativity researcher William Miller argues that people often don't recognize their opportunities to be creative. He suggests that the path to creativity begins by first recognizing all the ways in which we are or can be creative. People in organizations can channel their creativity into seven different areas: idea creativity, material creativity, organization creativity, relationship creativity, event creativity, inner creativity, and spontaneous creativity.[52] Steve Jobs' tenure at Apple is often given as an exemplar of creativity and market success. Let's examine how being creative in these seven areas may have helped Apple attain dominance in its industry under Jobs' creative leadership:

1. *Idea creativity* occurs when you think up a new idea or concept, such as an idea for a new product or service or way to solve a problem. Apple's invention of the iPhone was a very creative idea in the cellular phone industry. Previous cellular phones were for calls and texting. Now the world has a product that can deliver services for communication, entertainment, photos, and gaming all on one device.
2. *Material creativity* occurs when you invent or find new uses for materials for products, services, or processes. Creating the iPhone's unique face required

sourcing the unusually sturdy Gorilla Glass from Corning. Corning at the time didn't think they could deliver enough of the glass to meet Jobs' expectations, but within six months they were providing enough of the material to meet the product's first shipment deadline.[53] Rival companies were at a competitive disadvantage because they were still manufacturing phones with weaker glass that cracked when dropped.

3. *Organization creativity* occurs when you organize people or projects and come up with a new organizational form or approach to structuring things. Examples include organizing a project, starting a new business division, putting together or reorganizing a work group, redesigning the workplace, and changing the policies and rules of a group. The new Apple headquarters in Cupertino, California, stands as Jobs' last great achievement. The circular 2.8-million-square-foot building sits on a 175-acre property landscaped to resemble a national park. Chief designer Jonathan Ive says Jobs wanted the building to be his final contribution to the company. It would provide a workplace to inspire Apple employees for the next 100 years. The Ring, as it's affectionately called, will be a location where "people can connect and collaborate and walk and talk. The value is not in what went into the building. It's what will come out."[54]

4. *Relationship creativity* occurs when you take a creative approach to achieving collaboration, cooperation and win–win relationships with others. The person who handles a difficult situation well or deals with a particular person in an especially effective manner is being creative in a relationship or one-on-one context. Although accused of creating a "reality distortion field" during tense one-on-one meetings, Jobs pushed people to achieve feats that they didn't believe were possible. In the aforementioned Gorilla Glass example, Corning CEO Wendell Weeks told Jobs that Apple's production and shipment request was impossible. But Jobs responded, "Don't be afraid. Yes, you can do it. Get your mind around it. You can do it." Weeks did get his mind around it, and the Gorilla Glass orders were eventually met. A less creative executive than Jobs might not have had the same persuasive sway.

5. *Event creativity* occurs when you produce an event such as an awards ceremony, team outing, or annual meeting. The creativity here also encompasses décor, ways in which people are involved, sequence of happenings, setbacks, and so forth. A product launch by Apple and Steve Jobs was always an event. Media, company employees, and technology fans filled an auditorium to watch Jobs evangelize the latest Apple inventions. Most executives probably couldn't even pay an audience to show up for such an event.

6. *Inner creativity* occurs when you change your inner self; you're open to new approaches to how you do things and think about yourself in different ways; or you achieve a change of heart or find a new perspective or way to look at things that's a significant departure from how you've traditionally looked at them. Jobs credits much of his flexible thinking to his experiences as a young man traveling India and embracing the counterculture movement of the 1970s. Although he moved on from those free spirit activities, he still

practiced Zen Buddhism and listened to Bob Dylan and the Beatles to keep his mind limber and open to new possibilities in the world.

7. *Spontaneous creativity* occurs when you act in a spontaneous or spur-of-the-moment manner, such as coming up with a witty response in a meeting, delivering an off-the-cuff speech, offering a quick and simple way to settle a dispute, or making a creative appeal when trying to close a sale. Jobs' most famous example of spontaneous creativity occurred when he recruited Pepsi CEO John Sculley to Apple. Jobs felt he could learn a lot working with the successful and experienced Sculley, but the senior executive didn't want to leave his comfortable position leading a Fortune 500 company. That's when Jobs delivered a challenge that haunted Sculley for days: "Do you want to spend the rest of your life selling sugared water, or do you want a chance to change the world?" This off-the-cuff question caused Sculley to change his mind in that instant and agree to join Apple. Although the relationship would flounder in the future, Sculley did help the company through its growing pains in the 1980s and laid the groundwork for the more mature company Jobs rejoined in 1997.

Think about creative leaders you admire. Which of these seven areas do they excel in? What examples can you come up with that illustrate this? When you're working in one of these seven areas, remember to apply the principles of creativity covered in this chapter. Better yet, think of ways to bring each of these types of creativity into your work and company culture. Immerse yourself in topics you're curious about, use divergent thinking to generate new ideas, apply convergent thinking to choose a path, and believe in your abilities to reach your goals. If you consistently practice these principles in your personal and professional lives, you'll become more creative.

Summary

This chapter examined the importance of creativity in generating new business ideas. The nature of creativity was explained by first examining the common mythology behind it. Once we understood what creativity isn't, we explained what it actually is. The three elements needed to increase creativity were then covered. The four phases of the creative process were also presented. The chapter concluded with the seven areas where people can generate new ideas.

Innovation-in-Action

Scientific Research on the "Aha!" Moment

Recent research in neuroscience is shedding light on how the brain works. Scientists used to believe the only way to understand mental mechanisms was by indirectly studying behavior and attitudes; however, medical technology in the form of magnetic resonance imaging (MRI) has provided a new set of tools to peer into the once mysterious realms of the brain. Using a technique called functional magnetic resonance imaging, or fMRI, neuroscientists can study what areas of the brain become activated by different thoughts and stimuli. Researchers Read Montague and Gregory Berns took special interest in utilizing the technology to answer the question, "What do people find rewarding?" Or put another way, what do people really want? The way to finding the answer to this age-old question is by measuring the amount of dopamine released in the brain. Dopamine is the "feel good" chemical in the brain, and is your body's way of reinforcing behaviors. In a sense, it's natural "dope." Those things that bring a dopamine release are repeated because they feel good. If a thought, action, or stimuli is enjoyable to the person, it's due to dopamine being released in greater quantities. It's your body's way of telling you what to pursue and what to avoid. While it's difficult to actually measure dopamine itself, scientists do know that the striatum—a small area in the brain with the densest dopamine concentration—lights up during an fMRI when dopamine is released. Scientists from all realms, including economics, are searching to see what things stimulate the striatum.

So after all these studies, what have scientists found that stimulates the striatum the most? Novelty. When you go into new territory, whether physically or mentally, new information comes into your brain and your striatum goes into overdrive. The challenge and the risk of new situations stimulate an increased release of dopamine that focuses your attention on the new stimuli. As you contemplate and address the new situation or topic, your brain changes at the molecular level, and lays down new tracks and connections. The new neuronal networks we build are the foundation of learning, which brings satisfaction with ourselves and our world. As a result, we are driven to seek new challenges and accept the risk involved if we subconsciously calculate that the rewards of the search outweigh the costs. Some people get these feelings through risky, physical activities like sky diving and rock climbing, while others find it through more cerebral pursuits that stretch their minds.

Even the expectation of something good can release dopamine. This is the source of curiosity, and once piqued we feel compelled to follow through. Thus, when we seek an answer to a problem that we think could bring future rewards, we search until we find a solution. When we finally find a solution to a problem, we are rewarded with a larger release of dopamine. This dopamine release is the essence of the "Aha!" moment. In a sense, we can become addicted to this experience—but in a good way. When we've experienced this pleasurable, satisfying moment, we seek out further challenges. This incredible mechanism leads us to conquer new lands, markets, and fields. It may also be why some people are serial entrepreneurs, because they return again and again to the exciting challenges and thrills found during the early days of a startup company.

(Adapted from: Berns, Gregory. 2005. *Satisfaction: Sensation Thinking, Novelty, and the Science of Finding True Fulfillment*, New York: Henry Holt and Company.)

Key Terms

convergence

creativity

deferral of judgment

divergence

domains

evaluation

ideas

implementation

incubation

intrinsic motivation

knowledge accumulation

passion

Discussion Questions

1. Describe creativity. Explain how it is important for managers in a company.
2. What are the eight myths of creativity?
3. What are the three elements of creativity? How could a manager incorporate these elements into their company? How could a manager use these elements to become more creative themselves?
4. What is the difference between divergent and convergent thinking? Why are these important skills?
5. Why is Disney such a creative company?
6. What role does a mentor or teacher play in shaping creativity?
7. Explain each phase of the creative process.
8. How does your brain come up with new ideas?
9. Describe the seven areas in which people can be creative.
10. What steps can you take today to become more creative in your own work?

Notes

1 Lynch, David. 2006. *Catching the Big Fish: Meditation, Consciousness, and Creativity*, New York: Penguin.
2 Kao, John. 2007. *Innovation Nation: How America Is Losing Its Innovation Edge, Why It Matters, and What We Can Do to Get It Back*, New York: Free Press.
3 Christensen, Clayton M. 2003. *The Innovator's Dilemma: The Revolutionary Book that Will Change the Way You Do Business*, New York: HarperBusiness Essentials.
4 Schwartz, Evan I. 2004. *Juice: The Creative Fuel that Drives World-Class Inventors*, Boston: Harvard Business School Press.

5 Andreasen, Nancy C. 2005. *The Creating Brain: The Neuroscience of Genius*, New York: Dana Press.

6 Vance, Ashlee. 2015. Elon Musk: Tesla, SpaceX, and the quest for a fantastic future. *Ecco*, p. 140.

7 Robinson, Ken. 2001. *Out of Our Minds: Learning to Be Creative*, Mankato, MN: Capstone.

8 Sawyer, R. Keith. 2006. *Explaining Creativity: The Science of Human Innovation*, Oxford: Oxford University Press.

9 Ibid, p. 18.

10 Gladwell, Malcolm. 2008. *Outliers: The Story of Success*, Boston: Little, Brown, and Company.

11 Colvin, Geoff. 2008. *Talent Is Overrated: What Really Separates World-Class Performers from Everybody Else*, Boston: Portfolio.

12 Ericsson, K. Anders. 1996. The acquisition of expert performance: an introduction to some of the issues, in Ericsson, K. Anders (ed.), *The Road to Excellence: The Acquisition of Expert Performance in the Arts and Sciences, Sports and Games*, Hillside, NJ: Lawrence Erlbaum Associates.

13 Sawyer, R. Keith. 2006. *Explaining Creativity: The Science of Human Innovation*, Oxford: Oxford University Press, p. 22.

14 Torrance, E. Paul. 1998. The nature of creativity as manifest in its testing, in Sternberg, Robert J. (ed.), *The Nature of Creativity: Contemporary Psychological Perspectives*, Cambridge: Cambridge University Press.

15 Sterberg, Robert J., Kaufman, J.C. & Perez, J.E. 2002. *The Creativity Conundrum*, Hove, UK: Psychology Press.

16 Thompson, Derek. 2017. *The Hit Makers: The Science of Popularity in an Age of Distraction*, London: Penguin.

17 Goleman, Daniel, Kaufman, Paul & Ray, Michael. 1993. *The Creative Spirit*, New York: Plume, p. 26.

18 Csikszentmihalyi, Mihaly. 1996. *Creativity: Flow and the Psychology of Discover and Invention*, New York: HarperCollins.

19 Goleman, Daniel, Kaufman, Paul & Ray, Michael. 1993. *The Creative Spirit*, New York: Plume.

20 Johnson, Steven. 2008. *The Invention of Air: A Story of Science, Faith, Revolution, and the Birth of America*, New York: Riverhead.

21 Harford, Tim. 2008. *The Logic of Life: The Rational Economics of an Irrational World*, New York: Random House.

22 West, Geoffrey. 2017. *Scale: The Universal Laws of Growth, Innovation, Sustainability, and the Pace of Life in Organisms, Cities, Economies, and Companies*, London: Penguin, p. 252.

23 Weiner, Eric. 2016. *The Geography of Genius: A Search for the World's Most Creative Places, from Ancient Athens to Silicon Valley*, London: Simon & Schuster, p. 8.

24 Ibid, p. 62.

25 Ibid, p. 148.

26 Ibid, p. 218.

27 Johnson-Laird, P.N. 1988. Freedom and constraint in creativity, in Sternberg, Robert J. (ed.), *The Nature of Creativity: Contemporary Psychological Perspectives*, Cambridge: Cambridge University Press.

28 The Imagineers. 1996. *Walt Disney Imagineering: A Behind the Dreams Look at Making the Magic Real*, New York: Disney.

29 Basadur, Min, Graen, G.B. & Scandura, T.A. 1986. Training effects on attitudes toward divergent thinking among manufacturing engineers. *Journal of Applied Psychology*, 71(4): 612–617.

30 Basadur, Min. 1999. *Simplex: A Flight to Creativity*, Buffalo, NY: The Creative Education Foundation Press.

31 Biondi, Angelo M. 1986. *The Creative Process*, Buffalo, NY: The Creative Education Foundation.

32 Murray, W.H. 1951. *The Scottish Himalayan Expedition*, London: Dent.

33 Smith, Dave. 2001. *The Quotable Walt Disney*, New York: Disney.

34 Ibid.

35 Surrell, Jason. 2007. *The Disney Mountains: Imagineering at Its Peak*, New York: Disney.

36 Dubos, R.J. 1995. *Louis Pasteur*, New York: Little, Brown, and Company.

37 Goleman, Daniel, Kaufman, Paul & Ray, Michael. 1993. *The Creative Spirit*, New York: Plume.

38 The Imagineers. 2003. *The Imagineering Way: Ideas to Ignite Your Creativity*, New York: Disney.

39 de Bono, Edward. 1992. *Serious Creativity: Using the Power of Creativity to Create New Ideas*, New York: HarperBusiness.

40 Mellow, Eleni. 1996. The two conditions view of creativity. *Journal of Creative Behavior*, 30(2): 126–143.

41 de Bono, Edward. 1985. *Six Thinking Hats*, New York: Little, Brown & Company; see also de Bono, Edward. 1995. Serious creativity. *Journal for Quality and Participation*, 18(5): 12.

42 Ardichvili, A., Cardozo, R. & Ray, S. 2003. A theory of entrepreneurial opportunity identification and development. *Journal of Business Venturing*, 18(1): 105–123; see also Davidsson, Per & Honig, Benson. 2003. The role of social and human capital among nascent entrepreneurs. *Journal of Business Venturing*, 18(3): 301–331.

43 Raudsepp, Eugene. 1981. *How Creative Are You?* New York: TarcherPerigee; see also Van Gundy, Arthur B. 1983. *108 Ways to Get a Bright Idea and Increase Your Creative Potential*, New York: Prentice Hall; and see Firestein, Roger L. 1989. *Why Didn't I Think of That?* United Education Services.

44 Johnson, Steven. 2008. *The Invention of Air: A Story of Science, Faith, Revolution, and the Birth of America*, New York: Riverhead.

45 Pinker, Steven. 1997. *How the Mind Works*, New York: Norton.

46 Hawkins, Jeff & Blakeslee, Sandra. 2004. *On Intelligence*, London: Times Books.

47 Stevenson, Leslie. 2004. *Ten Theories of Human Nature*, Oxford: Oxford University Press.

48 Burton, Robert A. 2008. *On Being Certain: Believing You Are Right Even When You're Not*, New York: St. Martin's.

49 Harman, W.W. & Rheingold, H. 1984. *Higher Creativity: Liberating the Unconscious for Breakthrough Insights*, New York: Tarcher; and see Goleman, Daniel, Kaufman, Paul & Ray, Michael. 1993. *The Creative Spirit*, New York: Plume.

50 Osborn, A.F. 1963. *Applied Imagination*, 3rd ed., New York: Scribner's; see also Gordon, William J. 1961. *Synectics*, New York: Harper & Row; and see also Pollock, Ted. 1995. A personal file of stimulating ideas, little-known facts and daily problem-solvers. *Supervision*, 4(April): 24.

51 Keil, John M. 1985. *The Creative Mystique: How to Manage It, Nurture It, and Make It Pay*, New York: Wiley; and Brandowski, James F. 1990. *Corporate Imagination Plus: Five Steps to Translating Innovative Strategies into Action*, New York: Free Press.

52 Miller, William C. 1999. *Flash of Brilliance*, New York: Perseus Books.

53 Isaacson, Walte. 2011. *Steve Jobs*, New York: Simon & Schuster.

54 Levy, Steven. 2017. One more thing. *Wired*, June: 56.

4

MANAGERIAL SKILLS FOR THE INNOVATION PROCESS

Whenever I look at a problem, I have this one simple lens, which is innovation should help here.
~Bill Gates, co-founder of Microsoft and the Bill and
Melinda Gates Foundation[1]

Introduction

As we discussed in Chapter 1, creativity and innovation can be very similar concepts, but there are some differences. *Creativity is typically described as the process of generating new ideas, while innovation is a process that turns those ideas into reality. It's for this reason that some people refer to innovation as applied creativity.*[2] To further complicate the concept, innovation is conceptualized as not only a process, but also as an outcome based on change. As Donald Marquis clarifies:

> *When an enterprise produces a good or service or uses a method or input that is new to it, it makes a technical change. The first enterprise to make a given technical change is an innovator. . . . Another enterprise making the same technical change is presumably an imitator. . . . Thus, an innovation can be thought of as the unit of technical change.*[3]

Therefore, change is the key word in innovation. The more you do something that fundamentally changes your market and forces your competitors to react to you, the more innovative you are. While efficiency and cost control are important for effectively running a business, companies eventually reach a plateau where increased efforts on improving current products, services, and processes bring minimal improvements on return. Innovation, therefore, is required to take a company to new heights. Legendary track and field athlete Sergei Bubka understood the value of using innovation to go to new heights. After pole vaulting to a world record height of 6 meters (19 feet 8 ¼ inches), he was asked if he would ever reach

7 meters (22 feet 11 ¾ inches). He replied, "No, there will have to be another technical revolution before that height can be reached. There's only so high you can jump using a bending fiberglass pole."[4] There's also only so high a company can go in its market if it continues to offer the same products and services. In order to raise the bar, a company must embrace innovation, but this isn't always easy.

The first step in changing attitudes and behaviors is to use a diagnostic tool to identify your personal innovation style. Table 4.1 provides an adapted version of the Kirton Innovation-Adaption instrument for gauging whether you embrace routine or change.[5]

After taking the inventory, add up your scores. Kirton has concluded that the mean score across the general population is 96. If you scored less than 96, you're

TABLE 4.1 Adapted Kirton Adaption/Innovation Inventory

The following questions are about your style of work behavior (for example, decision-making) in your organization. Please respond to the question based on your assessment of yourself. Please read all the questions first, and then respond.

1 = Not at all (NA)

2 = To a slight extent (SE)

3 = To a moderate extent (ME)

4 = To a great extent (GE)

5 = To a very great extent (VGE)

You are a person who:	NA	SE	ME	GE	VGE
1. Conforms.	1	2	3	4	5
2. Will always think of something when stuck.	1	2	3	4	5
3. Enjoys detailed work.	1	2	3	4	5
4. Would sooner create than improve.	1	2	3	4	5
5. Is prudent when dealing with authority.	1	2	3	4	5
6. Never acts without proper authority.	1	2	3	4	5
7. Never seeks to bend or break the rules.	1	2	3	4	5
8. Likes bosses and work partners who are consistent.	1	2	3	4	5
9. Holds back ideas until obviously needed.	1	2	3	4	5
10. Has a fresh perspective on old problems.	1	2	3	4	5
11. Likes to vary set routines at a moment's notice.	1	2	3	4	5
12. Prefers change to occur gradually.	1	2	3	4	5
13. Is thorough.	1	2	3	4	5
14. Is a steady plodder.	1	2	3	4	5
15. Copes with several new ideas at the same time.	1	2	3	4	5
16. Is consistent.	1	2	3	4	5

17.	Can stand out in disagreement against others.	1	2	3	4	5
18.	Is stimulating.	1	2	3	4	5
19.	Readily agrees with the team at work.	1	2	3	4	5
20.	Has original ideas.	1	2	3	4	5
21.	Masters all details painstakingly.	1	2	3	4	5
22.	Proliferates ideas.	1	2	3	4	5
23.	Prefers to work on one problem at a time.	1	2	3	4	5
24.	Is methodical and systematic.	1	2	3	4	5
25.	Often risks doing things differently.	1	2	3	4	5
26.	Works without deviation in a prescribed way.	1	2	3	4	5
27.	Imposes strict order on matters within your control.	1	2	3	4	5
28.	Likes precise instruction.	1	2	3	4	5
29.	Fits readily into the system.	1	2	3	4	5
30.	Needs the stimulation of frequent change.	1	2	3	4	5
31.	Prefers colleagues who never 'rock the boat'.	1	2	3	4	5
32.	Is predictable.	1	2	3	4	5

Source: Abbas Monavvarrian (2004), "Administrative Reform and Style of Work Behavior: Adaptors-Innovators," *Public Organization Review: A Global Journal*, 2: 141–164.

an adaptor who tends to focus on reducing conflict, minimizing risks, and solving problems in a disciplined manner. Adaptive skills are very helpful in structuring work and getting results. If you scored above 96, you're a more natural innovator who is comfortable with increased risk, uncertainty, and imprecision. Innovators are more flexible in where they search for opportunities and are constantly toying with ideas. The further south you are of 96, the more adaptive you are. The further north of 96, the more naturally innovative you are. Table 4.2 presents the common behaviors of adaptors and innovators. It's important to note that adaptors are very capable of making innovative breakthroughs, but it might not come as easily to them as it does for natural innovators. As Kirton notes, "Everyone is a *potential* agent of change."[6] However, adaptors may find innovative activities a bit messy, taking them out of their comfort zone.

Organizations benefit by having both adaptors and innovators in their ranks. Uber founder Travis Kalanik constantly addressed this mix within his fast growing company:[7]

> *You need to create mechanisms and cultural values so that you feel as small as possible. That's how you stay innovative and fast. But how you do that at different sizes is different. Like when you're super small, you go fast by just tribal knowledge. But if you did tribal knowledge when you're super big it would be chaotic and you'd actually go really slow. So you have to constantly find that line between order and chaos.*[8]

The adaptors are skilled at building structures and procedures to ensure the innovators' ideas find a supportive home where they can thrive. But an overreliance on rules and routines by adaptors can sometimes frustrate the innovators inside the organization. By mixing the following ingredients for innovation into their work life, adaptors can become more innovative and open to change. Innovators will benefit from these conditions too.

TABLE 4.2 Behavior Descriptions of Adaptors and Innovators

Adaptor	Innovator
Characterized by precision, reliability, efficiency, methodicalness, prudence, discipline, conformity.	Seen as undisciplined, thinking tangentially, approaching tasks from unsuspected angles.
Concerned with resolving problems rather than finding them.	Could be said to discover problems and discover avenues of solution.
Seeks solutions to problems in tried and understood ways.	Queries problems' concomitant assumptions; manipulates problems.
Reduces problems by improvement and greater efficiency, with maximum of continuity and stability.	Is catalyst to settled groups, irreverent of their consensual views; seen as abrasive, creating dissonance.
Seen as sound, conforming, safe, dependable.	Seen as unsound, impractical; often shocks others.
Liable to make goals of means.	In pursuit of goals, treats accepted means with little regard.
Seems imperious to boredom, seems able to maintain high accuracy in long spells of detailed work.	Capable of detailed routine (system maintenance) work for only short bursts. Quick to delegate routine tasks.
Is an authority within given structures.	Tends to take control in unstructured situations.
Challenges rules rarely; cautiously, when assured of strong support.	Often challenges rules, has little respect for past custom.
Tends to high self-doubt. Reacts to criticism by closer outward conformity. Vulnerable to social pressure and authority; compliant.	Appears to have low self-doubt when generating ideas, not needing consensus to maintain certitude in face of opposition.
Is essential to the functioning of the institution all the time, but occasionally needs to be "dug out" of his or her systems.	Can handle unscheduled crises.
When collaborating with innovators: supplies stability, order and continuity to the partnership.	*When collaborating with adaptors:* supplies a break from the past and accepted theories.
Sensitive to people, maintains group cohesion and cooperation.	Insensitive to people, often threatens group cohesion and cooperation.
Provides a safe base for the innovator's riskier operations.	Provides the dynamics to bring about periodic radical change, without which institutions tend to ossify.

Source: Michael J. Kirton, "Adaptors and Innovators: Cognitive Style and Personality," in *Frontiers of Creativity Research*, Scott G. Isaksen, ed. (Buffalo, New York: Bearly Limited, 1987), p. 285.

Ingredients for Enhancing Innovation at Work

As we learned in the last chapter, good ideas do not come out of thin air, but rather occur from a combination of knowledge, new information, creative thinking skills, and hard work. Innovation can also be enhanced by incorporating the tried and true practices of the world's most innovative companies. In this section, we'll more closely examine some of the best practices in innovation.

Innovation Mentorship

For innovative behavior to take place in a company, it must be supported by upper management. One way of demonstrating this support is by providing mentorship. Employees benefit from a coach or teacher who can guide them in developing the skills required to be more innovative. This process will not always be easy, and may require pushing the employee out of their comfort zone. Consider the example of Jack Welch and General Electric. In 1988, GE faced a crisis when millions of compressors in their refrigerators were recalled. Welch and human resources chief Bill Conaty put a young and upcoming manager named Jeff Immelt in charge of this situation. Immelt had no experience with recalls, but he handled the crisis well. Welch guided him through the recall process, and 12 years later he replaced Welch as CEO. Immelt credits Welch's coaching of him through the experience as a major reason he became CEO later.[9,10] Companies should provide similar leadership in developing innovative employees. If the company's executives do not have the ability to mentor employees in this way, they should hire talent to do so and/or contract with innovative and applied creativity consultants to provide such guidance. And as a manager, you should be continuously building a network of the most innovative people you can find who can offer feedback on your ideas.

An effective technique for developing an employee's innovative leadership capabilities is to hold regular debriefs with them at the end of meetings. If employees are working on a project for you, set aside a few minutes and ask the following three questions:

1. What went well for you on this project?
2. What didn't go so well for you on this project, or what could have gone better?
3. What did you learn on this project that you didn't know before?

Allow them to reflect on their answers to these questions. Emphasize that you're not looking for one right answer, but rather you want them to take a moment to think about their work.

With minimal rewording, the three questions can be tweaked for a variety of situations. For example, a very beneficial exercise during a break or at the end of a shift is to simply ask an employee what they've learned that day. The following three questions can guide this daily practice:

1. What's going well for you today? (Or, another way to phrase this question if it's asked at the end of a shift is, "What went well for you today?")
2. What's not going so well for you, or what could go better for you today? (Or, if asked at the end of a shift, "What didn't go so well for you today? What could have gone better?")
3. What have you learned today on your job that you didn't know before?

The debrief is a very effective technique because it empowers the employee to take an active role in their own development.[11] In many organizations, employees are told what to do, which limits their growth as decision-makers. These environments can create a state of learned helplessness within the ranks. Managers who train their employees to rely on them for their answers send a message that taking initiative is not encouraged here. This situation isn't good for anyone in the organization. Employees don't think for themselves, and managers become exhausted dealing with a constant barrage of minor issues.[12] Bottlenecks rapidly develop and production is constrained. The manager who practices debriefs with their employees, however, plays the role of a "guide on the side" instead of a "sage on the stage" or the "know-it-all boss." Picture Michael Scott from *The Office*, and you get a better understanding of what a "know-it-all boss" is.

Debriefs permit the employee to take ownership of their development, which leads to increased engagement in the workplace. This is no light matter. The Gallup Organization pinpoints workplace engagement as the most critical issue in organizations today. Their research found that only 28 percent of the American workforce is engaged in their work. That means only a quarter of managers and employees are deeply committed to their job and organization. And even worse, another 53 percent are "not engaged" and 19 percent are "actively disengaged." Unengaged employees simply don't care about what happens to the company and perform their jobs to meet minimal expectations. And worse, the actively disengaged actually work to sabotage the results of the company. As Gallup CEO Jim Clifton states:

> The 28% of engaged employees are the best colleagues. They cooperate to build an organization, institution, or agency. They are the creative force behind everything good that happens in an organization. They are the only people in your organization who create new customers.[13]

One of your major responsibilities as a manager is to increase engagement among your employees. Given the paucity of engagement in most businesses, the organization that can support employee growth will have a major advantage in their industry. If the debrief technique becomes a regular practice in your managerial toolkit, you'll find more engaged employees performing innovative activity in your area of responsibility.

Incentives for the Innovative Employee

A company's culture has significant impact on its innovative activity. Small companies often have a loose culture that provides employees more situations to spot opportunities. Discoveries of new ways to deliver products and services are a frequent occurrence in a startup. Without the more formalized organizational structures and policies, employees have more flexibility to work on all aspects of a project. In the process, a good team can uncover new angles on problems that larger competitors are overlooking. However, not all large firms are lumbering dinosaurs. A major advantage large organizations can have over smaller competitors is their wealth of human capital within business units. People often think of smaller companies as being naturally more entrepreneurial, but commanding vast human resources sometimes gives large corporations the edge in innovation. Large companies are storehouses of experience and expertise. This experience reservoir is an investment companies make over many years. It doesn't come cheap, and it isn't easy. K. Anders Ericsson has extensively studied high achievers and found it takes ten years in a field before someone attains expert status.[14] Clearly, corporations have a large wealth of experienced talent from which to draw. If you're working in an established company, you have a large selection of experts to shape ideas with. You may also have access to more resources to develop those ideas. However, the critical factor in whether that happens is if your company has a flexible or rigid culture for innovation. If it's hard to access the people or resources needed to bring new ideas to market, innovation becomes an exhaustive exercise. And if innovative behavior is not rewarded or positively acknowledged, it will cease. Employees and managers will either dial back their innovation or go elsewhere where they can pursue their ideas with more support.

The key for any department, division, or company is to examine how they support and reward the development of innovative and entrepreneurial pursuits. Do senior managers of the organization select, develop, and reinforce innovative behaviors among their employees? Do the organizational structure and practices foster and facilitate innovative activity? Do senior managers adequately reward such behavior? Because of fear of failure, lower-level managers are often risk averse and must be encouraged to take reasonable risks. Rewarding innovative behavior is a signal that senior managers value and support it.[15] At Koch Industries, for example, corporate innovators who develop a successful product, service, or process are entrusted with larger decision rights over future company activity. It's similar to Stephen Covey's concept of the "Circle of Influence and the Circle of Concern." The Circle of Influence encompasses those matters we can actually impact, whereas the Circle of Concern includes everything of interest to us. Covey believed that if we spend time on issues we're concerned about but that we can't influence, we'll find ourselves wasting our time. However, if we focus our efforts on issues within our Circle of Influence, we'll get results, and people who get results are afforded more opportunities to work on matters they care about. Thus, a culture of corporate innovators who are always increasing their circle of influence will be able to tackle customers' problems at levels their rivals can only imagine.

Innovative Behavior

Innovative behavior can also be enhanced through deliberate practice. *Deliberate practice* is the use of regular, structured, and intense repetitive activities aimed at developing high skills in someone. Top performers not only work harder, but also work on the right things to make themselves better.[16] By studying what separates great innovators from their peers, you can replicate the daily practices that led to some of history's greatest achievements. Some of the most common best practices of legendary innovators include enthusiastic immersion in a domain, collaboration with others in the sharing and development of ideas, and a clear understanding of what priorities to address.[17]

Let's look at how some of history's big breakthroughs happened within networks of motivated people who were excited about some common issue. The European Renaissance, for example, happened largely because the Medici family funded and coordinated many of the era's top artists and scientists.[18] The Medici family created an environment that brought many of history's greatest minds together. Michelangelo, Galileo, and Botticelli were all beneficiaries of the Medicis' support of the advancement of civilization. In more modern times, many leading innovations were supported through large-scale communities. The Manhattan Project is one example of collaboration that had a massive impact on the world. The atomic bomb would never have been built during World War II without bringing together the country's greatest scientists in the deserts of New Mexico. Project director Robert Oppenheimer understood the power of collaboration, motivating and organizing perhaps the most brilliant, and eccentric, group of individuals ever brought together. In the business landscape of the twentieth century, Bell Labs was the corporate version of the Manhattan Project, housing many of the world's top scientists. During its heyday, Bell Labs held research seminars and invited guests to exchange knowledge with its research scientists and technicians; however, this setting was not purely for the advancement of science. Many breakthroughs occurred from informal interactions in the hallways and on lawns of this corporate campus setting that were later commercialized with great success, such as cellular telephone technology, lasers, and transistors. As these examples illustrate, the lone genius making a breakthrough in an isolated lab in the mountains is largely myth. Most moments of insight are not made in seclusion but are the result of collaboration. Exchanges of information affect the future thought of those in the group.[19] Legendary investor Warren Buffett offers these words of wisdom to guide you in finding collaborative opportunities:

> *You will move in the direction of the people you associate with, so it's important to associate with people better than yourself. You want to associate with people who are the kind of person you'd like to be. You'll move in that direction.*[20]

Today, Google is able to attract some of the brightest technology experts by creating an environment that encourages its employees to pursue innovative ideas. At Google headquarters, a.k.a. the Googleplex, you might find employees sharing work cubes and huddle rooms, outdoor seating for idea sessions, and health food cafes. For many years Google famously supported its employees to spend 20 percent of their work time on innovative projects that interested them. The practice led to breakthrough products such as Gmail, Adsense, and Google Talk. The company no longer needs to put an exact number on this activity anymore because its culture has become built around self-motivated innovators.[21] The results have been astounding. Google's stock price has risen from $279/share in 2009 to $1,024/share in 2017. Google understands that innovation comes from all ranks in the company. You should search for or create areas in your company where people can get together to discuss ideas. If there aren't too many options currently available for you, organize salon-style get-togethers where colleagues can socialize and share their thoughts, whether that's at a home, bar, or ball game.

Another practice that is critical for innovation is *opportunity recognition*, or the ability to find or create untapped sources of potential profit.[22] Research reveals that entrepreneurs are more alert to opportunities than managers in traditional organizations. Clearly, managers would benefit from thinking like an entrepreneur and developing skills to recognize opportunity. Fortunately, *entrepreneurial alertness* is a skill that can be improved with more experience recognizing and developing opportunities. Professors Dawn DeTienne and Gaylen Chandler help their students improve this skill by having them keep an opportunity alertness notebook. Each day students are required to capture five to ten business opportunities in the world around them in their notebook.[23]

Consider the examples of Leonardo da Vinci and Thomas Edison, two of history's greatest innovators. While Leonardo was famous for his artistic and scientific break-throughs, historians often have more interest in his notebooks. His great paintings were the result of his active scholarship on light, matter, form, and function, all captured in his journals. Edison also believed every idea should be captured for possible future development. He was so committed to this principle that he had notebooks positioned throughout his workshops, so that his team got into the practice of writing down all possible ideas regarding problems in the laboratory. As Leonardo and Edison worked on large-scale projects, they also kept their minds open to serendipity or insights. It was one of those unexpected observations that led to the invention of the phonograph, one of Edison's greatest inventions.[24]

If the aforementioned ingredients are adhered to, you will become more innovative. As you pursue innovation, however, there are two different approaches you can take. The following section explores closed innovation and open innovation.

Approaches to Innovation

Innovation occurs when two questions are successfully answered: "*What is possible?*"—which concerns research, discovery, and invention—and "*What is needed?*"—which concerns business and social needs. Answering these questions is complicated because developing new products, services, and experiences may take a while, and what is wanted in the future may be different from what customers want now. As Mark Stefik and Barbara Stefik observe, "You can't easily ask a future customer what they will want."[25] There are two approaches you can take in getting to these answers. Closed innovation is a more traditional approach that utilizes in-house resources on secret projects until new products or services are brought to market. Apple is a good example of closed innovation. Only a handful of designers and executives know the actual products being developed at the Apple campus. Engineers and project managers are given specific components to create for that product, but they're not privy to the entire design. Open innovation, on the other hand, is an approach where collaboration rules. External parties are even included to help develop new ideas. Tesla is a good example of open collaboration. Elon Musk has provided open access to all the company's patents, in order to promote the development of electric vehicles. He believes that any advancement in electric vehicle technology is good for the industry in general.[26] There are pros and cons with each approach. The traditional approach protects intellectual property well, but often proceeds in a calculated, slow way. The open approach embraces the advantages of social and digital networks, but makes company activities more transparent. In a quickly changing world, companies are increasingly turning to open innovation and accepting the tradeoff of collaboration for loss of ownership. Many executives believe more conversations among colleagues spur faster innovation cycles. Both approaches have been found successful by different companies, so it's a manager's call as to which they want to use.

Closed Innovation

The questions "What is possible?" and "What is needed?" are typically answered by different people at different times in the innovation process. In traditional research and development models, there is a linear process to innovation: basic research to applied research to development to production. Basic research begins the process by asking "What is possible?" Led by their curiosity, scientists search for answers to this question without any thought of practicality. While this may seem antithetical to business success, many of today's most common products and services such as microwave ovens and wireless communication are the result of such scientific searches. As Donald Stokes found in his survey of breakthrough innovations, basic research is the "powerful dynamo of technological progress as applied research and development convert the discoveries of basic science into technological innovations to meet the full range of society's economic, defense, health, and other needs."[27] When interesting discoveries are made, applied scientists, researchers, and engineers seek ways to make them practical for everyday life. There may be a considerable time lag between scientific discovery and practical application, but, once found, technological revolutions can occur in an industry. Sometimes entire new markets and industries are created, and, as a result, the economy becomes invigorated and grows. It's for this reason that the government and other large institutions commit large resources to basic science projects. Once possible applications are found, the discoveries, inventions, and insights can be developed into new commercial products, services, and experiences. Companies then put the organizational support in place to produce and deliver the commercial offering. New plants and headquarters are built. Suppliers increase their production and logistics companies expand their fleets. Retailers open new locations. New employees are hired and wages grow. The spillover effects of innovation bring positive externalities to other parties associated with the host company.

The closed approach to innovation is an attempt to generate new business break-throughs through full utilization of the people, knowledge, and technology within the company's boundaries. Figure 4.1 demonstrates the traditional approach to R&D.

Closed innovation is internally focused and based on the following principles:[28]

1. Hire the best and brightest people, so that they work for you and not your competitors.
2. Make discoveries in secret, so that your company has a head start on rivals in your market.
3. Release new products and services in spectacular fashion to generate public-ity for your company. Most reporters are bored with their daily beat and are happy to go to fun promotional events for a change. The publicity can bring a good return on the money invested in such an event.
4. Invest great amounts in R&D, in order to ensure that your company generates the best ideas and stays ahead of the competition
5. Control and protect intellectual property, in order to ensure that your com-pany profits from the innovations, not your competitors.

Open Innovation

While closed innovation is still the dominant paradigm in industry, some companies are starting to rely on an approach variously known as open-source innovation,

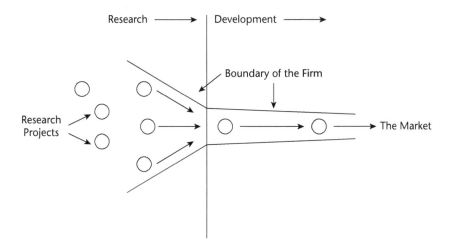

FIGURE 4.1 The Closed Paradigm for Managing Industrial R&D.

Source: Adapted from Henry Chesbrough (2006), *Open Innovation* (Boston: Harvard Business School Press), p. xxii.

open-market innovation, or, more simply, open innovation. Open innovation implies that the firm is not solely reliant upon its own resources for new technology, product, or business development purposes. Rather, the firm acquires critical inputs to innovation from outside sources. Additionally, the firm may choose to commercialize its innovative ideas through external pathways, such as partnerships and alliances with other companies, that operate beyond the bounds of the firm's current business(es). Open innovation abides by a collaborative win/win mindset among its practitioners.

It's a move away from the traditional closed system model of innovation, where ideas are generated, developed, and commercialized in secret, to one in which the organizational boundaries of innovation are porous, allowing innovative ideas to flow in and out of the organization with ease. Figure 4.2 demonstrates this dynamic.

The open innovation model encourages firms to exploit creative ideas through different modes. For example, open innovation can entail licensing arrangements in which the firm sells its technology and/or acquires technology from others. A firm can arrange a joint venture with a competitor. It can spin off new businesses that are supported by the parent firm's resources but operate with their own strategies. Spin-offs can also seek venture capital investments and participate in external R&D consortia and alliances. In short, open innovation considers and adopts others' ideas. As Keith Sawyer observes:

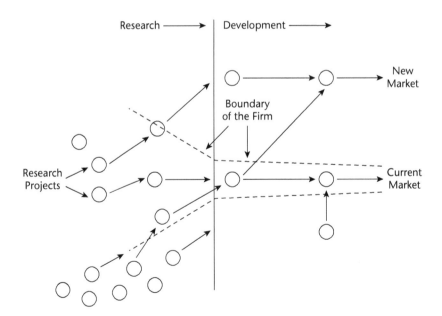

FIGURE 4.2 The Open Innovation Paradigm for Managing Industrial R&D.

Source: Adapted from Henry Chesbrough (2006), *Open Innovation* (Boston: Harvard Business School Press), p. xxv.

Innovation today isn't a sudden break with the past, a brilliant insight that one lone outsider pushes through to save the company. Just the opposite: Innovation today is a continuous process of small and constant change, and it's built into the culture of successful companies. When I ask creators where their ideas come from, they always tell stories about collaboration and connection, about innovations that emerge from a creative space that spreads out across the entire company—and sometimes beyond its boundaries.

(p. 155)[29]

Collaboration has always been the key to great breakthroughs, and companies are realizing that communication technology and enhanced supply chains provide more possibilities for innovation. A firm's innovation processes, activities, and capabilities depend on the information resources provided by its social networks. Being "plugged in" to information networks allows a firm to be alert to new opportunities in its environment. This is a "give and take" approach that is not entirely accidental. Successful managers strategically influence their information networks. The more a manager is connected to others, both inside and outside the firm, the better their chance to obtain superior information about opportunities in their environment. Useful intelligence can come from anywhere, so the savvy manager must remain alert to new sources of information. Consider how some of today's corporate titans have benefited from these types of interactions. In 1979, Steve Jobs toured the Xerox PARC laboratories and learned about GUI (graphical user interface). For three days, he and his engineers studied the GUI interface, eventually developing the concept for the Apple Lisa. Although the Lisa was a market failure, the knowledge and technology garnered from its development led to Apple's later successes. Proctor & Gamble is another innovation leader in its industry. P&G is a company with a $224 billion market cap that sets an annual goal of increasing its revenues 5 percent each year. This isn't an easy task, as it's equivalent to creating a market-leading brand like Tide each year. How does P&G accomplish this feat year in and year out? The company uncovers big customer problems that haven't been addressed yet within their industry. And to do this, they must have extensive knowledge about what their customers really care about and are concerned with. The company interacts with its customers in many settings. Managers are even willing to immerse themselves in their customers' life experiences, visiting their workplaces and joining them in recreational activities. And sometimes employees will actually live with consumers for several days in their homes and take part in their daily routines. By going to these lengths, P&G learns what its customers' real needs and wants are.[30] Other times the company brings its customers to them. At its GYM facilities, where new ideas are hatched and tested, target customers can shop for products in mock grocery stores where designers and researchers can watch how products are bought. Laboratory homes are also on the premises that allow customers to use products in a realistic living environment. Designers can look for quirky behaviors that new products can address. P&G also generates relationships with other stakeholders as well.

Distributors may have more insight into what end users want. Suppliers may have new materials that could revolutionize products. The key is to be open to opportunity wherever it presents itself. As open innovation advocate Henry Chesbrough observes:

> *Today it is not necessary or even feasible to lock up vital knowledge and ideas in silos, where they will only be used when and if a company's internal business needs dictate. A world of opportunity awaits the company that can harness ideas from its surrounding environment to advance its own business and that can leverage its own ideas outside its current business.*
>
> *(p. 195)*[31]

So, whether a company uses closed or open innovation, it shares a similar goal with its rivals: finding and seizing market opportunities. Unfortunately, many managers do not know how to pursue and develop opportunities. There are many books that provide direction on how to work with existing intellectual property or how to commercialize new technology, but little guidance is given with regard to opportunity recognition. This chapter now provides you guidance on how to find and develop opportunities from scratch. And the first step in finding opportunity is knowing where to look for it.

Sources of Opportunity

All innovative activity begins with an opportunity where a favorable set of circumstances creates a need or an opening for a new business concept or approach. Sometimes the opportunity is clear and other times it's revealed through a rigorous search. The reality is that many new business ideas fail because there was no opportunity in the first place. In these situations, the management team likely didn't have a true understanding of who their customer truly was. While past products may have been successful for the company, there is no guarantee the next one will be. You increase your odds of success by grounding your ideas with good customer research. The following questions are examples that can help guide you in gaining insights about your customers' background, attitudes, and behavior:

What common physical features do the customers have, if any?

What common activities do they do?

What do they typically wear?

What are typical jobs they hold?

Where do they typically live?

What is the most interesting thing about these customers?

What one word or phrase best describes these customers?

Interviews, observation, and consultation can be used in answering these questions. Apply the principles from the previous chapter on creativity. Use divergent thinking to list as many answers to the questions as you can, and then converge on the most intriguing facts, gaps, and revelations. Answers can come from fellow employees, outside experts, suppliers, customers, and yourself. If you already have intellectual property that you wish to develop into a commercial opportunity, first diverge and converge on potential markets and customers for the technology. Once you have selected a target market, answer the questions.

Once we have a profile of our potential customer, our next step in identifying opportunity is to understand why our target market buys particular goods and services in the first place. The simplest and most accurate answer is that everyone buys things in order to make their life better. Some transactions are simply to meet the physiological and safety needs of survival, such as food, water, sex, a constant body temperature, safety from dangerous elements, and medical attention.[32] People need to eat, need to clothe themselves, and need to have shelter. A market for satisfying these needs will always exist. And since everyone has different tastes, life goals, and means, how they satisfy these needs will vary too. When survival and safety needs are met, most people turn their attention to buying things to meet their desires and wants. These transactions often account for a large share of people's consumption, as they buy products they want but don't necessarily need. As social critic Arthur Asa Berger summarizes, "It boils down to this: Needs are finite but desires are infinite. We don't need all the stuff we buy; but we feel that having things will make our lives better, make us feel more alive."[33] So in a capitalist society where desires are never fully met, companies will always have the opportunity for product and service innovation.[34] Goals for living a better life and being accepted or admired in society are two of the most common sources of these desires. Unsolved problems are another popular source of innovation potential. Most customers' buying patterns can be captured by one or more of these three categories. By considering these categories, you'll have a better understanding of how to satisfy the customer. The three categories of opportunity (social goals, life goals, and problems) are next examined in more depth.

Social Goals

One way customers pursue their vision of the "good life" is by buying products and services that signal to others their values, rank, and preferred self-image. Everyone covets their uniqueness and wants to feel special. This goal is often achieved in our society through the purchase of the things we wear, the objects we use, and the things we do. Evolutionary psychologist Geoffrey Miller asserts that the underlying drive of this consumer behavior is to demonstrate to others your worth. The clothes you wear, the car you drive, and the house you live in are visible indicators of your professional and financial status. From an evolutionary perspective, these are signs or proxies of good genes, good health, and good social intelligence, which others are drawn and attracted to. As Miller notes:

Almost every animal species has its own fitness indicators to attract mates, intimidate rivals, deter predators, and solicit help from parents and kin. Male guppies grow flag-like tails, male lions sport luxuriant manes, male nightingales learn songs, male bowerbirds build bowers, humans of both sexes acquire luxury goods.

(p. 13)[35]

In a consumer society, this will likely be an ongoing shopper arms race that will offer unlimited innovative opportunities for companies, with marketing providing the vehicle for persuading customers that the new products and services meet these underlying desires. Corporations even evidence this behavior through branding and symbols of prestige. Banks are often housed in large, marble buildings to show stability and wealth, Fortune 500 companies host professional golf events that bring celebrities and athletes together under a corporate presence, and companies like Apple and Google build modern corporate campuses that signal "the smart innovators work here."

While Miller addresses the competitive nature of people in pursuing mates, status, and possessions, he also notes the social side of human nature. As social creatures, we seek products and services that allow us to communicate and socialize more frequently and easily with others. Music preferences, web pages, and clothing help us to advertise our interests, so that we can interact with people like ourselves. Coffee shops and other social settings allow us to have places to meet and socialize. Tablet computers, smartphones, and social media make it easier for people to stay in touch on a regular basis. Uber and Airbnb provide social platforms and shared resources that bring independent contractors and customers together to exploit underutilized assets like empty car seats and bedrooms. There will always be business opportunities for creating new ways to help people come together to leverage new technologies and address customer concerns and problems. The following questions can offer insights into your customers' social goals:

How does this customer usually communicate with others?

Where are this customer's favorite places to go?

Why do they like these locations so much?

What about the locations they frequent stand out to you?

Is there anything unusual about these locations?

Is there anything about these locations that could be applied in different settings?

Is there anything interesting about the people that could be applied to a different group of people?

Is there anything from a different setting or a group of people that could apply to this setting?

How do the people interact with each other in this setting?

Do they have access to unused resources they could have others rent, share, or buy?

In answering these questions, apply the principles from the previous chapter on creativity. Use divergent thinking to list as many answers to the questions as you can, and then converge on the most intriguing facts, gaps, and revelations. Answers can come from fellow employees, outside experts, suppliers, customers, and yourself. You might be surprised by what trends begin to appear. Uncovering an unmet, and perhaps consciously unknown, want is a big step in making a break-through innovation.

Life Goals

Beyond the social nature of consumption, shopping plays an immensely personal role in people's lives. As author Jim Pooler asserts:

> *Shopping is important, and it is underestimated. It's one of the most common things we do, and it dominates our lives. . . . Never before has so much emphasis been placed on shopping, and never before has it assumed the central place in our lives that it now does. Shopping for emotional and psychological reasons has become the new mantra of modern society.*[36]

In short, shopping has become a pathway toward the good life and feeling ful-filled . . . at least in the short term. People shop to attain health and alleviate illness, to achieve gusto and thrills and reduce sluggishness and misery, to feel secure and avoid physical threats, to feel loved and admired and not hated and shunned, to be considered an insider and not an outsider looking in, to feel confident and not insecure, to feel serene and relaxed and not tense and anxious, to feel beautiful and not ugly, to feel rich and not poor, to feel clean and not dirty, to feel knowledge-able and not ignorant, to feel in control of life and not at the mercy of events, to feel entertained and not bored, among other reasons.[37]

Shopping can also be a self-reward for enduring the trials and challenges of life.[38] In a busy world where people take on the responsibilities of work and family, they often don't receive the recognition from others they feel they deserve. Shopping provides an opportunity to reward themselves, to indulge in buying something extra like an unneeded tool, gadget, or piece of clothing. The purchase might not be nec-essary for survival, but it might provide temporary enjoyment in a hectic, stressful world.[39] Savvy marketers advertise this theme in many commercials broadcast in the middle of people's busy days.

Although at opposite ends of the entertainment spectrums, Las Vegas and the Disney theme parks capitalize on meeting this underlying motivation with *escapism and self-renewal*. They pamper the masses with world-class service and fun-filled experiences. But customers don't have to go to Orlando or Las Vegas to find escape. They can drive to their local mall and hunt for good deals. Some people even reward themselves for doing a good job of shopping. Finding bargains gives compulsive shoppers psychological comfort for buying more goods and services.[40] While some managers struggle for new business ideas, the aforementioned discussion on shopping motivations should be proof that there will never be a shortage of opportunities. The following questions can serve to find out more about your customers' life goals:

What do they seem to enjoy doing?

What are their hobbies?

What activities do they pay to do?

What are they passionate about?

How could the customer improve themselves physically, intellectually, or spiritually?

What seems to be missing in their lives?

What changes, issues, problems, and opportunities for improvement do you visualize?

What keeps your customers up at night? What do they worry about?

What does a good day look like for them?

What do they hope to be doing in the future?

In an ideal world, what would their life look like?

Again, apply the principles from the previous chapter on creativity. Use divergent thinking to list as many answers to the questions as you can, and then converge on the most intriguing facts, gaps, and revelations. Answers can come from fellow employees, outside experts, suppliers, customers, and yourself. This is an important fact-finding stage of your innovation journey.

Problems

Problems are great sources for innovation. A problem is a situation where there is a gap between where a person is now and where they want to be, but they don't know how to find a way to cross that gap.[41] The bigger that gap is and/or the more difficult it is to figure out how to cross it, the bigger the problem. If it's a big enough problem, finding a solution to it will be very important to a person. They need help from someone in crossing that gap, and they'll pay a lot to a person or company for a good solution. If enough people have the same problem, there's a great market opportunity for the company that can solve it well. On the other hand, companies fail when: (1) they offer solutions that don't adequately cross the gap; (2) the gap isn't considered much of a problem in the first place; or (3) there aren't enough people who have the problem to make it profitable for the company. So keep the following heuristics in mind when you're thinking about offering a new product or service:

1. Am I offering something people would really buy? Am I offering something that's really better than what other companies are providing customers? Or is it just a clever, cute idea that they wouldn't actually want to spend money on?
2. Is this really a problem for people? Does my solution make any real impact in their lives?
3. Do enough people have this problem to warrant investing resources into its solution? Would these resources be better invested toward another problem where I'll get better results?
4. When I offer this solution, will it have a long window of future purchases or is it just a "flash in the pan"? In other words, what's the return on investment (ROI) on putting my resources into this solution? How do I measure success with offering this solution? What evidence do I need to show that it's working?
5. What are the opportunity costs of providing this solution and not offering something else? What will you have to give up to do this?

Thus, innovation requires finding the right problems to solve and offering solutions that are worthwhile to enough people. The astute manager can ask the following questions to have a better idea as to what worthwhile problems to pursue for innovation opportunities:

Is there anything that appears to be frustrating this customer?

What activities or responsibilities are placing unwanted financial strain on the customer?

Where are bottlenecks in the customer experience?

What red tape does the customer face in their daily life?

The following questions apply more to business-to-business situations:

What performance goals are being missed regularly in the industry?

What issues and problems could be alleviated through partnerships with other organizations?

What will be the biggest challenges companies in the industry will face over the next three years?

What technology issues are hindering progress in the industry?

Again, apply the principles from the previous chapter on creativity. Use divergent thinking to list as many answers to the questions as you can, and then converge on the most intriguing facts, gaps, and revelations. Answers can come from fellow employees, outside experts, suppliers, customers, and yourself.

Fact-Finding

Once we have identified a need, want, or problem that we think is worth exploring, we need to learn more about it. Professor Min Basadur emphasizes the importance of fact-finding on an opportunity before creating a solution. Fact-finding gives us a better idea of what we're dealing with and also uncovers issues we might have overlooked in our previous analyses. Before we take action, we should do our *due diligence* to make sure we know all we can about the problem we're addressing. As Professor Basadur likes to say, "You can never go wrong with more fact finding. Sometimes you have to slow down to speed up. The better you understand a problem, the better solution you'll come up with in the end." Due diligence prevents us from launching products that, with a little more thought, could have been more pleasing to our customers. Perform your due diligence by delving into the following questions. These questions will help you gather more facts about the need, want, or problem you selected:[42]

What do you know, or think you know, about this opportunity?

What do you not know about this opportunity (but you'd like to find out)?

Why is this a problem for the customer?

Why is this an opportunity for you (or your company)?

How does the customer currently deal with this problem?

What have you and your competitors already thought of or tried regarding this problem?

If this problem were solved, what would the customer have that they don't have now?

Are you making any assumptions about the problem you don't have to? In other words, what might you be assuming about the need, want, or problem that may or not be true?

The second question above often requires more follow-up fact-finding (what do you not know about this opportunity (but you'd like to find out)?). The best way to get answers to this question is to talk to experts that have additional knowledge on the issues you're concerned about. Some useful questions to ask experts are:

1. Can you tell me a little about your job and how you got into this field?
2. What's your background?

3. What are the hot trends in your industry today? What has changed in the industry during your time with the company? What big changes are happening in the industry today?
4. Where do you source your supplies from?
5. How do you reach your customers? What do you try to do to make these customers happy with your company?
6. Are you often surprised in your work? When?
7. What do you find your customers struggling with the most?
8. What keeps you up at night? What issues or problems in the market occupy your mind the most? What issues or problems regarding your company occupy your mind the most?
9. Is there something you'd like to work on but can't? Because of technical limitations? Money? Manpower?
10. What are the *critical success factors* that must be addressed in this industry? In other words, what do companies have to do to make sure they survive in this market?
11. Where is your company currently stuck?
12. What are the current technological limits in your industry? What limits companies from being more innovative?
13. *Broadly explain your idea to the expert, and ask:* Do you think this idea is feasible? What suggestions do you have for me regarding my idea? What obstacles might I come across in pursuing this idea? Do you have any suggestions for overcoming these obstacles?
14. *If you have a specific problem you need an answer to, explain the issue and ask:* Do you have any advice for me in how I can solve this problem? Am I overlooking something important about this issue?

Experts will appreciate you having prepared questions, as it shows respect for their time. The above questions help the interview to get off to a good start, but serendipity must be allowed to happen too. A good interview will flow to other topics the expert wants to share with you as well. Be open to the free-flowing exchange of ideas that can happen in an engaging interview. In fact, you probably won't cover all the above questions in an interview. Pick the ones that make the most sense for who you're meeting with at that time.

Another important step wraps up the interview. MIT professor Eric Von Hippel suggests innovators initiate a "search on the fly" by concluding the interview by asking the expert, *"Who in your organization or elsewhere has more insight on this problem that could be helpful to me?"* This powerful question asked at the end of each interview creates a path to getting new answers to the inquiries you have.[43] Ask the expert's permission to contact that person and continue moving forward collecting more information. It won't be long before you start feeling like an expert on the topic yourself.

When approaching a new lead, you should try to set up the next meeting by acknowledging the person who gave you the contact information and what you would like to talk about. The referral, indication of preparation for the interview, and respectful demeanor will open many doors for you. It's amazing how quickly you can build a network using *pyramiding*.[44] The ongoing use of the question requesting contact with someone who has more information on the subject can even lead you to the top figures in an industry. Once you're at that level, the experts may not be aware of anyone having more knowledge than themselves in the company, so they'll often suggest an expert in another company or field. The movement from one domain pyramid to another offers possibilities for new insights into the problem space, and, in the process, you expand your vocabulary and perspectives on the issues. With a thorough immersion, you gain trust among relevant experts and executives by speaking their language. Engaging experts in this way will later prove useful when you seek resources and support from others in your company. After pyramiding, you'll better understand who your customers are, the problems they have, and the solutions others are currently providing. With good fact-finding skills and techniques, you won't be building from scratch in generating solutions. As Isaac Newton said, "If I have seen further than others, it is by standing upon the shoulders of giants."

Ignorance and Discovery

After finding answers to your questions, you should have a better idea of the underlying structure of the opportunity you're considering. Fact-finding sheds more light on what your idea can become, but it also sheds light on new possible paths as well. In fact, you may want to fact-find and research more than one opportunity, and then select the one that has the most market potential. Therefore, fact-finding helps you make an informed decision as to which need, want, or problem you should pursue by removing what Austrian economist Israel Kirzner calls "the fog of ignorance."

Kirzner instructs us that "insights operate toward dispelling this fog."[45] And admitting ignorance on a subject is the first step toward making a worthwhile discovery. Neuroscience professor Stuart Firestein even teaches a class at Columbia University entitled "SNC3429 *Ignorance*." His goal is to teach his students to welcome and embrace periods of ignorance in their lives because it is in those situations where discoveries are made. He explains:

> *How does a scientist use facts beyond simply accumulating them? As raw material, not as a finished product. In those facts is the next round of questions, improved questions with new unknowns. Mistaking the raw material for the product is a subtle error but one that can have surprisingly far-reaching consequences. Understanding this error and its ramifications, and setting it straight, is crucial to understanding science. . . . As Erwin Schrodinger, one of the great philosopher-scientists, says, "In an honest search for knowledge you quite often have to abide by ignorance an indefinite time."[46]*

Business breakthroughs are no different. Impactful market discoveries don't always follow a set timeline. *Insights can't be forced.* But with persistence, facts and insights build on top of each other until one day a clear picture appears that compels you to take action. Again, when this moment of clarity will happen is unpredictable.

A new idea brings excitement and can generate passion to pursue a project. But excitement and passion aren't always enough to win others over to your cause. Fact-finding provides the foundation for building the composure and confidence needed to sell your idea in a convincing fashion. Think of the President of the United States. He faces a slew of challenges every day from all over the world and must make informed decisions. How is it possible for one person to appear knowledgeable on so many complex issues? The answer lies in the President's Daily Brief, which he receives as soon as he arrives in the Oval Office each day. The CIA and National Security Agency compile the most essential information in the brief that they think the President will need to know that day. Former intelligence briefer David Priess explains that:

> *The President's Daily Brief contains the most sensitive intelligence reporting and analysis in the world. The Central Intelligence Agency's spies, the National Security Agency's listening posts, and the nation's reconnaissance satellites gather secrets for it, while America's enemies send undercover agents to try to unearth its classified content. Every working morning, intelligence briefers fan out from CIA headquarters to personally deliver copies of the PDB to the president and the handful of senior advisors he has designated to see its Top Secret pages. No major foreign policy decisions are made without it.*[47]

If fact-finding is good enough for the President of the United States, it should be good enough for us too. Fact-finding builds confidence in an opportunity. If an opportunity still looks good after the due diligence of fact-finding and discovery, it's time to seize it and move forward in developing your innovation.

Seizing Opportunity

Once an opportunity has been recognized, a company must capture it. Occasionem Cognosce! Seize the opportunity! The best way to develop an innovation is to collaborate with others on a clearly stated challenge. And the more simply stated the challenge is, the better. Business teams perform better when they have specific issues to address rather than working on ambiguous goals.[48] If we've accepted that our customers have a clear need, want, or problem, it's time to provide a commercial solution for it. Let's try an example to better understand how this process works. Assume we found out from our research that runners find it difficult to get motivated to run after a long day at work. They want to get their workout in, but they feel drained when they leave their desk at the end of the day. We could address this problem by asking, "How might we help runners find the motivation they need to get their runs in after work?"

Now we can pursue a solution to the problem. There are five ways a company can fulfill a customer need or want. It can sell a commodity that provides the materials or ingredients the customer can use for fulfilling their need or want; it can sell a finished good that is already assembled and can be put to immediate use by the customer; it can provide a service that accomplishes a specific task for the client; or it can stage an experience that more fully engages the customer. At the highest level of offerings is transformation, where the business makes a deeply personal impact on a customer, but this is rare. So, let's assume we found that the running customer would like a drink they could consume that would pep them up and give them a good workout. We decide that coffee could meet this need, and we start thinking about what type of coffee product would interest these runners. Let's also assume we found a coffee bean that not only wakes the person up but has a performance benefit as well. We could sell these coffee beans, which are a commodity, directly to the runners, and have them grind them up themselves and brew the coffee at home before their workout. Of course, that takes a little time, so the customers may be willing to pay a little more for an instant version of coffee at the grocery store that they can put right into their Keurig machines. This more finished product will bring a higher price tag at the store than a scoop of coffee beans would. Busier people may bypass the brewing process altogether and pay a service fee for someone else to make it. The runner may go through a drive-through at a coffee chain that serves it, and take the drink with them on the way to the park where they'll do their run. However, they may want to socialize with other runners before they workout, so they're willing to pay a little more for the experience of drinking the coffee at the Endorphin Café. Providing a transformative experience with coffee would be difficult, but maybe we offer coaching and motivational talks at the café that inspire the runner to do better workouts and run personal records. Because of this transformative approach, the runner feels more confident and proud, which carries over into the rest of their lives. They receive promotions at work and set new records on the course, all which they credit to the Endorphin Café. The Endorphin Café becomes hugely successful in the running community, and we realize we can charge country club memberships to customers who drink coffee there. After considering who our customers are, we decide that the best approach to meeting the customers' needs is to offer a coffee product that boosts endurance performance. We package it so that it can be drunk cold or easily warmed up in a microwave, and sell it in supplement stores, on running websites, and at marathon expos. We are intrigued by the Endorphin Café idea but decide that there are very few areas in the country with a large enough population of runners to support it.

Considering whether to offer a commodity, product, service, experience, or transformation can be applied to any customer need, want, or problem we're addressing. It ensures that we're offering a solution to our customers that generates the most profits for us. The form of commercial offering we deliver is a critical business decision. It's important that you understand the nature and benefits of each approach, so let's look at each one more closely. In the previous example, you may have noticed that each offering became more involved as it was scaled up. B. Joseph Pine II and James H. Gilmore point out, "each successive offering greatly increases in value because the buyer finds each more *relevant* to what he truly wants."[49] Sometimes companies move from one category into another. For example, McDonald's commoditized the restaurant business by standardizing its food products and counter services. McDonald's became very popular—and profitable—by offering cheap hamburgers and fries and essentially created the fast food category. Starbucks on the other hand created an experience for the coffee drinker by placing emphasis on product variety, quality, and customer service in a relaxing, hip atmosphere. As a result, McDonald's prices products at a low price while Starbucks charges a premium. Both are hugely successful but take much different approaches to satisfying their customers. The following discussion examines offerings in more detail.

Commodities and Materials

Commodities are resources that are obtained from the natural world, such as animals, minerals, and vegetables, and are the first source of opportunity in an economic system. All products are made from something, and great fortunes can be made in acquiring and selling commodities in great quantities to others. The market for commodities is immense. We're a society of producers and consumers endlessly digging up and moving the earth's resources. Sometimes we recycle those materials into repurposed commodities. But regardless of whether we dig or recycle, the world we live in today is a human-created environment—a built environment. We design, build, and plan things to satisfy our needs and wants. Look outside your window, and chances are that even the grass and trees you see were engineered, grown, and planted by someone.[50] Table 4.3 presents a breakdown of common materials used in manufacturing and building.

TABLE 4.3 Family of Materials

Group	Subgroup	Examples
Metallics (metals and alloys)	Ferrous	Iron
		Steel
		Cast iron
	Nonferrous	Aluminum
		Tin
		Zinc
		Magnesium
		Copper
		Gold
	Powdered metal	Sintered steel
		Sintered brass
Polymerics	Human-made	Plastics
		Elastomers
		Adhesives
		Paper
	Natural	Wood
		Rubber
	Animal	Bone

(continued)

TABLE 4.3 *(continued)*

Group	Subgroup	Examples
Ceramics	Crystalline compounds	Skin Porcelain Structural clay Abrasives
	Glass	Glassware Annealed glass
Composites	Polymer based	Plywood Laminated timber Impregnated wood Fiberglass Graphite epoxy Plastic laminates
	Metallic based	Boron aluminum Primex
	Ceramic based	Reinforced concrete CFCC
	Cermets	Tungsten carbide Chromium alumina
Others	Other	Reinforced glass
	Electronic materials	Semiconductors Superconductors
	Lubricants	Graphite
	Fuels	Coal Oil
	Protective coatings	Anodized aluminum
	Biomaterials	Carbon implants
	Smart materials	Shape memory alloys Shape memory polymers

Source: Adapted from James A. Jacobs, Thomas F. Kilduff (2000), *Engineering Materials Technology: Structures, Processing, Properties, and selection* (New York: Prentice Hall), p. 57.

Commodities trade primarily at low prices and in large quantities, and since most commodities are bought in a raw state and easily acquired, their economic value is usually at the bottom of the value chain. Innovation in commodities can occur, however, when new compounds and materials for medicine, architecture, and manufacturing are discovered; however, since most of the land on earth has been explored, there are fewer chances of discovery of new materials and compounds. A few remote rain forests, the deep ocean, and other planets may hold the opportunity for new discoveries, but increasingly scientists and researchers are exploring ways to create new materials in laboratories, such as: material scientists creating new resources for manufacturing and building; bioengineers designing new foods; and nanotechnologists changing the molecular structure of compounds. Once these new materials and composites are created, they are patented and, if embraced by technology companies, can generate tremendous financial returns.

Another source of innovation is finding new ways to use existing commodities and materials. Many entrepreneurs today are building companies that specialize in sustainable business practices and construction. As the green movement takes hold, there will be increasing needs for retooling existing structures and building new houses and facilities that are sustainable. The innovative companies will gain an edge in those markets, but it is likely that once a dominant design has taken hold, green building technologies will standardize, and more companies will enter the market. These building materials will then become more of a commodity and lose some of their economic value. Additionally, commodities require the purchaser to shape and mold the materials themselves. If you want more compensation from customers, you must offer them something they can put to immediate use—a product.

Products

A common way to seize opportunity is to create a unique product—one that is not being offered today but would be in great demand if it were. The next-best way is to modify or upgrade something that is currently on the market or extend the offering into a new market. The first approach is often referred to as *new-new*, the second as *new-old*.

The new-new approach is a more innovative way to enter a market. Typical examples include smartphones, tablet computers, and driverless cars. These products were introduced as a result of research and development (R&D) efforts by major corporations. However, unique products and services are produced by small companies as well, as they are often able to more easily fill product niches overlooked by bigger firms. Therefore, there will always be a place for small and large companies in our economic system to deliver new-new products.

How does one discover or invent new products? One of the easiest ways is to make a list of annoying experiences or hazards encountered with various products during a given period of time. Common examples include objects that fall out of one's hands, household chores that are difficult to do, and items that are hard to store. Can certain innovations alleviate these problems? Indeed, people often get ideas for new products this way. For example, an engineer once observed the mechanism for recording the revolutions of a ship's propeller. As he watched the device tally the propeller's revolutions, he realized that the idea could be adapted to the recording of sales transactions—a problem he had been trying to solve for some time. The result led eventually to the development of the original cash register.

Most business ideas tend to come from people's experiences. In general, the main sources of ideas are prior and current jobs, hobbies or interests, and personally identified problems. This new-new approach indicates the importance of people's awareness of their daily lives (work and free time) for developing new business ideas.

Most new products, however, aren't based on a totally unique idea. Instead, a company "piggybacks" on someone else's ideas by improving a product—hence the term "new-old." There are several ways this can be done. First, competitors may not be offering products that fully meet the needs of the customer, opening the door for another company to deliver more value with better products. Second, there may be locations that are being overlooked by other companies, which warrant selling the product there. Walmart is a classic example of this type of scenario. When Sam Walton focused on towns of less than 50,000 people to build his business, his critics said he would fail. The small town platform, however, helped him to gain a foothold in communities across the country, which led to Walmart's current position as a retail leader. Third, sometimes being a follower to a new-new innovation can pay off. In markets where the product is considered radically innovative, early pioneers often run out of cash trying to develop an original concept. With radical innovation, customers usually aren't demanding the new product because they have no experience with it, and thus don't realize the impact it would have on their lives. As a result, the potential market can be quite small for a while until the product starts to catch on.

An established firm struggles with balancing their mix of old and new products. It becomes quite a paradox. It must focus on generating enough revenues to support current operations and planned growth, and if it pursues a lot of different avenues, it may become unfocused and lose efficiency in its operations. But if it doesn't maintain its exploratory activities, it may miss out on profitable markets in the long term.[51] The route many companies take then is to stay abreast of new trends and acquire entrepreneurial small companies that have developed a winner. The small company benefits from the support of the parent company, and the larger company develops the new market with its stable of experienced professionals. It's for this reason that many startups have acquisition as their exit strategy. Table 4.4 shows examples of innovators that were idea explorers and market creators.[52]

TABLE 4.4 Two Types of Innovators: Idea Explorers and Market Creators

Industry	Innovator That Came up with the Idea	Innovator That Created the Mass Market
35mm cameras	Leica	Canon
ATMs	DeLaRue	IBM/NCR
Diapers	Chicopee Mills (J&R)	P&G
Personal computers	Osborne/Apple	IBM
Online bookselling	Charles Stack	Amazon
Online brokerage	Net Investor	Schwab
VCRs	Ampex	JVC
Copiers	(Haloid) Xerox	Canon
CAT ccanners	EMI	GE
Videogames	Magnavox/Atari	Nintendo
Operating systems	Digital Research	Microsoft
Pocket calculators	Bowmar	TI
Mainframes	Atanasoff's ABC Computer	IBM

Source: Constantinos C. Markides, Paul A. Geroski (2002), "Fast Second" in *Authors' Research*, (2005) Tellis and Golder, and Schnaars (1994), ed., (London: John Wiley & Sons, Inc), p. 67.

Therefore, sometimes it pays to be a fast second in the market rather than an original developer. So, while the new-new approach is the one we often associate with innovation, we must be open to the benefits of the new-old approach as well.

Services

In the latter half of the twentieth century, the economy moved from being industrial-based to being service-based. Sometimes customers want more from companies than merely products. In a service-based business, companies provide specific tasks customers want done but don't want to do themselves. It's a step beyond products, because there's usually more interaction between the company and the customer. They want companies to perform tasks for them they would rather not do themselves, or they seek out expert counsel on matters they don't understand. Companies that provide services that better meet the individual needs of their clients will receive more compensation. Services tend to be much more personal than selling products. Therefore, listening to the customer and finding out what their needs and problems are is essential. It's then up to the company to offer a service that leaves the customer satisfied in meeting those demands.

Just as products can be new-new and new-old, services can be as well. One hot area of service innovation in the twenty-first century is social media. Facebook was founded by Mark Zuckerberg, a Harvard University student who was frustrated by the lack of networking facilities on campus. The company was founded in February 2004 and is now the largest source for social interaction and one of the most trafficked sites on the internet. In two short years, the company attracted offers of $750 million from Viacom[53] and $900 million from Yahoo.[54] Zuckerberg turned down the acquisition offers. It was a smart move. His net worth in 2017 stood at $64 billion and the market cap of Facebook was $449 billion. Zuckerberg doesn't expect the company to slow down. He intends for it to remain relevant as social media evolves with new technologies and reaches new markets around the world.

Common new-old examples of service offerings are offering new varieties of restaurants, clothing stores, or similar outlets in homogenous shopping districts. Of course, these kinds of operations can be risky because competitors can easily move in. Potential companies considering this kind of market should try to offer services that are difficult to copy. For example, an online billing and accounting service can be successful if the business serves a sufficient number of doctors to cover the cost of programmers and administrative expenses. Better yet, if a company wants a sustainable advantage in its market, it will transform its services into a hard-to-match experience.

Experiences and Transformations

Services increasingly resemble commodities as companies search for new ways to handle tasks for customers in cheaper and more efficient ways. Airlines once offered a high-end service, but now more resemble bus travel. Many people no longer have a personal relationship with an insurance agent, but rather search for the best deals on the internet. Fast food restaurants continue to pop up all over

America, offering quick and cheap ways to get daily calories. Taco Bell, for example, offers nachos supreme for $2.49 and cheesy double bean burritos for $1.19, and proclaims, "Why pay more?" But some people want more than the basics and are willing to pay more for it. And many companies are meeting that challenge by offering experiences rather than merely services. In fact, some social observers say we live in an "*experience economy.*"

As Pine and Gilmore state, an experience

> *occurs whenever a company intentionally uses services as the stage and goods as props to engage an individual. While commodities are fungible, goods tangible, and services intangible, experiences are memorable. Buyers of experiences—we'll follow Disney's lead and call them guests—value being engaged by what the company reveals over a duration of time.*[55]

This observation was quite evident during the 2008–2009 recession. Few would consider theme parks one of life's necessities, and during a time of cash crunch we would expect people to curtail their spending on such activities. Most did, and theme parks like Six Flags, which offers thrill rides to its customers, filed Chapter 11 bankruptcy, but, amazingly, the Disney theme parks didn't miss a beat during the same period.[56] They maintained their attendance level, and from 2008 to 2016, Disney actually increased its revenue from $36 billion to $56 billion. How can this be? The main reason is that Disney stages an experience that goes beyond rides to consider how to interact with every guest in a positive way throughout the entire park. Through the whole day Disney delivers ongoing "magic moments," from the majestic photo ops in front of castles and mountains to the sweet smells being pumped into the air down Main Street. While some parks like Kings Island have a few cartoon characters strolling the grounds, the Disney parks put the characters in entirely themed worlds that suit them. This makes the visit more memorable and personal.

Pine and Gilmore provide Disney as the exemplar of customer interaction because they deliver on all four realms of what constitutes a premiere experience: esthetics, escapist, educational, and entertainment. Esthetics make an environment more inviting, and encourage a guest to enjoy the setting. The setting induces guests to sit down, relax, and hang out. Walt Disney World creates this setting by employing 5,000 maintenance and engineering workers, including 750 horticulturists and 600 painters, to keep the grounds clean and majestic.[57] No other resort employs the army of groundskeepers that Disney does. The escapist aspect of Walt Disney World draws guests in and encourages them to participate in the setting. Whether it's interacting with "tour guides" on the Jungle Cruise ride or getting a picture taken with Goofy, guests have many opportunities to feel connected to the park. The educational component occurs when guests learn something from taking part in the activities of the experience. Attractions at Disney's Animal Kingdom such as the Pangani Forest Exploration Trail and the Maharajah Jungle Trek present facts about nature in an exotic fashion. The entertainment aspect makes the experience more fun and enjoyable, as experienced by the smiles, oohs, and ahs guests emit during their visit. Pine and Gilmore point out that it's not required to deliver on all four of these realms to be successful, but the more you do the more memorable the customer's experience will be.

You don't have to operate a theme park to deliver a world-class experience. Companies from very different industries create memorable moments with customers that bring them back again for future purchases. Southwest Airlines, for example, is well known for turning discount air travel into an experience. Funny and caring flight attendants can actually make hours in the air fun and relaxing. On the other end of the price spectrum, British Airways and Singapore Airlines pamper travelers with luxuries and access to services not found on traditional flights. Their customers are willing to pay significantly more money to make travel time more pleasant and satisfying. In the food industry, the Hard Rock Café provides a dining experience where customers can interact with hip food servers and bartenders while checking out museum quality artifacts from the music industry. Many people make it a point to dine at these theme restaurants when on vacation and purchase memorabilia to commemorate the visit. And if luxurious quarters are what you desire, Four Seasons Hotels and Resorts promises the best customer service in the hospitality industry.

In an increasingly competitive world, developing innovative experiences can help differentiate a company from its competitors. Pine and Gilmore believe the highest stage of experience is even transformative in nature, in that the customer changes in some fundamental way from the interaction. In a transformation, the customer is the product. Weight Watchers and Alcoholics Anonymous are two famous examples of transformative organizations. All attention is placed on helping the customer change a behavior or mindset that brings a better life in the future. The organization looks for ways to help clients realize their aspirations along the physical, emotional, intellectual, and spiritual dimensions of their lives. To make a big change in life requires first starting with a diagnostic tool that allows the customer to find a baseline on an issue. Then it's the company's responsibility to lead and guide the customer to the desired change. This approach is quite common in good university programs and churches, and may account for the strong attachments and loyalties people have with those institutions. People build loyalty with organizations that change their lives in a positive way. Companies that develop innovative transformative experiences have very appreciative customers who pay a premium for the desired results. For example, imagine an innovative healthcare company focusing on changing its clients into healthy and productive individuals instead of focusing only on efficient, cost-based treatment. A transformative hospital might be more expensive, but patients might also travel great distances to be treated in an inspirational, caring way.

This section examined sources of possible opportunities for new innovations. We first examined who the customer is, and then uncovered their wants, needs, and problems. We then explored ways to meet those opportunities. A company can find, develop, or use new materials, create new products, offer unique services, deliver experiences that fully engage their customers, and/or transform their behaviors and attitudes. As evidenced in this section, needs, wants, and problems are prime opportunities for innovation. After developing a list of the best opportunities, it's time to offer an actual product or service to the customer. The following section provides a methodology for shaping the idea into something customers will buy.

Converting Opportunity into Innovation

Assuming that you've found an opportunity for commercialization, it's time to convert it into an actual product, service, or experience. We now examine new product development. *Keep in mind that what a commercial offering actually becomes in the market is rarely identical to the original idea it was based on.* Blue sky ideas are much different than their real world design. Attributes and features might be added or subtracted and modifications will occur as a natural result of iterations in R&D efforts and commercialization.

New Product Development

Concept Development

The first step in converting an opportunity into an innovation is to develop a clear concept of what you want to achieve. The opportunity must be developed into a clear concept that can be defined and evaluated. For example, using the coffee example from earlier in this chapter, we could frame a challenge such as "What type of coffee product could we offer runners that would give them pep and boost endurance?" We can now explore different ways to meet this challenge by utilizing the creativity skills of divergence and convergence.

Leading design and development company IDEO employs this approach as a regular way of doing business. At IDEO, creative teams address challenges by undergoing a *"deep dive"* and immersing themselves in the problem space. With a specific challenge in mind, they study and interact with the customers and their surroundings in any way possible. General Manager Tom Kelley says designers at IDEO act like anthropologists, "getting out of the office, cornering the experts, and observing the natives in their habitat."[58] You can see this practice in a classic *Nightline* episode in which Ted Koppel presents IDEO with a distinct challenge, "Take something old and familiar, like say the shopping cart, and completely redesign it in just five days."[59] After visiting grocery stores, talking to managers, watching parents and children use shopping carts, interviewing professional buyers who purchase shopping carts, and visiting a shopping cart repairman, three goals emerged from the research: make the cart more child-friendly, redesign the shopping experience so that it's more efficient, and increase safety. The team then broke into different teams and diverged on possible ways to meet these goals in a new shopping cart design. After each team had developed their solutions, they shared them with the larger group. Each individual then selected the solutions they thought best met the stated goals of the project. After everyone converged on their favorite solutions, the group as a whole discussed why they chose what they did. After much discussion, the group came to agreement on what the best concept would be for the new shopping cart design.

Once a concept is defined, it can now be tested with relevant audiences, including customers, to gauge potential interest in the new product. Focus groups, interviews, and surveys are often used to do this. Industry analysis can also be helpful in preparing the product for new market entry. Areas such as competition, customer definition, technological assessment, regulatory concerns, and economic measures are all considerations for such research.[60] Once potential benefits are identified, marketing and sales are then considered before moving forward with product development. How much will shipping and handling cost to sell the product? Where will the product be stored? How can you get the product into proper distribution channels? How tough is the competition in this sector, and what are they doing to deliver products, services, and experiences?[61] If these factors are addressed and the idea still holds up, business cases can be prepared for the most promising concepts that survive this preparation and due diligence. A preliminary outline of the business case can include the concept and the related goals it meets; the needs, wants, or problems it addresses; the milestones you'll need to achieve in bringing the concept to market; and the potential obstacles you'll have to overcome to be successful.[62]

Prototyping

Once the concept is well defined and evaluated, it's time to start to transform it into a physical product, service delivery model, or customer experience. Managers must assemble a team who can establish the exact technical requirements for designing and producing the product, and ensure that these requirements can be met on a reasonable time and cost schedule. Design professionals may conceive different versions of the product (or service delivery system) based on the many tradeoffs that must be made among product attributes. Next comes technical product or service testing, which subjects the innovation to a rigorous examination of tolerances and performance capabilities under differing circumstances. Designers and engineers put a product through tough tests to make sure it holds up in everyday use. Once in-house tests show promise, products, services, and experiences can then be placed in customer locations (or beta test sites) for further testing and monitoring.

Final Evaluation

After a prototype is modeled, profitability analysis is performed to determine breakeven points in terms of initial investment as well as rates of return that will be realized through selling the product. Projected cash flows can help with these calculations. To confirm initial sales projections and finalize decisions regarding price, packaging, promotion, and distribution, test marketing is performed using a representative subset of the intended market. Market launch efforts are then planned and staged, often requiring a year or more before the product or service hits the market.

A Unique SWOT Analysis Approach

In this section we offer another approach to uncovering opportunities by utilizing a SWOT (Strengths, Weaknesses, Opportunities, and Threats) analysis, performed in an unconventional manner. A SWOT analysis is predominantly used in strategy sessions, but it can also be helpful as a tool for generating new product or service ideas. Following the steps below will help uncover additional opportunities:

Step 1: Diverge on the strengths, weaknesses, opportunities, and threats of your organization. You have probably performed these steps before. It will look familiar, but we provide a few twists to SWOT analysis. First, gather a diverse group of organizational members and diverge on your company's strengths, weaknesses, opportunities, and threats; i.e., capture all the strengths the group can come up with on large sheets of easel paper, and then do the same with weaknesses, opportunities, and threats. Be sure to write each fact in a complete sentence. For example, "Communication between the sales force and the marketing team is bad" is a better stated fact than "bad communications." Full sentences discipline us to think in more clear and precise terms, and ensure we understand what each other is saying. As you fill a page, have another participant tape the page to a wall in the room. Continue until the group comes to a standstill. Remember there are no wrong answers. The key is to capture as many ideas as possible.

Step 2: Converge on the main strengths, weaknesses, opportunities, and threats. After you have developed a full list of each factor, count how many facts were obtained in each segment. Multiply each segment's total by 10 percent and write that number at the top of each segment. For example, if a group had 22 strengths, 35 weaknesses, 10 threats, and 18 opportunities, write 2 on strengths, 4 (rounding up) on weaknesses, 1 on threats, and 2 (rounding up) on opportunities. Now ask each participant to put a sticky dot on the 2 strengths, 4 weaknesses, 1 threat, and 2 opportunities that they think will have the biggest impact on the company's future wellbeing.

Step 3: Clarify and select the key strengths, weaknesses, opportunities, and threats. Now look at the statements in each column that received the most "sticky dots" and ask the people who selected them why they did so. When there is consensus among the group as to the most important strengths, weaknesses, opportunities, and threats, circle the selections, and ask if there are any facts that were overlooked by the group that should be given further consideration. Once consensus is reached, draw a line under the strengths column and write underneath it "core competencies."

Step 4: Add core competencies to the strengths column. Explain to the group that core competencies are another type of strength that can be useful for capitalizing on opportunities. Core competencies are specific factors your company does well that are central to the way it delivers benefits to its customers. Core competencies separate your company from its competition, and are applied over a range of products and services. If the company has an official list of what its core competencies are, write them in the strengths column. If not, have the group diverge and converge on what the core competencies of the company should be.

Step 5: Explore how strengths and core competencies can be leveraged. Ask the group to diverge on how the company can leverage its strengths and core competencies to take advantage of the opportunities that were converged on. Once a list is generated, have the group converge on the ideas with the most market potential.

Step 6: Explore ways to improve weaknesses. Ask the group to consider how it could improve weaknesses in the company. For example, there may be process or service improvements that could be pursued for innovative solutions.

Step 7: Discuss threats. Ask the group to consider how it could build barriers to prevent threats from hurting the company. You can also ask what alternatives the company has for minimizing the threats it faces.

Steps 5, 6, and 7 provide participants after they leave the meeting with a list of general challenges that they can start designing solutions for. When the group meets again, each person will present their ideas. Write the ideas on easel paper, and then ask each participant to converge on the two ideas that they think have the most potential for the company. Ask the group why they made the selections they did. The group should now discuss which ideas they want to move forward.

Commercialization

The moment that management has decided the product, service, or experience is ready to launch is called the *point of commercialization. Final designs are confirmed, manufacturing and operations requirements are put in place, and distribution channels are authorized.* It is now critical that the marketing component of the innovation be firmed up. Chapter 8 will explore this component in more detail.

Summary

An innovative company is composed of innovative employees. Innovation is a way of life for people in these organizations. While scientists discover and inventors create, innovators find ways to adapt new products and services so that they're accepted in the market. This chapter examined how a manager can become more innovative. The ingredients for innovation were first covered. The approaches of closed innovation and open innovation were then examined. Sources of opportunity were also covered in depth. The chapter then explained how to recognize and seize an opportunity. It concluded with guidelines on how to develop an opportunity into an innovation.

Innovation-in-Action

Nike's History of Innovation

Since his graduation from Stanford University, Phil Knight, the founder of Nike, has changed the way everyone thinks about athletic shoes. With $500 and a handshake, Knight and his college track coach, Bill Bowerman, created Nike in 1964 and the innovations began immediately. The two made their first shoe order and began ripping the shoes apart, trying to find ways to improve the running shoe. Before long, Nike was revolutionizing running shoe technology and changing the way runners and the general public looked at the gym shoe.

Nike's innovative spirit has always played a key role in developing the athletes who utilize the technology. Athletes including Michael Jordan, Steve Prefontaine, Tiger Woods, and Michael Johnson have sought Nike for their design techniques, looking to better their already incredible talents. In the 1970s, Steve Prefontaine, one of the greatest track runners of all time, was one of the first to sport Nike's innovative technology. Bowerman drew inspiration from a common kitchen appliance when he created a shoe with an outsole that had waffle-type nubs for traction but were lighter than traditional training shoes. Prefontaine served as Nike's first international spokesman.

Perhaps Nike's most influential ambassador, Michael Jordan began his relationship with Nike in the 1980s and created his first signature basketball shoe. The Jordan brand launched in 1986 after Jordan was drafted into the NBA. Nike and the Jordan brand are still creating custom shoes today. His footwear remains the standard for not just basketball shoes, but for popular culture as well.

Olympic gold medalist Michael Johnson asked Nike to design a shoe that was light enough to shave a tenth of a second off of his personal best sprint times. Nike created a 112-gram track spike, the lightest track shoe ever made. The lightweight shoe proved to be the perfect catalyst, and at the 1996 Olympics, Johnson set the world record in the 200-meter sprint and also won gold in the 400-meter sprint.

The list of athletes who wear Nike shoes and clothes and sport the Nike swoosh on their chest goes on and on. Nike continues to design and create the world's most important sports technology and to push the limits of what the athlete can achieve.

(Adapted from: NikeBiz, *Company Overview: History*. Retrieved January 5, 2018, from: www.nikebiz.com/company_overview/history.)

Key Terms

adaptor

change

closed innovation

commercialization

commodities

concept development

deliberate practice

education

entertainment

escapism

esthetics

evaluation

experiences

fact-finding

innovation

innovator

life goals

needs

open innovation

opportunity

problems

products

prototyping

services

social goals

transformations

wants

Discussion Questions

1. What is the difference between creativity and innovation?
2. What is the difference between an adaptor and an innovator?
3. Why is mentorship important?
4. What are the deliberate practices of innovation?
5. What is the difference between closed innovation and open innovation?
6. When would a company use closed innovation?
7. When would a company use open innovation?

8. Why is collaboration important for innovation?
9. Where can managers find opportunities for new business?
10. Why do customer wants provide opportunities for new business?
11. What is the difference between a need and a want?
12. What avenues do managers have for seizing opportunity?
13. Provide your own example of a customer experience. What makes it unique?
14. Explain the four realms of customer experience. Provide your own example of a company that delivers value in these four realms.
15. Provide your own example of a transformative experience. Why are transformative experiences like this rare?
16. What is the process for converting an opportunity into an innovation?

Notes

1 Gates, Bill. 2017. A conversation about friendship, failure, and the future. *Gates Notes*, www.gatesnotes.com, February 1.
2 Basadur, Min. 1999. *Simplex: A Flight to Creativity*, Buffalo, NY: The Creative Education Foundation Press.
3 Marquis, Donald. 1972. Innovation, in E. Mansfield (ed.), *Research and Innovation in the Modern Corporation*, New York: Norton.
4 Foster, Richard. 1986. *Innovation: The Attacker's Advantage*, Philippines: Summit Books.
5 Monavvarian, Abbas. 2002. Administrative reform and style of work behavior: adaptors-innovators. *Public Organization Review: A Global Journal*, 2: 141–164.
6 Kirton, Michael J. 1987. Adaptors and innovators: cognitive style and personality, in Isaksen, Scott G. (ed.), *Frontiers of Creativity Research*, Bearly Limited.
7 Lashinsky, Adam. 2017. Riding shotgun with Travis Kalanik. *Fortune*, 175(7): 43.
8 It appears at the time of this writing that Kalanick stepped over the line into chaos. He resigned as CEO due to controversy over his management style and questions about the work culture inside Uber. While his management tenure might be questioned, his startup stage of the company was quite successful, as Uber had the highest market value of any startup in US history ($63 billion). He may have had more success as a manager if he had followed his own advice to stay on the line between order and chaos. Kalanick may have benefitted by relying on more adaptors as the company matured, or even developed more adaptor skills himself as his leadership role evolved. His presence will still remain at Uber, but he will be in a reduced role from daily operations as a member of the board of directors. Situations like this often have a maturing effect on ousted founders, who are forced to modify their style if they are to have a second chance at running future companies. Steve Jobs, for example, was a much more competent executive after his stints at NeXT Computers and Pixar. Time will tell if this happens to Kalanick.
9 Colvin, Geoff. 2008. *Talent Is Overrated: What Really Separates World-Class Performers from Everybody Else*, New York: Portfolio.
10 Welch's mentorship and preparation for crisis with Immelt paid off later as well. Just four days after Immelt took the reins as CEO from Welch, he was faced with leading GE on September 11, 2001, when the United States was attacked by terrorists. Immelt saw the company through the crisis and went on to have a successful 16-year run as CEO. In 2017, Immelt retired, and the leadership of GE was passed onto John L. Flannery.
11 Basadur, Min. 1999. *Simplex: A Flight to Creativity*, Buffalo, NY: The Creative Education Foundation Press.
12 Seligman, Martin E.P. 2011. *Learned Optimism: How to Change Your Mind and Your Life*, New York: Vintage.
13 Clifton, Jim. 2011. *The Coming Jobs War: What Every Leader Must Know About the Future of Job Creation*, New York: Gallup Press, p. 103.

14 Ericsson, K. Anders. 2006. The influence of experience and deliberate practice on the development of superior expert performance, in Ericsson, K. Anders, Charness, N., Feltovich, P.J. & Hoffman, R.R. (eds.), *The Cambridge Handbook of Expertise and Expert Performance*, Cambridge: Cambridge University Press.

15 Hayton, James C. & Kelley, Donna J. 2006. A competency-based framework for promoting corporate entrepreneurship. *Human Resource Management*, 45(3): 407–427.

16 Ericsson, K. Anders, Prietula, Michael J. & Cokely, Edward T. 2007. The making of an expert. *Harvard Business Review*, 85(7/8): 114–121.

17 Colvin, Geoff. 2008. *Talent is Overrated: What Really Separates World-Class Performers from Everybody Else*, New York: Portfolio.

18 Johansson, Frans. 2006. *The Medici Effect: What Elephants and Epidemics Can Teach Us About Innovation*, Boston: Harvard Business School Press.

19 Sawyer, Keith. 2007. *Group Genius: The Creative Power of Collaboration*, New York: Basic Books.

20 Gates, Bill. 2017. A conversation about friendship, failure, and the future. *Gates Notes*, www.gatesnotes.com, February 1.

21 Wright, Casey. 2017. Ten things to know about Google's awesome culture. *Huffington Post*, www.huffingtonpost.com/entry/10-things-to-know-about-googles-awesome-culture_us_59088802e4b03b105b44bbfd, May 2.

22 Hills, G.E. & Shrader, R.C. 1998. Successful entrepreneurs' insights into opportunity recognition, in Reynolds, P.D. et al. (eds.), *Frontiers of Entrepreneurship Research*, Babson Park, MA: Babson College Press, pp. 30–43.

23 DeTienne, Dawn R. & Chandler, Gaylen N. 2004. opportunity identification and its role in the entrepreneurial classroom: a pedagogical approach and empirical test. *Academy of Management Learning & Education*, 3(3): 242–257.

24 Psychology professor Richard Wiseman has found that *positive serendipitous moments*, also known as "luck," can happen more frequently to those who believe they'll have good fortune in the future. Keeping a journal and carrying notebooks are practices that build awareness of what's going on in your world. Writing down your thoughts allows you to reflect on how the moving parts in your life might connect. Once an underlying order appears, you gain confidence in what might be coming your way, and, in the process, develop positive expectations about what will happen to you. When an opportunity does arise, people with positive expectations are more likely to take action, thus giving themselves a chance of a good outcome. Therefore, a positive state of mind leads to action that makes a person more "lucky" or "fortunate" than an overly cautious, withdrawn individual who only takes what is given to them. The most surprising aspect of Professor Wiseman's research is just thinking you're lucky actually does make you "lucky."

25 Stefik, Mark & Stefik, Barbara. 2004. *Breakthrough: Stories and Strategies of Radical Innovation*, Boston: MIT Press.

26 Vance, Ashlee. 2015. *Elon Musk: Tesla, SpaceX, and the Quest for a Fantastic Future*, New York: Ecco.

27 Stokes, Donald. 1997. *Pasteur's Quadrant: Basic Science and Technological Innovation*, Washington, DC: Brookings Institution Press.

28 Chesbrough, Henry. 2003. *Open Innovation: The New Imperative for Creating and Profiting from Technology*, Boston: Harvard Business School Press.

29 Sawyer, Keith. 2007. *Group Genius: The Creative Power of Collaboration*, New York: Basic Books.

30 Laffley, A.G. & Charan, Ram. 2008. *The Game-Changer: How You Can Drive Revenue and Profit Growth with Innovation*, New York: Crown Business.

31 Chesbrough, Henry. 2003. *Open Innovation: The New Imperative for Creating and Profiting from Technology*, Boston: Harvard Business School Press.

32 Maslow, Abraham. 1943. A theory of human motivation. *Psychological Review*, 50: 370–396.

33 Berger, Arthur Asa. 2005. *Shop 'til You Drop: Consumer Behavior and American Culture*, New York: Rowman & Littlefield.

34 This condition of a constantly changing array of unmet needs and desires is the underlying rationale of a capitalist society. Since people are rarely satisfied, there will always be a

place for new innovations that grow the economy. Capitalist critics call this state of living the "hedonic treadmill." Supporters of capitalism call it progress.

35 Miller, Geoffrey. 2009. *Spent: Sex, Evolution, and Consumer Behavior*, New York: Viking.

36 Pooler, Jim. 2003. *Why We Shop: Emotional Rewards and Retail Strategies*, Santa Barbara, CA: Praeger.

37 O'Shaughnessy, John. 1987. *Why People Buy*, Oxford: Oxford University Press.

38 How many times do you find yourself buying something under the rationale of "I deserve it"? For example, "I put up with my boss all week, I deserve this," or "I got an A on my test, I deserve this"? If you do this often, you're in good company. Most people have spectacular justifiers in their brains and can find reasons to support their behavior. And research has even shown that the smarter a person is, the better they are at coming up with rationale to support their actions. This cognitive capacity might explain why so many successful people who were smart enough to build a fortune can also find themselves bankrupt due to unwise investments or lavish purchases.

39 In the movie *True Stories* directed by musician David Byrne, one of the characters puts on a fashion show at a mall and tells the crowd, "Shopping is a feeling." And like other feelings, it can be fleeting. The purchase of products and services as a self-reward rarely brings long-term satisfaction. But this impulse is nothing new. The stoic philosopher Seneca offered words of wisdom for this condition thousands of years ago when he said, "True happiness is to enjoy the present, without anxious dependence upon the future, not to amuse ourselves with either hopes or fears but to rest satisfied with what we have, which is sufficient, for he that is so wants nothing. The greatest blessings of mankind are within us and within our reach. A wise man is content with his lot, whatever it may be, without wishing for what he has not."

40 "I just saved 50% on a pair of shoes. That gives me more money to make more good purchases. In fact, I deserve to buy another pair. That's two for the price of one. What a good shopper I am!"

41 Hayes, J. 1980. *The Complete Problem Solver*, Philadelphia, PA: The Franklin Institute Press.

42 Basadur, Min. 1999. *Simplex: A Flight to Creativity*, Buffalo, NY: The Creative Education Foundation Press.

43 Von Hippel, Eric, Franke, Nikolaus & Prügl, Reinhard. 2009. Pyramiding: efficient search for rare subjects. *Research Policy*, 38(9): 1397–1406.

44 Von Hippel calls this technique "pyramiding" because an organization often resembles a pyramid with a lot of people at the base and a lone leader at the top. As you continue to ask who else you can talk to about a problem, you move up the pyramid to higher-ranking people in the organization. The earlier conversation with lower-ranking managers and employees builds your knowledge to take part in richer conversations with executives, thus building your credibility in the industry.

45 Kirzner, Israel M. 2016. *Discovery, Capitalism, and Distributive Justice*, Carmel, IN: The Liberty Fund.

46 Firestein, Stuart. 2012. *Ignorance*, Oxford: Oxford University Press, pp. 16–17.

47 Priess, David. 2016. *The President's Book of Secrets: The Untold Story of Intelligence Briefings to America's Presidents*, New York: PublicAffairs, pp. xi–xii.

48 Sawyer, Keith. 2007. *Group Genius: The Creative Power of Collaboration*, New York: Basic Books.

49 Pine II, B. Joseph & Gilmore, James H. 1999. *The Experience Economy: Work Is Theatre and Every Business a Stage*, Boston: Harvard Business School Press.

50 McClure, Wendy R. & Bartuska, Tom J. 2007. *The Built Environment: A Collaborative Inquiry into Design and Planning*, New York: John Wiley & Sons.

51 Christensen, Clayton. 2003. *The Innovator's Dilemma: The Revolutionary Book that Will Change the Way You Do Business*, New York: Harper.

52 Markides, Constantinos C. & Geroski, Paul A. 2005. *Fast Second: How Smart Companies Bypass Radical Innovation to Enter and Dominate New Markets*, New York: Jossey-Bass.

53 Rosenbush, Steve. 2006. Facebook's on the block. *BusinessWeek Online*, March 28, www.businessweek.com/technology/content/mar2006/tc20060327_215876.hum (accessed October 3, 2006).

54 Hansell, Saul. 2006. Yahoo woos a social networking site. *New York Times Online*, September 22, www.nytimes.com/2006/09/22/technology/22facebook.html?ex=1316577600eten=09f3d5e70aa0r977etei=5008epartenr=rssnyetemic=rss (accessed October 3, 2006).

55 Pine II, B. Joseph & Gilmore, James H. 1999. *The Experience Economy: Work Is Theatre and Every Business a Stage*, Boston: Harvard Business School Press.

56 Barnes, Brooks. 2009. Struggles at the box office weigh on Disney's profit. *New York Times Online*, May 5, www.nytimes.com/2009/05/06/business/media/06disney.html?_r=1&ref=media (accessed July 21, 2009).

57 Disney by the Numbers. 2009. www.disneybythenumbers.com/wdw/wdw.html (accessed July 21, 2009).

58 Kelley, Tom & Littman, Jonathon. 2001. *The Art of Innovation: Lessons in Creativity from IDEO, America's Leading Design Firm*, New York: Currency Books.

59 *Nightline: Deep Dive*, www.youtube.com/watch?v=z6z-3ejvvGE.

60 Gruenwald, George. 1997. *How to Create Profitable New Products—from Mission to Market*, Lincolnwood, IL: NTC Business Books.

61 Gorman, Tom. 2007. *Innovation*, New York: Adams Business.

62 Nochur, Kumar. 2009. *Executing Innovation*, Boston: Harvard Business Publishing.

PART 3

The Design Function in Innovation (*I-Design*)

5

THE DESIGN THINKING PROCESS

Engineers are not the only professional designers. Everyone designs who devises courses of action aimed at changing existing situations into preferred ones.

~Herbert A. Simon, professor and 1978 Nobel
Laureate in Economics[1]

Introduction

Design has become one of the most popular topics in business today. *Fast Company* magazine prints its annual Innovation by Design issue every October, the Mayo Clinic publishes a book about how design transformed its medical practices, and universities offer a growing list of design courses in colleges outside of architecture and engineering. But design is not a new practice. It's been around a long time and continues to be used whenever people envision new possibilities of what the future can be. The Great Pyramids of Egypt and the Hoover Dam, while separated by thousands of years, are both magnificent achievements in design. We marvel at their appearance and imagine the labor that went into building them. But the immense structures would not be there at all if someone had not first devised a plan to build them. The plans were not perfect, and no doubt many mistakes were made in the construction of both. Slaves were likely crushed by the huge blocks of limestone that canvassed across the sloped faces of the pyramids and, in building the Hoover Dam, the US Department of the Interior cites 96 "industrial fatalities," such as drowning, blasting, rock falls, slides, falls from the canyon walls, truck accidents, and equipment issues.[2] But through tremendous perseverance and investment, each great vision was achieved. Although most things around us aren't on par with these manmade marvels, everything around us is an outcome of a design of some sort. We pass our days living in a built environment.

A good business idea is important in getting the innovation process going, but it's design that brings it into reality. *Design, therefore, is the process that converts ideas into form, whether that is a plan of action or a physical thing.* The Mayo Clinic uses the *Wikipedia* definition to guide their work:

> *Design thinking is the ability to combine empathy for the context of a problem, creativity in the generation of insights and solutions, and rationality to analyze and fit solutions to that context.*[3]

In the previous chapters, we covered issues that relate to the context of the opportunity you're considering pursuing. Customers, industry, supply chains, company capabilities, and a host of other business considerations define this context. The more up-front work you've done on these considerations, the better equipped you are to design a great product or service. Now you might be asking yourself, what constitutes a great product or service? Well, the answer is determined by your customers. Great products and services make their lives easier, better, and more interesting. When a company offers a product or service that delights and surprises its customers, it's hit its mark. Perhaps no group better understands how to do this than the acrobatic performance company Cirque du Soleil. Cirque du Soleil's design goal is to develop shows and acts that delight the 5-year-old child within all of us. If the audience is held spellbound for two-and-a-half hours, they know they've put together a good show. Attention to detail and pride of their craft helps performers and choreographers create shows that both a 5-year-old and an 85-year-old can enjoy. Take for example how one of their performers meticulously approaches his fire act:

> *I've been doing this for twenty-five years, so you can't avoid getting burned at some point. Plumbers get wet, beekeepers get stung every once in a while. I use the best materials I can, the right fuels and clothes and stunt gels. But even with those things, it's dangerous. The world record for being on fire is two minutes and thirty seconds, and I burn for two minutes and fifteen seconds every night. We time it to the exact second, because you can only go so long before the material breaks down. . . . I take my time, shuffling along, which creates the illusion that I've been burning for a long time, when it isn't that long. The rest of the troupe does a great job of distracting the audience with all this fast stuff, which helps to cloud their perception of time. It seems agonizing—to you![4]*

Some companies, like Cirque du Soleil, are much better at design than others because they know how to make their customers happy and satisfied. In the circus world, agony is a desirable feeling performers want you to have. Will the tightrope walkers make it to the other side? How long can the clown endure being on fire? Will the BMX bike rider be able to jump over the break dancers? In another context, agony would be a horrible business outcome. Agonizing at your next dental appointment, for example, would not be a good experience; neither would waiting hours for a meal at a restaurant. So each design challenge requires recognizing what will be accepted and what will be frustrating in that particular setting.[5]

No one understood this principle better than industrial design legend Raymond Loewy. There are two eras of modern American capitalism—one before Raymond Loewy and one after. Before Loewy, American companies focused almost exclusively on efficiency and costs. Products were bland and packaged in generic boxes, as assembly lines housed in gigantic factories applied scientific management practices, cranking out cheap products to a growing middle class. Loewy appeared on the scene in post-World War I America. It was the "Roarin' Twenties," and people were open to new styles. Loewy was motivated to elevate American taste in this new golden age of business. He had grown up in France and developed a rich aesthetic sense to go along with his technical knowledge of engineering. When he arrived in New York City in 1925, the styles immortalized in the television series *Mad Men* didn't exist yet. The city had a very industrial feel to it. It was dirty and utilitarian. There was no elegance to what people wore and used. Loewy saw an opportunity to offer consumers more elegant products that would better fit a cosmopolitan lifestyle. Many historians of twentieth-century America believe Loewy may have had more impact on influencing American culture than just about any other business figure. Biographer Derek Thompson explains that Loewy was the first designer to understand "what made things cool."[6] For example:

> His firm designed mid-century icons like the Exxon logo, the Lucky Strike pack, and the Greyhound bus. He designed International Harvester tractors that farmed the Great Plains, merchandise racks at Lucky Stores supermarkets that displayed produce, Frigidaire ovens that cooked meals, and Singer vacuum cleaners that ingested the crumbs of dinner. The famous blue nose of Air Force One? That was Loewy's touch, too. "Loewy," wrote Cosmopolitan magazine in 1950, "has probably affected the daily life of more Americans than any man of his time."[7]

Loewy's reign as the king of industrial design, however, didn't garner the press that today's rock stars of design receive. There was no *Fast Company* magazine to do behind-the-scenes coverage or cable business channels to promote new product launches. But corporate executives knew who Loewy was, and sought him out to create new products that Americans would love. Thompson explains that Loewy landed on a formula for product design that still works today:

> To see more stuff, American industrialists needed to work hand in hand with artists to make new products beautiful—even "cool." Lowey had an uncanny sense of how to make things fashionable. He believed that consumers are torn between two opposing forces: neophilia, a curiosity about new things; and neophobia, a fear of anything too new. As a result, they gravitate to products that are bold, but instantly comprehensible. Loewy called his grand theory "Most Advanced Yet Acceptable"—MAYA. He said to sell something surprising, make it familiar, and to sell something familiar, make it surprising.[8]

In other words, know your customers and how they think. Surprise them but don't confuse them. *It's a fine line, but great designers push their ideas just enough to be interesting but not so far to be ridiculous.* They respect the intelligence of their audience.

Design

In previous chapters, we examined the concepts of creativity and innovation. We also discussed entrepreneurial activity within an organization. In this chapter, we turn to the role design can play in increasing our innovation capabilities. Creativity, design, innovation, and entrepreneurship are related terms and influence each other. Let's clarify what makes each one different. *Creativity is a set of thinking skills that generates novel (but acceptable) ideas into the world.* Using divergent and convergent thinking we can be more creative in everything we do. *Design is the process of shaping an idea into an actual artifact.*[9] In other words, we create something we can observe and manipulate. We make the new idea real. Keep in mind that this artifact could be a product, a service, a process, or a business model. So when we design, we bring an idea into the world for others to comprehend. We don't have to ask the designer what the idea means. The artifact speaks for itself. A well-designed artifact is embraced by the target audience, whereas bad design leaves the user confused and/or uninterested in it. *Innovation is the extended process of providing the artifact to a larger audience.* The more impact a product or service has on a society, the more innovative it's deemed to be. However, for an innovation to reach a customer, entrepreneurship must take place. An entrepreneur must champion the product or service or it will never make it to market.

Figure 5.1 demonstrates how the concepts are related. Understanding the differences and interrelationships of these concepts will help you develop each skillset. A designer—which can be anyone who comes up with a new artifact—has an idea and then tweaks and transforms it into a desirable or needed form. They become an innovator when they convert the design into a marketable product for production. That same person becomes an entrepreneur when they solve problems and overcome obstacles, garner the resources for manufacturing the product, and present the innovation to the target audience.

Now let's see how the different skillsets build on each other. A manager who is more creative can design more interesting products and services. And a manager who is more proactive has the discipline and grit to move projects forward. Designing a product or service that's worthwhile drives innovation, and the more innovation a company generates the more entrepreneurial it can be. Therefore, a design that's shepherded by a proactive and creative entrepreneurial champion can be shaped into a viable commercial product or service. So, if a manager applies creativity and is ruthlessly proactive, then all three elements will be amplified. *Thus, being more creative and proactive leads to better design, better design leads to more innovation, and more innovation leads to increased entrepreneurial activity.*

Let's see how Peter Drucker explained the interrelationship of these concepts by looking at McDonald's:

> *Hamburger stands have been around in the United States since the nineteenth century, but in the McDonald's hamburger chain, management was being applied to what had always been a hit-and-miss, mom-and-pop operation. McDonald's first designed the*

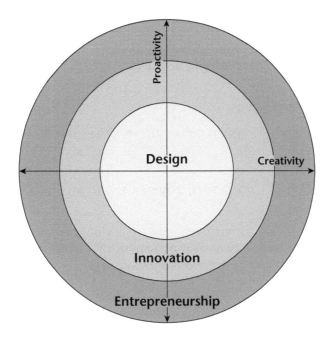

FIGURE 5.1 Relationship between Design, Innovation and Entrepreneurship.

end product; then it redesigned the entire process of making it; then it redesigned or in many cases invented the tools so that every piece of meat, every slice of onion, every bun, every piece of fried potato would be identical, turned out in a precisely timed and fully automated process. Finally, McDonald's studied what "value" meant to the customer, defined it as quality and predictability of product, speed of service, absolute cleanliness, and friendliness, then set standards for all of these, trained for them, and geared compensation to them.

(p. 17)

McDonald's is the global giant it is today because Ray Kroc utilized thoughtful design, innovation, and entrepreneurship to create a new industry. The McDonald's hamburger was designed to be affordable and tasty to a wide market. McDonald's innovations in the preparation of hamburgers transformed the grease cook's grill into an assembly line in the kitchen. Finally, the company professionalized the way restaurants were operated and created a profitable model that could easily be replicated in multiple locations. The system was designed to prepare hamburgers that met Kroc's standards anywhere in the world, which quickly scaled McDonald's into a global corporation. As Drucker notes, if hamburger stands can be transformed into business empires, nearly anything can be if enough creativity and proactiveness are applied to the practices of design, innovation, and entrepreneurship.

Now that we've examined the concept of design, we turn to one of the main reasons why design is often *not* pursued by managers: the misconceptions associated with it. Much like we have seen in previous chapters, myths and misconceptions can hinder managers from developing new skills.

Design Misconceptions

There are many misconceptions that keep people from pursuing design in their work, such as:

Misconception 1: Only artists, engineers, and architects use design.

Artists, engineers, and architects are most commonly associated with design because they build things that we can see. Artists work with different mediums to bring what's inside their minds onto the canvas. Engineers provide solutions to a variety of product and operational problems to improve a company's performance. Architects design buildings to satisfy client requests and make philosophical and aesthetic statements to society at large. While these professions do incorporate design, they need not be the only ones who can do so. Managers can also bring a design mindset to their work by utilizing the same principles the artists, engineers, and architects do to their realms. Doing so, however, requires a different approach to work. Design requires a flexible approach with others to improve what the company can be. The manager must become a facilitator during the design process rather than just a boss.

Misconception 2: Research and development departments are where companies should do design.

It is true that a lot of design takes place in the R&D departments of companies, but it's time for more managers outside the lab to engage in the design process as well. Markets are changing rapidly, and keeping design solely in R&D labs limits opportunity. While R&D departments will always play an important role in large corporations, other employees must be allowed to participate in the innovation process with scientists and engineers. Everyone in a company has unique insights that could lead to new products and services if they're allowed to develop an idea. Twenty-first century business leaders can unleash a wealth of new product ideas by informing employees about what's going on in their laboratories. Design, like entrepreneurship and creativity, is the practice of a universal set of principles that can be applied in any domain. *Therefore, the more that people are involved in the design process, the more likely the company is to uncover hidden opportunities.* Like corporate entrepreneurship and creativity, design is quickly becoming a practice that will become democratized by forward-thinking companies.

Misconception 3: Design is too complex to be used by the average manager in the company.

This misconception is related to the first one. Since technical professionals use design in their daily jobs, design is seen as the province of craftsmen and artisans. Indeed, if a manager were to attempt to design a building or engineer a product, they'd find it an arduous task. But there are equally challenging aspects of their jobs that engineers and architects would find perplexing as well. Once managers appreciate what design is, they can work more easily with the technical professionals in their company. The best managers may not have the technical expertise of their scientific colleagues, but they have an appreciation for what they do, which fosters more collaboration. When managers incorporate design principles into their work, they'll also gain more technical literacy of what scientists and engineers do. On the flip side, when technical professionals are working more closely with managers, they'll gain a better understanding of the economic issues of the company. Design collaboration brings the often opposing worlds of technology and business together.

Misconception 4: Design would cut into a manager's daily schedule and lead only to frustration.

Managers often spend their days thinking about hitting financial targets and achieving organizational goals. Coupled with the demands that come with leading employees in their business units, managers may believe they don't have time to introduce design into their jobs. While this is an understandable concern, utilizing design principles actually helps managers improve their department's work processes and policies to be more effective and efficient. Too many managers give their employees orders without taking the time to consider the true impact of their decisions. Design principles can help a manager build a better functioning team. Additionally, managers that get involved in designing new products and services are more likely to enjoy their work. In *Drive*, Daniel Pink explains that while financial incentives are effective for motivating manual labor, meaning and purpose lead to better performance in cognitive work. Thinking about new products and services actually helps managers become more engaged in their work.[10]

Misconception 5: Design will slow down the innovation process.

In today's competitive world, time may be our most valuable resource. Executives are expected to get quick results or else. Under these conditions, managers may not feel they have the luxury to be involved in design. They may say to themselves, "Better to leave it to the experts in the R&D department. We've got work to do." This sentiment is understandable, but it may actually lead to setbacks in the innovation process. Good design speeds up the innovation process. Customers, experts, technicians, and other managers should be brought into product discussions.

By incorporating a diverse group of relevant stakeholders early in the innovation process, later setbacks can be averted or minimized. Design requires that managers face the reality of what really matters to their customers and what their company can realistically produce. Thus, design is the mixing of what currently exists with a possible future that can be realized.

Misconception 6: Design is too fuzzy and will take the manager away from the realities of business.

Many managers may think that design is a practice for eccentric artists or engineers, but design properly understood is grounded in the realities of business. While the early stages of design can be fuzzy, fact-finding, seeking feedback, and fixing concerns creates viable products and services. The best managers develop the ability to manage and lead their organizations to hit current goals while looking for new opportunities. This mindset doesn't happen overnight, but the more managers integrate design into their work, the better they will be at it. Managers must develop the discipline to make their daily practices and workplace better than they were the day before.

Misconception 7: Design is just another business fad.

Many business practices seem to be the "flavor of the month" in management theory. In the 1980s, total quality management and continuous improvement were the rage. The 1990s brought the re-engineering movement and e-commerce. In the twenty-first century, design appears to be the most popular topic in the business press. While critics may cynically call these movements "fads," experienced managers know that these trends are now established as ways their companies do business. It's almost second nature now for managers to consider quality and cost-efficiency in delivering their products and services. The re-engineering movement is still evident today as companies seek ways to become more lean and productive. With companies operating with better efficiencies, executives now realize they must become entrepreneurial to increase their revenues. As a result, they're turning their attention to design to create new products and services. It's likely that in ten years, the world's leading companies will have more designers spread throughout their ranks.

Misconception 8: Design is the same thing as innovation.

Design and innovation are quite often used interchangeably in conversation. While the terms are related, there are some differences. Innovation covers the entire process of bringing an idea to market, whereas design encompasses the iterative component of shaping the idea into a finished product or service. The critical reason for covering design is that too many companies rush an idea into the marketplace before it's had the opportunity to evolve into a better product or service. In fact, in meeting the call for more innovation, some companies actually hurt their business by bringing worse products than they already have to market. Good design slows a company down in the short run but speeds up the innovation process in the long run. Business history is riddled with the New Cokes and Ford Edsels that weren't embraced by the market because of poor design. Understanding these subtle differences will help the manager become more effective in the innovation process.

Misconception 9: Design is too quirky for a business environment.

Design often gets a bad rap in business. This may be because professions traditionally related to design often comprise flamboyant characters. At the Walt Disney Company, for example, there's a big difference in the cultures found among the Imagineers and the business executives. The Imagineers often wear wild clothes and jewelry while the executives look the part of Fortune 500 business people. But when it comes to developing a new ride or hotel for one of their parks, the executives appreciate the big ideas of the Imagineers. While there's some creative tension between the groups, co-development on projects bridges aesthetics with economics. This collaboration gives Disney a huge advantage over its competition. As a result, a Disney theme park rarely misses its mark, and their guests come back repeatedly to see what the company dreams up next. While Disney is in an industry focused on delivering high-quality experiences, every company has the opportunity to include design in their business as well.

These misconceptions have been presented to provide a background for today's current thinking on design. By sidestepping the folklore, we can build a foundation for better understanding what design thinking is and how the design process works.

Design Thinking

Now that we've examined what design is and what it isn't, we can look at how to think like a designer. Design has become a hot topic in the business world. The demand has become so great that universities now offer programs in design for everyone rather than just concentrating it in technical schools like architecture and engineering. Mirroring the general approach of design firms like IDEO, Stanford University has founded an Institute of Design (also known as the d school) and the Rotman School of Management at the University of Toronto has built a curriculum based on "harnessing the power of design thinking."[11] The goal of such programs is to train future business leaders to incorporate design thinking into their general practices. Companies such as Procter & Gamble and Microsoft are also embracing this approach, but any company can utilize design principles through their ranks if they employ the following elements of design thinking offered by IDEO CEO Tim Brown.[12]

Elements of Design Thinking

Accept that Constraints Are Part of the Design Process

Designers are always faced with choices in how they develop a new product or service. They'd like to be able to make a product good, fast, and cheap, but it's almost impossible to meet all three of these goals in one product. Typically they must choose two of the three to pursue. For example, if a product is made good and fast, it requires committing a lot of resources to pull off the accomplishment in such a short time. If a product is made good and cheap, it may take a while to produce because organizational resources are committed elsewhere. And if it's made fast and cheap, the quality may suffer. This is the reality of design, but the best designers see constraints as invigorating challenges to master. The best designers take a can-do attitude about "wicked problems," almost as if they're puzzles to be solved. They view constraints as a chance to test and demonstrate their abilities.[13] As Brown explains:

> *The mark of a designer is a willing embrace of constraints. Without constraints design cannot happen, and the best design—a precision medical device or emergency shelter for disaster victims—is often carried out within quite severe constraints. The willing and even enthusiastic acceptance of competing constraints is the foundation of design thinking.*

Seek a Harmonious Balance between Desirability, Feasibility, and Viability

A designer must be a big picture thinker. Details must fit together that meet the expectations of different stakeholders. The best-designed products and services meet these expectations when they are desired by their customers, can be reasonably produced by employees, and make economic sense for the company. This exercise in optimization is best attained by designing the product with the user in mind. When a designer observes, researches, and interacts with the customer, good ideas of what they find desirable in a product or service spring forth. Aesthetics are an important consideration for creating a design that's pleasing and interesting to a particular geographic region or market segment. Products should also be reliable and easy to use for the intended customer. Additionally, an idea must be feasible for a company to pursue. If a product is too complicated, intricate, or time-consuming to be produced, the company should pass on the opportunity. What might be a good idea for one company may be a potential disaster for another. Thus, a major aspect of commercializing a product is deciding what materials, components, and fabrication techniques make the most sense for manufacturing and whether the company has the capability to adequately produce it. With regard to a new service concept, a company should consider whether it has the expertise and capacity to deliver it well. And finally the economic viability of the product must be considered. A product or service might be interesting and well received, but if it doesn't make economic sense to produce it (or fit within the mission and strategy of the company at large), it may need to be modified or dropped. Tim Brown points out that "a competent designer will resolve each of these three constraints, but a design thinker will bring them into a harmonious balance."

So three sets of questions that are good to ask yourself when you're screening your design are:

1. *Desirability questions:* Will our customers love this? Will it surprise and delight them? Will it make their lives easier, better, or more interesting? Is it a lot better than their current options? What are the benefits of this product or service? What are the costs associated with this product or service? After considering the benefits and costs, will this be a valuable and unique product or service in the market?
2. *Feasibility questions:* What will it take to do this? Are we capable of providing this? Do we have the expertise needed to do this? Do we have the capacity to do this? If not, what resources and people do I need to meet this capacity?
3. *Viability questions:* Is it worthwhile for us to do this? Will it bring a good return on investment if we sink resources into this project? Resources are always limited, so if we do this, what are we going to have to give up to do it? What would be our next best alternative if we didn't do this? Is it worth our time to do this? Is it worth the effort to do this? After all these considerations, is it still worth it?

If your ideas fall short in one or more of these three areas, you may need to drop it or modify it. In an upcoming section, we'll explain how this can be accomplished using iteration.

Next, we provide additional elements of design thinking we've found useful in working with clients and students on new product ideas.

Inspiration

In Chapter 4, we learned how to discover good ideas to work on, which is the first critical step of design. All designers are inspired by a problem they want to solve or an opportunity that they feel motivated to pursue. Without working on meaningful projects, people won't be willing to put in the long hours of work required to shape an idea into an innovative product. But designers are also inspired by the work of others that they wish to emulate in their own projects. Authors are inspired by other writers' styles, filmmakers influence other directors, and architects design buildings to embody philosophical schools of thought, for example. Sometimes designers even cross over one field's ideas into their own, such as when Elon Musk fashioned the first Tesla electric cars after the look of the iPhone. If you look at a Tesla from above, you'll see that it indeed has the same appearance as the iPhone. This is how inspiration works. You never know where it may come from, but you have to be open to it. A trip could inspire you, a movie could inspire you, or a particular product you love could inspire you. Steve Jobs, for instance, loved driving his silver Mercedes SL55. He liked how it handled when he drove over the winding roads of northern California, he liked the engineering that delivered power when he called on it, and he enjoyed the features within easy reach of his fingertips. His daily commute to Apple in the well-designed sports car put him in the right frame of mind to pursue excellence in his own work. He may have even thought of the iMac as the "Mercedes" of computers.

So what inspires you? What are your favorite products and services? Which companies do you think "get it right"? How can you incorporate that excellence into your own work? What places in the world invigorate you? What works of art speak to you? And most importantly, why do these sources inspire you? These are the types of questions you should ask yourself to enhance your design skills. And once you've identified what inspires you, start learning more about the people and companies that created the sources of your admiration. Or if it's a place, learn more about the culture, people, architecture, politics, and geography of the location. Your consciousness of what's possible in your own work will be elevated.

Proactiveness

Inspiration is an important starting point for working on a project, but a more important element of design is proactive behavior. Most people get excited by the possibility of where an idea can go, but they often don't have the grit to persevere through the difficult challenges that arise. One source of reticence is the struggle many people have with the unknown. Thus, being proactive means embracing risk. Simply put, some ideas may not pan out, and a person will be proven wrong. People who see failure as a learning opportunity handle these consequences better than others do. Action, though, brings understanding. Anyone who's made a big discovery did so by moving forward and taking their chances. If you're inspired by an idea and believe you've done your due diligence, it might be time to take a leap of faith and pursue it. Designers don't live in the past. They create the future.

Humility

A humble approach helps in designing products or services. While seemingly con-tradictory to what we think achievement requires, humility properly understood leads to better results. As Charles Koch, CEO of Koch Industries, told one of the authors recently:

> *Humility doesn't mean looking down at your shoes and saying, 'Aw Shucks.' It means knowing what you don't know and turning to those who do. It's being willing to admit to yourself and others that you don't have all the answers. From that state of mind, you can get the answers you need to get things done.*

When you approach others for knowledge that you lack, you accelerate the design process. Using the pyramid approach discussed in Chapter 4, you can approach experts with specific questions. Consider what specific issues you need to know more about to proceed further on your project. Remember, experts are busy people, so they'll appreciate your consideration of their time by coming to the meeting prepared with a list of questions. Showing up with a clear agenda will make the most of your time with the expert, and if you're well prepared, you may find the expert enjoying themselves too. Since the chance to self-reflect and share insights is rare in most people's busy day, you may find the expert quickly warming up to you, which might open up the door for follow-up meetings in the future.

At the end of the meeting, an interesting question to ask is what book, video, website, or film they've recently found interesting. The answer will cue you into other resources that will benefit your work. And never forget the most important phrase you can utter at the end of a session with an expert: *"Thank you for your time. Is there anyone else you know who might be helpful to me on these issues?"*

Author Stephen Covey states that this type of behavior is one of the seven habits of highly effective people:

> *If I am intellectually interdependent, I realize that I need the best thinking of other people to join with my own. As an interdependent person, I have the opportunity to share myself deeply and meaningfully with others, and I have access to the vast resources and potential of other human beings.*[14]

Chip Heath and Dan Heath tell the tale of how this type of thinking helped Sam Walton build Walmart. They explain that, "Again and again in his career Walton found clever solutions by asking himself, *'Who else is struggling with a similar problem, and what can I learn from them?'*"[15] This is an amazingly powerful question and one that can guide you in finding answers to problems that spring up on your design journey. Imagine you're having a hard time finding a good supplier. You could ask yourself, "Who has the best supply chain? What can I learn from them? How did they build it? What benchmarks are they setting in their industry?" Or maybe you're having a hard time getting your team to be more creative. You could ask yourself, "Which companies keep creating breakthrough products? How do they do it? How can I learn more about them?" Here's how the Heath brothers explain how Sam Walton used this question to turn Walmart from a small business in Arkansas to the corporate giant it is today:[16]

> *Throughout Walton's career, he kept his eyes out for good ideas. He once said that "most everything I've done I've copied from someone else." In the early days of discount store chains, he crisscrossed the country in search of insights, visiting discounters from Spartan and Mammoth Mart in the Northeast to FedMart in California. Through conversations with one of FedMart's leaders, Walton clarified his thinking on distribution, which would eventually become a defining strength of Walmart. And he admired the merchandise mix and displays in Kmart, founded in Garden City, Michigan, by S.S. Kresge. "I'll bet I've been in more Kmarts than anybody," Walton said. Again and again in his career, Walton found clever solutions by asking himself, "Who else is struggling with a similar problem, and what can I learn from them?"*

A helpful twist on this question is, *"Who's already doing something like I want to do? What can I learn from them? Do I have to make any modifications to what they do to make it work for me? What's not so good about what they do? How would I do it differently? What could I do better than them? How would I do that? How can I work it in with what we already have or do? How can we combine it with something else outside our company and make it our own?"*[17]

We recently spoke with a Walt Disney Parks and Resorts executive who shared with us that whenever they come up with a concept for a new attraction, they'll ask themselves these same types of questions. When they're considering using a design, they first look at technologies that already exist to see if they want to include them in their attractions. For example, one attraction they considered adding at their DisneyQuest location at Walt Disney World featured an indoor skydiving machine. They immediately visited other places around the country that were already using the machines as stand-alone businesses. After doing some fact-finding on the technology, they decided that while it was a fun experience for guests, it didn't make economic sense for Walt Disney World. One person getting the experience of a free fall from the sky for five minutes didn't warrant investing millions of dollars into one of their locations. At Walt Disney World rides have to be "people eaters." Disney parks are designed to move hundreds, and sometimes thousands, of guests through each ride every hour to maintain traffic flow. Therefore, attraction capacity is a major consideration in the Walt Disney Parks and Resorts system.[18] So what works for iFly Indoor Sky Diving in Chicago won't work for Disney in Orlando, but that decision was informed by the executives' road trip to those outside locations.

Fact-finding road trips by executives and Imagineers is a practice at Walt Disney Parks and Resorts that was firmly established by Walt Disney himself. He did a lot of exploring when he was dreaming up what Disneyland could become. Todd James Pierce's *Three Years in Wonderland* covers the exploratory road trips Walt took to gather intelligence for building his theme park:

> On Saturdays and Sundays, Walt and his new WED employees began their great experiment: the quest to see if men with absolutely no experience in the amusement industry could teach themselves how to build an amusement park that would rival the most famous parks in the world. They visited parks in Southern California, including the Los Angeles Fair in Pomona and Knott's Berry Farm in Buena Park, both for inspiration and to better understand the site layout of such facilities. "Funny thing," Imagineer Marvin Davis later revealed, "we visited Knott's Berry Farm, and at this time they had no idea of what was going to happen. They were so congenial and pleasant to Walt and all of our group, you know, and showing us everything." Walt was particularly interested in traffic flow, the way people moved through open space and narrow streets, what grabbed their attention, how landscape architecture affected their mood.[19]

Again, we see a legendary entrepreneur admit he didn't have all the answers and go looking for them. We've placed a lot of attention on the subject of humility throughout this book, but the principle can't be emphasized enough. Great ideas are built on the foundation of the hard work others have done before you. You must know what that tradition is so that you can determine what your contribution to that flow of achievements can be. If a humble mindset of learning from others is good enough for Sam Walton, Charles Koch, and Walt Disney, it should be good enough for us too. Embrace what you don't know as the starting point for exploration, learning, and creation. Treat it like your own personal adventure. Eventually you'll have insights that others will want to copy too.

Flexibility

One of the biggest pitfalls of people working on an idea is that they hold too tightly to their original insight. But a good designer maintains an open mind about the possibilities of what an idea can become by seeking and using the input of others. The idea that inspires you is just your beginning point to get the design process started. Too many people think the idea is everything, but few products or services turn out the way they were originally imagined. And those that do are usually failures in the marketplace. As a caveat, if you attain a successful product launch, remember to maintain a humble outlook. Sometimes success can cause a person to think they have all the answers. Becoming arrogant and shutting out ideas from others is a recipe for failure.[20] If you continue to stay humble and hone the way of thinking that made you successful in the first place, you can have even greater success in the future.[21]

Focus on the idea, not on yourself. Focusing on an idea and not on yourself is one of the hardest skills to master in design. Always remember, you and the idea are separate. Criticism about the idea is not criticism about you—although it may feel like it! As you receive feedback from others, you'll want them to know you won't be offended by their comments. Good designers want honest feedback about their ideas. If you approach design with this mindset, you'll amass information and opinions that will help you build a better product or service. You might endure a few emotional bruises along the way, but you'll be happier in the long run. This approach can be difficult because we often perceive feedback as criticism of us. After all, isn't criticism just a backhanded insult? No! That's a very limiting perspective to have. And if you have that thought a lot, you'll need to ignore it when it arises. Successful people know that one person can't have all the answers. When others criticize your idea, appreciate that they care enough to give you feedback. It's one of the best favors they can do for you. But it's still your call to decide what you do with it.

Increasingly research supports this position. More wisdom occurs when projects are collaborative. In the book *Smart Swarm*, Peter Miller explains how groups are correct more often than individuals are. He uses the game show *Who Wants to be a Millionaire?* as evidence of this phenomenon. Contestants have three "lifelines" they can use on questions they are unsure of. They can poll the audience, phone a friend, or ask for a 50/50 (the option of taking two of the answers away). When contestants called a trusted friend as their lifeline, they were right 63 percent of the time, but when they polled the studio audience for help they were right 91 percent of the time. Peter Miller points out that there may not be any particular person in the audience as intelligent as the friend on the other end of the phone, but as a group the audience knows more than the smart friend.[22] Keep the same perspective in your projects. The opinions of others should be considered. If you do this, you'll find yourself far more successful in your final result. It's still your decision how you choose to use the information, though. Your experts might not be right, but if you start to see a pattern of consistent answers and insights, you'd be wise to seriously consider those positions and work them into your project.

Design Guidelines

Once we know how successful designers think, we can now look at how they act. Tilman Lindberg, Christine Noweski, and Christoph Meinel of the Hasso Plattner Institute at the University of Potsdam provide design thinking education specifically to nondesigners. The curriculum adheres to the following guidelines. Each guideline includes insights from our own experience of teaching design as well.[23]

Set a Clear Vision of a Design Challenge by Defining Its Project Pillars

As discussed in the previous section, the original design concept is a starting point. Once you've received feedback from others, you may find that major revisions are required. When your idea receives general support from others, it's time to take more serious design steps. In a study of more than 700 product development teams, Gary S. Lynn and Richard R. Reilly found that the most successful product launches come from a clear vision of what a product should be. They also found that vision is clarified through the use of "project pillars" that focus the design effort down to key challenges to solve. For example, the project pillars for the Palm Pilot were: (1) fits in pocket; 2) synchronizes seamlessly with a PC; (3) is fast and easy to use; and (4) costs no more than $299. Within those constraints, the Palm Computing Company was able to build the world's first successful personal digital assistant (a forerunner of the smartphone). Meeting those constraints required a lot of trial and error, but it provided targets to focus the team's creative energies.[24] Once you've nailed the general design concept, project pillars lead to more innovative outcomes than wandering aimlessly from one idea to another does. This is a tricky guideline to master because you have to balance direction with an open mind. Lindberg, Noweski, and Meinel point out that it may require a lot of formulating and reformulating of the vision and criteria before you move forward on a project. Project pillars give a project direction.[25]

Utilize Restriction-Free Thinking to Avoid Premature Judgments

All actions start with a thought. Thus, if we think like a designer, we can act like one too. Our awareness of the need to think with an open mind to what's possible betters our odds of designing truly innovative products and services. In Chapter 3, we discussed divergent thinking. This thinking skill is critically important during design. We have to be open to where an idea can go. As Biz Stone, a co-founder of Twitter, says, "Everyone should study design because you learn that every problem has many good possible solutions."[26]

Gather Information from a Variety of Sources and Arrange the Knowledge into an Associative Network of References for Future Use

As you research and seek feedback on your idea, document everything you learn. The designer's best friend is their notebook. Capture everything you come across that pertains to your topic. As you pursue your idea, you may at times be overwhelmed by the mass of information you gather. Keeping information and thoughts in notebooks and folders can alleviate that problem. After all, your memory is fallible. If you don't maintain notebooks, you're likely to recall the information incorrectly later or forget it altogether. Another good practice is to periodically re-examine your notebooks, so that you can pull together new ideas and insights from what you've studied before. Notebooks are a wonderful way to remind ourselves of important points on our projects that might be forgotten as we come across new information. Maintaining notebooks also reduces stress because you don't have to worry about forgetting something. It's in your notebook! Note-taking and journaling can also move projects along much faster because you can go directly to what you've already written instead of recollecting information again.

Refine Ideas to Fit the Context Where They'll Be Embedded

Always be aware that even though you may think you have a great idea, your target audience and bosses may disagree with you. Design is sometimes different than straight problem-solving because you might be bringing something new into the world that's never existed before. People may not be able to get their heads around what you're trying to do, so before you commit substantial resources to a project, it's beneficial to get signals from your target audience that you're moving in the right direction. Consequently, if you include the customer in the design process, you can get the feedback you need to make quick (and often cheap) fixes. An innovation will always be a bit of a gamble, but we lessen the risk when we include a wide variety of perspectives to help us pivot when needed.

However, this doesn't mean that you *have* to deliver what the customer expects or asks for. In the *Innovator's Dilemma*, Clayton Christensen explains that simply meeting expectations can lead to stale product development. To surprise customers, sometimes it's better to think about what they'll buy rather than what they're asking for. Understanding your customers' deepest values and interests will help you get there. Think about where you can take the customer on their purchasing journey.[27]

Ideas should be translated into different prototypes (e.g., visualization, mock-ups, models). This is perhaps the heart of the design process because it's so effective in advancing an idea into a more refined form. When you have an insight, it's only in your head, so you need to communicate that idea in a way others will understand. Verbal communication is a start but it's not enough. A better way to communicate your idea is to capture it in a visual format. This can be accomplished through sketches, mechanical drawings, or 3D computer programs. After all, as the old saying goes, a picture's worth a thousand words. However, if a picture's worth a thousand words, an actual physical model is worth a million words. If you want to get great feedback on your idea, build a prototype. Nothing gets your idea across better than something people can view from different angles. It prompts great questions as they move it around in their hands and examine it. One of the reasons managers struggle with prototyping is that they fear a lot of craftsmanship and expertise is required to build a prototype, but this is not necessarily true. Prototypes can be inexpensive and basic, and anyone can build one. Chapter 6 will provide more information on how this can be accomplished.

Good Designers Break a Big Problem into Smaller Problems on Their Way to a Solution

Once you move a project along you're likely to face unexpected design issues. This is the point where success or failure is often determined. Some people may give up because the problems seem too overwhelming to solve.[28] Too many projects are ended prematurely because the designer wasn't persistent enough to work through the problems. The key for working through these tough patches is to recognize each stumbling block as a design challenge of its own. Big problems comprise a lot of little problems. Good designers break big problems into groups of smaller problems they can take action on. Different groups can even be assigned to work on each sub-problem, and then brought together to discuss how their solutions fit into the overall design.

Search for Feedback and Involvement from People with Diverse Backgrounds and Talents

Search for feedback from a diverse group of potential customers, suppliers, fellow managers, employees, and content experts to see if you're on track. You may get a lot of suggestions, but only a few might be really useful (that's okay, design is a journey). But you never know when someone will give you an unexpected insight that sets you on a new design path. When an idea starts to consistently interest others, you'll know you're on the right track.

Iteration: The Secret Sauce

How does a manager make an idea a successful reality? And more importantly, how do they learn to design? The key practice that accomplishes all this is iteration. Iteration is what all great innovators do as they transform rough concepts into polished products and services. Take Picasso, for instance. Novelist Tess Calahan explains how the great painter's iterative work style inspires her own habits:[29]

I recently found wordless inspiration for the writing craft in a short documentary about Picasso called The Mystery of Picasso. *The film is simply footage of Picasso painting— but what comes across is his extraordinary ruthlessness with regard to his images. He might start with a vase, for example. Seeing it, you might think to yourself, That's amazing! It's a Picasso vase! But in an instant he goes back in and reworks the vase, transforming it into a hen. Wow. Even better. Surely he's not going to mess with it more. He does, of course. He obliterates the hen and makes it into a demon with horns. What's stunning to see is his complete detachment from the endgame. It's all process. He has no loss aversion, no preconceived notions that bind him. Although he began with a kind of underpainting—the vase—he follows each new brushstroke like a hunter who has no idea what he's chasing but is determined to catch it.*

Like Picasso, you can create a masterpiece too, if you're willing to iterate and rework your ideas. The iterative process is composed of three steps that occur over and over until a design is polished and refined for consumption. In the first step, you work with an idea and tinker with it until you think it's worth showing to others. We call this step "play" because it requires the designer to be playful and work with many possible combinations until something feels right. When designers like what they have, they show it to others for feedback. We call this step "display." After designers display their ideas, they analyze the feedback they received and think about how to use the suggestions to make their product better. We call this step "replay," because the activity is reminiscent of coaches who break down a replay and figure out how to improve a player's performance.[30]

So, iterative means rework. Take the feedback you received and go back to the drawing board to address the suggestions you were given. After playing with the new information, redesign your idea and display the idea to the group again. You may also want to display your reformulated idea to a different group that might have another perspective. Continue the iterative process until it appears that you're receiving consistent approval from others. Now it's time to display your idea to the appropriate decision-makers. You're seeking endorsement and sponsorship that will propel the idea further through the system. You might only get one shot to sell it, so when you display the idea to an executive team, you want to create a "wow" effect in the room.[31] *The iterative process polishes the idea and shapes it into presentation form.* Once approved, your real work begins. You'll need to continue to play, display, and replay until the idea reaches the market or is implemented into company practice. The iterative process is present in all aspects of design. In the following sections we examine the three steps of iteration in more detail.[32]

Step 1: Play

Play is a vital aspect of the design process. It's a natural act that can be tapped for creativity. Play can even be witnessed throughout nature. A famous example of play is the dolphin that rides the waves in front of large sea vessels. The activity is actually quite dangerous for the dolphin, and offers little in regard to survival needs, but it appears to be done for the sheer sake of thrill and enjoyment. Successful entrepreneurs often describe a similar rush of enthusiasm when considering market opportunities. They enjoy the startup game. They don't need the money, but they want to stay in the game and continue to pursue new ventures long after they've made their initial fortune. Although some entrepreneurs may have been lucky enough to have had success with an instant market insight, it's more likely that most learned from trial and error and playful contemplation in developing a hit.

Unfortunately, while play is a natural behavior, it's often conditioned out of people over time, especially inside large organizations. Thus, it's imperative that managers regain a playfulness to working with ideas. If not, companies will find it difficult to renew themselves and remain competitive in the marketplace. To gain a perspective of playfulness, you must understand that a business idea needs to go through an evolutionary development. Avoid being locked into protecting an idea. Instead, see it as something to be played with. You must set aside your ego and work with different variations of the idea in different contexts until you're sure you have a possible winning combination.

Like entrepreneurs who dream big, you should also set high aspirations for your ideas. *Aim for excellence.* Creativity expert Keith Sawyer has found that more creative outputs occur when people set expectations that their ideas be truly unique and valuable. If your idea doesn't pass that test, you should continue playing with it until it does. In business, unique means something new to a market or something that's better than rival products or services. Valuable means that the customer feels that the derived benefits from the product or service exceed the costs of purchasing it. If the value of your idea is low, you'll need to search for ways to provide more benefits or reduce costs, such as:[33]

- adding more useful features or services;
- removing or modifying confusing and frustrating features;
- promoting ease of adoption;
- lowering switching costs;
- providing better customer service;
- increasing ease of use;
- refining its aesthetic appeal;
- lowering the price to the customer.

Once the product is determined to be unique and valuable, the designer should consider whether their company is capable of bringing it to market. It's possible that the product's technical requirements exceed your company's capability. If so, partnering with another company with the needed capability should be considered.[34] Another key question you must consider is whether you have enough legitimacy in the market among the necessary stakeholders—such as customers, suppliers, investors, and the media—to make the product successful. You may need to look for other markets where the product will be accepted, or you may need to adjust the idea to better fit your technical capabilities. Scaling back the idea may even be required. Again, partnering or cross-promoting with another company with an established reputation in a market may be the best route. With time though your company may be able to go alone on future projects as you gain market traction and master new capabilities.

Many companies make the mistake of going to market with an underdeveloped idea. The play stage is for better defining the market problem and solution to be created. Calling this stage "play" may contain a bit of irony because good old-fashioned hard work and a substantial commitment of time and energy is required to do this. It takes a tremendous amount of genuine passion and love of the business idea, passion and love that will sustain you through the most difficult times of developing a truly innovative product or service. To find the right combination of customer problems and solutions requires a "stick to it, never give up" attitude.[35] You can strengthen your resolve by being sure that you've chosen a business idea that you absolutely love. Avoid choosing a business idea *solely* because you think you'll acquire a promotion or a raise because of its success. Intrinsic motivation trumps extrinsic rewards in the long run. In the *Art of the Start*, Guy Kawasaki says he's never seen a business be successful when it was built with money in mind rather than the creation of something meaningful.[36] Meaningfulness sustains cerebral work.[37]

Once you have a solid idea, it's time to more fully develop it. After all, it'll most likely require further refinement. The hard work continues, but it has a different quality to it. There may be unforeseen contingencies with the idea, or it may just simply appear to be missing something to make it more feasible. Confusion and frustration may result, and you may be tempted to call a halt to the process. But always keep in mind: those who persist and solve problems receive the reward of insight. Experienced designers understand, seek, and relish that insight moment (also known as the Eureka! or Aha! moment). When you attain a sudden deep understanding of a situation, you're flooded with feelings of joy and relief because you've finally found the solution that's been eluding you. Dale Meyer describes this moment as a time when "a problem solver goes suddenly from a state of not knowing how to solve a problem to a state of knowing how to solve it."[38] Or, as Roger Dominowski and Pamela Dallob state, "to gain insight is to understand (something) more fully, to move from a state of relative confusion to one of comprehension."[39] Good designers find the challenge of solving problems stimulating and enjoyable. As you discover how to solve problems more efficiently, you'll become more confident and proficient in your design skills and you'll also seek out more opportunities to design new products and services in the future.[40]

Step 2: Display

Once a concept has been fully developed, it's now ready to be displayed. It's time to see if what's in your head matches up with the hard realities of the world. Will others like the concept like you do? You can find out by giving a short pitch to anyone who's willing to provide insight on your idea. A physical representation of the business idea helps here. It can be a diagram, flow chart, architectural model, prototype, feasibility study, business plan, I-Solution, or anything else that gets across what you want to do.

You must be very open to constructive criticism at this stage. This is where *your* conception of what will be accepted in the outside world is tested against the reality of what *others* think. You may be tempted to simply seek confirmation of your concepts in this stage, but that would be a mistake.[41] Be open to complaints and criticisms others may have with the product or service. It's the best way to improve it. The more we engage with the world, the more we can test and adapt our ideas by learning from others.

This reasonable approach to feedback is easier said than done because our cognitive wiring isn't set up to do this well. It's actually an acquired skill. Nobel Prize-winning behavioral economists Daniel Kahneman and Amos Tversky explain that our brains have two modes of thought: System 1 and System 2. System 1 intuitively makes quick, emotional decisions driven by the subconscious, while System 2 makes slower, more deliberate, and conscious decisions.[42] Both modes of thought have their benefits to you. In most cases, System 1 works quite well and gets you through the day. You don't have to use the effortful System 2 thinking all the time. If you did, every decision you made would require slow, effortful thought before you did anything. You'd be exhausted, and you'd get little done.[43] So automatic System 1 thinking is used most of the time, and it generally works quite well. The problem arises when we have a complex decision that we don't give enough thought to. Rushing to a decision without fully utilizing System 2 thinking can lead to people making major mistakes in judgment. Psychologist Jonathon Haidt says these two systems operate like a person riding an elephant.[44] The elephant is your quick, intuitive, emotional subconscious System 1 thinking, and the rider is your more conscious, rational, deliberate System 2 thinking. Using this metaphor, Haidt warns that the elephant is more powerful than the rider. Although the rider may feel like he's in control, if the elephant gets spooked and decides to take over there's not much the rider can do to stop it. Kahneman, Tversky, Haidt, as well as behavioral economist Richard Thaler and psychologist Daniel Gilbert, all recommend the same course of action to ensure your rider tames the elephant and keeps it on track: be aware of these two modes of thinking and how they work, train yourself to slow down before making a big decision, and talk to others who can offer perspectives that you might be overlooking.

Ultimately, when you engage with the world more you open yourself up to others' opinions, which can change your perspective. And breakthroughs happen when someone sees the world in a different way than others have. When you're open to addressing issues others point out to you, you'll change your perspective and approach opportunities from a new angle. When seeking feedback on your ideas, good questions to ask others are, *"What stinks about this idea? What do you think will be major headaches for me if I do this? What would you do differently if you were me?"* The answers you receive don't necessarily mean that you *have* to change your idea, but at least you'll be making a more informed decision of what your concept can be. And if a decision-maker brings up the same point later in your big presentation, you'll be able to give a thoughtful response to justify what you want to do. Criticism won't shake you when you officially pitch the idea.

In *Thanks for the Feedback*, Douglas Stone and Sheila Heen say that evaluation like this "tells you where you stand, aligns expectations, and informs decision making. . . . It answers the questions '*How do you think I'm doing on this? Am I on track based on where I should be at this stage?*'"[45]

But after thorough review, some projects may need to be scrapped. Starting over with an empty slate can sometimes be a very smart move.[46] As Seth Godin points out in *The Dip*, the most successful people persevere through challenges that others might give up on, but they also stop when it's clear they're on the wrong path. They don't waste time continuing with something that won't work or where their effort would be better placed somewhere else. Steve Jobs always believed that saying "no" and stopping was the sign of true discipline. Everyday he asked his chief designer Jony Ive, "How many times did you say 'no' today?" Jobs only wanted to work on excellent projects. Hearing criticism of things you've worked on doesn't come easy, and it doesn't feel good, but it comes with the pursuit of excellence.

How can you develop the tough mindset to openly accept tough feedback? Well, it helps if you always remember that you are *not* the product. It exists separate from you, so don't internalize criticism of it. *Focus your attention on the product, not on yourself.* Remove your feelings and ego from the process. Instead, embrace feedback. Seek it out, so that what you bring to market is as good as you can make it. It's like a book. No one buys the first rough draft; they always buy the finished novel that's gone through numerous revisions and edits. Any creative endeavor goes through the same editorial process. Humbling yourself to receive this feedback is difficult, but it pays dividends later. It's what separates the successful innovators from the deluded dreamers. In the end, you'll be happy you took this humble approach when your product is selling well for the company. In the next step, we'll see how to work with feedback to refine your idea so that it's ready for launch.

Step 3: Replay

The third step of the iterative process is called "replay" because it's time to reflect on the feedback you've gathered so far. It's like a coach who breaks down a player's performance on tape. As every sports fan knows, the best coaches watch a lot of game film to improve their performance. They are ruthless about finding weaknesses to exploit in games. You should take the same approach with your projects. Think of feedback like it's your game film. Let's see how the best football minds use game film to get more wins on the field:[47]

1. *The best players and coaches are humble and willing to take feedback in whatever way will help their performance. They look at constructive criticism as information for improvement.* Sportswriter Michael Holley explains how Roman Phifer, a linebacker for the New England Patriots, developed a humble frame of mind by being around his legendary coach Bill Belichick:[48]

   > "God opposes the proud, but gives grace to the humble," Phifer said. He had become a dutiful notetaker, and his notebook pages were filled with painstaking instructions

from Belichick. He thought to himself, "This could be an MBA program. It's like I'm going to grad school for football, and Bill is the professor." He knew that Belichick and the other coaches got to the stadium long before the players did, and departed who knew when. They had watched more film than the players had. Given that, it always amazed Phifer that the professor could stand in front of the group and condense that mass of information into three things. It was always, Do these three things and we should be in position to win.

2. *The best coaches are fact-finding machines. They look for areas of improvement that go beyond the obvious.* Like a designer who devotes immense attention to detail in making a great product, great coaches know that small improvements and adjustments in a game plan can lead to big wins on the field. Take Bill Belichick and Nick Saban, the best coaches in professional and college football. Saban used to be an assistant coach for Belichick at the Cleveland Browns, and the two still watch game film together to this day. ESPN analyst Louis Riddick, who played for Saban and Belichick, explains what it's like:[49]

   Nick would say that coaching for Bill didn't leave time for anything else. He would look at me and say, "You ever watch film with Bill?" Belichick was notorious for the amount of film he watched, of other teams and his own players, taking the time to pore over some things that to other coaches would be of little consequence. I'd come in at ten p.m. and Nick and Bill would be watching film of our bag and agility drills from practice. It was amazing.

3. Why would a coach watch film of practice drills? Aren't drills just meant to improve skills and conditioning? What could possibly come out of those sessions that's worthy of a $7.5 million per year coach's time? In *War Room*, another book that goes behind the scenes of professional football, sportswriter Michael Holley explains that they're looking for indicators of other factors that determine good performance in a game:[50]

   They love to see how a player reacts when he's beaten in a drill or dominates it; how he responds to instruction from the coaches; how he interacts with teammates who make him look either good or bad. It's a great way of getting information that has innocently slipped through the cracks.

   Executives want the same out of the people leading their projects. Someone who is calm, cool, and collected when taking questions during a pitch sends a signal that a lot of preparation and research is behind a presentation.

4. *The great coaches are serious note-takers. They write down their insights from sessions and file them away for future use.* Biographer Monte Burke provides an overview of Nick Saban's note-taking habit:[51]

   Saban is an obsessive and meticulous note taker. At practices, whenever he sees something he doesn't like, he reaches into his back pocket and pulls out a flip-top notebook, then makes a quick note, determined to never make that mistake again.

He has piles of notebooks from years past, all dated, and frequently he refers to them to see what happened on that exact date on any given year. He has kept notes on nearly every game he's been involved in as a head coach, and files on the programs and individual coaches against who he's coached, laying out the specific tendencies and strategies that those teams and coaches used against them.

5. As these examples demonstrate, *great coaches sweat the small stuff.* Jim Schwartz, a former assistant coach and scout for Belichick, describes what it's like to work with a meticulous coach:[52]

    Probably the biggest thing I learned from Bill is that there isn't anything that is not important. That philosophy of "Don't sweat the small stuff?" Yeah, that was never his philosophy.

The above quotes are provided as inspiration for paying attention to the details needed to win. A lot of hard work goes on behind the scenes. We only see the game on the field, but its outcome is the result of meticulous analysis and preparation in film rooms and adjustments on the practice field. Great coaches place their attention on their product, not on themselves. And they want all involved in a project to have the same commitment to excellence. Yet, this pursuit for superior performance isn't limited to sports. You'll read more about it later in this chapter when we cover Steve Jobs and his approach to design. Jobs always focused on the product first and foremost. As his chief designer Jony Ive stated about what it was like to work with Jobs:

> *He wanted smart answers, and he didn't waste time on niceties when it was simpler to be clear, no matter how critical his response. He would talk directly about the work. That's the way Steve was. That's why he'd say, "That's s---!" But then the next day or the day after, he also would as likely come back saying, "Jony, I've been thinking a lot about what you showed me, and I think it's very interesting after all. Let's talk about it some more."*[53]

It's clear that whether in sports, the arts, military, science, or business, innovators want excellent performance in their respective fields.

But why is excellence so important? Why won't good enough do? And why do innovators obsess over the smallest of details? Is it purely for fame and fortune? Is it for vanity? Perhaps for some people these reasons are why they pursue excellence. But many scientists believe we chase our dreams because it's part of what makes us human. In fact, it may be that we even feel most alive when we're throwing ourselves into new territory, like it's what we're meant to do. As biologist Charles A. Pasternak explains in *Quest: The Essence of Humanity:*[54]

> *The story of the last 100,000 years is man's unceasing search, the propensity for quest. The behavioral differences between human and chimpanzee stems from nothing*

more than man's superior means to engage in the primeval act of quest. His brain questions and dreams up new challenges: his hands respond. The exploratory drive of humans, from walking out of the Great Rift Valley in east Africa to landing on the moon is evidence that some people are not content to remain where they are.

And what exactly is a quest? Pasternak explains that:

The word is derived from the Latin verb quaerer, to search, to seek. From it we have query and inquisitiveness on the one hand, conquest on the other. Together the words describe the qualities that have made us masters of life on earth: we search for new horizons, we seek explanations for the phenomena around us, but we also search for no apparent reason at all: it is curiosity alone, not need, that has led men to seek the source of the Nile and to unravel the origin of the stars.[55]

Are you content to remain where you are? Or are you someone who likes to explore and bring new things into the world? Do you want to go on a quest? When you start working on a new product, service, or process, you'll be on yours. Enjoy the journey. *Embrace your quest and be open to where it takes you.* Play, display, and replay will help you on that quest. And after you watch the replay, you might find that you have to:

1. Go back and rework major areas of the concept where the experts say you fell short.
2. Search for another market for the idea and adapt it as needed.
3. Scrap the idea and pursue new ideas to explore.
4. Scrap the idea and put your focus on projects that you have previously set aside.
5. Or, fix any minor issues that the experts think need refinement and move forward into the next stage of development.

Always remember that if one of the first four options is taken, the hard work was not done in vain. New skills were gained and, additionally, future losses of investment may have been prevented. As you innovate, you'll continually cycle through these steps—playing with an idea, displaying it to others for feedback, reflecting on the advice, and refining the concept for showing again. *Ultimately, design is a gamble, which requires calculated risk taking.* A creative project ventures you into new territory, but you must also be wary of making overly risky moves. In the end it's your call. Ideally, though, if you have taken an intellectually honest approach in getting feedback from others, you'll have increased your odds of making the right design decisions. If you still have a good gut feeling about your idea after displaying it, it's time to reflect on how you'll refine the concept and continue moving forward. You may even need to seek out new experts, who can point you in the right direction on new problems that pop up. Design is not only a creative process but a learning one as well. The experience of leading new projects will change your personal outlook on how you operate in the world as well.

An Important Caveat to the Beginning Designer

We've found the following traits among successful designers:

- They become immersed in their projects.
- They're playful in working with their ideas.
- They're excited to show what they have to others.
- They're appreciative of feedback they receive.
- They carefully consider what the feedback means for their idea's success.
- They're willing to go back and play with the feedback to create a better version of the product than they had before.

On the other hand, we've found novice designers are often:

- overly confident about their original idea;
- or on the other end of the spectrum, lack confidence and work with the first idea they get because they fear they may not get another;
- lacking good judgment of which ideas are feasible and viable for the company to pursue.

Clearly, companies should encourage creative thinking among their employees. However, for a design to be taken further in the organization, it must fit with the company's strategy. Given limited time, money, and other resources, you must ensure that the design meets the vision, mission, and goals of your company. From a strategic perspective, the design may be interesting, but not good for the present competitive situation. If this situation occurs, you may find yourself frustrated with the company and consider leaving to build your own startup where you can implement the idea. The decision to leave should be seen as beneficial for both parties. You need to feel fulfilled, and the company doesn't need a disgruntled employee in its ranks.

Some companies love venturing into unknown territory and rely on design as the vehicle for doing so. These companies may be the ones you want to work for. And perhaps no company better demonstrates the power of design in business than Apple. We close this chapter by looking at the company all others use as the benchmark for design. Specifically, we'll examine how its founder Steve Jobs embraced design as its source of competitive advantage.

The Apple Design Dozen

If you're going to learn about innovation, it's worthwhile to study the company most recognized for its design prowess. Apple is widely accepted as the most innovative company among its peers, due mostly to its signature design philosophy. Apple products are sleek, powerful, and fun to use, and, as a result, the company's revenues have shot up from $36 billion in 2009 to $215 billion in 2016. For comparison, Dell had $51 billion in revenue and Hewlett-Packard had $48 billion in 2016. There may be other reasons for these differences in performance, but design is no doubt a major driver of Apple's success in its industry. After all, computers in their essence are data and information machines. Most teenagers in the 1970s did not put the Altair 8080 at the top of their Christmas lists, but much has changed over the last 40 years. iPhones, iMacs, iPods, and iPads are now icons of hipness. Apple through its design process has made plastic boxes of silicon cool.

Steve Jobs is most responsible for Apple's focus on design. And to better understand Apple's approach to design, we need to know more about the designers who influenced Steve Jobs' philosophy. Jobs' design sensibility can be traced to 12 key historic figures: Bill Hewlett and David Packard, Walt Disney, Edwin Land, Dieter Rams, Akio Morita, Hartmut Esslinger, Jony Ive, Tim Cook, the Beatles, Bob Dylan, and Bill Gates. Let's call this group the Apple "Design Dozen," and examine how each of these influences can be seen in their products today:

1. **Bill Hewlett and David Packard**. These two legends of Silicon Valley created the Hewlett-Packard Company (commonly known as HP) in a garage in 1939. HP was a major player in the early days of the semiconductor business, and a young Steve Jobs contacted Bill Hewlett directly when he needed parts for an electronics project he was working on in school. Hewlett was so impressed with his initiative that he offered Jobs a summer job doing basic work on electronic components. It was a formative experience for the future tech entrepreneur because at the age of 14 he learned about electronics and computers from the best company in the industry. Hewlett and Packard would forever inspire Jobs to weave innovation into Apple's DNA.

2. **Steve Wozniak**. When Jobs was 15 years old, he met Steve "Woz" Wozniak, an older kid in the neighborhood. Without Woz, there would be no Apple or Steve Jobs legacy. While Jobs had a basic understanding of electronics and computers, Woz was a genius when it came to technology. He was designing systems well ahead of his age. Jobs learned a lot about computers by hanging out with Woz. And it was in a Silicon Valley garage like HP started in that Apple was founded too. Woz handled the circuit boards as the design engineer, and as the entrepreneur Jobs made sure that the product was successful on the market.

   The presence of Woz in Jobs' younger years cannot be overestimated. In *The Powers of Two*, Joshua Wolf Shenk documents how the most creative breakthroughs happen when two innovative people partner together to pursue a common dream. Shenk calls this chemistry *"creative intimacy,"* citing Paul McCartney and John Lennon, Walt and Roy Disney, Charlie Munger and Warren Buffet, and even Matt Stone and Trey Parker of *South Park* fame as sharing this dynamic. Creative partners talk, think, and even look like each other over time. And like other intimate relationships, conflicts often arise and some partnerships even burn out. But in that cauldron of creative energy, great works can be created.[56] This cycle happened to Jobs and Wozniak as well, and they eventually parted ways. But they always viewed each other as brothers even as they pursued their own individual paths later in life. Finding a thought mate who can shape and test your ideas is one of the most valuable lessons we can learn from Jobs' and Woz's partnership.

3. **Walt Disney**. Jobs wanted to build a company that would last like Walt Disney did, and they had much in common in how they established their legacies. Like Disney, Jobs thought of business as an art form. His products had to not only work well but also be beautiful. They each possessed an artist sensibility in how they designed their products, and they both paid meticulous attention to detail. They wouldn't release anything that bore their names unless they thought it was excellent.

   They both also wanted to create products that would be reassuring to customers in a stressful world. Jobs did this by building electronic products that were simple and fun to use. He shunned instructional manuals and wanted customers to intuitively "get" what the product did. Disney wanted his movies to be good, clean family fun for people around the world. The uplifting themes were continued in the design of Disneyland. Legendary Imagineer John Hench called Disney's design style "the architecture of reassurance."[57]

   And, they also shared experiences of betrayal in their companies. Walt Disney felt betrayed a number of times in his career. His original hit cartoon *Oswald the Lucky Rabbit* was taken from under his control by Universal Pictures. In the process, his animators deserted him to start a rival studio. It was during this trying time that Mickey Mouse was created, which helped the Disney studio stay in business. Later his animators went on strike when he needed them most, which also felt like a betrayal. Jobs always felt betrayed by CEO John Sculley and the board of directors who ousted him from control of Apple in 1985. Jobs often used Disney as a role model for how to run a creative company. In the last chapter, we examined closed innovation. Because of the betrayals, Jobs and Disney both closely controlled the design process inside their companies.

4. **Edwin Land**. Edwin Land isn't a name many people know today, but 50 years ago he was as famous as Steve Jobs in his day. Land was the inventor and founder of the Polaroid instant camera. Polaroid stunningly combined science, design, and business to create a product the world had never seen before. Land's patented Polaroid technology created a brand new product category that went head-to-head with the more established Kodak film brand. Jobs admired Land's maverick ways and Polaroid's pirate philosophy. Land's biographer Christopher Bonanos believes that Jobs had much in common with the photography innovator. He observes:

   > Both fetishized superior, elegant, covetable product design. And both their companies exploded in size and wealth under an in-house visionary-godhead-inventor-genius. At Apple, that man was Steve Jobs. At Polaroid, the genius domus was Edwin Herbert Land.[58]

   Jobs sought Land for his advice during his early years at Apple, and he always felt he and Land had a lot in common. Later in his life, Jobs reflected back to Land's influence:

Edwin Land of Polaroid talked about the intersection of the humanities and science. I like that intersection. There's something magical about that place. There are a lot of people innovating, so that's not the main distinction of my career. The reason Apple resonates with people is that there's a deep current of humanity in our innovation. I think great artists and great engineers are similar, in that they both have a desire to express themselves. In fact, some of the best people working on the original Mac were poets and musicians on the side. In the seventies, computers became a way for people to express their creativity.[59]

And perhaps that's the secret to Jobs' success as an entrepreneur and designer. He put himself at the intersection of creative technical experts and business people and found new market opportunities where he could channel their creative energies together. Jobs' biographer Randall E. Stross states that:

he defined his role as the matchmaker, shuttling between those who create new technology and those who will use it. While at Apple, in early 1984, he said, "Computers and society are out on a first date in this decade, and for some crazy reason, we're in the right place at the right time to make that romance blossom."[60]

The lesson here for you is that if you want to create new markets, think about how you can facilitate a diverse group of creative people to build on each other's ideas and come up with the next big thing. Being in the right place at the right time helps too, but knowing what that is is a tricky endeavor.[61] Land's breakthrough moment was the result of combining truly original science in chemistry with leaps of technological design. Jobs, on the other hand, mastered finding the right place at the right time by adopting what already existed and making it better. In a *New Yorker* profile of Jobs' innovation style, Malcolm Gladwell believes Apple's breakthroughs happened because he was a master at tweaking what already existed. He explains:

Jobs's sensibility was editorial, not inventive. His gift lay in taking what was in front of him—the tablet with stylus—and ruthlessly refining it.

After looking at the first commercials for the iPad, he tracked down the copywriter, James Vincent, and told him, "Your commercials suck."

"Well, what do you want?" Vincent shot back. "You've not been able to tell me what you want."

"I don't know," Jobs said. "You have to bring me something new. Nothing you've shown me is even close."

Vincent argued back and suddenly Jobs went ballistic. "He just started screaming at me," Vincent recalled. Vincent could be volatile himself, and the volleys escalated.

When Vincent shouted, "You've got to tell me what you want," Jobs shot back, "You've got to show me some stuff, and I'll know it when I see it."

I'll know it when I see it. That was Jobs's credo, and until he saw it his perfectionism kept him on edge.[62]

So being an innovator doesn't require you to create a whole new science like Land did. Breakthroughs can happen by simply moving around and having conversations with people to see what's possible, and then deciding what can be done better.[63] Fact-finding and pyramiding can help you find those places of opportunity like Land, Disney, and Jobs did.

5. **Dieter Rams**. Simple. Functional. Minimal. These words capture Apple's philosophy of what products should be, but these ideas didn't begin at Apple. These values were first embedded in the design philosophy of a German thinker named Walter Gropius. Gropius founded a school called the Bauhaus in the 1920s and 1930s in Weimar, Germany, which was conceived "to provide the larger world with sensible designs in which form followed function, and ornament and fluff were eradicated."[64] Jobs had an appreciation for Bauhaus design, and one company that followed that approach very well was Braun.[65] In particular, German designer Dieter Rams headed Braun's new product development from 1955 to 1977.[66] Rams is famous for his sleek designs of everyday products like electric razors, toothbrushes, and watches. Jobs was a big fan of his work and wanted computers to have the same appeal.

It's possible to understand how Braun products were designed. Rams provided a manifesto for others to follow in designing iconic products. He called it his "Ten Principles of Good Design."[67] The ten principles are:[68]

1. *Good design is innovative.* A designer should always be aware of new technologies that can be used to create better products.
2. *Good design makes a product useful.* Anything that distracts from good use of a product should be removed. The design philosophies of Braun and Bauhaus emphasize "less is more." A product shouldn't have superfluous features that might confuse, frustrate, or distract a user from fully enjoying it. Therefore, remove unneeded features. "Extras" might be good on a Blu-ray disc, but it's an evil word in Bauhaus design. A product is enjoyed to its fullest when it delivers key functions at an excellent level. This is how excellence is attained in Bauhaus product design.
3. *Good design is aesthetic.* Well-crafted products are beautiful. Products that are put together in a sloppy, lazy way or that have unnecessary features are ugly. When a product or service delivers a coherent set of features and is produced with care, customers will notice and appreciate the attention to detail. It will have a feeling of wholeness to it.
4. *Good design makes a product understandable.* Well-designed products are intuitive and easy to use. Jobs fully embraced this principle. He wanted his products to be so intuitive that instructions weren't even needed in their packaging. This objective kept his designers and engineers focused on creating consumer-friendly products. If instructions were needed, more thought needed to go into how to make the design better. This tactic was unheard of previously in the computer and consumer electronics industry. But Apple was making products for the rest of society, not just scientists and engineers. If a product was complicated, the average customer

wouldn't love it. This philosophy opened up much larger markets for Apple than just traditional computers.

5. *Good design is unobtrusive.* The products should fit naturally into the customer's world. It shouldn't look out of place in its setting. The German design philosophy finds garish displays of adornment and ornamentation disturbing. An appreciation for superior engineering, advanced technology, and ease of use are to be pursued in good design.

6. *Good design is honest.* A product must deliver on what the consumer expects of it. Overpromising and underdelivering is the most egregious sin a designer can make. A good product not only meets but exceeds the expectations of the customer. This creates surprise and delight, which is needed to separate well-designed products from competitors' mediocre offerings.

7. *Good design is long-lasting.* Well-designed products are not faddish. Their use should hold up over many years. Because of their simple features, designs by Braun and Apple stand the test of time. German companies are famous for their iconic products, like Porsche sports cars and Adidas Gazelle tennis shoes that have remained popular for decades with the same basic designs.

8. *Good design is thorough down to the last detail.* Every aspect of a product must be considered. Every detail matters. Consumers know when a product is complete and isn't missing something that could make it better. Architect and design theorist Christopher Alexander calls this wholeness "the quality without a name." A customer might explain a product in this way by saying, "It just works. It feels right. I like it." When it doesn't have this quality, they may say, "It doesn't feel right. Something is off about it." German psychologists such as Fritz Perls called this state a "gestalt," when all the parts come together into a pleasing unified whole.

9. *Good design is environmentally friendly.* Well-designed products are constructed of the most environmentally friendly materials that make sense for it. The product's appearance also shouldn't detract from the scenery around it. It should fit well with its environment and design context. Poorly designed products pollute their setting.

10. *Good design is as little design as possible.* Again, simple is the chief goal for designing a great product. Only essential details are to be included in a minimalist design. However, it should be noted that for the designer, simple doesn't necessarily mean easy. It can take a lot of design iterations to figure out what is essential and what isn't. The simpler a product is for a customer to use, the more likely it is that a lot of hard work and thought went into deciding what would be included in its design. A product with a lot of features instead of only the essential ones is often a sign of lazy design. Complicated doesn't equate to good when it comes to this design philosophy.[69]

6. **Harmut Esslinger**. Although Jobs was a fan of Rams' work at Braun, he never hired the design legend to work at Apple. He did hire another German industrial designer to work for him, though. Harmut Esslinger had a successful

design firm in Germany called Frog Design. Some of his work included television sets he designed for Sony. He already had a solid global reputation when Jobs offered him a $2,000,000 contract to create a distinct design language for Apple products. But what is a "design language"? And why does a company need one? Esslinger explains:[70]

> In the most simple terms, a design language is a visual system made up of defining signature and shape elements, materials, colors, patterns and textures, which provides a lineup of products with a unique but consistent look and feel. A design language isn't about a specific product or style; it's about forming a visual brand DNA that expresses a company's true potential, as well as the founders' unique values and (hopefully) visionary goals.

When a company has a good design language, consumers can often recognize who made the product without even having to see the name on it. It gives a company and its products a distinct identity in a crowded marketplace. Thus, design not only helps a company create great products, it establishes its brand as well. To create a design language, Esslinger "starts with research to discover what's out there, and to explore the possibilities of what could be out there, but isn't." The design language that Esslinger developed with Jobs was called "Snow White," which looked much different than the beige computers on the market. Jobs wanted Esslinger to design computers that would appear sleek, clean, and modern. "When we launched the Snow White project, my intuition told me that the possibilities for improving the design and manufacture of personal computers were almost limitless."[71] One company in particular was a good model for inspiring what Apple's Snow White design could be, and it wasn't German. It was Sony in Japan.

7. **Akio Morita**. In the early 1980s when Jobs and Esslinger were creating a design language for Apple, Sony was producing the best-designed products on the market. The Japanese company created the enormously popular Walkman, which became a new product category in its own right. Besides its portable music player, Sony's televisions, stereos, and other consumer electronics were also doing very well with consumers worldwide. Jobs wanted the same impact with his computers. So he gave Esslinger and his designers this challenge: "What would Sony do if it built computers?" Esslinger said, "In 1982, Sony set the standard for producing high-tech consumer products that were smarter, smaller, and more portable, and Steve felt that their cool, sleek design language offered a good benchmark."[72]

Sony was founded by Akio Morita, a Japanese businessman who built the company from scratch shortly after World War II. Jobs admired the way Morita built Sony into a global powerhouse, and wanted Apple to follow the same path. He often flew to Japan to learn from Morita and tour Sony's facilities. He admired Sony's ability to design aesthetically pleasing technology that could be manufactured to the masses. Jobs wanted the same discipline and attention to detail in Apple that Morita instilled in Sony. In a sense, Apple became the American version of Sony in the computer industry, and Morita became a vision of what Jobs wanted to become in business.[73] It's safe to say Jobs accomplished these goals.

8. **Jony Ive**. When Steve Jobs was ousted from Apple by CEO John Sculley in 1985, it was a bitter experience for the young entrepreneur. However, one move Sculley made that Jobs appreciated upon his return back to the company was the hiring of Jony Ive, the company's future Chief Design Officer. When Jobs stepped back in to run Apple in 1997, he discovered a very underutilized design team at Apple headquarters. Jony Ive and his team were producing products that Ive admitted later weren't first rate, due mainly to a lack of inspired leadership from Apple's management team. Years later Ive stated he thought Jobs was going to fire him when they first met, but after having an engaging conversation Jobs left impressed with Ive. Jobs realized that the design team had a lot of potential if it was more engaged with the company's leadership. Quickly Jobs and Ive built a strong friendship and pursued a mission of making "insanely great" products. In 2015, reflecting back on his relationship with Jobs, Ive called his boss his "spiritual partner."[74] Jobs and Ive ate lunch together almost every day and spent a lot of time together in the design lab. They also shared an appreciation for Dieter Rams' work and believed in the same design philosophy. If Jobs' first run at Apple was defined by his partnership with Wozniak and a focus on circuit board wizardry, his second run might be defined by his partnership with Ive and better designed consumer products. As John Edson describes the relationship:[75]

> *Together they became Apple's tastemakers. Jobs promoted Ive to senior vice president, an acknowledgment of the central role Jobs ascribed to design. Within Apple the unusually tight bond between Jobs and Ive became crucial to spreading the company's design mantra and ethos throughout the organization.*

In the previous section, we looked at the importance of iteration for designing great products and services. Apple mastered iteration. For Jobs and Ive, iteration was the key to attaining the right details to make lasting products. As Ive explains:

> *The decisive factor is fanatical care beyond the obvious stuff; the obsessive attention to details that are often overlooked. . . . It doesn't go from thought to sketch to model to production even though, in simplistic terms, that is the general sequence of events. We'll go back and forth. We'll go all the way back to the concept model, we'll go to working with product development and operations groups on the engineering side.*[76]

It's not an understatement to say that the Steve Jobs and Jony Ive partnership saved Apple. The iMac, iPod, iPad, and iPhone were all huge successes and took the company's valuation from $3 billion when Jobs returned in 1997 to $350 billion at the time of his death. But another piece of the puzzle Jobs had to figure out was how to shore up the business side as well. For that, he turned to a smart southern gentleman with a sharp brain for operations.

9. **Tim Cook**. In the previous chapter, we mentioned that design answers two questions: "What's needed?" and "What's possible?" Steve Jobs and Jony Ive did an excellent job in answering the question "What's needed?", but it was Chief Operating Officer Tim Cook that did a splendid job addressing "What's possible?" Cook was the builder of the company architecture behind Apple's successful second run under Jobs. As a supply chain expert, he played a pivotal role in sourcing Asian factories for mass manufacturing Ive's and Jobs' creations at low costs. Without Cook's masterful and reliable sourcing of complicated technologies from Asia, Apple could not make their great products.

   Cook also had great instincts for ensuring the economic viability of the products because of his excellent accounting and finance skills. His mastery of Apple's operations and finances led Jobs to entrust him with the CEO role when he took leaves of absence for his illnesses. Cook did such a masterful job keeping the company strong, that upon Jobs' death he was picked as the heir apparent to run the company. In a sense, Cook fulfilled what Jobs had in mind when he channeled Aoki Morita and Sony as the inspiration for what Apple could become. Apple eventually did become the American version of Sony, due largely to Cook's management. Consider that at their pinnacle, Sony and Apple were companies that mastered design and built efficient, Asian manufacturing processes. Sony lost its luster after Morita's death, but Cook has kept Apple on course after Jobs' passing, as evidenced by the doubling of Apple's market value since 2010.

10. **The Beatles**. So far we've seen the influence business and design had on Jobs, but he saw himself first and foremost as an artist. He admired artists' views of the world and how they approach their work. And for him, the Beatles were the artists that represented what he wanted Apple to be like. As he said in a *60 Minutes* interview in 2003:

    > *My model for business is the Beatles. They were four guys who kept each other's kind of negative tendencies in check. They balanced each other and the total was greater than the sum of the parts. That's how I see business: great things in business are never done by one person, they're done by a team of people.*[77]

    You can see how Jobs would have been influenced by the Beatles. The Beatles never stood still. As John Lennon said about his group in 1974, "We were all on this ship in the sixties, our generation—a ship going to discover the new world. And the Beatles were in the crow's nest of that ship."[78] Imagine an impressionable 11-year-old Jobs in 1966, the year the Beatles took their art in a wild new direction. As Steve Turner notes in the book *Beatles '66: The Revolutionary Year*:

    > *Nineteen sixty-six was without question the pivotal year in the life of the Beatles as performers and recording artists. Before that they were the four loveable guys from Liverpool who wore identical suits on stage, played to packed houses of screaming*

(largely female) teenagers, played themselves in movie capers, and wrote jaunty songs chiefly about love. After 1966, they were serious studio-based musicians who no longer toured, wore individually selected clothes from Chelsea boutiques, wrote songs that explored their psyches and the nature of society, and were frequently considered a threat to the established order by governments around the world. During that twelve-month period they went through changes that would have crushed men with less resilience and vision.[79]

The Beatles are the epitome of what rock stars are. But in the computer world, Jobs was a rock star too, and he manned his company with fellow rock stars in the industry.[80] Apple was a super group in an industry of vanilla corporate goliaths. Steve Wozniak. Jony Ive. Tim Cook. And all the untold thousands that worked for these masters created a company that approached business like an art form. It may be for this reason that traditional artists choose Apple products for creating their own art work.

11. **Bob Dylan**. The other artist that greatly inspired Jobs was Bob Dylan. From the earliest days of Apple, Bob Dylan's presence was felt. As Jobs stated, "Woz and I very much liked Bob Dylan's poetry, and we spent a lot of time thinking about a lot of that stuff. This was California. . . . California has a lot of experimentation and a sense of openness—openness to new possibilities."[81]

Jobs was great at communicating to the masses, and part of this skill may have come from studying Dylan's lyrics.[82] Like the Beatles, Dylan was always reinventing his style and willing to take chances in creating new ways of expressing himself. Jobs found this very inspirational. At the end of his life he summed up the Beatles and Dylan's influence as:

You always have to keep pushing to innovate. . . . Dylan could have sung protest songs forever and probably made a lot of money, but he didn't. He had to move on, and when he did, by going electric in 1965, he alienated a lot of people. . . . The Beatles were the same way. They kept evolving, moving, refining their art. That's what I've always tried to do. Keep moving. Otherwise, as Dylan says, if you're not busy being born, you're busy dying. . . . What drove me? . . . It's about trying to express something in the only way that most of us know how—because we can't write Bob Dylan songs or Tom Stoppard plays. We try to use the talents we do have to express our deep feelings, to show appreciation of all the contributions that came before us, and to add something to that flow. That's what has driven me.[83]

In another interview, Jobs noted how he also found inspiration in the risk taking that great artists like Dylan do:

If you look at true artists, if they get really good at something, it occurs to them that they can do this for the rest of their lives, and they can really be successful at it to the outside world, but not really be successful to themselves. That's the moment that an artist really decides who he or she is. If they keep on risking failure they're still artists. Dylan and Picasso were always risking failure. This Apple thing is that way for me.[84]

After seeing how Jobs' success was heavily influenced by the Beatles and Bob Dylan, think about your own interests. *What artists inspire you? Why do you find their work so interesting? What can you learn from them? How can you apply that approach to your own work?*

12. **Bill Gates**. The final person we'll discuss in this section might not be a person who Jobs emulated in his design style, but there's no doubt that Bill Gates influenced it. If the other people we've discussed so far were figures he wanted to emulate, Gates was a person he reacted to. A major part of building an identity in business is not only to say who you are but also to say who you are not. Jobs admired the artists and the rebels of society. He wanted Apple to be reminiscent of pirates entering markets and sacking the competition. "Making a dent in the universe" was his ultimate objective. Gates, on the other hand, wanted to dominate the computer software industry with good old-fashioned business sense. Early accounts of Gates show a different mentality toward business than Jobs. While Gates was an excellent programmer himself, he left much of the technical work to Microsoft co-founder Paul Allen. In *Hard Drive: Bill Gates and the Making of the Microsoft Empire*, James Wallace and Jim Erickson explain:

> *At Harvard, Gates had read business books like other male students read Playboy. He wanted to know everything he could about running a company, from managing people to marketing products. He even checked out books on corporate law. He put his studies to good use at Microsoft. He not only negotiated the deals, he also wrote the contracts, as Wood found out one day when he met with Gates to discuss a nondisclosure agreement for FORTRAN, for which Wood had written the code. Gates quickly drafted the agreement. According to Wood, Gates seemed to know more than the lawyers did. Not only did Gates understand what needed to be done, but he was able to do a lot of the contract writing himself, saving Microsoft expensive legal advice.*

Gates was only 22 years old at that time. It's no wonder that Gates' combination of technology expertise, business acumen, and drive would lead him to become the richest person in the world in 1992 at the age of 37.[85] Much of the contentious feelings Jobs had towards Gates wasn't so much that Gates was so wealthy; it was how he built his fortune. Jobs believed that Microsoft had copied Apple's operating system when they created Windows. Furthermore, he thought Microsoft was too business focused and that their design was cold and functional. Jobs wanted to build beautiful products while Gates wanted to deliver reliable software that would be on every computer.

Jobs' ouster from Apple due to questionable business decisions caused him to reflect on how to build a company better the second time around. During the same time as Gates was becoming the richest person on the planet, Jobs was starting over from scratch and building NeXT Computers and Pixar.

While he still made some dubious business choices with NeXT, he was fortunate to work with Ed Catmull at Pixar. Catmull was a calm and reassuring computer scientist turned business executive who had a major influence on shaping Jobs' second run at Apple in 1997. He helped Jobs to see the value of building trust among a creative team and relying on more give and take in ideas. Indeed, Jobs' run at Pixar was helpful in making him a better executive at Apple in the twenty-first century.

However, the presence of Bill Gates throughout Jobs' life cannot be underestimated. They were both born in 1955 and entered the computer industry at the same time, and both dominated the media coverage of the industry. Every Jobs' failure happened in the sunshine of Gates' successes. And yet, if it hadn't been for Microsoft, Jobs' competitive drive may not have been as high as it was. Ultimately, Jobs was able to pull it all together and mature into a titan, though one not as wealthy as Gates. As Schlender and Tetzeli explain:

The iPod helped to propagate and commercialize the revolution in digital media first fomented by Internet file-sharing services such as Napster. To Jobs, though, it was also something else: the answer to Apple's existential crisis. In a world dominated by Microsoft, where did Apple fit? It turned out that a company's design talents, software prowess, and ability to exploit cheap but high-quality manufacturing in Asia could produce gorgeous and accessible consumer electronics.

As you can see in this section of the chapter, someone we see as a one-of-a-kind innovator is really the compilation of many influences and relationships. His wife Laurene called Jobs a "learning machine," who was curious and open to a wide range of ideas and people. He focused intensely on what people were saying to him and asked penetrating questions to learn all he could about things that interested him. As Jobs' biographers Brent Schlender and Rick Tetzeli observe:

He'd concoct a way to combine things with something else he'd seen, or perhaps to twist it in a way to benefit an entirely different project altogether. This was one of his greatest talents, the ability to synthesize separate developments and technologies into something previously unimaginable. It's a talent that he would call on to decide what came next.[86]

This might be the greatest lesson we can take from Jobs' life. Study the great innovators who came before you, and pick up the habits that made them successful. A good exercise for you is to find someone you admire and study who their influences were. There's something about that creator that resonates with you, and once you start putting together their story, you'll understand more deeply why you like them and what you can learn from them. Now think about yourself. *Who are your influences?* You'll gain a greater design sensibility by learning more about who influenced the creators you admire.

Summary

Design is the process that converts ideas into form. A designer is anyone who comes up with a new artifact by tweaking and transforming an idea into a desirable or needed form. Designing a product that is worthwhile drives innovation, and the more innovation a company generates, the more entrepreneurial it can be. Ten myths of design were covered in this chapter. This chapter explained how designers think. Guidelines were also given to assist people with becoming designers in their own work environments. Steps were also given for converting ideas into innovations using the design process. An overview of an iterative approach was given for designing products and services and solving problems. The chapter concluded with an examination of how Steve Jobs attained his design philosophy and inspired Apple to make great products.

Innovation-in-Action

From Designers to Design Thinkers

IDEO is one of the most famous names in the design world today. They are a design and consulting firm responsible for thousands of products, services, retail environments, and digital experiences you probably take for granted. IDEO has influenced products like the computer mouse, the modern toothbrush, and the first laptop. Companies like Anheuser-Busch, Gap, HBO, Kodak, Marriott, Pepsi, and PNC have sought the "design thinking" expertise of IDEO to redesign products that they can call their own.

The shift from being traditional designers to "design thinkers" proved to be the catalyst for IDEO's amazing success since its inception in 1991. "We moved from thinking of ourselves as designers to thinking of ourselves as design thinkers," explains co-founder David Kelley. Whether it's the redesign of a shopping cart, creating a new customer experience for a popular retailer, or creating the laptop from scratch, IDEO uses a long-proven method. According to Kelley, design thinking requires the utilization of a process very similar to the scientific method: a precise, refined system of steps that guide the designer. This method often contradicts common misconceptions about creativity and innovation. Rarely does a flash of insight spark the light bulb above the designer's head. Instead, design thinkers often start by asking a seemingly simple question: What is the problem? Only when that question is answered can design thinkers begin to reshape a product, process, or customer experience, and realizing the nature of that problem is generally half the battle.

The idea of rethinking the status quo isn't unique to IDEO's clients. IDEO itself is often forced to reshape its own processes. As often as fashion trends change, so also do consumers' wants and needs. Even today, after over 30 years of experience, IDEO has to analyze markets of consumers and shift its own approaches in order to truly benefit its clients. This self-evaluation and recalculation is often the most important lesson IDEO can teach its clients. While IDEO may be redesigning a child's toothbrush, they are teaching their customer to become design thinkers, and in the end, that is the true advantage.

(Adapted from: Tischler, L. 2009. Designer. *Fast Company*, February(132): 78–101.)

Key Terms

artifact

breakthrough

business viability

commercialization

concept

constraints

consumer desirability

design

design challenge

design thinking

display

evaluation

feedback

flexible mind

humility

inspiration

iteration

play

proactive

prototype

refinement

replay

research and development

solution path

supply chain

SWOT analysis

technical feasibility

Discussion Questions

1. What is the difference between design and creativity?
2. What is the difference between design and innovation?
3. What factors can enhance design, innovation, and entrepreneurship?
4. What is design?
5. How does a designer think?
6. How does a designer handle challenges and opportunities?
7. What was Peter Drucker's favorite entrepreneurial example? Why?
8. What are five myths of design? Why are they myths?
9. What role do constraints play in design?
10. What is humility? Why is it good for design?
11. What guidelines do good designers follow?
12. How do designers convert opportunities into innovations?
13. Why is iteration such an important part of design?
14. Describe the three steps of iteration.
15. What caveat must the designer consider when working on an idea?

Notes

1 Simon, Herbert. 1996. *The Sciences of the Artificial*, 3rd ed., Boston: MIT Press.
2 U.S. Department of the Interior. 2017. www.usbr.gov/lc/hooverdam/History/essays/fatal.html
3 LaRusso, Nicholas, Spurrier, Barbara & Gianrico Farrugia. 2015. *Thing Big, Start Small, Move Fast: A Blueprint for Transformation from the Mayo Clinic Center for Innovation*, New York: McGraw Hill, p. 99.
4 Heward, Lyn & Bacon, John U. 2006. *The Spark: Igniting the Creative Fire That Lives Within Us All*, New York: Doubleday, p. 107.
5 Again, *context matters with design*. What fits one setting may not be appropriate in another. For example, Walt Disney World closed its Pleasure Island area of bars and nightclubs because it didn't fit with Disney's brand. Las Vegas, on the other hand, turned away from its failed family entertainment strategy with its successful "What Happens in Vegas, Stays in Vegas" campaign. This consideration is why social psychology and cultural anthropology are popular areas of interdisciplinary science in design. *Better understanding of a people and their culture and place leads to good design that fits within that context.*
6 Thompson, Derek. 2017. What makes things cool. *The Atlantic*, January/February: 70.
7 Ibid.
8 Ibid.
9 "Artifact" is a formal word in design that means the same thing as "creation." So an artifact, or creation, in design can be anything that comes from a person's mind and is brought out into the world in a form others can observe and experience. This could be a product, service, building, plan, show, experience, etc.
10 Pink, D.H. 2005. *A Whole New Mind: Moving from the Information Age to the Conceptual Age*, New York: Riverhead Books.
11 www.rotman.utoronto.ca/index.html
12 Kelley, Tom & Littman, Jonathon. 2005. *The Ten Faces of Innovation: IDEO's Strategies for Beating the Devil's Advocate and Driving Creativity throughout Your Organization*, New York: Random House.
13 Ibid.
14 Covey, Stephen R. 1999. *The 7 Habits of Highly Effective People: Powerful Lessons in Personal Change*, New York: Simon & Schuster.
15 Heath, Chip & Heath, Dan. 2013. *Decisive: How to Make Better Choices in Life and Work*, New York: Crown Business, p. 69.

16 Ibid.
17 Harvard psychologist Daniel Gilbert covers this question in more depth in his book *Stumbling on Happiness.* He devotes the book to examining how people make "*the three most important decisions in their lives: where to live, what to do, and with whom to do it.*" He offers the same advice on these personal choices as we offer on design decisions: Learn from those who have already faced similar decisions and study how their choices worked out for them. Gilbert notes that while our imagination is a wonderful cognitive tool, it's also fallible to *biases and misperceptions.* Therefore, it's wise to study cases that have already happened to help you make more informed decisions.
18 Consider that in 2017, 139 million guests visited one of the Disney theme parks. The Magic Kingdom alone has 20 million guests who pass through its gates each year.
19 Pierce, Todd James. 2016. *Three Years in Wonderland: The Disney Brothers, C.V. Wood, and the Making of the Great American Theme Park*, Jackson, MS: University of Mississippi Press, p. 37.
20 This cognitive misstep is known as "*survivorship bias.*" Past success can sometimes lead to overconfidence in your abilities and cause you to overestimate your chances of future success with an idea. Use the screening questions from earlier in this chapter to help with future decisions.
21 Roman *stoicism* is experiencing a revival in modern culture because of its principles of keeping your ego in check and approaching the world with a humble attitude. See *The Obstacle is the Way* and *Ego is the Enemy* by Ryan Holiday if you're interested in learning more about stoicism.
22 Miller, Peter. 2010. *The Smart Swarm: How Understanding Flocks, Schools, and Colonies Can Make Us Better at Communicating, Decision Making, and Getting Things Done*, New York: Penguin.
23 Lindberg, Tilmann, Noweski, Christine & Meinel, Christoph. 2010. Evolving discourses on design thinking: how design cognition inspires meta-disciplinary creative collaboration. *Technoetic Arts*, 8(1): 31–37.
24 Lynn, Gary S. & Reilly, Richard R. 2002. *Blockbusters: The Five Keys to Developing Great New Products*, New York: HarperCollins.
25 Ibid.
26 Biz Stone. 2017. www.twitter.com/biz.
27 Christensen, Clayton M. 2003. *The Innovator's Dilemma: The Revolutionary Book That Will Change the Way You Do Business*, New York: HarperCollins.
28 Yet, *sometimes shutting down a project may be the right thing to do*. Staying on a project just because you've sunk money into it isn't a good reason to move forward if the idea isn't going in the right direction. If you do terminate a project, keep all your notes. A change in conditions or new breakthroughs in technology may warrant revisiting the idea again in the future. Keep a project file you can refer back to in case this happens.
29 Calahan, Tess. 2017. Train your eye for better writing. *Writer's Digest*, September: 26.
30 If you're video (or audio) recording the feedback sessions, you can literally watch the replay. You can freeze the recording when needed as you play it back and consider each point someone is giving you, just like a coach does with game film.
31 When Imagineer Joe Rhode was trying to convince Disney CEO Michael Eisner and the management team to greenlight the Animal Kingdom theme park, he brought a Bengal tiger into the room so that the executives could feel what it was like to be in the presence of wild animals. Before the presentation, the concept looked like it might be turned down, but when Eisner looked into the eyes of a tiger, he understood what Rhode was trying to sell them. The "wow" effect worked, and Eisner approved construction of the park.
32 Everything leading up to the "play" step could be considered "pre-play." Fact-finding and discovery set the stage for the quality of play to come. The more time you've spent preparing to play, the more "toys" you'll have in your sandbox. "Sandbox," by the way, is also a metaphor many innovators use to denote where they'll do their work. So as you're preparing to play with your ideas, think about what your sandbox is and what's in it. What sandbox are you playing in? What do you have in your sandbox to play with?

33 Sawyer, R. Keith. 2007. *Group Genius: The Creative Power of Collaboration*, New York: BasicBooks.

34 We've often heard executives say the reason they partnered or outsourced with another company is that, "That's not the business we're in. We'll turn to others who already do that, so we can focus on what we do well."

35 And the good health needed for the designer to work a demanding schedule. The manager needs to remember the *self-care* they need to maintain their wellbeing as they work on tough projects. Good health is needed to sustain a demanding schedule that comes with running operations and working on innovative ideas. Know your limits and what you need in your life to function well over the long haul. In today's world, people often overcommit and get nothing completed well, which further adds to their stress. Good intentions but poor results can dent a person's self-esteem. Good guidance on this modern phenomenon comes from the example Steve Jobs set for his company. Everyday he asked his chief designer Jony Ive, *"What have you said 'no' to today?"* Jobs' point was that there are a lot of interesting things people can work on, but to do something at an excellent level requires focus and the discipline to turn down opportunities that distract from the ultimate objective. Again, great designers are big picture people. They keep their eye on what they want to accomplish and make their decisions with their grand goal in mind. If something doesn't contribute towards that goal, they're likely to say "no."

36 Kawasaki, Guy. 2004. *The Art of the Start: The Time-Tested, Battle-Hardened Guide for Anyone Starting Anything*, New York: Penguin.

37 We don't mean to disparage financial rewards, since money enables you to pursue higher goals of interest. But when it comes to the day-to-day grind of working on a project, intrinsic motivation improves the quality of the work in the long run.

38 Mayer, Richard E. 1995. The search for insight: grappling with Gestalt psychology's unanswered questions, in Sternberg, Robert J. & Davidson, Janet E. (eds.), *The Nature of Insight*, Boston: MIT Press, pp. 3–32.

39 Dominowski, Roger L. & Dallob, Pamela. 1995. Insight and problem solving, in Sternberg, Robert J. & Davidson, Janet E. (eds.), *The Nature of Insight*, Boston: MIT Press, pp. 33–62.

40 And more people will seek you out to do the same with their projects. Opportunity comes to problem solvers—not problem creators—in the workplace.

41 This mental flaw is known as "confirmation bias" and is one of the biggest reasons people make bad choices. We subconsciously disregard things that counter our position and accept what confirms it. It's as if people don't even hear something that goes against what they want. Don't fall into this cognitive trap. Be aware of the need to be open to hearing and considering others' points. It may prevent you from overlooking a vital piece of information that could have made your idea much better. Companies with good customer relations, for example, train their employees to listen to *what* customers are saying, not *how* they say it. Don't let strong emotions steer you away from hearing information that might be useful to you. Again, recording sessions and taking notes can help you better capture what is being said.

42 Kahneman, Daniel. 2011. *Thinking, Fast and Slow*, New York: Farrar, Straus, and Giroux.

43 The premise behind why the brain has quick and slow modes of thought is based on evolutionary "fight, flight, or freeze" responses. When our ancestors lived in the wild, quick judgments were necessary to avoid becoming lunch for a predatory animal. Slowly thinking through whether the sound in the bush was due to a large dangerous animal or a harmless one could lead to a quick death. That cognitive system that is biased toward quick action on the Savannah is still preloaded in our heads even though the environment we live in today has changed. Mindfulness is a cognitive practice that has become popular today as a way of helping people manage day-to-day stressors. Simply recognizing that the ancestral part of your brain is going into "fight or flight" mode can help you slow down, regroup, and handle situations better. Labeling the brain activity as it takes place changes your response to it.

44 Haidt, Jonathon. 2006. *The Happiness Hypothesis*, New York: Hachette.

45 Stone, Douglas & Heen, Sheila. 2014. *Thanks for the Feedback: The Science and Art of Receiving Feedback Well*, New York: Penguin, p. 300.

46 People who move forward on ideas just because they've invested a lot of resources into it fall victim to the "*sunk cost fallacy.*" They don't want to feel like they're throwing away what they've already worked on. However, this isn't a rational way to think about past work. Resources should always be put to productive use where positive results can happen. Continuing to sink resources into a failed idea just leads to more waste. Move resources to where you'll get a better return. The phrase "cut your losses" aptly fits here. Ask yourself, "*What's in it for me, my boss, and the company if I keep moving forward on this?*"

47 Football coaches are often used as leadership role models, due mainly to their motivational approaches and team building skills. However, we believe much of their success is due to their off-the-field preparation that others don't see. The best coaches (and players) tend to be voracious consumers of game film. It's those countless hours in the film room that often highlight what they'll focus on in games. We can also see similar practices in the military, where field operations are planned in great detail based on intelligence and capability reports. Where great risks and stakes exist, we find the most meticulous minds poring over information that will help them be successful. Business should be no different.

48 Holley, Michael. 2016. *Belichick and Brady: Two Men, the Patriots, and How They Revolutionized Football*, New York: Hachette, p. 55.

49 Burke, Monte. 2015. *Saban: The Making of a Coach*, New York: Simon & Schuster, p. 96.

50 Holley, Michael. 2011. *War Room: The Legacy of Bill Belichick and the Art of Building the Perfect Team*, New York: itbooks, p. 272.

51 Burke, Monte. 2015. *Saban: The Making of a Coach*, New York: Simon & Schuster, pp. 284–285.

52 Fleming, David. No more questions. *ESPN Magazine*, 10(17): 43.

53 Kahney, Leander. 2013. *Jony Ive: The Genius Behind Apple's Greatest Products*, New York: Portfolio, p. 231.

54 Pasternak, Charles. 2004. *Quest: The Essence of Humanity*, West Sussex, England: Wiley, pp. 7–8.

55 Ibid, p. 1.

56 Wolf Shenk, Joshua. 2014. *Powers of Two: Finding the Essence of Innovation in Creative Pairs*, Boston: Houghton Mifflin Harcourt.

57 Hench, John. 2003. *Designing Disney: Imagineering and the Art of the Show*, New York: Disney Editions.

58 Bonanos, Christopher. 2012. *Instant: The Story of Polaroid*, New York: Princeton Architectural Press, p. 11.

59 Isaacson, Walter. 2011. *Steve Jobs*, New York: Simon & Schuster, pp. 567–568.

60 Stross, Randall E. 1993. *Steve Jobs & the NeXT Big Thing*, New York: Macmillan, p. 23.

61 We recently spoke with a former product manager for RCA in Bloomington, Indiana, who worked on the ill-fated VideoDisc player. The VideoDisc was a 12-inch vinyl album that played video. The grooves in the VideoDisc were 48 times smaller than a record LP and were read with a diamond needle. The technology had superior picture quality to videotape and was on the market before the LaserDisc by Panasonic, but it failed because of three key reasons: (1) big screen televisions were not common in households, so superior video clarity wasn't an issue on 27-inch TV sets; (2) the market wasn't prepared to pay higher costs for the better product; and (3) the company struggled with achieving quality standards in its manufacturing process. A few years later, Philips and Sony launched the compact disc format to music fans, which helped the market become familiar with the small shiny disc format. The compact discs were round discs that played music, so that was deemed acceptable and affordable, and it had better sound quality than vinyl LPs. DVDs and Blu-ray discs were more natural progressions to video than their predecessors VideoDisc and LaserDisc.

62 Gladwell, M. 2011. The tweaker. *The New Yorker*, November 14.

63 Walt Disney operated in the same manner. He had master animators and engineers working for him at his company and relied on them to generate ideas he could take forward. When he was asked what he did all day, he answered, "Sometimes I think of myself as a little bee. I go from one area of the studio to another and gather pollen and sort of stimulate everybody. I guess that's the job I do."

64 Fox Weber, Nicholas. 2011. *The Bauhaus Group: Six Masters of Modernism*, New Haven, CT: Yale University Press, p. 5.

65 Although founded and headquartered in Germany, Braun is now a subsidiary of Procter & Gamble. It still maintains its German design and management practices though.

66 Edson, John. 2012. *Design Like Apple*, Hoboken, NJ: Wiley.

67 Rams, Dieter. Ten principles of good design. *Vitsoe*, www.vitsoe.com/en/gb/about/dieterrams/gooddesign.

68 You can watch Rams explain his ten principles in the documentary about industrial design called *Objectified*.

69 It should be noted that the Bauhaus philosophy is only one school of design thought. Settings exist where simple and basic wouldn't fit, and a different design philosophy might work better. For example, in some cultures, the context that products must fit into is one where clothes, interior design, and architecture are very ornate and decorative. Scandinavian minimalist furniture might not fit well in a setting like the Taj Mahal. Like with any other design decision, you'll need to consider the market you're creating your products for.

70 Esslinger, Harmut. 2013. *Keep It Simple: The Early Design Years of Apple*, Stuttgart: Arnoldsche Art Publishers, p. 32.

71 Ibid, p. 35.

72 Ibid, p. 35.

73 Nathan, John. 1999. *Sony*, Boston: Mariner.

74 D'Onfro, Jillian. 2015. Steve Jobs used to ask jony ive the same question almost every day. www.businessinsidercom/this-is-the-question-steve-jobs-would-ask-jony-ive-every-day-2015-10.

75 Edson, John. 2012. *Design Like Apple*, Hoboken, NJ: Wiley.

76 Kahney, Leander. 2013. *Jony Ive: The Genius Behind Apple's Greatest Products*, New York: Portfolio.

77 Thomas, Alan Ken. 2011. *The Business Wisdom of Steve Jobs*, New York: Skyhorse Publishing, p. 59.

78 Turner, Steve. 2016. *Beatles '66: The Revolutionary Year*, New York: HarperCollins, p. 1.

79 Ibid.

80 It should be noted that the Beatles' recording company was called Apple too. While Jobs always said his company's name was inspired by an apple orchard he spent a lot of time in during his youth, one has to wonder if his company's name was paying homage to the artistic inspiration of the Beatles.

81 Esslinger, Harmut. 2013. *Keep It Simple: The Early Design Years of Apple*, Stuttgart: Arnoldsche Art Publishers, p. 21.

82 Bob Dylan was a good role model for Jobs to study for lyricism. In 2016, Dylan won the Nobel Prize for Literature. A lifetime of studying Dylan would hone Jobs' ability to craft a message that resonated with his customers like Dylan's songs resonated with his fans.

83 Isaacson, Walter. 2011. *Steve Jobs*, New York: Simon & Schuster, p. 570.

84 Schlender, Brent & Tetzeli, Rick. 2015. *Becoming Steve Jobs: The Evolution of a Reckless Upstart into a Visionary Leader*, New York: Crown Business, p. 213.

85 Gates has remained at or near the top of the Forbes 400 list of wealthiest individuals in the world ever since claiming number 1 in 1992. At the time of this writing, he is still number 1, with a net worth of $89 billion. Jeff Bezos, the founder and CEO of Amazon, is rapidly closing on Gates, though, with an $84 billion fortune.

86 Schlender, Brent & Tetzeli, Rick. 2015. *Becoming Steve Jobs: The Evolution of a Reckless Upstart into a Visionary Leader*, New York: Crown Business, p. 298.

6

DESIGN-DRIVEN INNOVATION

Prototyping and Manufacturing

Google is run by engineers, and engineers are people who ask why: Why must we do things the way they've always been done?

~Ken Auletta[1]

Introduction

In the previous chapter, we discussed how to utilize design principles to shape an idea into a commercial concept. The next challenge is how to get the product actually manufactured. If you're like many other managers, you may not have an extensive mechanical background. That's okay. You don't have to attain technical expertise to get a product manufactured. All you have to do is gain some basic technology literacy, so that you can communicate with the people in your company who have that expertise. In this chapter, we provide an overview of engineering and prototyping, so that you can gain a bit of fluency in the language of technology. You'll learn the basic principles engineers employ in their daily practices. You'll also be given guidelines on how you can prototype your ideas. Although it would take a long time to become an expert in these areas, our goal is to help you become technology literate so that you can interact better with engineers and other technical experts. This knowledge will help you to get your ideas through the corporate system better.

Your main role as a corporate innovator is to be a facilitator. Your success will be determined by how well you shepherd good ideas—your own or your employees'—through your organization. This may seem like a daunting task if you've been trained to read financial statements and develop marketing campaigns; however, being able to take part in discussions with technology-based colleagues holds advantages for a corporate innovator. The manager who can speak geek, as well as talk money, will be able to acquire needed feedback and gain the support of technical colleagues. Engineers and production managers can become valuable partners in your innovation journey. They'll help you shape your ideas into more feasible and exciting products and services.

If you've traveled to another country, you know that having a rudimentary knowledge of the local language helps you get around easier. When you enter the laboratory or machine shop, you may feel like you just landed in a foreign land, but you'll be able to navigate through the labs and the shop floors better by speaking the language of the locals. A more thorough understanding of what the technical people in your organization do will help you gain their support, involvement, and feedback as you design your product. We first examine engineers—the chieftains of the technology landscape—in order to gain an appreciation for how they contribute to innovation and design.

Engineering

Woody Norris is an inventor who has made millions creating products like a non-lethal acoustic weapon that has been used to ward off pirates, a bone-induction headset, radar that can scan the human body, and a tapeless tape recorder—and yet he says, "Virtually nothing has been invented yet. We're just now starting to understand the laws of nature."[2] Popular science writer Matt Ridley, after interviewing the world's leading technologists and economists, also concluded that innovation is limitless. He encapsulates this view with the following observation:

> There is not even a theoretical possibility of exhausting the supply of ideas, discoveries, and inventions. This is the biggest cause of all for my optimism. . . . If you were to combine any of the 100 chemical elements into different alloys and compounds in different proportions ranging from one to ten, you would have 330 billion possible chemical compounds and alloys to test, or enough to keep a team of researchers busy testing a thousand a day for a million years. Yet if innovation is limitless, why is everybody so pessimistic about the future?[3]

Better yet, why do so few people offer solutions? We believe a major reason most people are pessimistic and apathetic is that they don't possess entrepreneurial and innovative skills. Most people feel more comfortable with the status quo. They fear change instead of embracing it. That's unfortunate, because a structural shift is taking place in the economy. Just as a manufacturing economy replaced agrarianism in the nineteenth century and was later replaced itself by an information society, the economy of the latter twentieth century is being supplanted by one based on creativity and entrepreneurship. Richard Florida captures this economic transformation in his seminal book *The Rise of the Creative Class*. He envisions a world where people with artistic and technical knowledge thrive:

> If you are a scientist or engineer, an architect or designer, a writer, artist, or musician, or if you use your creativity as a key factor in your work in business, education, health care, law or some other profession, you are a member. . . . Because creativity is the

driving force of economic growth, in terms of influence the Creative Class has become the dominant class in society.[4]

If managers are going to succeed in this new economic reality, they must be able to work in technical and artistic domains that they may have ignored in the past. Understanding design can help in bringing about this transformation. As Roger Martin, dean of the Rotman School of Management, said, "Business people don't need to understand designers better. They need to be designers."[5] One way business people can become better designers is by becoming more proficient in technology. If managers embrace technology, they'll find the economic shift providing more opportunities than ever before. At a round table discussion, investor Warren Buffett, longtime Microsoft CEO Steve Ballmer, and recently retired General Electric CEO Jeff Immelt predicted a bright future based on more technological advancement and invention than during the internet era. Ballmer stated, "I am very enthusiastic about what the future holds for our industry and what our industry will mean for growth in other industries." Buoyed by new technologies that tie together computers, phones, internet platforms, big data, and artificial intelligence, new products and services are spinning out at an amazing rate. Immelt added that more manufacturing may take place in the country as well due to better production technologies and service centers. And Buffet resolutely stated, "This country works. The best is yet to come."[6] Unfortunately, many managers do not have the same view. New opportunities bring new challenges. Managers will have to stretch themselves to learn design and technology. They'll have to gain a more artistic sensibility to go along with their comfort of numbers and analyses. This terrain may be disconcerting to a lot of managers, but if they embrace the future they may find it better than anything they've experienced before.

So what's a good first step for better understanding technology? We suggest the manager acquire a rudimentary knowledge of engineering because it's the profession that designs, builds, and maintains the objects in our world. Engineering has been around in some form for thousands of years, but in recent history the impact of the engineer has been huge. Alfred P. Sloan Jr., the longtime president of General Motors, stated, "Without his genius and the vast contributions he has made in design, engineering, and production on the material side of our existence, our contemporary life could never have reached its present standard."[7] But, as C.C. Furnas and Joe McCarthy observed in 1966:

Despite the essential part the engineer plays in the progress and well-being of humanity, to many he is a blurred figure, his exact role imperfectly understood. One reason for the hazy impression left by the modern engineer is his close association with the scientist. Both men look alike, talk alike, worry over similar mathematical equations; the guard at the gate who checks their identification badges often cannot tell which is which. In fact, in such industries as plastics and communications, it is difficult to determine where the scientist's work ends and the engineer's begins.[8]

Aside from the gender insensitivity of the quote, much of Furnas and McCarthy's sentiments hold today, but that need not be the case if one understands the different goals that a scientist and engineer pursue. Jay B. Brockman, an engineering professor at Notre Dame University, clarifies the difference that:

> *When geologists, physicists, or chemists analyze natural things, they generally seek answers to questions such as: How does this thing work? What is it made of? How did it get to be that way? By comparison, the man-made things on the planet—and elsewhere in our solar system—are all designed with a purpose: to satisfy mankind's complex needs and desires. The main business of engineering is to apply technology in concert with natural phenomena to develop these things that we need or want. Whereas the natural sciences traditionally seek to discover how things are, engineering focuses on the question, what form should we give to this thing so that it will effectively serve its purpose?*[9]

As the above quote points out, scientists focus on discovery in the natural world whereas engineers are trained to utilize a problem-solving process to address issues in the constructed world. Therefore, you can sum up engineering in one phrase: problem-solving. So, understanding more about engineering also teaches you more about problem-solving. And since most design issues are actually problems to be solved, you can quickly see why you would benefit from having a basic comprehension of engineering. Yet, everyone is taught science in school but not engineering, even though we are affected every minute of the day by the handiwork of engineers. It's not in the scope of this book to provide a complete education on engineering, so we'll simply summarize some of the basic approaches engineers apply in their jobs.

Engineers are very goal oriented. If you approach an engineer with an idea, give them a good summary of what you intend to accomplish and what's important in the project. Engineers want to know that they're working towards clearly defined goals, and they want to know what constraints must be adhered to. They also want to know the parameters of the tasks and goals they're pursuing. Ranges of values with which to work within are helpful. It's also important that the criteria are in alignment with the project mission. If you don't come to them with this information, you may find the engineer becoming frustrated with you, and they will not be interested in working on your project. The eternal conflict between marketing and engineering can be curtailed with a little understanding and empathy on your part. Keep in mind that marketing professionals often believe engineers are not creative, and engineers often believe that marketers' ideas are too fuzzy and unrealistic. However, coming prepared to a meeting with an engineer with a well-formed idea, design goals, evaluation criteria, and project constraints will ensure better interactions.

To better understand how engineers define and tackle big challenges, let's look at how Steve Wozniak applied goal-oriented thinking to design the world's first user-friendly personal computer. Before the PC revolution, computers were large machines known as "main frames" that were purchased by large data-driven institutions like insurance companies, universities, and government agencies. However, in 1975, the Altair 8800 "microcomputer" appeared on the scene. It was the world's first small computer, but you'd probably not recognize it as one today. The customer had to toggle switches and interpret flashing red lights to operate the computer. In *Becoming Steve Jobs*, Brent Schlender and Rick Tetzeli explain how Wozniak created a more accessible personal computer:[10]

> *Spurred by a geek's natural competitive instincts, he roughed out some new designs for what he knew would be a better microcomputer, one that would be easier to program, control, and manipulate. . . . Why not input commands and data values more directly with a typewriter keyboard? And why not have the computer project your typing and results onto an attached television monitor? And for that matter, why not plug in a cassette tape recorder to store programs and data? The Altair had none of these features that would make computing far less intimidating and far more approachable. This was the challenge Woz decided to tackle.*

Steve Wozniak had a clear idea of what he wanted to accomplish with the first Apple computer. He also knew what design problems needed to be resolved to bring about his greater vision. And engineering provided him the solutions to those problems to build the first modern PC. So if you're going to work with engineers on your idea, you'll need to think the same way as Woz. Then you'll need to communicate with precision and clarity what you need help with.

Engineers approach problems like an economist. Engineers understand the old economic adage that "there is no such thing as a free lunch." Time is money. As such, an experienced engineer will first search for solutions that may already exist for the problem. If the solution adequately fits the situation, they'll likely advise that route be followed, since time can be saved and used on other problems requiring more thinking. A very important point for managers new to technology to understand is: Most inventions and new products are simply a unique combination of what already exists. That's why very few products are made of truly original components. When possible, the engineer will use off-the-shelf components to build a product. As you more closely examine how products are designed, you'll quickly discover that most are simply made with already existing parts with a new innovation or two added in. The aesthetic qualities may appear original, but the inside components are usually from pre-existing products. Why do engineers use already existing technology instead of innovating totally original products? It saves a lot of money. Why put a lot of dollars into R&D when a parts distributor can sell you something that already works?

Engineers seek the most efficient solution to a problem. Complexity expert W. Brian Arthur points out that understanding this important fact makes technology a much less daunting subject:

> *If you open up a jet engine (or aircraft gas turbine powerplant, to give it its professional name), you will find components inside—compressors, turbines, combustion engines. If you open up other technologies that existed before it, you find some of the same*

components. . . . Technologies inherit parts from the technologies that preceded them, so putting such parts together—combining them—must have a great deal to do with how technologies come into being. This makes the abrupt appearance of radically novel technologies suddenly seem much less abrupt. Technologies somehow must come into being as fresh combinations of what already exists.

Solutions that have been useful in the past may be useful to working on new design projects. However, while efficiency and economics are common design constraints, an innovative engineer is always on the lookout for a better way to do something. Balancing the new with the tried and true is the ultimate design challenge.

With knowledge of how engineers approach their jobs, you can ask questions in a way to get more help on the technical aspects of your product. You'll also approach opportunities with the eye of an engineer as well as a designer. As technology experts often say: You'll know just enough to be dangerous. With that in mind, we now provide information about the different engineering disciplines, so that you'll have a general idea of who to go to for help.

The Engineering Disciplines

If you're turning to an engineer for help in developing your product, you'll want to approach one who is from the discipline that pertains most to your design question. In *Engineering Your Future*, William Oakes, Les Leone, and Craig Gunn provide new university students with an overview of the most common areas of engineering. Their descriptions are also useful to managers new to engineering.[11]

Chemical Engineering

Chemical engineers apply chemistry to industrial processes. They change the composition or properties of substances for the manufacturing of drugs, cements, paints, lubricants, pesticides, fertilizers, cosmetics, and foods. Chemical engineers also work with oil refining, combustion, extraction of metals from ores, and assist with the production of ceramics, brick, and glass. They can be very helpful in explaining what materials would work best in your product. They may also help create new materials needed for producing the product you're designing. Some industries are transformed by the use of more efficient or affordable materials, such as aerospace, automotive, biomedical, electronic, environmental, space, and military applications. Material innovation is one of the greatest sources of new technology in our society.

Civil Engineering

Civil engineers design the infrastructure that supports our communities. They deal with the design, construction, and maintenance of structures in built environments, such as buildings, bridges, roads, canals, and dams. They're very engaged in projects involving rapid transit systems, highway systems, skyscrapers, industrial plants, and recreational facilities. Because of their involvement in construction, they also often work in materials science and deal with concrete, aluminum, steel, polymers, and carbon fibers. Civil engineers also help lay out roads, tracks, and pipelines as surveyors. If a new facility needs to be built, a civil engineer is a likely first expert to consult.

Electrical Engineering

Electrical engineering is the largest discipline of engineering. 301,500 engineers design and develop electronic systems and products.[12] They may work on electronics, solid-state circuitry, communication systems, computers, instrumentation, power generation and transmission, and industrial applications. If a product needs power to operate, it's likely an electrical engineer had a hand in the development. We can expect electrical engineering to continue to grow, especially as the "internet of things" develops. Plus, with advances in medical technology, electrical engineers will be called upon to power up new devices that will be used in prosthetics and implants.

Computer Engineering

Computer engineering combines electrical engineering with computer science to develop new computer systems. Robotics, artificial intelligence, industrial automation, and computer hardware and software are just a few of the many areas that computer engineers work in in today's digital world. As new digital technologies become utilized in more areas of work and leisure, the role of the computer engineer will continue to grow.

Industrial Engineering

If you've designed a product, chances are an industrial engineer will assist in the manufacturing stage. Industrial engineering applies engineering principles and techniques to efficiently produce goods. As such, they're very concerned with the optimal allocation of people, materials, and equipment to increase productivity in their areas. Industrial engineering is also known as management science, systems engineering, or manufacturing engineering. The information they provide on the manufacturing needs of your product will be very helpful when you put together a plan later.

Mechanical Engineering

Mechanical engineering is a vital area of new product development. It deals with the design, development, production, control, operation, and service of machines and mechanical devices. Mechanical engineers provide detailed layout and assembly of the components of products and machines. They ensure that the parts of a product fit together and operate as intended. Because of their expertise on components and parts, they can be found in many related areas such as bioengineering, robotics, aerospace engineering, nuclear engineering, ocean engineering, applied mechanics, and manufacturing.

Industrial Designers

Although not technically an area of engineering, industrial design is an area that applies many engineering concepts to designing products. Ergonomics, usability, design-for-manufacturing, and design for end-of-life management are some of the areas involved in industrial design. Industrial designers work to improve the function, value, and appearance of products. Since they focus on the form of the product, they can come from different backgrounds such as architecture, art, and engineering. Industrial designers such as Sir Jony Ive of Apple and Tinker Hatfield of Nike have garnered worldwide recognition for their products. Their products are admired for their artistic relevance as well as their commercial success. Other aesthetic professionals, such as graphic designers, set designers, and fashion designers, are influencing new product development as well. As prototyping technologies become more accessible in price and availability and design principles propagate through the greater public, we'll see more companies and innovators implementing the principles of industrial design into their products.

Understanding the basic roles of the aforementioned engineers will be very useful when you try to develop a product in the future. As you design the function, shape, and components of your product idea, you may need to turn to one of these experts to help you work through design issues. You should be aware that we didn't provide you with an exhaustive list of engineering categories. Many fields and industries have their own engineering specialists as well, such as nuclear engineering and petroleum engineering. If you're interested in learning more about engineering and technology, you can obtain free online lectures by visiting the following websites: TED (www.ted.com), Udacity (www.udacity.com), the Kahn Academy (www.kahnacademy.org), MIT's OpenCourseWare (ocw.mit.edu), and the Stanford Technology Ventures Program (stvp.stanford.edu). For up-to-date information on the latest technologies and science trends, visit www.wired.com, news.cnet.com, www.popsci.com, www.technologyreview.com, and www.popularmechanics.com. The Bureau of Labor Statistics also provides more information on the engineering disciplines at www.bls.gov/ooh/architecture-and-engineering/home.htm.

In the following section, we'll examine another important aspect of new product design: prototyping. To the average person, prototyping seems like a task best left to technical professionals; however, as we'll see, prototyping technologies have been democratized where anyone can build basic prototypes. This skill set will come in very handy as you work with your product idea.

Prototyping

Burt Rutan, the American aerospace engineer who won the Ansari X Prize, believes that experimentation and exploration are important aspects of the human condition. He said, "I think we need to explore. I think if we stop exploring that we will run into mediocrity and we all will get bored." Yet, how many companies are mediocre because managers and employees through the ranks accept the status quo and hold back their ideas? One key reason why managers may hold back their ideas is that they're not quite sure what to do with the ones they have. Their reticence to explore the practical side of technology was not always the case in the developed world. Peter Wright, former Assistant Director of MI5—the British intelligence service—once observed that World War II was won by having a large group of inquisitive people who sought practical solutions to complex problems. He states:

> *Science in wartime is often a case of improving with the materials at hand, solving a problem as best you can at the time, rather than planning ten or fifteen years ahead, when it may be too late. The war shaped my later approach to technical intelligence. It taught me the value of improvisation and showed me, too, just how effective operations can be when men of action listen to young men with a belief in practical, inventive science. Sadly, by the end of the war this attitude had all but disappeared, the dead hand of committees began to squeeze the life out of England.*[13]

These sentiments pertain to many businesses today as well. How many managers behave like the committees Wright describes? Overanalyzing and micromanaging employee activities can squeeze out any innovation taking place in a company. Managers should instead be role models for innovative behavior and support their employees in exploring the development of ideas.

In previous chapters, we discussed the general principles that managers and employees can follow to design new products and services. Unfortunately, most books that cover innovation stop there, and the reader is not given any direction on how to actually shepherd the idea into production. We rectify this gap by providing practices you can employ to shape an idea into an actual product. As Chapter 4 covered, the innovation process begins with an insight of an opportunity to explore. Chapter 5 discussed how to apply the design process to develop the insight into a practical and refined concept. This chapter extends the design process into prototyping and manufacturing.

A prototype is a physical representation of your idea, and is useful for attaining more in-depth feedback. A model of your idea makes it more realistic. It's no longer just on paper, so others can look at it from every angle. Therefore, *a prototype is rich with details of what you're hoping to build.* After all, visual communication is usually more informative than verbal communication. If a picture is worth a thousand words, a prototype is worth a million words. The next time you have a meeting with your boss to discuss an idea, bring a prototype. If you start off describing the idea with a polished pitch, they'll probably nod and say something like, "Okay, sounds interesting." But if you then put a well-designed prototype in their hands, they might respond, "Oh, wow! Now I get it! Let me see more. Tell me how this works." If you've piqued their interest with the prototype, the floodgates might open with feedback and support to make the next version better. And you'll probably start to separate yourself from the rest of the managers in your company who just talk about their big ideas.

Prototyping in Five Steps

Many people avoid learning about prototyping because they think it's too complicated or expensive. This need not be the case. Prototypes do vary in their sophistication and costs, but in the early stages of design, anyone can create inexpensive models made of simple materials like paper and tape to capture the most basic elements of an idea. As we display the prototype for feedback, we can easily modify the concept with another inexpensive model. As you can see, the iterative process of play, display, and replay holds true for prototyping as well. Once enthusiastic support has been received for the simple prototype, we can build a more advanced conceptual prototype. The *conceptual prototype* is not necessarily polished or expensive, but it is more sophisticated than the earlier rough prototypes. Conceptual prototypes are also known as surface prototypes, because on the surface they start to take on the appearance of what the final product may look like. You may have to create a few conceptual prototypes until you have a winning concept. When you're pleased with the conceptual prototype, you can begin building a *working prototype*. Although it doesn't necessarily have to be the case, it's likely that more costs will be incurred on this model, because a working prototype has to actually *work*. It goes beyond merely looking like the final product, so it needs to demonstrate how it functions. After a working prototype is found acceptable, some designers build a *presentation prototype* to demonstrate a polished version of how the actual product will look and work. It doesn't have to be an exact replica of the real product, but it should appear to be. Sometimes companies substitute less costly materials that wouldn't be used in the actual product, but paint and final detailing is applied to give it a polished look. If the working prototype gets across enough information and garners support for follow-through, some executives may give the go-ahead to bypass the presentation model and go straight to production with the technical drawings, concepts, and working prototype as guides for setting up the manufacturing process.

Now that you have a basic understanding of what prototyping is and the various types of prototypes, you're now ready to learn how to actually build one. The following five steps provide guidance on how to take your idea through the various stages of prototyping and ready your concept for production.

Step 1: Drawing

Sketches

When you get an idea, the first thing you should do is draw a quick sketch and jot down notes. The sketch doesn't have to be particularly artistic or technical. It just needs to get a basic point across to someone else. This exercise doesn't require much in terms of materials or costs. A good pen and something to write on will get you going. Many great companies were founded by someone having an idea for a new business and writing it on the back of a napkin. For example, market leader Southwest Airlines was started this way. When Rollin King and Herb Kelleher met for dinner in 1967 at a San Antonio restaurant, they had an idea for a new airline. Grabbing a napkin, King drew a triangle representing flight routes between Dallas, Houston, and San Antonio. They would offer airline services that catered to frequent fliers who did business between the three cities. Southwest would later be innovative in its company culture and operations as well, but it all got started when King and Kelleher drew out the idea on a napkin.

Sketching is also a good way to document your ideas. Whenever you have an idea, draw it out and capture it in a notebook. Notebooks are also important for writing as well as drawing. It's important to write notes on the parameters, criteria of success, and possible issues and ideas in your notebook. This is why engineers, designers, and inventors keep notebooks handy. They know that an idea is safe and won't be lost if it's written down. Another benefit of keeping an active notebook is that it supports the design principles of play, display, and replay. You can track the changes in your idea. Plus, if someone suggests you do something you've already tried, you can pull out your notebook and show them what you did and explain why it didn't work. Therefore, whenever you have an idea, draw it out, and capture it.

A wealth of popular resources is available for improving your drawing skills. Four very accessible books are The Back of the Napkin: Solving Problems and Selling Ideas with Pictures, Drawing Ideas: A Hand-Drawn Approach for Better Design, The Sketchnote Handbook: The Illustrated Guide to Visual Note Taking, and The Doodle Revolution: Unlock the Power to Think Differently.

The authors of these books—Dan Roam,[14] Mark Baskinger and William Bardel,[15] Mike Rhode,[16] and Sunni Brown[17]—all emphasize the power of adding visual language as a complement to numerical and verbal languages. Roam states that:

> *Visual thinking means taking advantage of our innate ability to see—both with our eyes and with our mind's eye—in order to discover ideas that are otherwise invisible, develop those ideas quickly and intuitively, and then share those ideas with other people in a way that they can simply "get."*[18]

Baskinger and Bardel offer a powerful explanation for the benefits of drawing:

> *Your ability to draw is a fast, powerful means for thinking, reasoning, and visually exploring ideas—providing visual information for self-reflection and focused discussion with your colleagues, teams, and clients. Whether it is of a product, service, information, or system, a hand-drawn sketch communicates the essence of your idea and illustrates its potential. The simplicity of connection between mind, eyes, hand, and pencil shrugs off the layered burden that complex technology often adds.*[19]
>
> *Rhode developed a method called "sketchnotes" that focuses on capturing the essence of an idea through drawing. He encourages us to go back to our roots as children (17–18): "Kids draw to express ideas. They don't worry about how perfect their drawings are, as long as their ideas are conveyed. Ideas, not art!"*[20] *But while your drawings may appear childlike on the surface, they can still communicate some*

deep thought behind them. As Sunni Brown explains: A doodler is engaging in
deep and necessary information processing. A doodler is concentrating intently, sifting
through information, conscious and otherwise, and—much more often than we real-
ize—generating massive insights." She further encourages the reader to "seriously
elevate your skill in doodling: because you'll be elevating your skill in thinking and
problem solving, too.[21]

It's beyond the scope of this book to teach you how to draw; however, these books offer very accessible ways to develop this ability. However, if you're good at drawing, you might consider expanding your artistic skills into the mediums of gouache paint, acrylic paint, and rendering markers. These colorful mediums are popular with concept artists because they dry quickly, provide a rich artistic appearance, and are fairly easy to learn. Perspective drawing is another valuable skill to have in your artistic toolkit. If you're interested in learning more about these illustration styles, visit a bookstore and peruse the entertainment section for books on movie concept art. Books featuring Ralph McQuarrie (the concept artist for the first three *Star Wars* films), Syd Mead (the concept artist for *Blade Runner*), and Ron Cobb (the concept artist for *Alien*) will inspire your creative work.

Technical Drawing

As you progress with an idea, you may want the assistance of an engineer or draftsman to draw more technical sketches of the product. Drawings that capture the width, height, and depth along with measurements, parts, and components will communicate how an object should be made. Rudimentary skills in technical drawing can be developed by taking art classes and mechanical drawing courses; however, open-source software such as SketchUp can be used to craft digital 3D drawings of your idea as well.

The best way to gain proficiency in drawing is to do it whenever you have an idea. Rest assured that even if you don't see yourself as artistic, the more you draw, the better you'll get at it. Simply carry a notebook through the day and draw what you see around you. Examine objects on your desk, such as a computer mouse, pens, and coffee cups, and study with a designer's eye the shape, colors, and small details of the object. Try drawing them. Observe how the object reflects light. Take a guess at what it's made of. Try to figure out how it was put together. Think about the characteristics of objects as you draw them, and as you do so you'll develop a *designer's eye* for detail. *Ask yourself how the product could have been made better. What are its weaknesses? What are the good characteristics of the object? Why? What's interesting about the object? What do you think the designer was trying to achieve when the concept was developed? Did they hit their intended mark? How would you modify the object for a different market?* Drawing the world around you with a critical eye will help you develop skills that will be helpful when you design your own products.

Step 2: Model Building

Making It Real

A complement to drawing is model building. Karl Aspelund describes a model as:

> *any kind of sample, mock-up, or attempt at physical representation of an idea, ranging from a standard architectural model to a sample garment on a mannequin. The creation of models and samples at this stage of any design is an attempt to bring the idea into the real world and help us understand how the design will function there.*[22]

Again, like drawing, model building can be an informal and relaxed method for capturing your idea, except now instead of being on paper it will be captured in three-dimensional physical form. As Apelund points out, "The model is real, but it's not the real thing."[23]

If there were one phrase to sum up this stage of prototyping, it would be "build it." You may have had a good conversation with someone on a business idea and even drawn it on the back of a napkin, but if you want to really get across your idea, get some paper, cardboard, tape, and a pair of scissors and start building a *mock-up*. The same principles you used in drawing apply here. Use whatever is available that you can piece together to capture your idea. As Tom Kelley, general manager of IDEO, states, good designers "delight in how fast they take a concept from words to sketch, to model, and yes, to a successful new offering."[24] In *The Ten Faces of Innovation*, he recalls how IDEO used modeling to develop a concept for a break-through medical instrument for nasal surgery. IDEO met with the medical advisory board of surgical tool company Gyrus ENT to discuss what surgeons wanted in the new device. Ideas were flying around the meeting about what the instrument should look like, but the group was having a hard time grasping the general design of the product. Kelley recalls:

> *Then one of our young engineers had a flash of inspiration and bolted from the room. Outside the conference room, seizing on the "found art" of materials lying around the office, he picked up a whiteboard marker, a black plastic Kodak film canister, and an orange clothes-like clip. He taped the canister to the white board marker and attached the orange clip to the lid of the film canister. The result was an extremely crude model of the new surgical tool. Five minutes after his mysterious departure, he returned to the meeting and handed his kindergarten-quality prototype to a respected surgeon. He asked, "Are you thinking of something like this?" To which the surgeon replied, "Yes, something like THIS!" That initial crude prototype got the project rolling.*[25]

Materials for Model Building

As the IDEO example demonstrates, you can make mock-ups with whatever is handy around you. However, if you want to be more adept at building models, you may want to invest a little money into a few basic tools and materials that can be found at any good art store or craft shop. Paper, illustration board, heavy cardboard, poster board, bristol paper, chipboard, museum board, foamcore, canson paper, balsa wood, and basswood are good materials to have on hand. A utility knife, a craft knife, a retractable blade knife, a handheld board cutter and beveler, dividers, a metal ruler, a T-square, a 30-degree by 60-degree triangle, a 45-degree triangle, and an ample supply of pencils, pens, markers, and charcoal are handy tools to design and shape the parts and frames of your prototype. Adhesives are important to hold your creation together. White glue, rubber cement, spray adhesive, balsa wood cement, and sticky tape can work wonders in building fairly sturdy prototypes.

Tips for Building Models

Building models comprises gathering materials, drawing out what you want to cut, cutting out the pieces, and gluing or fastening them together. Be sure to carefully measure your drawings on the materials, so that you ensure the parts fit well together. When extracting parts out of the materials, slice against a metal straight edge such as a T-square to ensure an even cut, and put a protective object underneath the material you're cutting so that you avoid damaging your table surface and dulling the knife blades. It's also important to wear safety goggles. Just snipping a metal container can shoot a metal shard into an eye. Attentiveness during any cutting maneuver is essential. If you use glue to attach the parts, only apply as much as is minimally necessary, in order to avoid making messy models. And replace blades whenever they become dull.[26]

The materials at this stage are inexpensive, so don't be afraid to make mistakes. That's the only way you can learn to develop prototyping skills. You'll get better with time. If you're particularly adventurous and want to build a small model shop, you might consider purchasing some fairly inexpensive power tools and machines. A scroll saw and a chop saw are easy to use and very effective in working with wood and foamboard to build slightly more realistic prototypes. Portable hand drills, a rotary shaft tool, a floor model drill press, and a hacksaw are worth considering as well. A shop vacuum cleaner and a draftsman table will complete your workshop. Clay and plaster are other materials you might also want to add to your supply shelf. A small shop in your home will allow more opportunity to experiment with your ideas.

As you begin to build inexpensive prototypes, you'll start looking differently at the world around you. You'll become curious as to how something was made, why it was made that way, and how it could have been made better. You might even find yourself picking up a copy of *Make* magazine or *Popular Mechanics* instead of the *Wall Street Journal*. Technology will no longer be a foreign concept to you. Also, as you iterate and build more models, you'll learn prototyping shortcuts and new ways to display the details of your ideas. And, as your prototyping skills improve, people will get a better idea of what's going on inside your head. You'll no longer have to struggle with trying to find the right words to get across your ideas. Your models will do the talking for you.

Business Viability

In the previous chapter, we noted how IDEO defines good design as a product or service that meets the constraints of consumer desirability, technical feasibility, and business viability. The consumer desirability component of design has been covered in Chapter 4. Chapter 5 extended coverage of this component when it provided guidance on how to design products with customer feedback. The early part of this chapter has addressed technical feasibility. The rough prototype stage is an excellent time to cover business viability. You now have enough information about what materials and manufacturing your product requires to estimate costs and financial margins. Figure 6.1 provides a simple method for getting a general idea about the business viability of your product. Experienced innovators, executives, investors, and designers can run these numbers in their head, but you'll likely need to work these calculations out on paper.

These are rough calculations. When you address financial aspects in your plan, you'll apply more sophisticated techniques. But for now, you just want to get an overall idea of whether your idea is on the right financial path. If you frequently use this method to test the business viability of your ideas, you may find you can get to where you can run the numbers in your head like more experienced innovators and executives. For now, though, work the calculations out on paper. You'll find that once you know the basic formulas you can run them anywhere. The back of an envelope or napkin is all that's needed to do these calculations. Your goal is to just get a basic idea of whether the idea makes business sense. If you're testing the viability of an employee's idea, you'll find it will take about a half hour to hour to work through the calculations and debrief on your conclusions and any next steps they may need to take on the project. The following steps will help you in determining the business viability of your project:

1. *Define what your product is.* What problem, need, or want does it address? How does it address it? Describe who the average customer of the product is. What do the customers have in common? That is, what characteristics do the customers share? If you could provide a profile of the average customer, what would it be?
2. *Determine how many of these customers are in your reachable market.* Your reachable market is the target market you can reasonably market to and service. For a small company, this might be a particular side of town, whereas for a large corporation it could be a particular part of the world. For example, the local Pita Pit in Muncie, Indiana, considers its reachable market to be local customers who are health conscious and active adults north of the river that runs through town. Roche Applied Sciences, a worldwide manufacturer of medical products, is located in the same part of Indiana as the Pita Pit, but considers its local market to be life scientists in government, private, and university labs in North America. Some companies such as ExxonMobil may even consider the whole world to have reachable customers for its products.
3. *Once you've determined how many potential customers are in your reachable market, calculate how many of these customers you think you can reasonably convince to buy your product.* This is just an estimation. You'll do more thorough market research when you write your plan. There may be different ways you're going

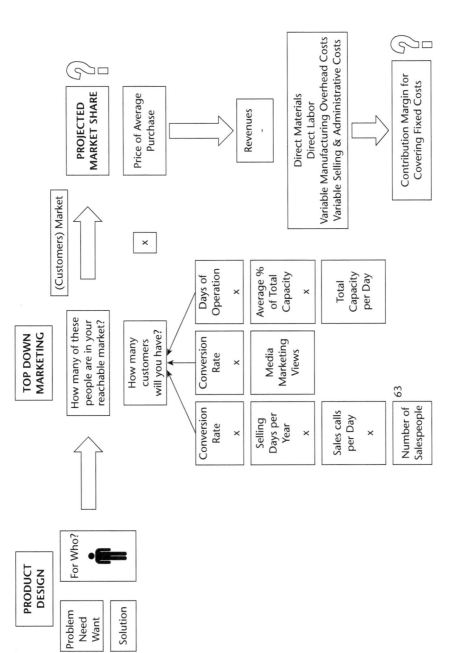

FIGURE 6.1 Business Viability Calculations.

63

to try to reach the customer. For example, if you use a sales force, how many salespeople can you devote to selling the product? How many sales calls can they make in an average day? How many days per year will they try selling the product? Multiply the number of salespeople by the sales calls per day by the number of days the sales force will talk to customers. Now multiply that number by the percentage of sales calls that you reasonably think you can convert into a sale. This is just an educated guess based on past experience, so don't stress over the exactness of your number. If you're using television, newspaper, radio, or internet marketing, estimate how many of your potential customers see the advertisements and multiply that number by the percentage of people you think will go ahead and make a purchase of your product. If you're offering a service, you can calculate this figure based on how much you can deliver of it. This is your total capacity. Then estimate the average percentage of total capacity you'll have on an average day. Multiply the total capacity by the average percentage of total capacity by the number of days you can offer the service during the year. For example, a new computer software support service may consist of three people who can potentially make five visits to clients per day. If we assume that they only get two calls per day for the service and that they work 200 days per year, we can estimate that they'll have 400 visits per year. There may be some considerations regarding customers being reached by multiple marketing channels or having service contracts that need to be taken into account in your calculation. Take those adjustments into account, and perform the calculations without getting too hung up on small details. The key is to get a general idea of *business viability* in this exercise.

4. *Divide the number of customers you think you can attain by the estimated number of target customers in your reachable market.* This is your *projected market share*, and is a good first check on the business viability of your idea. Is the market share large enough to make the business worthwhile? If not, will you need to hire more salespeople to sell the product? Will you have to use more advertising? Would you reasonably be able to do this? These are just a few of the insights you can gain by considering how much of the market you can attain with your idea.

5. *After you've estimated your market share, you can examine the economic logic of your idea.* What price will you charge for the product? Multiply the price by the number of customers you project for the product. If you think some customers will be repeat customers, make the appropriate adjustment to your calculation. This total gives you your *projected revenues* for the product.

6. *Estimate the cost of goods sold for your product.* What will *materials* cost for the product? How much will it cost for *labor* used in making the product? What are the *variable manufacturing overhead costs*? These are the additional costs incurred due to the manufacturing of a product, such as electricity. What are the *variable selling and administrative costs* incurred because the product is being manufactured? This may be the most difficult calculation of the business viability process. If you have pretty good knowledge of operations, you can probably make a reasonable estimate for cost of goods sold. If you struggle with this calculation, an engineer, cost accountant, or production manager may be able to provide

good estimates of these figures. However, for a quick calculation, you can make a ball park estimate to get a general idea of the viability of your concept.

7. *Subtract the cost of goods sold from revenues.* The resulting number is the *contribution margin* for covering fixed costs. This figure gives you an idea of how much the product clears internally after covering its manufacturing costs.

If the contribution margin is small, the product may not make sense for the company to pursue. Don't give up though. This information may simply tell you that you need to tweak some of the product and financial variables. For example, what happens to the revenues and gross margin if you raise price? What are the costs of the product if you use a different material? Establishing business viability is akin to trying to solve a Rubik's Cube. Keep working the variables around until something makes business sense. Apply design principles again, iterating and tweaking the technical, marketing, and financial components until you have a viable idea. You should probably continue testing business viability throughout the rest of the prototyping stages as well, but meeting this design constraint early in the prototyping process gets you off to a good start. Once you've developed a rough prototype that appears to be technically feasible and economically viable, it's time to develop a more advanced prototype.

Step 3: Conceptual Prototyping

A conceptual prototype advances the best elements of your previous rough prototype. The rough prototype should have given you a general idea of what the product might end up being, but the conceptual prototype starts to take on more detail of the form, fit, and function of the final design. This does not mean that you have to invest significant amounts of money into prototyping yet. In fact, it doesn't necessarily have to have all the working parts of what you envision the final version being. However, it should start to at least *resemble* what you think it might become. That's why a conceptual prototype is sometimes called a *surface prototype*, because on the surface the observer can get a better idea of what the product will look like. When the Palm Pilot was being developed at Handspring Inc., company co-founder Jeff Hawkins carried a conceptual prototype of it in his shirt pocket for weeks to see how it felt. He whittled the prototype out of wood. The dimensions of the wooden Palm Pilot were very similar to the final version that went to market.[27] Capturing the anticipated look of the product can be further attained by putting together a more realistic version of the prototype by adding vinyl overlays, paint for the overall appearance, and buttons and accouterments from other products.

Rapid Prototyping Techniques

In centuries past, craftsmen carefully built prototypes using hand tools and machine tools, a process that required much skill and time. However, modern technologies are available today for rapid prototyping (RP), which allow a three-dimensional prototype to be constructed in considerably less time, and without demanding a high level of technical skill. Rapid prototyping typically employs a computer-aided drafting (CAD) program that allows the user to create virtual spheres, rectangular prisms, and other solids. These images are repositioned and scaled, duplicated and arrayed, squashed, twisted, or folded. Sometimes they're joined together or subtracted from one another. The resulting digital object is then saved in a format that can be transferred to a prototyping machine for an actual physical "build."

Rapid prototyping technologies can be classified as either subtractive, where we cut away unwanted material, or additive, where we build a model, typically by stacking up different layers of materials, each a horizontal cross-section. One additive process is laminated object manufacture (LOM), where one layer of a material is placed on top of another; these may be paper or paperboard with glue on one surface, for instance, each piece the exact shape of a horizontal cross-section at a different elevation within the object. This same "slicing" is used for most other additive RP technologies. Stereolithography (SLA refers to StereoLithography Apparatus) is a process where photo-curable plastic resin is drawn from a vat to selectively place a thin layer of the liquid down where it's cured by a laser beam, one layer at a time; this polymerizes and solidifies the part, growing it from the bottom up. Another RP additive technology is fused deposition modeling (FDM), where a spaghetti-like strand of material is heated and extruded onto a platform to build the first layer of a product; a second layer is extruded on the first, and so on until the entire object has been built. Solid object printing (SOP) is a technique where print heads are used to selectively place material. In some instances, we can use a plaster-like powder and have a colored or clear binder agent printed on a thin layer of the powder, on which is wiped the next layer of the powder until the entire part is built. In other instances, we can have the build material itself, sometimes a wax, placed down by the same mechanism seen in some printers. Selective laser sintering (SLS) uses a laser to make certain areas of powder, often plastic or metal powder, stick together. Each of these methods has specific advantages and disadvantages, so you'll want to consult an expert in selecting the one that's best for your project. In general, while the specialized materials are somewhat costly, prices for rapid prototyping machines have dramatically decreased over the last decade.

In addition to 3D additive RP technologies, there are subtractive technologies. Some of these methods are primarily two-dimensional, while others are 3D. Two-dimensional subtractive technologies cut out wanted areas from sheet stock according to digital information. These include lasers, plasma arc cutters, electrical discharge machining, routers, milling machines, water jets, and more. For some systems, a programming language known as G-code is used to tell a computer numerically controlled (CNC) machine to turn on, where to cut, and how fast to cut. In other instances, specialized computer interfaces are used, and some of these are as easy as sending data to a printer. Cutting out parts from a flat sheet is generally a two-axis system. Full movement to cut shapes through all axes is possible on a three-axis system, and it's even possible to have a four-axis system (where it's possible not only to machine along paths for curves generated in the x, y, and z axes, but to add a different motion, such as a turntable, which is considered a different degree of freedom, even though the object really only exists in three-dimensional space), or a five-axis system. Lathes are also used to create parts with circular cross-sections.

CNC machines build prototypes from images captured with computer-assisted design (CAD) programs or machine languages such as G-code. A G-code program may appear intimidating to the untrained eye, but with a little training the fundamentals of the language can be quickly picked up. Although there's a bit of a learning curve to the programs, the technology is becoming increasingly easy to use. There are computer-aided manufacturing (CAM) systems that let you generate a complex G-Code program by starting with a CAD drawing and using the features of that drawing to create tool paths. If you're interested in learning machine languages and running rapid prototyping equipment, visit your local university or community college. Most public institutions of higher education provide courses on how to write milling programs and run machinery. A short programming course that includes 10 hours of lab time and 25 hours of training in a machine shop can make you proficient enough to start building more sophisticated prototypes. You'll need to devote an additional five hours per week at home writing programs to run in the machine shop.

A helpful feature of modern prototyping software is that you can write the program in Microsoft Word and save it to a flash drive that can later be brought to a programming lab. You can then verify that you wrote a good program to build your prototype by testing it in a virtual milling machine on the computer screen. The screen will show a digital version of your part and the tool that will be used to cut out shapes for your prototype. When you activate the program, you'll see how the cutting tool would operate in the real world on your object. The verifying program lets you know if your design will be successful in the machine shop.

Even if you don't learn how to do rapid prototyping yourself, a basic understanding of the process may help you to get a prototype made. Knowing the different processes and machines will enable you to approach the appropriate technology experts who can build your prototype. You'll also have a better idea of the costs and time involved in the process. Still, if you wish to advance your design skills and become more innovative in your company, we encourage you to learn rapid prototyping. As the rapid prototyping technologies become more available and easy to use and as design becomes a more common business practice, managers may use prototyping machines in the future like they do LaserJet printers today. Like any technology movement, the spoils will go to those who adopt the new ways sooner.

The Three Dimensions of a Good Prototype

Now that you have a more refined prototype, you'll be able to receive even better feedback on whether your idea is hitting the mark, and how it might really work. Be open to the feedback and make changes as needed. Even though you're much further along in the design process, it's okay to continue making changes. Use simulations when you can, but also build a prototype at an intermediary phase of your design if it's helpful. The purpose of a prototype is to facilitate learning for improving your idea. As A.G. Lafley, former chairman and CEO of Procter & Gamble, tells his employees:

The essence of prototyping is try and try again, iterate and reiterate. The key is not to seek perfection at any single step, but, through trial and error, to get a little improvement all along the way. Learn; get closer; learn more; get a little closer. And continually build on the insights of the user.[28]

He adds:

Prototyping is the process of finding mistakes, and of adding value, so don't worry about perfection . . . the key is to get the ideas out there in tangible form; the more people are comfortable with this show-and-tell, the more ideas that will be generated, which is the point.[29]

Advanced prototypes are judged by higher expectations of quality. *The three criteria that determine the quality of a prototype are functionality, expressivity, and credibility. Functionality* is met if the product is able to do what the customer expects of it. The product "must be able to function as a useful, effective and also perhaps a desirable object."[30] For example, carabiners are very useful tools for rock climbers to hook their ropes through. They trust that the carabiner will not break if they fall off the side of a mountain. *Expressivity* means that the product looks like what the customer expects it to. It can be original, but it must not be too far away from the norm or else customers may be confused by its appearance. If a customer has to ask, "What is it?" you're probably missing the mark in your design. Regarding the carabiner example, a climber wants to know that their equipment meets traditional standards. With their lives depending on their equipment, they don't want to take a chance on using carabiners that look too experimental or unreliable. *Credibility* means there's a seamless interaction between the product and the customer. When a product is reliable, the customer can get to the point where they use it without thinking. For example, when a skilled climber secures a rope, they want to effortlessly reach for a carabiner off their belt and attach it to a bolt in the side of the rock. Therefore, if a climbing aficionado wanted to design a new carabiner, they would want to take functionality, expressivity, and credibility into account. You'll want to take the same approach as you design your prototype.

Manufacturability

Manufacturability of the product is also worth exploring. The best design is a collaborative process between the designer and manufacturers and technicians who understand the material requirements and production processes needed for manufacturability. Material requirements include: *hardness*, which is the material's resistance to surface penetration (or local plastic deformation); *toughness*, which is the material's ability to absorb energy without breaking; *elasticity*, which is the ability of a material to spring back to its original shape after being subjected to force; *plasticity*, which is the ability to permanently take on a new shape after being subjected to a force; brittleness, which is the likeliness a material will break; *ductility*, which is the ability of a material to bend, stretch, or twist without breaking; *strength*, which is the ability to withstand a force without changing shape or breaking;

tension, which is the pulling force a material can withstand from both ends; *compression*, which is how much a material can withstand pushing or squeezing; *torsion*, which is the degree of twisting the material utilizes; and *shear*, which is the amount of force that splits a material.[31] As you can see, there are many considerations for ensuring that the materials in your product meet your expected standards. Manufacturing considerations include the volume of production that can be undertaken in a batch, material costs, the speed of production, and the manufacturing applications that will be used to build the product.[32] Knowing what materials and manufacturing processes to use will give you a better idea about the costs and requirements that need to be met to build your product.

Step 4: Working Prototype

Now that you have decided what the product will look like and what its function is, it's time to build a working version of it. Depending on the complexity of the product and your experience, you may need to enlist help from engineers and craftsmen to help you develop a working model of your idea. A *corporate sponsor*[33] inside the company might be needed to help you get the expertise and money you require for building your working prototype. Again, the working prototype is probably not the final version of the idea, but it's very close to what will go into production. A working prototype doesn't necessarily have to look like the final version, but it has to successfully demonstrate the principle of the product.[34] Most of the bugs need to be worked out, and it needs to be easy to use.

Building a Working Prototype

Although a working prototype will be more sophisticated than a conceptual prototype, it doesn't have to cost a lot of money to build. *Wired* magazine provided its favorite examples of iconic working prototypes of famous products. They weren't the most polished objects, but they worked. Examples included the Super Soaker squirt gun and the Apple I computer. The Super Soaker was built with an air pump, a series of check valves, PVC pipes, plastic tubing, and a 2-liter soda bottle. The Apple I consisted of a motherboard and keyboard attached to plywood.[35] The concepts hit their mark. The Super Soaker tallied over $200 million in sales, and the Apple I provided the technical foundation for Steve Jobs and Steve Wozniak to revolutionize the computer industry. As these iconic models demonstrate, *the main focus of the working prototype is demonstrating how the product gets the job done.*

You may even find toys in your attic that can be helpful in building prototypes. K'Nex, Legos, and Erector sets are easy-to-use, inexpensive materials that have been used by many inventors and engineers to address design issues. If you've been to the Epcot theme park at Walt Disney World, you've probably seen an example of this practice. Soarin' Around the World is a ride that lifts guests' seats into the air and gives them the sensation of flying by placing them in front of an IMAX-sized screen. Wind blows through their hair and the smell of pine needles wafts through the air to add to the effect. The ride runs at 100 percent capacity from the moment the park opens to the minute it closes. Epcot sometimes even opens a half hour early to allow guests the chance to get in the line early to get a ticket for the ride. What you probably didn't know was that an Erector set is responsible for overcoming its design challenges. While IMAX theatres exist in most major cities, the moviegoer always remains seated on the ground. But not at a Disney park. Walt Disney Imagineering had to devise a way to create the sensation of fly-ing. Imagineer Mark Sumner figured it out. He used an Erector set to design the basic seat and lift mechanism. A cantilever system hoists the guests off the floor and into the air. Guests "ooh" and "ah" as they sail over world landmarks. It's one of Disney's most popular rides, but it never would have been built if Sumner had not pulled out his Erector set and experimented with the ride mechanics.

Machine Principles

A basic understanding of machines may come in handy as you develop proto-types. The Naval Education and Training Program Development Center defines a machine as:

> *any device that helps you to do work. We use machines to transform energy. Another use is to multiply force. Machines may also be used to multiply speed. There are only six simple machines: the lever, block, wheel, axle, inclined plane, screw, and gear. When you're familiar with the principles of these simple machines, you can work on better understanding the operation of complex machines. Complex machines are merely combinations of two or more simple machines.*[36]

A little understanding of technology, machinery, and power can provide you with a toolkit to move an idea further along. Of course, you'll want to work with tech-nical experts, but you'll have a better interaction with them if you understand some basics about machinery.

Presentation Prototyping

After you build a successful working prototype, you may decide to produce a presentation prototype that you can show to potential customers. A presentation prototype is a selling tool that shows what the product will look like and how it will function. It may not be entirely the same as the product sold, but it will be a close facsimile. When Altair Product Design conceived a bus that would revolutionize public transportation, it decided it had to make a believable prototype to convince government officials that the bus was worth purchasing. The company imagined building a bus that would be to public transformation what a Frank Gehry building is to architecture. The company utilized CAD drawings for demonstrating how the innovative hybrid power train system would work inside a novel bus frame. Altair received positive response from a few potential customers, but company chairman James R. Scapa decided that because of the extreme innovativeness of the product, it would need to be experienced firsthand to win more customers over to the new concept. He told his engineering team to "get physical and get physical fast."[37] So instead of going to customers with CAD drawings and 1:10-scale models, Altair built a bus around an inexpensive aluminum bus frame. Transit buses are made out of stainless steel to endure the wear and tear accumulated over an average 20-year life span, but building the demonstration bus out of steel would have been prohibitively costly. Also, by actually building a less costly version of the bus, Altair was able to more easily identify potential structural flaws in the design. Altair would not sell the aluminum bus on the market, but it proved helpful in selling the product concept to venture capitalists and government officials.

Deeper Considerations for Prototyping

If you've gotten to this point in the book, you can see that a structured design process can guide you in systematically developing a unique business concept. You must be open to where the process takes you. This approach may be intimidating at first because it may force you to enter new domains you have little experience with. However, addressing the following considerations will help you get the answers you need for better product development.

Consideration 1: What's Already Out There?

Once you have an idea for a product, you can ask yourself, *"Is my company currently capable of making this happen? What's currently possible for us?"* You'll need to know what you're capable of accomplishing with your company's resources before you move forward. Answering the following questions ensures you're ready to manufacture your product:

Do I have the capability to do this?

Do other people in the company have the capability to help me do this?

Is there intellectual property on the market I have to be aware of?

What are the technological needs of the product?

Will we have to invent technology for the product or use someone else's?

If we need to use someone else's, can we get access to it?

Will we have to license or buy it from another company?

Can we partner with another company somehow with a win/win arrangement?

Is the supply chain accessible for making and delivering this product?

Do we have the knowledge to pull this off?

Do we have to hire people for my project team to make this happen?

Can we contract with someone who has the knowledge we need for this product?

Do we need to acquire another company who has the technology and knowledge we need to make this product?

Do we need to acquire another company to get access to their existing customers?

These are just a few of the questions you might ask yourself as you assess your company's capability to bring the product to market. You can get answers to these questions, but it's going to take a lot of hustle talking to people from many different disciplines and industries. It can be done. You see, rarely do you need to invent a product from scratch. There are people inside and outside your company who you can bring on board, contract with, acquire, or partner with.

And as you do this, you need to focus on how your company can be different and better than your competition. Remember, companies are always making design decisions as to what their product can do, how it can look, how long it will last, and how much it will cost. There are a lot of possibilities for what a product can be, so chances are that your competition has missed things some customers might want.

Let's consider an example of how you might better hone in on your product design. Imagine you're working on an idea for a new audio product for cars. You might seek answers to these questions:

"What audio equipment is already out there?"

"What cars are using this equipment?"

"What are the features of these cars? What's their size? What type of cars?"

"Can all cars use our audio equipment? Or will only certain types of cars have it?"

"What's the age group of the customers who usually buy this equipment?"

"Is this product 'after market' or does it come with the purchase of the car?"

"Is it a Do It Yourself (DIY) product or does a professional have to install it?"

"Is it sold directly to the consumer (B2C) or is it a business to business (B2B) product?"

Consideration 2: How Close Is This Product to Getting to Market?

Okay, so let's say you've gotten answers to a lot of those questions, and you're moving forward with the product. Is everything going to be great now? Probably not, but that's alright. The product may not be perfect, but it will probably be refined once it's on the market. However, you do want to make sure that any glaring problems are addressed before launching. This is where engineers come in.

If possible, to avoid making any catastrophic mistakes, you'll most likely need to bring on board your team, contract with, or seek the advice of the following experts:

1. *Someone with expertise in technical specifications.* Engineers really appreciate looking at diagrams and descriptions that capture what the product is. It's one of the key tools that helps them think through your product.
2. *A marketing specialist* who knows how to bring the product to market.
3. *Financial experts* who understand the economic reality of bringing a product like yours into existence.
4. *A project manager* who can work with the different groups and move the project forward (if you're not given that responsibility by senior management).
5. *A human factors expert* for tweaking the technical specifications to address how a person actually uses the product.

So, how do you find these subject matter experts? Well, it's not easy, and it's this consideration that often separates the serious manager from one that just has a good idea. You'll have to put some miles on your shoes, car, and frequent flyer membership. If they're not inside your company, you'll have to go where these types of experts meet, such as clubs, trade shows, and hangouts like cafes and coffee shops. You want to seek out people with different backgrounds, knowledge, and connections.

Now if you're willing to do this, you'll be surprised how much people will help you. Go-getters are impressed by other go-getters. Just go up to them and start talking to them. People love to share their ideas and advice. Tell them what you need help with. A good way to say this is, *"I need help with X. Do you know anyone who can help me with this?"* And then follow the trail. You'll be amazed at how things come together when you do this.

The following resources can also be helpful in producing an advanced prototype:

1. *MS Visio:* for flowcharts and basic PM processing.
2. *Arduino Chipset:* Arduino can integrate with various platforms and can be expanded as needed. It's limited only by your creativity.
3. *Raspberry Pi:* It's a mini computer that's pocket friendly as well.
4. *WBS:* Work breakdown structure.
5. *US Patents (www.uspto.gov):* You can search for patents here.
6. *Google Scholar Search:* You can search for research about technology and R&D here.
7. *IEEE:* A good source of extensive technology news.

Now that we've covered prototyping, the next step is to manufacture the product. Manufacturing is included as a step in prototyping because it should always be considered in the design process. Keeping the manufacturing end in mind will help you as you design your prototype. The next section will provide an overview of common manufacturing techniques. There are many techniques available, but we'll just cover the most common ones utilized in going from prototype to sellable product.

Step 5: Manufacturing Processes

Manufacturing Preparations

Once the prototype has been approved, it's time to manufacture it. You'll give guidance to production managers and shop operators on what to build. Working drawings are provided to show all the details a particular part must embody so that it can be properly manufactured. Shape, dimensions and sizes, locations of holes and bends, and special details are provided in the drawings. Special instructions on materials and surface finish may be included in a detail drawing as well. Assembly drawings show where the parts go and how they fit together. The picture looks like the object has been photographed a millisecond after exploding. All the parts of the product are separate in the drawing but very close to each other. This depiction of the product allows you to see every part on its own while also having an idea where it fits into the design. If electrical and hydraulic systems are used, schematic drawings may be used as well. It's important that the production line or machine shop have detailed drawings so that they can plan the most efficient production run of the product.[38]

Tooling Up

If your product has a unique shape, tools and equipment may need to be prepared to manufacture the object. This process is called "tooling up." A common practice is to make a mold of the final prototype. Silicone (or sometimes wax) is wrapped around the object to attain its shape. Then, the silicone is pulled away from the object and used to create a mold. Injection molding can now take place as plastic pellets are melted into liquid form and injected into the mold under pressure. Sometimes production of approximately 20 units is run to determine if it looks good to move forward with a full run. With this inexpensive mold, changes can still be made before investing in a full run. If the results look good, a metal mold is typically produced to make a full run of the object. Metal molds are more costly, but also stronger and can hold up for repeatable, long production runs. A strong metal mold can stamp out a large number of products during a milling cycle. Another popular method is known as blow molding, in which plastic is blown into a mold and expanded to match the mold's shape. Hollow containers such as shampoo bottles are commonly made in this fashion. There are many other production techniques, but these two are the most common in machine shops that specialize in designing unique products.[39] For further guidance on manufacturing issues, consult experts in manufacturing technology, production operations, and management science.

Prototyping Commodities, Services, Experiences, and Transformations

This chapter has focused primarily on prototyping products, but the principles of design can also be employed to prototype other economic deliverables. In Chapter 4, we discussed how Pine and Gilmore recognized five economic deliverables: commodities, products, services, experiences, and transformations. In the following section, we discuss how a manager can prototype the other economic offerings. Anything that can be sold can be improved with design.

Commodity Prototyping

Commodities are resources that are obtained from the natural world, and are typically utilized to manufacture products. Commodities are, thus, the ingredients of the products we use every day. Innovation can occur in commodities when companies find new uses for the materials they have. Koch Industries is one of the largest privately owned corporations in the world. The company's main source of revenues comes from using its materials and commodities in new product lines. This type of business may not receive as much press as iPods or Samsung Galaxy smartphones, but it's big business. It's estimated that Koch brings in $100 billion per year. Much of this is due to their innovation. An example of this success is the introduction of three- ply toilet tissue by their Georgia Pacific division. Quilted Northern Ultra Plush toilet tissue was a huge success in its first year, netting $135 million in sales. Ultra Plush was a successful proof of concept for utilizing three-ply tissue paper in a new range of products. As a result, the company invested $500 million to advance the proprietary tissue-making technology into other products.[40]

MBA Polymers, based in Richmond, California, is another company that has prospered by being a materials innovator. Looking for a way to help improve the environment, Mike Biddle built a recycling plant in his two-car garage, selling recycled plastic taken from junked electronics and automobiles. Now MBA Polymers is the world's most advanced recycler of plastics used in durable goods. Biddle is a business owner who started out with little more than a great idea. Designing new technologies and processes to convert junk into useable commodities showed what's possible with grit, creativity, and passion. Biddle says, "If you do something you love and you do something that makes a difference you will attract around you other people who will share your vision, and that is the secret to success."[41] Koch Industries and MBA Polymers demonstrate that design can be applied through a wide range of commodity goods.

Service Prototyping

Service-based businesses provide specific tasks customers want done but don't want to do themselves. Lance A. Bettencourt's advice for true service innovation is to "shift the focus away from the service solution and back to the customer. Rather than asking, 'How are we doing?' a company must ask, '*How is the customer doing?*'"[42] Therefore, good service innovation requires empathy. The service provider must be in tune with the deep, and sometimes unspoken, needs of the customer. Pollster Frank Lutz gives us some insight into what people may want in service innovation. In his book, *What Americans Really Want. . .Really*, he pinpoints five lifestyle attributes that really matter to Americans:

1. *More money:* Lutz found that products and services that help people make money reduces anxiety for women and provides a greater sense of freedom to men. If you can tie your service to showing how there's a financial benefit for using it or how it helps the customer make money, it will be embraced by the average American.

2. *Fewer hassles:* Americans always have a lot of responsibilities and perform many roles and duties. Services that make life easier are embraced.

3. *More time:* People's busy lives are making life more stressful than ever. Lutz said that when people make more money, they're afforded the luxury of being able to pay others to perform annoying duties. Time is then freed up to pursue things that are more satisfying.

4. *More choices:* Consumers like to have choices when they buy something. They also want to customize their purchases. One of the reasons Amazon is so popular is that their customers can buy movies, music, books, and just about anything else wherever and whenever they want. Instead of driving to multiple locations, they can peruse Amazon.com at their convenience, and select the exact offerings they want.

5. *No worries:* This phrase has become increasingly popular in modern conversations. Easing anxiety is important to Americans today. FedEx's slogan, "When it absolutely, positively has to get there overnight" delivers on meeting this want by today's consumer. FedEx customers pay a premium on deliveries for the assurance that a package will reach who it's supposed to when it's supposed to.

Two interesting examples of service design that encapsulate what Bettencourt and Lutz discuss come from two industries that most people would not think of when design is mentioned: banking and fast food.

Bank of America embraced design principles to enhance service at its retail branches. It use experiments to test ideas for improving customer interactions. With 4,500 banking centers in 21 states, it would be very risky to design a whole-scale change in the system without first testing it. In 1999, then CEO Kenneth Lewis oversaw the creation of the Innovation & Development Team. The I&D Team ran many of its experiments by reconfiguring 20 branches in Atlanta. Stefan Thomke reported in the *Harvard Business Review* that:

> *Five branches were redesigned as "express centers," efficient, modernistic buildings where consumers could quickly perform routine transactions such as deposits and withdrawals. Five were turned into "financial centers," spacious, relaxed outlets where customers would have access to the trained staff and advanced technologies required for sophisticated services such as stock trading and portfolio management. The remaining ten branches were configured as "traditional centers," familiar-looking branches that provided conventional banking services, though often supported by new technologies and redesigned processes.*[43]

The company then went through a five-step process to carefully design how the centers would look and work. Once an idea was approved for testing, a prototype

branch at the company's headquarters in Charlotte, North Carolina, was config-
ured whereby team members could design, rehearse, and measure each step of the
experiment. Then when the prototype seemed to work well, it was transferred
to experimental sites. Thomke said the principles of design and prototyping were
utilized extensively in the service innovations:

> *By the time an experiment was rolled out in one of the Atlanta branches, most of
> the kinks had been worked out. The use of the prototype center reflects an important
> tenet of service experiments: Design and production problems should be worked out
> off-line, in a lab setting without customers, before the service delivery is tested in a live
> environment.*[44]

When the new service design worked in its live settings in Atlanta, the innovation
was passed along to the other Bank of America branches across the country.

Another company that often invests in design makeovers is McDonald's. In
Chapter 5, we discussed how Peter Drucker admired Ray Kroc's conversion of a
hamburger stand into a multinational fast food chain. Kroc optimized the burger
business to a point never seen before in the food industry. However, at the end
of the twentieth century, the only innovations that were taking place were on the
menu. The company needed to find a way to grow sales beyond opening new
stores and offering new food. It needed to create a new way of delivering its service.
Enter Denis Weil, VP of Concept and Design for McDonald's. Weil utilized design
principles to overhaul the business. He did it very well. Tim Brown, IDEO's CEO,
paid Weil a strong compliment when he said, "There is a mythology that design is
a glamorous, personality-led activity. Denis really represents that you don't have to
wear a black turtleneck to do it. McDonald's has become one of the few companies
that does design management well." How did the company do it? Similar to Bank of
America's approach, McDonald's built a 250,000-square-foot warehouse in Chicago
that houses its Innovation Center. The facility houses three restaurant facsimiles
where it can test concepts and experiment. Different concepts are incorporated into
the models with target customers interacting with the designs. For example, a mother
and son may try to operate a self-order kiosk instead of talking to a person at the
counter. Ideas that receive enthusiastic response from customers are brought to stores
in the real world. Former McDonald's president Don Thompson said the company
embraced design to revolutionize the fast food industry because, "If you have a
restaurant that is appealing, contemporary, and relevant, the food tastes better." To
this end, the company is using design to transform the restaurants into a new format.
Weil describes the new restaurant concept as "a community center. The restaurant in
Oak Brook, for example, has been divided into four seating zones, each designed for
a different activity—chilling out, working, casual dining, and group events."[45] The
new service design has required the company to construct new buildings with chic
looks. But customers in the drive-through haven't been forgotten about during the
design process. Using insights about queuing behavior and information technology,
new design in drive-throughs has created a more convenient and fast service. Double
customer lanes help process more cars. Many McDonald's stores now utilize automatic

salutations and take orders at call centers in India. Automated soda machines make the drinks. Drive-through attendants are freed from the tasks of taking orders and making drinks, and can focus more on customer service. This innovation might appear to have a minimal impact on performance. However, the redesigned drive-through approach has helped McDonald's to become friendlier and more efficient, two key drivers of customer satisfaction in the fast food industry. McDonald's is an excellent example of how any service can be improved by understanding and applying the principles of design.

Experience Prototyping

Experiences are memorable encounters a company provides to its customers. Perhaps the best company at prototyping experiences is the Walt Disney Company. As we've discussed previously, Walt Disney Imagineering is an amazing corporate unit that dreams up the most original and fun experiences in the theme park industry. They do this through a time-tested design process, in which they're given a general project to work on with the executive team. For example, after the company had garnered tremendous success with its Typhoon Lagoon water park at Walt Disney World, it decided to open a second location at the Orlando site. The Imagineers were given the challenge of designing a water park that was different from its predecessor. They let their minds run free and drew many concepts, but none of them caught fire inside the company. Then one day Eric Jacobson looked at the snow globe collection in his office, picked one up, and said, "Too bad we can't make a park out of one of these." Another Imagineer said, "Why not?" and the team began to tinker with the idea of a snowy ski resort in Orlando, Florida. The concept of Blizzard Beach Water Adventure Park was born.[46]

Kevin Lansberry, Executive Vice President and Chief Financial Officer of Walt Disney Parks and Resorts, was in the concept pitch meetings for Blizzard Beach and said:

> You get this concept shown to you for a snow themed water park in the middle of Florida, and it seems crazy. But then you think about their track record and the many great experiences that the parks have, and you give them the go ahead to take it a little further. The leadership team provides feedback and the Imagineering team advances the design and builds models of the concepts. The concept helps set the feel and backstory for the attractions. Every Disney attraction, restaurant, and hotel has a backstory that provides a reason for why the attraction is there, and the aesthetic details and cast member attire and behavior inside that park are kept consistent with that theme.[47]

Models built by the Imagineers give the executive team a better understanding of what the attraction can be. The executive team then determines the project's estimated costs and timeline, which are then given back to the Imagineers as their design constraints. Typically, a "give and take" on the concept and costs takes place between the two groups.[48] Many adjustments are made to the models during the development stage, but eventually the Imagineers are given the "go-ahead" to move further in the design process. Once a conceptual model is approved, working prototypes of new ride technologies are developed and tested. All the bugs need to be worked out of a design before a ride is built. When everything seems to work and the Imagineers have gained proof of concept, the actual construction takes place. Imagineers often leverage past successes when possible, using concepts and technologies from past rides as proofs of concept to develop more thrilling attractions in other parks. For example, the widely popular ride Test Track at Epcot places the guest in a sportscar that undergoes various road tests. The apex of the experience is when the car leaves the ride building and hits a test track where it whips around turns and hits a top speed of 60 miles per hour down a long straightaway. During this stage of the ride, the car is actually travelling over the Epcot business headquarters and parking lot, but the guests don't seem to mind because they're flying down a track screaming at the top of their lungs. As a proven concept, Disney used the same ride format to build Radiator Springs Racers, an attraction in Cars Land at Disney California Adventure in Anaheim. Radiator Springs Racers utilizes the Test Track technology, but instead of racing over a parking lot, the ride takes guests through a re-creation of the southwest landscape found in the movie *Cars*. It's a themed masterpiece designed with the best storytelling, ride engineering, and set construction in the industry.

Another technique Disney uses to prototype experiences is 3D animation. By creating a virtual world based on the experience they want to put the guest in, they can experiment with different layouts and have the guest "move" through the animated environment. The virtual reality technology has become so advanced that many programs adhere to the laws of physics and show what happens if different weather conditions or activities take place in the built environment. Imagineers can manipulate the layout at will to test guest reactions to the designs. While Disney's technology is state of the art, basic 3D software is not costly for the rest of us. The more advanced programs may require machine language knowledge and animation training to operate for full effect, but most of this technology is now available for any company to use.

Transformation Prototyping

Transformations are experiences that help customers realize their aspirations and dreams. In a transformation, the customer is the product. One significant area of society that's focused on transformation is religion, and one of its most successful practitioners is Rick Warren. Rick Warren runs a very successful ministry because he used the principles of design and innovation to build his following. When he was in seminary, he attended a conference conducted by the popular but controversial pastor Robert Schuller. Schuller was an innovator himself. When most churches were competing among themselves for members, Schuller targeted non-church-goers as his audience. He developed messages that were appealing and delivered his sermons at a rented drive-in theatre. Schuller would stand atop the concession stand on Sunday mornings and deliver sermons to the congregation who were sitting in their cars and listening over the window-mounted speakers. He designed church services to be relaxing, easy to attend, and comfortable. It worked, and his popularity grew. In 1977, when his congregation reached 10,000, he built a $16 million mirrored glass and steel church called the Crystal Cathedral. To keep with his church's traditions, the walls were designed so that people could still choose to sit in their cars and see the sermon from the parking lot if they wanted. Schuller enjoyed immense popularity over the ensuing decades.

Impressed by Schuller's methods, Warren took a similar approach after he graduated seminary to build his own church. He studied the US Census along with other demographic data, and saw that Orange County, California, was the fastest-growing area of the United States at that time. And the fastest-growing part of Orange County was Saddleback Valley. He knew that this was where he should build his church. The Southern Baptist home office granted him the right to build his church there, and he began to plan how he would make it successful. Following Schuller's approach, he targeted non-church-goers to be his congregation. To better understand the local market, he went from door to door surveying residents in the area. He first asked if they went to church. If they said "yes," he moved onto the next house. But if someone said "no," he asked them "why not?" He then asked the person what they didn't like about church and what an ideal church would be like that would draw them in. After amassing a good database of customer information, he sifted through the data to recognize trends and profiles. He then crafted sermons and practices that would appeal to this target market. But before he opened the church, he prototyped the sermons by giving rehearsal services at a local high school. Warren mailed 15,000 letters inviting people from his database to the rehearsal. Sixty people showed up, and the service was a success. With positive feedback, Warren used the basic approach from that prototype to serve as his road map as he built the church. It worked. Today Saddleback Church has 20,000 members.[49]

While you may not have plans to lead a 20,000-member church, your business may be involved in having a substantial impact on people's lives. Prototyping your deliverables is a good practice to use. For example, if you run an executive coaching firm and have new instruments for assessing different leadership traits, ask some of your colleagues or clients if they would take the survey and give you feedback. When the survey is receiving enthusiastic comments and giving people valuable insights, start to include it as part of your paid practice. If part of your job is to give public talks and promote ideas, offer to give a free talk to a small group outside of your traditional venues. This is what standup comedians do to hone their acts. In the book *Talent is Overrated*, Geoff Colvin chronicles how Chris Rock works on a new act in small comedy clubs for months before he performs it in front of a large audience or on television.[50] Rock's flawless delivery on the big stage comes from ongoing practice and refinement in the small clubs spread across the country. If you're in the transformation business, you can take the same approach to your written materials, workshops, and talks.

Twenty-First-Century Innovation: The Emergence of the DIY Movement

In 1977, Ken Olsen, computer pioneer and founder of Digital Equipment Corporation, said to an audience at the World Future Society that, "There is no reason for any individual to have a computer in his house."[51] At that time, the dominant design in the industry was the large mainframe computer, which was used only by large organizations like the military and Fortune 500 companies. However, in areas like Cupertino, California, where a large number of engineers and technologists lived, an underground movement was taking place. Electrical hobbyists, including Apple founders Steve Jobs and Steve Wozniak, were building and selling computer kits. The kits were very basic, and required the customer to add their own case, keyboard, and video display, but with a little handiwork the setup worked. It was the start of the computer revolution. As more people bought computers for personal use, entrepreneurs began to enter the market offering better hardware and software. Many of the hobbyists who had bought the first kits rode the wave of growth to start computer-related companies of their own.

The 1970s and 1980s were a digital renaissance. More powerful computers needed advanced chips and circuitry, which in turn allowed programmers to create more advanced software. Prices were affordable enough that families and small businesses could buy a personal computer for their desks. And more importantly, customers didn't have to be expert programmers to operate the machines. The diffusion of computer technology into everyday life and business operations transformed society. The computer revolution was complete. Today nearly anyone who wants a computer has one, and prosperity has increased around the world.

Started during an era of stagflation and cynicism, the digital movement brought us out of the 1970s analog world and into a new one where people all over the world could communicate with each other, children could learn their ABCs playing games, and businesses could track their financial performance with spreadsheets. It's hard to find an area of life where computers are absent today.[52]

To many people, the early part of the twenty-first century is reminiscent of the 1970s. There has been much economic unrest. Trust in politicians is at an all-time low. Financial scandals and mismanagement have decimated the investment fabric of commerce. Banks have tightened up credit. It's no wonder so many people are pessimistic about the future. But are there any technological movements under way that might bring the same wave of innovation and entrepreneurial rejuvenation that computers did 30 years ago? We believe there is. Green technology is one field that's receiving increasing attention by government, corporations, and citizens. Innovations in new materials, manufacturing processes, and business models will support the formation of new companies and jobs in green industries. The green revolution is still in its infancy, but every industry that has transformed society has gone through the same growing pains. By all indications, the green movement will become an everyday reality in our lives, like computers are now. But there's another technical revolution taking place in garages and workshops around the world that's not receiving as much coverage: the DIY movement.

DIY stands for "do it yourself," and it's increasingly becoming an ethic that is filtering into all areas of life. You can see it on your television set. The Food Network teaches viewers how to prepare four-star meals in their own kitchens. HGTV shows homeowners what materials to buy at their local hardware store, how to tear down a wall, and what they need to do to renovate their bathroom. There is another DIY presence that is growing in popularity on television too: garage laboratories and workshops. Evidenced in such shows as *Mythbusters*, *Robot Wars*, *Everyday Edisons*, *American Chopper*, and *Monster Garage*, people of all ages are starting to take interest in using their hands for purposes other than tapping on a keyboard. They're getting them dirty again, working with machines, cars, and, most recently, manufacturing. You might respond to this trend with a bit of a surprise. Manufacturing? In a garage? Isn't manufacturing only done by large companies that have the money to buy millions of dollars of equipment and organize $100,000 production runs? Within the point of the view of the industrial economy, the answer would be yes. But within the point of the view of the emerging creative economy, the answer is no.

A revolution is taking place in DIY manufacturing similar to the one that took place in the 1970s with computers. Before desktop publishing, only newspapers, advertising agencies, and book companies provided printed materials. Most people didn't have the equipment or expertise to design layouts and produce high-quality print products. Personal computers, publishing software, and printers changed all that by turning every desk into its own printing press. A new movement is now under way in garages across the country that could be called "desktop manufacturing."

Desktop manufacturing enables you take an idea and, with a moderate investment in machinery, prototype a fairly sophisticated model in your home or office. With free open-source design programs such as Blender and SketchUp, home-based and office-based designers can transmit their ideas to 3D printers to be built. 3D printers are mini CNC rapid prototyping machines that allow you to make models of products you have in mind. The machines operate on the same model as the CNC devices described earlier in this chapter, but on a much smaller scale. It's called 3D printing because it's similar in concept to a laser printer. Whereas a laser printer prints on paper, a 3D printer lays down warm layers of acrylonitrile butadiene styrene (ABS) plastic that harden as it cools. ABS has the same texture and strength as a LEGO block. In effect, the mini CNC machine prints your prototype.

Companies such as MakerBot Industries are manufacturing DIY rapid prototyping kits that hobbyists can buy through the mail and assemble at home for less than $1,000. The kits are fairly easy to put together, requiring only minor soldering on non-critical parts in the machine. The parts are even labeled and step-by-step instructions are provided for constructing the 3D printer. However, most of today's mini CNC machines are already built for purchase. Once the machine is set up for operation, you can send designs to it. Sample designs can also be downloaded from open-source websites, which can be used to test the performance of the 3D printer as well as for making interesting objects for personal use. The first MakerBot machine was called the Cupcake CNC because the machine was fairly small compared with its industrial cousins. The machine gained a lot of interest among hobbyists and amateur designers because, with a little practice on the 3D printers, anyone could learn to prototype products. Skills learned on the home-based 3D printers are transferrable to the larger versions found inside industrial shops and larger design firms.

If there was ever a time to learn how to design and prototype, it's today. Companies are embracing design, and prototyping technologies are becoming easier to use, less expensive, and more available. If you have an interest in design and innovation, take classes, study online, or build your own workshop in your garage. You'll bring a skill set to your company that will be much appreciated. It won't be long before desktop manufacturing will be available to every garage. First movers in this technology may be rewarded with riding a wave of opportunity and prosperity like computer aficionados did in the 1970s. As home prototyping machines get cheaper, bigger, and more powerful, we expect the personal manufacturing movement to accelerate.

The computer industry provides us good insight into how the DIY revolution may take place. There's a time in an industry when only experts can participate in a field. The economies of scale and the complexity of technology in the industry preclude outsiders. However, when innovators find ways to provide kit models and home versions for the interested hobbyist, a new industry begins to grow. Those who are in the kit stage of an industry have the opportunity to learn how the machinery works at a basic level, and as the underground movement catches steam and a market evolves, more technology becomes available. Innovators ride the wave of technological advancement and become leaders when the movement spreads through society. Apple is still a leading innovator of hardware today, as is Microsoft in software. Garages are where great companies like Harley-Davidson, Hewlett-Packard, and the Walt Disney Company were founded. Will another round of great companies be started in garages in the twenty-first century? Bill Gates thinks so. When the business titan was once asked what he feared most, he said, "I fear someone in a garage who is devising something completely new."[53] Is your company prepared for the next innovation revolution taking place in garages all around the world? Are your executives aware of the design movement going on among everyday people? These are important questions that every firm must address if they're to keep up with the technology trends on the horizon.

Summary

This chapter focused on how to get products made. Technology and engineering were covered to assist the reader with gaining a basic technical literacy. The most common disciplines of engineering were explained. Prototyping was discussed in depth. Five steps for prototyping were given. Guidelines for prototyping commodities, services, experiences, and transformations were also provided. The emergence of the do it yourself (DIY) movement was covered as well. Applying all these design principles and guidelines will foster successful innovation processes. Good design encompasses technical feasibility, economic viability, and consumer desirability. Meeting these three constraints in the design process will also make it easier when you write an innovation plan. The odds of successful innovation go up with good design, and better design leads to more innovative achievement. This combination of skills will become more important as the marketplace becomes increasingly competitive.

Innovation-in-Action

Unleashed Designers Gone Astray

In 2004, LEGO, the company behind the internationally-successful and imagination-driving toy bricks, was struggling. Surprisingly, design, its prime competitive advantage, was at the root of its problems.

The problems began in the late 1990s. Hoping to extend the LEGO brand, executives promoted new product development that went beyond LEGO's traditional field of play and into a field already occupied by many other competitors. In 2002, for example, the company launched the "Galidor" toy line, which featured action figures and a concurrent Saturday morning cartoon. "Galidor" was a bold departure from LEGO's traditional lines, but it was also significantly similar to what competitors were already doing or had already done. In effect, it just was not LEGO.

Even in its core business, LEGO was struggling. For a while, managers had let designers run free with their ideas. Naturally, designers had seized upon that creative freedom, crafting imaginative but complex models and driving the number of individual LEGO components from 7,000 to 12,400 in just seven years. Unfortunately, the adult designers liked the ideas a lot more than kids. As a result, the uninhibited creative freedom resulted in increased supply costs and decreased sales. The "City" line, once a strength that had generated 13 percent of the company's total revenue, accounted for a negligible 3 percent.

Blame was correctly placed at the feet of the managers, not the designers. Managers' assumption that LEGO would thrive by allowing its designers to operate without constraints was incorrect. It turns out designers operate better with constraints than without.

Accordingly, LEGO reinstituted constraints on its designers. LEGO put each individual designer's request for components to a vote among all of its designers, with only the top vote-getters winning approval. LEGO also eliminated more than 5,000 rarely-used pieces. LEGO also required that designers work directly with marketing managers and manufacturing personnel when designing. The marketers brought designers information on the kinds of components kids wanted and the manufacturing personnel brought an understanding regarding feasibility of production.

In the end, LEGO rediscovered its "mojo." And, by 2008, "City" was back on top, accounting for 20 percent of the company's revenue. The company learned that management of innovation was an essential ingredient of success. The company continues to explore ways to remain relevant and impactful in the world. It's now exploring the use of corn and wheat instead of petroleum for manufacturing its toy bricks. Seeking to decrease its carbon footprint, LEGO wants to set not only a good example for the industry, but also to educate children about new sustainable manufacturing in the process. Clearly, the company intends to use its success to help its customers and employees have a better life.

(Adapted from: www.businessweek.com/innovate/content/jul2010/id20100722_781838.htm accessed January 10, 2011, and www.wsj.com/articles/lego-looks-to-plants-as-building-blocks-for-bricks-1489078385 accessed July 20, 2017.)

Key Terms

3D printing

business viability

chemical engineering

civil engineering

commodity design

computer numerical control

conceptual prototype

creative class

creative economy

DIY

drawing

electrical engineering

engineering

experience design

industrial design

industrial engineering

manufacturability

mechanical engineering

model building

presentation prototyping

rapid prototyping

service design

sketches

technical drawing

tooling up

transformation design

working prototype

Discussion Questions

1. Explain the profession of engineering.
2. Explain the different kinds of engineering.
3. What structural shift is taking place in today's economy?
4. What role will design play in this economic shift?
5. What basic approaches do engineers apply to problems?
6. How do engineers think like economists?
7. What is industrial design?
8. What role does drawing play in design?
9. How would you make a model of an idea?
10. What calculations can you perform to get a sense of the business viability of an idea?
11. What is conceptual prototyping?
12. How is rapid prototyping improving the design process?
13. What are the three dimensions of a good prototype?
14. What is the purpose of a working prototype?
15. When would you use a presentation prototype?
16. What does the term "tooling up" mean?
17. What should you consider before manufacturing a product?
18. Why is the DIY movement changing the world?
19. How could embracing the DIY movement help you to become a better designer?
20. How would design skills help your career?
21. How can design help create commodity innovations?
22. How can design help create service innovations?
23. How can design help create experience innovations?
24. How can design help create transformation innovations?
25. What impact do you foresee more widespread design having on the world?

Notes

1 Auletta, Ken. 2009. *Googled: The End of the World As We Know It*, New York: Penguin.
2 www.ted.com/speakers/woody_norris.html.

3 Ridley, Mark. 2010. *The Rational Optimist: How Prosperity Evolves*, New York: HarperCollins.

4 Florida, Richard R. 2002. *The Rise of the Creative Class: And How It's Transforming Work, Leisure, Community and Everyday Life*, New York: Basic Books.

5 Pink, Daniel H. 2005. *A Whole New Mind: Moving from the Information Age to the Conceptual Age*, New York: Riverhead Books.

6 www.usatoday.com/money/economy/2010-09-13-buffett-ballmer-immelt_N.htm.

7 Furnas, C.C. & McCarthy, Joe. 1966. *The Engineer*, New York: Time-Life Books.

8 Ibid.

9 Brockman, Jay. 2009. *Introduction to Engineering: Modeling and Problem Solving*, New York: John Wiley & Sons.

10 Schlender, Brent & Tetzeli, Rick. 2015. *Becoming Steve Jobs: The Evolution of a Reckless Upstart into a Visionary*, New York: Crown Business, p. 36.

11 Oakes, William C. & Leone, Les L. 2003. *Engineering Your Future*, Cottleville, MO: Great Lakes Press.

12 www.bls.gov/oco/ocos027.htm.

13 Wright, Peter. 1987. *Spycatcher: A Candid Autobiography of a Senior Intelligence Officer*, New York: Viking Adult.

14 Roam, Dan. 2013. *The Back of the Napkin (Expanded Edition): Solving Problems and Selling Ideas with Pictures*, New York: Deckle Edge.

15 Baskinger, Mark & Bardel, William. 2013. *Drawing Ideas: A Hand-Drawn Approach for Better Design*, New York: Watson-Guptill.

16 Rohde, Mike. 2012. *The Sketchnote Handbook*, New York: Peachpit Press.

17 Brown, Sunni. 2015. *The Doodle Revolution: Unlock the Power to Think Differently*, New York: Portfolio.

18 Roam, Dan. 2013. *The Back of the Napkin (Expanded Edition): Solving Problems and Selling Ideas with Pictures*, New York: Deckle Edge.

19 Baskinger, Mark & Bardel, William. 2013. *Drawing Ideas: A Hand-Drawn Approach for Better Design*, New York: Watson-Guptill.

20 Rohde, Mike. 2012. *The Sketchnote Handbook*, New York: Peachpit Press.

21 Brown, Sunni. 2015. *The Doodle Revolution: Unlock the Power to Think Differently*, New York: Portfolio.

22 Aspelund, Karl. 2014. *The Design Process*, New York: Fairchild Books.

23 Ibid.

24 Kelley, Tom & Littman, Jonathan. 2005. *The Ten Faces of Innovation: IDEO's Strategies for Beating the Devil's Advocate and Driving Creativity throughout Your Organization*, New York: Random House.

25 Ibid.

26 Sutherland, Martha. 1999. *Model Making: A Basic Guide*, New York: W.W. Norton & Company.

27 Lynn, Gary S. & Reilly, Richard R. 2002. *Blockbusters: The Five Keys to Developing Great New Products*, New York: HarperCollins.

28 Lafley, A.G. & Charan, Ram. 2008. *The Game-Changer: How You Can Drive Revenue and Profit Growth with Innovation*, New York: Random House.

29 Ibid.

30 Rusten, Grete & Bryson, John R. 2010. *Industrial Design, Competition, and Globalization*, Basingstoke: Palgrave Macmillan

31 Rogers, George E., Wright, Michael D. & Yates, Ben. 2010. *Gateway to Engineering*, London: Cengage Learning.

32 Central Saint Martins College of Art & Design. 2007. *Making It*, London: Laurence King Publishing.

33 Also known as a *champion*. And when managers sell their concept to their bosses so they can acquire resources to move their projects forward, they're being entrepreneurial *inside* the organization. Thus, we call managers who take the risk to pursue new ideas for the company (instead of accepting the status quo) *corporate entrepreneurs*. Like other forms of entrepreneurship, the corporate entrepreneur should gain something of importance to them

if the idea is successful. Raises, bonuses, company recognition, industry prestige, promotion, career opportunities, increased autonomy, a nicer office, first class flights, newer equipment, a company car, increased support for future projects, more personnel support, and more interesting assignments are possible rewards for the successful corporate entrepreneur. Successful risk taking should be rewarded if a company wants innovative behavior to continue.

34 Kivenson, Gilbert. 1977. *The Art and Science of Inventing*, New York: Van Nostrand Reinhold Company.
35 Leckart, S. 2010. Original models: a look at iconic tech prototypes. *Wired Magazine*, August: 11.
36 Naval Education and Training Program. 2008. *Basic Machines and How They Work*, www.bnpublishing.net, August, p. 22.
37 Vasilash, G.S. 2010. Developing a better bus. *Time Compression Magazine*, August 26: 12.
38 Brusic, S.A., Fales, J.F. & Kuetemeyer, V.F. 1999. *Technology: Today and Tomorrow*, New York: McGraw-Hill.
39 Rogers, George E., Wright, Michael D. & Yates, Ben. 2010. *Gateway to Engineering*, London: Cengage Learning.
40 www.kochind.com/files/DiscoveryApril2010.pdf.
41 www.bsu.edu/news/article/0,1370,--50891,00.html.
42 Betterncourt, Lance. 2010. *Service Innovation: How to Go from Customer Needs to Breakthrough Services*, New York: McGraw-Hill Companies.
43 Thomke, Stefan. 2003. R&D comes to service. *Harvard Business Review*, 81(4): 70–79.
44 Ibid.
45 Paynter, B. 2010. Super style me. *Fast Company*, October: 106
46 Sklar, Martin. 2010. *Walt Disney: Imagineering*, New York: Disney.
47 Goldsby, Michael G. 2017. Personal interview with Kevin Lansberry, July.
48 This "give and take" is common among the creative and business sides of a company. Some executives call it an internal negotiation process, as the creative team pushes to have more of its vision realized and the business team ensures that the concept fits the company's strategy and boosts its bottom line (more revenue with controlled costs = increased ROI on the project). The process can be adversarial or collaborative depending on the culture and history of the parties inside the company. But as an executive once told us, "Each dollar saved on a project is a dollar that can be used to fund another project. Efficiency and good returns lead to more creative projects for the company."
49 Sheler, Jeffrey L. 2009. *Prophet of Purpose: The Life of Rick Warren*, New York: Random House.
50 Colvin, Geoff. 2008. *Talent Is Overrated: What Really Separates World-Class Performers from Everybody Else*, New York: Penguin.
51 Gatlin, Jonathon. 1999. *Bill Gates: The Path to the Future*, London: Avon Books.
52 Innovation and technology have that effect on societies and economies. A successful product movement brings an influx of new needs and wants to satisfy a growing group of customers. Austrian economist Joseph Schumpeter called this entrepreneurial effect "*creative destruction*," as one set of consumer preferences gets replaced by another in the market.
53 Auletta, Ken. 2009. *Googled: The End of the World As We Know It*, New York: Penguin.

PART 4

Organizational Innovation (*I-Teams*)

7

MEASURING CORPORATE INNOVATION

. . . to be successful, entrepreneurial activity must be carefully integrated into the organization's overall strategies. In doing so, the internal environment of an organization (which can be influenced by managers) must be conducive to the initiation and sustainment of innovation-inducing strategies.

~Donald F. Kuratko, Jeffrey S. Hornsby, and Jeffrey G. Covin[1]

Introduction

The culture of an organization can be defined in several ways. Some of the best definitions of culture include:

- It is made up of the values, beliefs, assumptions, behavioral norms, artifacts, and patterns of behavior.
- It is a social energy that moves members to act.
- It is a unifying theme that provides meaning, direction, and mobilization for organization members.
- It functions as an organizational control mechanism, informally approving or prohibiting behavior.[2]

These definitions also apply to an innovative organizational culture. In order to strongly support a successful innovative strategy, there is the need for a focus on issues such as risk, reward and managerial support. For this reason, we are offering unique tools for assessing entrepreneurial and innovative cultures.

Assessing Innovation in Organizations

The existence of particular methods for assessing innovative culture has many uses. First, they will serve as a baseline for any organizational change efforts. Second, an assessment instrument can help key into problem points. Specifically it can help identify the particular organizational factors that may be serving as barriers to innovative activity. Once key problem areas are identified, change will successfully result in an improved culture.

Finally, an assessment instrument can help involve organizational members in the change process. The identification of employee perceptions is integral to the overall change process. There are numerous ways which could be used to assess a firm's innovative culture, each with its own advantages and disadvantages.

The critical nature of innovation and creativity as an important element of entrepreneurship points to the importance of being able to assess the level of innovative factors which exist in the organization. There are three methods which will be discussed here. For clarification purposes, we are separating them into two focus areas: entrepreneurial readiness and innovative readiness.

> *Entrepreneurial Readiness in Organizations*
>
> The Organizational Metaphor
>
> *Innovative Readiness in Organizations*
>
> Organizational Assessment of Innovation and Creativity
>
> The Corporate Entrepreneurial Assessment Instrument (CEAI)

Entrepreneurial Readiness

Researchers Michael H. Morris, Donald F. Kuratko, and Jeffrey G. Covin compared traditional and entrepreneurial cultures. This comparison suggests that companies with entrepreneurial cultures stress such activities as an immediate exchange of ideas, face-to-face interactions, ideas over hierarchy or status, "hard driving" method of operation, and a joy of discovery.[3] As discussed in Chapter 2, research conducted by the authors suggests five factors that foster an entrepreneurial culture. These factors include management support, autonomy, rewards/reinforcement, allocation of time, and organizational boundaries.[4]

The Organizational Metaphor

The organizational metaphor assesses a firm's entrepreneurial culture in an informal, non-threatening way.[5] Besides serving as an assessment method it also serves as an icebreaker and a way to open creative channels within groups of individuals. A review of the steps described in Table 7.1 shows how participants are asked to take factors of organizational life and translate them into metaphorical images. This allows employees to describe aspects of the firm that are not always positive in a way that is non-threatening and humorous.

TABLE 7.1 Organization Metaphor

Purpose: This exercise evokes a description of your organization from a dynamic living organism perspective.

Goal: To draw an animal that best represents our organization—real or imaginary?

Instructions: In your group. Reach some agreement with answers to the following questions or statements. The answers must be represented on the drawing . . . no words are allowed!

1. What animal (real or imaginary) really depicts the organization today?
2. Describe this animal in detail.
3. Is it male, female, neither, both?
4. Describe its temperament . . . gentle, domestic, wild, unpredictable.
5. What are its feeding habits, living routines, and other habits?
6. Describe its environment, how it succeeds in competition for food.
7. What are its strengths, weaknesses, vulnerabilities?
8. How does it relate to the internal systems which comprise it? Does it use its organs for functions to its advantage or cause harm to it?
9. How would you adapt or change the animal if you had the power to do so and why? (to be explained after the drawing is completed)

Several examples of images generated by previous training teams are presented in Figure 7.1. These are some common themes that are often depicted in these exercises. For example, Figure A shows a two-headed creature. Groups tend to draw this metaphor when employees perceive that their firm is moving in two different directions at the same time. Figure B depicts a creature with many legs and arms (somewhat similar to an octopus). This metaphor usually reflects a feeling that the firm has many uncoordinated activities that distract the organization from its main purpose. Finally, Figure C shows a metaphor where a large lumbering creature (somewhat similar to an elephant) has one leg chained down. This metaphor generally describes a firm that is slow to respond to changes in the environment and often burdened by a long tradition of red tape and bureaucracy.

While certainly not a systematic assessment of the firm, the organizational metaphor does provide an in-depth view of culture from the perspective of the firm as a living environment. The facilitator's role in this process is to provide participants with an open atmosphere where all comments are accepted in the light of friendly intercourse yet sincere concern for the organization. As suggested earlier, it is a way for individuals to be comfortable and open with each other.

The metaphor process also meshes well with the notion of creativity, which is addressed in the training process to be discussed later. Participants usually respond well and the process sets the stage and tone for thinking creatively.

The final benefit of the organizational metaphor is that it primes participants for the more systematic assessment that follows. The metaphor exercise highlights the attributes of the organization that makes up the factors in the survey instrument (the CEAI), which is completed later.

Organizational Metaphors:

A. Two-Headed Horse _____

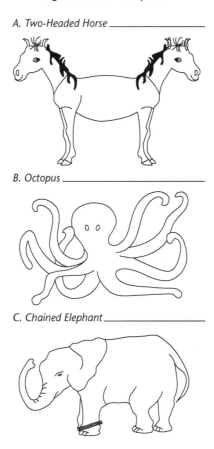

B. Octopus _____

C. Chained Elephant _____

FIGURE 7.1 Organizational Metaphors.

Innovation Readiness

One of the best ways to raise a good discussion about a firm's "innovative readiness" is to fill out the following questionnaire, called the Organizational Assessment of Innovation and Creativity. Just follow the instructions and when you are finished, you will be given further instructions on how to score the questionnaire.

Organizational Assessment of Innovation and Creativity

Instructions: Beside each item, place a number from 1 to 9 indicating the extent to which you disagree or agree with the statement. A score of 1 means strongly disagree and a score of 9 means strongly agree. A score of 5 means you neither disagree nor agree.

In my organization:

Score:

---

1. People take the time to develop creative ideas and new practices.
2. A lot of time is available to spend on innovation.
3. People are rewarded for innovative thinking even if it doesn't result in an immediate payoff.
4. We don't have time to be creative or innovative.
5. People are encouraged to attend seminars, workshops, and conferences outside the organization.
6. There is plenty of opportunity for training on, and application of, creativity and innovation skills and processes.
7. There are opportunities to get resources (money, staff help, work time) to support innovative projects.
8. Employees are encouraged to spend time talking with each other about their creative and innovative ideas.
9. We are encouraged to stay in touch with colleagues in other organizations in order to stay abreast of new developments.
10. Most employees have appropriate freedom and discretion to try new approaches or to improve old ones.
11. People who are more creative and innovative are given more responsibility.
12. People who spend time coming up with new and innovative ideas are seen as wasting valuable time that could be used to get their regular work done.
13. We have so much work to do there is little time to be creative or innovative.
14. People aren't encouraged to use their creativity.
15. While we do a good job of reworking and improving past practices, we don't try many really new things.
16. When suggestions for new and innovative ideas are made, they are usually shot down pretty quickly.
17. Most people believe innovative thinking takes too much time to be worthwhile.
18. People get blamed for being associated with something new that failed.
19. Managers drag their feet on new innovative projects for fear of being associated with a failure and thus limiting their careers.
20. Cross-functional teams routinely work together very effectively, putting the overall goals of the project ahead of their own personal and departmental objectives.

Instructions: Beside each item, place a number from 1 to 9 indicating the extent to which you disagree or agree with the statement. A score of 1 means strongly disagree and a score of 9 means strongly agree. A score of 5 means you neither disagree nor agree.

In my organization, senior management:

Score

1.	Drives innovation and expects everyone to join in.
2.	Sends a clear message that the organization is committed to innovation.
3.	Executes the same innovative behaviors they expect of others.
4.	Has clearly articulated the goals and strategies of the organization to all employees.
5.	Acts on innovative ideas regularly.
6.	Has included clear innovative performance goals in our strategic plan and how we will achieve them.
7.	Welcomes employees' unsolicited ideas on new ways to do things.

In my organization, employees are expected to:

Score

1.	Get their routine work done first and foremost, always before pursuing new developments.
2.	Bring their new and innovative ideas forward.
3.	Try new ways for solving problems.
4.	Share their ideas with others so they can be developed further.
5.	Leave creative and innovative thinking to those who are hired for it.
6.	Follow closely the work policies and procedures laid out for them and not stray from them.

Scoring Instructions

There are certain items in the questionnaire whose scores must be reversed. These are the following:

In the first section, called "In my organization," the scores for statements 4, 12, 13, 14, 15, 16, 17, 18, and 19 must be reversed. For example, if you gave statement 4 (we don't have time to be creative or innovative), a score of "2", you must reverse this to become a score of "8". If you scored it "6", you must reverse it to a score of "4".

In the second section, entitled "In my organization, senior management:" none of the seven items are reversed.

In the third section, entitled "In my organization, employees are expected to:" the scores for statements 5 and 6 (leave creative and innovative thinking to those who are hired for it, follow closely the work policies and procedures laid out for them and not stray from them) must be reversed prior to totaling.

Once you have made these reversals, simply add up the scores to create a grand total of the three sections.

How to Interpret the Scores

The highest possible overall score combining the three sections is 297. The lowest possible overall score is 33. If you scored your organization 200 or higher, you probably have a very entrepreneurial culture. If you scored 99 or lower, you probably have a culture that discourages entrepreneurship. If your score is somewhere between 100 and 199, your entrepreneurial culture is somewhere between very strong and very weak, with room for improvement.

How to Benefit from this Questionnaire

The way to achieve maximum benefit from this questionnaire is to discuss your scores with others in your organization. See if your perceptions are similar to or different from others. Discuss the strong points of your culture, and the weak points. Create suggestions for improving on the weak points and building on the strong points to create a stronger entrepreneurial culture in your organization.

Corporate Entrepreneurial Assessment Instrument (CEAI)

Another assessment instrument that has been proven successful among researchers is the Corporate Entrepreneurial Assessment Instrument (CEAI) developed by Donald F. Kuratko at Indiana University and Jeffrey S. Hornsby at the University of Missouri-Kansas City. It is one of the few research-based surveys that attempts to measure the innovative readiness within an organization. While the instrument has been through a number of iterations since its first publication,[6] the development of the survey items are extensively based on the research and writings to date.[7] The remainder of this section will provide a summary of the literature used to support item development; describe how the instrument was empirically derived; and outline the steps necessary to utilize the instrument for assessing innovative culture within an organization.

Research on Organizational Elements for Innovation

Research has examined the organizational elements that affect (either by promoting or impeding) the breadth and depth of entrepreneurial (innovative) actions that are taken within the firm at a point in time to pursue CE.[8] This research has studied different internal organizational factors including the firm's incentive and control systems,[9] organizational structure,[10] and managerial support.[11] Because they affect the nature of the firm's internal environment, these factors, both individually and in combination, are recognized as internal elements of the innovative behavior on which corporate innovation is built. An internal environment supportive of innovation tends to have strong elements of innovative behavior, while an environment that dismisses innovation and its importance yields weak elements of innovative behavior.[12]

Other research has contributed to our understanding of the organizational elements of innovative behavior. Researcher Danny Miller,[13] for example, correlated several macro-level variables (e.g., company type, environment, structure and decision-making) with the intensity of entrepreneurial activity. James Brian Quinn[14] identified several actions large corporations can take to develop the right "atmosphere" for entrepreneurial behavior to flourish. Some of these actions are oriented to changing the firm's structure in ways that will facilitate innovation. Another researcher[15] found a positive relationship between six management practices and performance for 100 new ventures in 17 organizations. There have been several factors that were associated with successful corporate innovation.[16] In addition, essential structural practices that firms need to use to facilitate entrepreneurial (innovative) actions have been identified.[17]

As mentioned earlier, it has been argued that corporate innovation (entrepreneurship) can take two primary forms—autonomous strategic behavior and induced strategic behavior. As an organizational antecedent, induced strategic behavior is a top–down process in which the firm's current strategy and structure shape the entrepreneurial actions taken to develop product, process, and administrative innovations. Autonomous strategic behavior is a bottom–up process in which product champions pursue new ideas, often through a political process, by means of which they develop and coordinate activities associated with an innovation until it achieves success. A top-level managerial decision to encourage risk taking and not to punish failure is a strong antecedent of autonomous strategic behavior on the part of managers' behavior as well as others in the firm. An important contribution of this work[18] is the recognition of the effect of the firm's culture, strategy, and structure as antecedents of autonomous strategic behavior—behavior that is grounded in innovative actions. Other research[19] has recognized the importance of managers in enhancing and cultivating autonomous strategic behavior. Thus, top-level managers should verify that organizational antecedents are in place that will elicit and support value-creating entrepreneurial behavior (in the form of autonomous strategic behavior) on the part of managers. See Table 7.2 for a compilation of the research that fostered the key elements.

While the literature illustrates a wide variety of entrepreneurial factors, there are a few elements that are consistent throughout the writings in this field. One is the appropriate use of rewards. Theorists stress that any reward system, in order to be effective, must consider goals, feedback, emphasis on individual responsibility, and rewards based on results. A second element is management support, which relates to willingness of managers to facilitate innovative projects. Resources (which include time) and their availability are a third element recognized in many of the writings. Employees must perceive the availability of resources for innovative activities. A fourth consistent element is organizational structure, which is identified in various ways yet always appears as an essential factor. Finally, risk taking appears as a consistent element in that employees and management must have a willingness to take a risk and have a tolerance for failure should it occur.

Much of our understanding of the impact of organizational architecture on individual-level innovative behavior is based on the empirical research of researcher

TABLE 7.2 Compilation of the research that fostered each of the key elements

Factor	Research Citations[20]
Rewards/ Reinforcement	Kanter, 1985; Sathe, 1985; Block & Ornati, 1987; Fry, 1987; Sykes, 1992; Barringer & Milkovich, 1998; and Kuratko, Ireland, & Hornsby, 2001; Kuratko, Hornsby, Goldsby, 2004; Ireland, Kuratko, Morris, 2006a, 2006b; Hornsby, Kuratko, Shepherd & Bott, 2009.
Top Management Support	Quinn, 1985; Hisrich & Peters, 1986; MacMillan, Block, & Narasimha, 1986; Sathe, 1989; Sykes & Block, 1989; Stevenson & Jarillo, 1990; Damanpour, 1991; Kuratko, et al., 1993; Pearce, Kramer, & Robbins, 1997; Antoncic & Hisrich, 2001; and Kuratko, et al., 2001; Kuratko, Ireland, Covin & Hornsby, 2005; Hornsby, Kuratko, Shepherd & Bott, 2009; Ireland, Covin Kuratko, 2009.
Resources/Time Availability	Kanter, 1985; Sathe, 1985; Burgelman & Sayles, 1986; Hisrich & Peters, 1986; Sykes, 1986; Sykes & Block, 1989; Damanpour, 1991; Stopford and Baden-Fuller, 1994; Slevin & Covin, 1997; Kuratko, Hornsby & Goldsby, 2007; Hornsby, Kuratko, Shepherd & Bott, 2009; Ireland, Covin, Kuratko, 2009.
Organizational Boundaries	Hisrich & Peters, 1986; Schuler, 1986; Sykes & Block, 1989; Guth & Ginsberg, 1990; Covin & Slevin, 1991; Damanpour, 1991; Zahra, 1991; Brazeal, 1993; Hornsby, et al., 1993; Hornsby, et al., 1999; Antoncic & Hisrich, 2001; Hornsby, et al., 2002; Hornsby, Kuratko, Shepherd & Bott, 2009.
Work Discretion (Autonomy)	Burgelman, 1983, 1984; Kanter, 1985; Quinn, 1985; Sathe, 1985; MacMillan, Block & Narasimha, 1986; Ellis & Taylor, 1988; Sathe, 1989; Sykes & Block, 1989; Stopford & Baden-Fuller, 1994; Hornsby, et al., 1999; Hornsby, et al., 2002; Hornsby, Kuratko, Shepherd & Bott, 2009.

Donald F. Kuratko and his colleagues.[21] In the original study, results from factor analysis showed that what had been theoretically argued and hypothesized to be five conceptually distinct factors that would elicit and support innovative behavior on the part of first- and middle-level managers (top management support for CE, reward and resource availability, organizational structure and boundaries, risk taking, and time availability) were actually only three in number. More specifically, based on how items loaded, they concluded that three factors—management support, organizational structure, and reward and resource availability—were important influences on the development of an organizational climate in which innovative behavior on the part of first- and middle-level managers could be expected. Although this study's results did not support the hypothesized five-factor model, the findings established the multidimensionality of antecedents of managers' innovative behavior.[22]

This original work was extended with an empirical study designed to explore the effect of organizational culture on innovative behavior in a sample of Canadian and US firms. In particular, the study wanted to determine if organizational culture creates variance in innovative behavior on the part of Canadian and US managers. The results based on data collected from all levels of management showed no significant differences between Canadian and US managers' perceptions of the importance of five factors—management support, work discretion, rewards/reinforcement, time availability, and organizational boundaries—as antecedents to their innovative behavior.[23] These findings partially validate those reported in the original study and extended the importance of organizational antecedents of managers' innovative behavior into companies based in a second (albeit similar) national culture.

The Corporate Entrepreneurship Assessment Instrument (CEAI) was developed to partially replicate and disentangle previously reported findings.[24] The instrument featured 48 Likert-style questions that were used to assess antecedents of innovative behavior. In this study, only middle-level managers, from both Canada and the United States, were surveyed. Results from factor analyses suggested that there are five stable antecedents of middle-level managers' entrepreneurial behavior. The five antecedents are: (1) *management support* (the willingness of top-level managers to facilitate and promote innovative behavior, including championing of innovative ideas and providing necessary resources); (2) *work discretion/autonomy* (top-level managers' commitment to tolerate failure, provide decision-making latitude and freedom from excessive oversight, and delegate authority and responsibility); (3) *rewards/reinforcement* (development and use of systems that reward based on performance, highlight significant achievements, and encourage pursuit of challenging work); (4) *time availability* (evaluating workloads to assure time to pursue innovations and structuring jobs to support efforts to achieve short- and long-term organizational goals); and (5) *organizational boundaries* (precise explanations of outcomes expected from organizational work and development of mechanisms for evaluating, selecting, and using innovations).

Numerous studies have been conducted by the authors to assess the reliability and validity of the CEAI. Research has established the extent to which these factors are used may be assessed using a reliable[25] and valid[26] measure—the Corporate Entrepreneurship Assessment Instrument (CEAI).

Using the CEAI to Diagnose Innovative Readiness

Completing the Corporate Entrepreneurial Assessment Instrument (CEAI) is an excellent diagnostic tool used to assess, evaluate, and manage the firm's internal work environment in ways that support innovative behavior. When using the CEAI to inventory the firm's current situation regarding innovation, managers identify parts of the firm's structure, control systems, human resource management systems, and culture that inhibit and parts that facilitate entrepreneurial (innovative) behavior as the foundation for successfully implementing a corporate innovation strategy.

The CEAI instrument consists of 48 Likert-style questions. As already mentioned, the instrument has been shown to be psychometrically sound as a viable means for assessing areas requiring attention and improvement in order to reach the goals sought when using a corporate innovative strategy. The instrument can be used to develop a profile of a firm across the dimensions and internal climate variables that we discussed earlier.

When interpreting the results of the CEAI, keep in mind that higher scores on the CEAI factors are related to increased entrepreneurial (innovative) activity. Low scores in an area of the CEAI suggest the need for training and development activities to enhance the firm's readiness for innovative behavior. With this in mind, the application of the instrument in an organization points out problem areas for further attention by upper management. The CEAI is intended for those employees in managerial, professional, and technical positions. While the CEAI could be used for operational workers, most organizations have not given those workers the mandate to act in an innovative manner. The specific steps for using the CEAI are described below.

Step 1: Distributing the survey instrument: Depending on the size of your organization, all managers can be surveyed or a random sampling of managers can be utilized.

Step 2: Individual scoring: In order to provide immediate feedback to the employee regarding their perceptions of the firm's innovative culture, each participant should be allowed to score the survey. Each scale has its own scoring box, where employees can transfer their answers and calculate an average score for each scale. Items 21, 36, 39, 40, and 46 are reverse-scored in order to prevent a response set in the positive direction.

Step 3: Organizational scoring: In order for the firm to assess their overall innovative culture, each participant's scoring sheets should be collected. However, it is extremely important that all information be kept confidential since some of the items are somewhat sensitive regarding the employee's feelings concerning management. The organization's score on each scale is simply calculated by averaging respondent scores. Each employee's scores should be verified before these calculations take place.

Step 4: Interpreting the scores: The highest score possible for any scale is a 5 and the lowest is a 1. Since the scores are based on averaging across employees, it is virtually impossible for the organization to score a perfect 1 or 5 on any scale. In general, the higher the score, the more the organization's culture supports these types of activities.

Step 5: Improving your innovative culture: This step is optional but may help managers take action steps toward improving the firm's innovative (entrepreneurial) culture. Each manager or group of managers could brainstorm and identify one to three suggestions that could improve the organization's scores in problem areas.

CEAI Assessment Instrument

Corporate Entrepreneurship Assessment Instrument

We are interested in learning about how you perceive your workplace and organization. Please read the following items. On the line to the left of each item please indicate how much you agree or disagree with each of the statements. If you strongly agree, write the number

"5." If you strongly disagree, write the number "1." There are no right or wrong answers to these questions, so please be as honest and thoughtful as possible in your responses. All responses will be kept strictly confidential. Thank you for your cooperation.

5 – Strongly Agree   4 – Agree   3 – Not Sure   2 – Disagree   1 – Strongly Disagree

Section 1: Management Support for Corporate Entrepreneurship

_____ 1. My organization is quick to use improved work methods.

_____ 2. My organization is quick to use improved work methods that are developed by workers.

_____ 3. In my organization, developing one's own ideas is encouraged for the improvement of the corporation.

_____ 4. Upper management is aware and very receptive to my ideas and suggestions.

_____ 5. A promotion usually follows from the development of new and innovative ideas.

_____ 6. Those employees who come up with innovative ideas on their own often receive management encouragement for their activities.

_____ 7. The "doers on projects" are allowed to make decisions without going through elaborate justification and approval procedures.

_____ 8. Senior managers encourage innovators to bend rules and rigid procedures in order to keep promising ideas on track.

_____ 9. Many top managers have been known for their experience with the innovation process.

_____ 10. Money is often available to get new project ideas off the ground.

_____ 11. Individuals with successful innovative projects receive additional rewards and compensation beyond the standard reward system for their ideas and efforts.

_____ 12. There are several options within the organization for individuals to get financial support for their innovative projects and ideas.

_____ 13. People are often encouraged to take calculated risks with ideas around here.

_____ 14. Individuals risk takers are often recognized for their willingness to champion new projects, whether eventually successful or not.

_____ 15. The term "risk taker" is considered a positive attribute for people in my work area.

_____ 16. This organization supports many small and experimental projects realizing that some will undoubtedly fail.

_____ 17. An employee with a good idea is often given free time to develop that idea.

_____ 18. There is considerable desire among people in the organization for generating new ideas without regard for crossing departmental or functional boundaries.

_____ 19.   People are encouraged to talk to employees in other departments of this organization.

Section 2: Work Discretion

_____ 20.   I feel that I am my own boss and do not have to double check all of my decisions with someone else.

_____ 21.   Harsh criticism and punishment result from mistakes made on the job.

_____ 22.   This organization provides the chance to be creative and try my own methods of doing the job.

_____ 23.   This organization provides the freedom to use my own judgment.

_____ 24.   This organization provides the chance to do something that makes use of my abilities.

_____ 25.   I have the freedom to decide what I do on my job.

_____ 26.   It is basically my own responsibility to decide how my job gets done.

_____ 27.   I almost always get to decide what I do on my job.

_____ 28.   I have much autonomy on my job and am left on my own to do my own work.

_____ 29.   I seldom have to follow the same work methods or steps for doing my major tasks from day to day.

Section 3: Rewards/Reinforcement

_____ 30.   My manager helps me get my work done by removing obstacles and roadblocks.

_____ 31.   The rewards I receive are dependent upon my work on the job.

_____ 32.   My supervisor will increase my job responsibilities if I am performing well in my job.

_____ 33.   My supervisor will give me special recognition if my work performance is especially good.

_____ 34.   My manager would tell his/her boss if my work was outstanding.

_____ 35.   There is a lot of challenge in my job.

Section 4: Time Availability

_____ 36.   During the past three months, my workload kept me from spending time on developing new ideas.

_____ 37.   I always seem to have plenty of time to get everything done.

_____ 38.   I have just the right amount of time and workload to do everything well.

_____ 39.   My job is structured so that I have very little time to think about wider organizational problems.

_____ 40.   I feel that I am always working with time constraints on my job.

_____ 41.   My co-workers and I always find time for long-term problem-solving.

Section 5: Organizational Boundaries

_____ 42. In the past three months, I have always followed standard operating procedures or practices to do my major tasks.

_____ 43. There are many written rules and procedures that exist for doing my major tasks.

_____ 44. On my job I have do doubt of what is expected of me.

_____ 45. There is little uncertainty in my job.

_____ 46. During the past year, my immediate supervisor discussed my work performance with me frequently.

_____ 47. My job description clearly specifies the standards of performance on which my job is evaluated.

_____ 48. I clearly know what level of work performance is expected from me in terms of amount, quality and timelines of output.

Scoring Scales

Scale 1: Management Support for Entrepreneurship
Statement

1.	1	2	3	4	5	
2.	1	2	3	4	5	
3.	1	2	3	4	5	
4.	1	2	3	4	5	
5.	1	2	3	4	5	
6.	1	2	3	4	5	
7.	1	2	3	4	5	
8.	1	2	3	4	5	
9.	1	2	3	4	5	
10.	1	2	3	4	5	
11.	1	2	3	4	5	
12.	1	2	3	4	5	
13.	1	2	3	4	5	
14.	1	2	3	4	5	
15.	1	2	3	4	5	
16.	1	2	3	4	5	
17.	1	2	3	4	5	Total
18.	1	2	3	4	5	Score
19.	1	2	3	4	5	(Scale 1)
Sub-Totals	+	+	+	+	=	

Scale Score = Total Score (19)

Scoring Scales (continued)

Scale 2: Work Discretion

Statement

20.	1	2	3	4	5	
*21.	5=1	4=2	3	2=4	1=5	
22.	1	2	3	4	5	
23.	1	2	3	4	5	
24.	1	2	3	4	5	
25.	1	2	3	4	5	
26.	1	2	3	4	5	
27.	1	2	3	4	5	Total
28.	1	2	3	4	5	Score
29.	1	2	3	4	5	(Scale 2)
Sub-Totals	+	+	+	+	=	

Scale Score = Total Score (10)

*Item 21 revised scores.

Scale 3: Rewards/Reinforcement

Statement

30.	1	2	3	4	5	
31.	1	2	3	4	5	
32.	1	2	3	4	5	
33.	1	2	3	4	5	Total
34.	1	2	3	4	5	Score
35.	1	2	3	4	5	(Scale 3)
Sub-Totals	+	+	+	+	=	

Scale Score = Total Score (6)

Scale 4: Time Availability

Statement

*36.	5=1	4=2	3	2=4	1=5	
37.	1	2	3	4	5	
38.	1	2	3	4	5	
*39.	5=1	4=2	3	2=4	1=5	Total
*40.	5=1	4=2	3	2=4	1=5	Score
41.	1	2	3	4	5	(Scale 4)
Sub-Totals	+	+	+	+	=	

Scale Score = Total Score (6)

*Items 36, 39, 40 are revised scores

Scoring Scales *(continued)*

Scale 5: Organizational Boundaries
Statement

*42.	5=1	4=2	3	2=4	1=5	
*43.	5=1	4=2	3	2=4	1=5	
*44.	5=1	4=2	3	2=4	1=5	
*45.	5=1	4=2	3	2=4	1=5	
46.	1	2	3	4	5	Total
*47.	5=1	4=2	3	2=4	1=5	Score
*48.	5=1	4=2	3	2=4	1=5	(Scale 5)
Sub-Totals	+	+	+	+	=	
Scale Score = Total Score (7)						

*Items 42, 43, 44, 45, 47, and 48 are revised scores

(*Source*: CEAI is adapted from original work done by D.F. Kuratko, R.M. Montagno, and J.S. Hornsby (1990), "Developing an Entrepreneurial Assessment Instrument for an Effective Corporate Entrepreneurial Environment," *Strategic Management Journal*, 11: 49–58; and J.S. Hornsby, D.F. Kuratko, and S.A. Zahra (2002), "Middle Managers' Perception of the Internal Environment for Corporate Entrepreneurship: Assessing a Measurement Scale," *Journal of Business Venturing*, 17: 49–63.)

Essentially concerned with a firm's "innovative readiness," the CEAI can significantly benefit organizations as managers search for ways to initiate innovation inside the organization. For managers, the CEAI provides an indication of a firm's likelihood of being able to successfully implement an innovation strategy because it indicates how the members of the organization "perceive" the five major elements. Therefore, the CEAI highlights areas of the work environment that should be the focus of ongoing development efforts. Further, the CEAI can be used as an assessment tool for evaluating corporate training needs in entrepreneurship and innovation. Determining these training needs can set the stage for improving managers' skills and increasing their sensitivity to the challenges of prioritizing and supporting corporate innovative activity. Beyond this, the CEAI can be used at different points in time to measure the actual change in perceptions by managers within the organization. Perceptions are critical to the reality that exists in the organization.

The perception of managers at the executive, middle, and operating levels regarding the role of innovation within the firm and what the firm is explicitly doing to reinforce innovative behavior is critical. Managers are most likely to engage in innovative behavior when the organizational antecedents to that behavior are well designed and they are aware of their existence.[27] Individuals assess their innovative capacities in reference to what they perceive to be is a set of organizational resources, opportunities, and obstacles related to innovative activity. Determining that the value of innovative behavior exceeds that of other behaviors leads managers to champion, synthesize, facilitate, and implement.

Managers and employees across a firm are most likely to engage in innovative behavior when the organizational antecedents to that behavior are well designed, widely known, and accepted. Individuals assess their innovative capacities in reference to what they perceive to be is a set of organizational resources, opportunities, and obstacles related to innovative activity. Determining that the value of innovative behavior exceeds that of other organizational behaviors and causes managers and their employees to continuously champion, facilitate, and nurture innovative behavior.

Improving Your Firm's Innovative Readiness

Once the scores of the CEAI have been calculated for the organization as a whole, teams can be formulated to outline suggestions for improvements on each of the dimensions. Teams can use the following template for identifying *one to three* suggestions that could lead to higher scores on the five innovation factors.

1. Management Support for Entrepreneurship

   1. _____
   2. _____
   3. _____

2. Work Discretion

   1. _____
   2. _____
   3. _____

3. Rewards/Reinforcement

   1. _____
   2. _____
   3. _____

4. Time Availability

   1. _____
   2. _____
   3. _____

5. Organizational Boundaries

   1. _____
   2. _____
   3. _____

A full discussion of these suggestions and how they might improve the specific element in the organization is another critical step in establishing employee support for the innovative strategy. It also enhances employees' perceptions of the commitment that management displays towards the effective implementation of innovative actions.

Create an Understanding of Corporate Innovation Processes

Having assessed the degree to which its internal work environment supports innovation and the innovative behavior, the next step in the innovation audit determines the degree to which a corporate innovation strategy and innovative behavior are understood and accepted by the employees. A corporate innovation strategy is successfully implemented only when all affected individuals are committed to it. Of course, commitment to any strategy increases when those involved with and affected by a strategy are fully aware of the outcomes being sought by using that strategy. The readiness of each employee to display innovative behavior should be realistically assessed. Actions to enhance innovative skills of employees should then be set into motion. These commitments and processes help to shape a common vision around the importance of an innovative strategy and the innovative behavior that is critical to its successful use.

Our experience suggests that firms should develop a program with the purpose of helping all parties who will be affected by an innovative strategy to understand the value of the innovative behavior that the firm is requesting of them as the foundation for a successful corporate innovation strategy. To illustrate how this can be accomplished, we outline the elements of this type of training program.

A Corporate Innovation Employee Development Program

1. *Introduction to Corporate Innovation*—A review of managerial and organizational behavior concepts, definitions of corporate innovation and a corporate innovation strategy, examination of the innovation in established companies, and a review of several innovative cases.
2. *Innovative Breakthroughs*—An overview of innovative breakthroughs in the company and in other organizations. Best practices in terms of highly innovative initiatives can be reviewed. This challenges participants to think innovatively and emphasizes the need to take risk and be proactive in order to do so. Importantly, employees must be given a reference point in terms of the types of innovative behaviors that are expected of them.
3. *Creative Thinking*—The process of thinking creatively is foreign to those working in firms that have not attempted to implement an innovative strategy. Misconceptions about thinking creatively should be reviewed and a discussion of the most common creativity inhibitors should be presented and evaluated. After completing a creativity inventory, participants engage in several exercises to facilitate their own creative thinking.
4. *Innovation Development Process*—Participants should generate a set of specific ideas on which they would like to work. Issues of strategic fit can be examined, together with a review of the types of criteria the organization uses to evaluate new concepts. Additionally, participants can identify the resources they will require to complete their projects.
5. *Barriers, Facilitators and Triggers to Innovative Thinking*—Culture factors from the CEAI are reviewed. This is done to discuss the most common barriers to innovative behavior. This effort includes examining a number of aspects of the firm's culture including structural barriers and facilitators. Specific types of internal and external triggers for different forms of innovation can be explored. Participants can complete exercises that will help them deal with barriers in their internal work environment. In addition, video case

histories are shown to describe the innovative behaviors of innovators in companies similar to the participants' firm that have positively contributed to implementing innovative actions. Time in this module might be devoted to strategies for soliciting sponsors and leveraging internal corporate resources. In addition, it is important here to review the firm's structure, control systems and human resource management system to verify that each is oriented to facilitating innovative behavior.

6. *Innovation Planning*—After participants examine several aspects of facilitators and barriers to behaving innovatively in their organization, groups are asked to begin the process of completing an innovation plan. The plan includes setting goals, establishing a work team, assessing current conditions, developing a step-by-step timetable for project completion, and evaluation.

Final Thoughts

Finally, we should note that experience suggests to us that the type of program we are outlining here should be ongoing in nature. As new innovative opportunities surface in a firm's external environment, as the internal work environment changes simply from being used, and as new employees join the organization, it is appropriate for those from whom innovative behavior is expected to work together to find the best ways to proceed to implement a corporate innovation strategy. In this sense, efforts to successfully engage in corporate innovation must themselves be entrepreneurial—changing in response to ever-changing conditions in the firm's internal and external environments.[28]

The innovative audit can be used by firms competing in all types of industries as well as by not-for-profit organizations. In all instances, the audit provides insights to an organization's decision-makers about the three core issues we are describing. These insights are very helpful to firms interested in understanding what can be done to improve their ability to compete in today's complex, rapidly changing competitive environments. In many instances, decision-makers believe that innovation is a path to improved performance.

Summary

Innovation and creativity are important elements of entrepreneurship; however, being able to assess the level of innovative factors which exist in the organization is critical for any sustained activity. There are three methods which we discussed in this chapter. For clarification purposes, we separated them into two focus areas: entrepreneurial readiness and innovative readiness. With the *entrepreneurial readiness in organizations* segment we introduced "the organizational metaphor." Then for the *innovative readiness in organizations* segment we introduced the following two instruments: "Organizational Assessment of Innovation and Creativity" and "the Corporate Entrepreneurial Assessment Instrument (CEAI)." It is through the use of these instruments that an organization can begin to audit the entrepreneurial and innovative readiness of an organization.

Innovation-in-Action

What Executives Say about Measuring Innovation

In a recent McKinsey Global Survey, over 800 senior executives were asked the following questions: which types of innovations their companies pursue; which ones they measure and with what metrics; what goals they have in using metrics; and how satisfied they are with the metrics they choose.

In general, 65 percent of those reporting said that measuring innovation was one of their top three priorities. Companies reporting the highest contribution to growth from their innovation projects were more interested in measuring their innovations and used metrics across the whole innovation process (including inputs, process, and outcomes). They were also more satisfied than others with the ability of such metrics to help their organizations do everything from developing individual performance incentives, improving innovation performance, and communicating with investors. On the other hand, 16 percent of the respondents said that they don't use any metrics to assess innovations.

Among those that do measure innovation, most are satisfied but the findings suggest they aren't effectively using these metrics. Companies are much likelier to rely on metrics for outputs than for inputs, so they aren't assessing the whole process of innovation. Forty-five percent don't track the relationship between spending on innovation and shareholder value. Further, although many companies are satisfied with their use of innovation metrics in general, far fewer are satisfied with specific uses, such as aligning individual performance incentives.

Some Specific Interesting Findings . . .

- Respondents say that their companies use about eight metrics to assess innovations.
- When asked which metric is the single most important among those used, executives focused on a few simple outcome metrics than input metrics or performance metrics, such as time to market or time to breakeven.
- For companies that track the relationship between shareholder value and spending on innovation, the three most important metrics are externally focused and include: revenue growth, customer satisfaction, and the percentage of sales from new products or services.
- For companies where innovation is the most important strategic priority, the top three metrics are: customer satisfaction, the number of ideas in the pipeline, and R&D spending as a percentage of sales.
- While companies typically benchmark their performance in most areas relative to that of their peers, many companies don't do so with innovation metrics.
- Regardless of the combination of innovation metrics respondents use, more than 70 percent of them say they at least somewhat agree that their organizations are satisfied with the usefulness of these metrics

- Just over half of all respondents say their companies are spending about the right amount on innovation and just 7 percent said their companies are spending too much.
- Less than a third of the respondents track the relationship between spending on innovation and shareholder value.

What Successful Companies Do . . .

One group of respondents reported that at least 31 percent of their organic growth comes from innovation. These respondents have a somewhat different approach to using innovation metrics than the other respondents. They tend to measure their innovations as a portfolio and are more likely to pursue and measure all types of innovation with the goal of a balanced portfolio.

- These high-performing organizations use only one more metric than other respondents.
- They are likelier to use metrics across the whole innovation process, such as assessing the number of people actively devoted to innovation, the number of new ideas sourced from outside the organization, and the percentage of innovations that meet their development schedules.
- Like most other respondents, the high-performing ones also track the financial returns from innovation in general and customer satisfaction with specific innovations.
- High-performers are satisfied with their use of metrics across a wide range of activities, including allocating resources, aligning metrics with individual performance incentives, and communicating with investors. According to the survey report, these companies may be more satisfied because they make greater use of metrics that, taken together, assess the whole process of innovation.

(Adapted from: *Assessing Innovation Metrics: McKinsey Global Survey Results*, www.mckinseyquarterly.com/McKinsey_Global_Survey_Results_Assessing_innovation_metrics_2243. Accessed January 20, 2011.)

Key Terms

Corporate Entrepreneurial Assessment Instrument (CEAI)

corporate innovation training program

entrepreneurial readiness

innovative readiness

Organizational Assessment of Innovation and Creativity

organizational metaphor

Discussion Questions

1. Briefly describe what is meant by "culture."
2. What is the concept of assessment of entrepreneurial readiness?
3. What is the organizational metaphor? Describe some of the results.
4. How can innovative readiness in an organization be assessed?
5. Describe the "Organizational Assessment of Innovation and Creativity."
6. How do you interpret the scores from that instrument (in question 5)?
7. What does CEAI represent?
8. Outline the factors that are identified in the CEAI.
9. How would you use the CEAI in your organization? Be specific.
10. What is the overall value of assessing the organization for innovative readiness?

Notes

1 Kuratko, Donald F., Hornsby, Jeffrey S. & Covin, Jeffrey G. 2014. Diagnosing a firm's internal environment for corporate entrepreneurship. *Business Horizons*, 57(1): 37–47.
2 Deal, T. & Kennedy, A. 2000. *Corporate Cultures*, Reading, MA: Perseus Publishing.
3 Morris, Michael H., Kuratko, Donald F. & Covin, Jeffrey G. 2011. *Corporate Entrepreneurship and Innovation*, 3rd ed., Mason, OH: Cengage/SouthWestern Publishers.
4 Ibid.
5 The *Organizational Metaphor* was developed by the authors.
6 Kuratko, D.F., Montagno, R.V. & Hornsby, J.S. 1990. Developing an intrapreneurial assessment instrument for an effective corporate entrepreneurial environment. *Strategic Management Journal*, 11, Summer: 49–58; and Kuratko, D.F., Hornsby, J.S. & Covin, J.G. 2014. Diagnosing a firm's internal environment for corporate entrepreneurship. *Business Horizons*, 57(1): 37–47.
7 Hornsby, J.S., Kuratko, D.F. & Zahra, S.A. 2002. Middle managers' perception of the internal environment for corporate entrepreneurship: assessing a measurement scale. *Journal of Business Venturing*, 17(3): 253–273; and Hornsby, J.S., Kuratko, D.F., Shepherd, D.A. & Bott, J.P. 2009. Managers' corporate entrepreneurial actions: examining perception and position. *Journal of Business Venturing*, 24(3): 236–247.
8 Zahra, S.A. 1991. Predictors and financial outcomes of corporate entrepreneurship: an exploratory study. *Journal of Business Venturing*, 6: 259–285; Zahra, S.A. & Bogner, W.C. 2000. Technology strategy and software new ventures' performance: exploring the moderating effect of the competitive environment. *Journal of Business Venturing*, 15(2): 135–173; and Zahra, S.A. & Covin, J.G. 1995. Contextual influences on the corporate entrepreneurship performance relationship: a longitudinal analysis. *Journal of Business Venturing*, 10: 43–58.
9 Sathe, V. 1985. *Managing an entrepreneurial dilemma: nurturing entrepreneurship and control in large corporations.* Frontiers of Entrepreneurship Research. Wellesley, MA: Babson College: 636–656; Hisrich, R.D. & Peters, M.P. 1986. Establishing a new business venture unit within a firm. *Journal of Business Venturing*, 1: 307–322; Brazeal, D.V. 1993. Organizing for internally developed corporate ventures. *Journal of Business Venturing*, 8: 75–90; and Kanter, R.M. 1985. Supporting innovation and venture development in established companies. *Journal of Business Venturing*, 1: 47–60.
10 Covin, J.G. & Slevin, D.P. 1991. A conceptual model of entrepreneurship as firm behavior. *Entrepreneurship Theory and Practice*, 16(1): 7–25; Dess, G.G., Lumpkin, G.T. & McGee, J.E. 1999. Linking corporate entrepreneurship to strategy, structure, and process: suggested research directions. *Entrepreneurship Theory and Practice*, 23(3): 85–102; and Naman, J. & Slevin, D. 1993. Entrepreneurship and the concept of fit: a model and empirical tests. *Strategic Management Journal*, 14: 137–153.

11 Kuratko, D.F., Hornsby, J.S., Naffziger, D.W. & Montagno, R.V. 1993. Implementing entrepreneurial thinking in established organizations. *SAM Advanced Management Journal*, 58(1): 28–33; and Stevenson, H.H. & Jarillo, J.C. 1990. A paradigm of entrepreneurship: entrepreneurial management. *Strategic Management Journal*, 11(Special Issue): 17–27.

12 Hornsby, J.S., Kuratko, D.F. & Zahra, S.A., 2002. Middle managers' perception of the internal environment for corporate entrepreneurship: assessing a measurement scale. *Journal of Business Venturing*, 17(3): 253–273.

13 Miller, D. 1983. The correlates of entrepreneurship in three types of firms. *Management Science*, 27: 770–791.

14 Quinn, J.B. 1985. Managing innovation: controlled chaos. *Harvard Business Review*, 63(3): 73–84.

15 Souder, W. 1981. Encouraging entrepreneurship in large corporations. *Research Management*, 24(3): 18–22.

16 Fry, A. 1987. The Post-it Note: an intrapreneurial success. *SAM Advanced Management Journal*, 52(3): 4–9; and Kanter, R.M. 1985. Supporting innovation and venture development in established companies. *Journal of Business Venturing*, 1: 47–60.

17 Schuler, R.S. 1986. Fostering and facilitating entrepreneurship in organizations: implications for organization structure and human resource management practices. *Human Resource Management*, 25: 607–629.

18 Burgelman, R.A. 1983a. A process model of internal corporate venturing in the diversified major firm. *Administrative Science Quarterly*, 28: 223–244; Burgelman, R.A. 1983b. Corporate entrepreneurship and strategic management: insights from a process study. *Management Science*, 23: 1349–1363; and Burgelman, R.A. 1984. Designs for corporate entrepreneurship in established firms. *California Management Review*, 26(3): 154–166.

19 Floyd, S.W. & Wooldridge, B. 1990. The strategy process, middle management involvement, and organizational performance. *Strategic Management Journal*, 11: 231–242; Floyd, S.W. & Wooldridge, B. 1992. Middle management involvement in strategy and its association with strategic type. *Strategic Management Journal*, 13: 53–168; and Floyd, S.W. & Wooldridge, B. 1994. Dinosaurs or dynamos? Recognizing middle management's strategic role. *Academy of Management Executive*, 8(4): 47–57.

20 Antonic, B. & Hisrich, R.D. 2001. Intrapreneurship: constructive refinement and cross-cultural validation. *Journal of Business Venturing*, 16: 495–527; Barringer, M.W. & Milkovich, G.T. 1998. A theoretical exploration of the adoption and design of flexible benefit plans: a case of human resource innovation. *Academy of Management Review*, 23: 305–324; Block, Z. & Ornati, O.A. 1987. Compensating corporate venture managers. *Journal of Business Venturing*, 2: 41–51; Brazeal, D.V. 1993. Organizing for internally developed corporate ventures. *Journal of Business Venturing*, 8: 75–90; Burgelman, R.A. 1983a. A process model of internal corporate venturing in the diversified major firm. *Administrative Science Quarterly*, 28: 223–244; Burgelman, R.A. 1983b. Corporate entrepreneurship and strategic management: insights from a process study. *Management Science*, 23: 1349–1363; Burgelman, R. & Sayles, L. 1986. *Inside corporate innovation: strategy, structure, and managerial skills*. New York: The Free Press; Burgelman, R.A. 1984. Designs for corporate entrepreneurship in established firms. *California Management Review*, 26(3): 154–166; Burgelman, R.A. 1994. Fading memories: a process theory of strategic business exit in dynamic environments. *Administrative Science Quarterly*, 39: 24–57; Covin, J.G. & Slevin, D.P. 1991. A conceptual model of entrepreneurship as firm behavior. *Entrepreneurship Theory and Practice*, 16(1): 7–25; Damanpour, F. 1991. Organizational innovation: a meta-analysis of effects of determinant and moderators. *Academy of Management Journal*, 34: 355–390; Ellis, R.J. & Taylor, N.T. 1988. *Success and failure in internal venture strategy: an exploratory study*. Frontiers of Entrepreneurship Research. Wellesley, MA: Babson College; Fry, A. 1987. The Post-it Note: an intrapreneurial success. *SAM Advanced Management Journal*, 52(3): 4–9; Guth, W.D. & Ginsberg A. 1990. Corporate entrepreneurship. *Strategic Management Journal*, 11(Special Issue): 5–15; Hisrich, R.D. & Peters, M.P. 1986. Establishing a new business venture unit within a firm. *Journal of Business Venturing*, 1: 307–322; Hitt, M.A., Ireland, R.D., Camp, S.M. & Sexton, D.L. 2001. Strategic entrepreneurship: entrepreneurial

strategies for wealth creation. *Strategic Management Journal*, 22(Special Issue): 479–491; Hornsby, J.S., Naffziger, D.W., Kuratko, D.F. & Montagno, R.V. 1993. An interactive model of the corporate entrepreneurship process. *Entrepreneurship Theory and Practice*, 17(2): 29–37; Hornsby, J.S., Kuratko, D.F. & Montagno, R.V. 1999. Perception of internal factors for corporate entrepreneurship: a comparison of Canadian and U.S. managers. *Entrepreneurship Theory and Practice*, 24(2): 9–24; Hornsby, J.S., Kuratko, D.F. & Zahra, S.A. 2002. Middle managers' perception of the internal environment for corporate entrepreneurship: assessing a measurement scale. *Journal of Business Venturing*, 17: 49–63; Hornsby, J.S., Kuratko, D.F., Shepherd, D.A. & Bott, J.P. 2009. Managers' corporate entrepreneurial actions: examining perception and position. *Journal of Business Venturing*, 24(3): 236–247; Ireland, R.D., Covin, J.G. & Kuratko, D.F. 2009. Conceptualizing corporate entrepreneurship strategy. *Entrepreneurship Theory and Practice*, 33 (1): 19–46; Ireland, R.D., Kuratko, D.F. & Morris, M.H. 2006a. A health audit for corporate entrepreneurship: innovation at all levels – part I. *Journal of Business Strategy*, 27(1): 10–17; Ireland, R.D., Kuratko, D.F. & Morris, M.H. 2006b. A health audit for corporate entrepreneurship: innovation at all levels – part 2. *Journal of Business Strategy*, 27(2): 21–30; Kanter, R.M. 1985. Supporting innovation and venture development in established companies. *Journal of Business Venturing*, 1: 47–60; Kuratko, D.F., Hornsby, J.S., Naffziger, D.W. & Montagno, R.V. 1993. Implementing entrepreneurial thinking in established organizations. *SAM Advanced Management Journal*, 58(1): 28–33; Kuratko, D.F., Ireland, R.D. & Hornsby, J.S. 2001. Improving firm performance through entrepreneurial actions: Acordia's corporate entrepreneurship strategy. *Academy of Management Executive*, 16(4): 60–71; Kuratko, D.F., Ireland, R.D., Covin, J.G. & Hornsby, J.S. 2005. A model of middle-level managers' entrepreneurial behavior. *Entrepreneurship Theory and Practice*, 29(6): 699–716; Kuratko, D.F., Hornsby, J.S. & Goldsby, M.G. 2004. Sustaining corporate entrepreneurship: a proposed model of perceived implementation/outcome comparisons at the organizational and individual levels. *International Journal of Entrepreneurship and Innovation*, 5(2): 77–89; Kuratko, D.F., Hornsby, J.S. & Goldsby, M.G. 2007. The relationship of stakeholder salience, organizational posture, and entrepreneurial intensity to corporate entrepreneurship. *Journal of Leadership and Organizational Studies*, 13(4): 56–72; MacMillan, I.C, Block, Z. & Narasimha, P.N. Subba. 1986. Corporate venturing: alternatives, obstacles encountered, and experience effects. *Journal of Business Venturing*, 1: 177–191; Pearce, J.A., Kramer, T.R. & Robbins, D.K. 1997. Effects of managers' entrepreneurial behavior on subordinates. *Journal of Business Venturing*, 12: 147–160; Quinn, J.B. 1985. Managing innovation: controlled chaos. *Harvard Business Review*, 63(3): 73–84; Sathe, V. 1989. Fostering entrepreneurship in large diversified firm. *Organizational Dynamics*, 18(1): 20–32; Sathe, V. 1985. *Managing an entrepreneurial dilemma: nurturing entrepreneurship and control in large corporations.* Frontiers of Entrepreneurship Research. Wellesley, MA: Babson College, 636–656; Schuler, R.S. 1986. Fostering and facilitating entrepreneurship in organizations: implications for organization structure and human resource management practices. *Human Resource Management*, 25: 607–629; Slevin, D.P. & Covin, J.G. 1997. Time, growth, complexity, and transitions: entrepreneurial challenges for the future. *Entrepreneurship Theory and Practice*, 22: 43–68; Stevenson, H.H. & Jarillo, J.C. 1990. A paradigm of entrepreneurship: entrepreneurial management. *Strategic Management Journal*, 11 (Special Issue): 17–27; Stopford, J.M. & Baden-Fuller, C.W.F. 1994. Creating corporate entrepreneurship. *Strategic Management Journal*, 15: 521–536; Sykes, H.B. 1992. Incentive compensation for corporate venture personnel. *Journal of Business Venturing*, 7: 253–265; Sykes, H.B. & Block, Z. 1989. Corporate venturing obstacles: sources and solutions. *Journal of Business Venturing*, 4: 159–167; Sykes, H.B. 1986. The anatomy of a corporate venturing program. *Journal of Business Venturing*, 1: 275–293; and Zahra, S.A. 1991. Predictors and financial outcomes of corporate entrepreneurship: an exploratory study. *Journal of Business Venturing*, 6: 259–286.

21 Kuratko, Donald F., Monagno, Ray V., & Hornsby, Jeffrey S., 1990. Developing an intra-preneurial assessment instrument for an effective corporate entrepreneurial environment. *Strategic Management Journal*, 11, Summer: 49–58; Hornsby, J.S., Kuratko, D.F. & Montagno, R.V. 1999. Perception of internal factors for corporate entrepreneurship: a comparison

of Canadian and US managers. *Entrepreneurship Theory and Practice*, 24(2): 9–24; Hornsby, J.S., Kuratko, D.F. & Zahra, S.A. 2002. Middle managers' perception of the internal environment for corporate entrepreneurship: assessing a measurement scale. *Journal of Business Venturing*, 17: 49–63; Kuratko, D.F., Ireland, R.D., Covin, J.G. & Hornsby, J.S. 2005. A model of middle-level managers' entrepreneurial behavior. *Entrepreneurship Theory and Practice*, 29(6), 699–716; and Hornsby, J.S., Kuratko, D.F., Shepherd, D.A. & Bott, J.P. 2009. Managers' corporate entrepreneurial actions: examining perception and position. *Journal of Business Venturing*, 24(3): 236–247.

22 Kuratko, D.F., Monagno, R.V. & Hornsby, J.S., 1990. Developing an intrapreneurial assessment instrument for an effective corporate entrepreneurial environment. *Strategic Management Journal*, 11, Summer: 49–58.

23 Hornsby, J.S., Kuratko, D.F. & Montagno, R.V. 1999. Perception of internal factors for corporate entrepreneurship: a comparison of Canadian and US managers. *Entrepreneurship Theory and Practice*, 24(2): 9–24.

24 Hornsby, J.S., Kuratko, D.F. & Zahra, S.A. 2002. Middle managers' perception of the internal environment for corporate entrepreneurship: assessing a measurement scale. *Journal of Business Venturing*, 17: 49–63; and Kuratko, D.F., Hornsby, J.S. & Covin, J.G. 2014. Diagnosing a firm's internal environment for corporate entrepreneurship. *Business Horizons*, 57(1): 37–47.

25 Rutherford, M.W. & Holt, D.T. 2007. Corporate entrepreneurship: an empirical look at the innovativeness dimension and its antecedents. *Journal of Organizational Change Management*, 20(3): 429–446.

26 Holt, D.T., Rutherford, M.W. & Clohessy, G.R. 2007. Corporate entrepreneurship: an empirical look at individual characteristics, context, and process. *Journal of Leadership and Organizational Studies*, 13(4): 40–54.

27 Morris, Michael H., Kuratko, Donald F. & Covin, Jeffrey G. 2011. *Corporate entrepreneurship and innovation*, 3rd ed., Mason, OH: Cengage/SouthWestern Publishers.

28 Ireland, R.D., Kuratko, D.F. & Morris, M.H. 2006. A health audit for corporate entrepreneurship: innovation at all levels – part 2. *Journal of Business Strategy*, 27(2): 21–30; and Ireland, R.D., Kuratko, D.F. & Morris, M.H. 2006. A health audit for corporate entrepreneurship: innovation at all levels – part 1. *Journal of Business Strategy*, 27(1): 10–17.

8

HUMAN RESOURCE MANAGEMENT IN CORPORATE INNOVATION

Human resources are like natural resources; they're often buried deep. You have to go looking for them; They're not just lying around on the surface.

~Ken Robinson[1]

Introduction

As we have discussed in previous chapters, creative, innovative, and entrepreneurial behaviors are rapidly becoming desired in organizations as they face economic uncertainty, international competition, and technological advances. As Hamel suggests, "In these suddenly sober times, the inescapable imperative for every organization must be to make innovation an all-the-time, everywhere capability."[2] Zahra, Kuratko, and Jennings noted that:

> *Some of the world's best-known companies had to endure a painful transformation to become more entrepreneurial. They had to endure years of reorganization, downsizing, and restructuring. These changes altered the identity or culture of these firms, infusing a new innovative spirit throughout their operations . . . change, innovation, and entrepreneurship became highly regarded words.*[3]

Furthermore, Dess, Lumpkin, and McGee noted that, "Virtually all organizations—new startups, major corporations, and alliances among global partners—are striving to exploit product-market opportunities through innovative and proactive behavior"[4]—the type of behavior that is called for by innovation and entrepreneurship. We have been focused on finding ways to create and facilitate this innovative behavior throughout the chapters of this book. However, what human resource practices play a major role in initiating and sustaining this type of behavior? The goal of this chapter is to discuss the important human resource management (HRM) elements necessary for initiating and sustaining innovative behavior.

In this chapter we will first outline a model of the critical organizational characteristics involved with HRM. Next, each element of the model is discussed. Finally, we present some conclusions about applying the model for increasing desired innovative behaviors.

An Organizational Innovation Characteristics Model

In order for an organization to achieve an innovation ideology, it must focus on the organizational factors that have been successfully linked to increasing innovativeness. The model in Figure 8.1 depicts many of the critical elements for altering the human, structural, and cultural/environmental variables necessary for implementing the innovation required. The model suggests that creating a high-performance work system (HPWS) and effective human resource management (HRM) practices play a mediating role between critical antecedents or an innovative environment and actual changes in the entrepreneurial orientation of the organization. The model also suggests that organizational level plays a key role in creating an innovative organizational posture. Specifically, the model makes the following assertions:

- Environmental antecedents including top management support, rewards/reinforcement, autonomy/discretion, time availability, and organizational boundaries impact the human resource practices of an organization. The concept of high-performance work systems (HPWS) is utilized to highlight the critical organizational and human resource practices necessary to initiate innovative and entrepreneurial behavior. The environmental antecedents are necessary for creating HPWS.
- HPWS leads to an organizational entrepreneurial orientation causing increased strategic entrepreneurial behaviors including proactiveness, risk taking, and innovativeness.
- The link between the environment, human resource practices, and entrepreneurial orientation is moderated by the level of the person(s) in the organization and the type of job(s) performed.

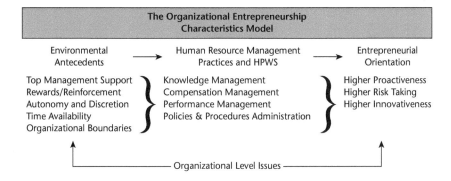

FIGURE 8.1   The Organizational Entrepreneurship Characteristics Model.

Environmental Antecedents for Innovation

Corporate innovation occurs when the organization strives to "exploit product-market opportunities through innovative and proactive behavior."[5] An effective corporate innovation strategy facilitates the firm's efforts to exploit its current competitive advantages and explore the opportunities and the competencies required to successfully pursue them.[6] Some firms foster an environment that is more entrepreneurially intense than others.[7] As we presented in Chapter 7, assessing an innovative (entrepreneurial) environment has become an important element for successfully implementing a corporate innovation strategy. An organizational change effort such as implementing an innovation strategy requires an analysis of the current environment or state of readiness/antecedents for encouraging proactive corporate innovative behavior. In Chapter 7 we introduced one instrument that has been utilized to assess environmental issues related to implementing a corporate innovation strategy: the Corporate Entrepreneurship Assessment Instrument (CEAI). Hornsby, Kuratko, and Zahra developed the 48-item CEAI to assess the innovative readiness of an organization.[8] Reviewing from Chapter 7, there were five stable antecedents or elements of managers' innovative actions. These antecedents are as follows:

1. *Top management support:* The willingness of top-level managers to facilitate and promote innovative behavior, including the championing of innovative ideas and providing the resources people require to take innovative actions.
2. *Work discretion/autonomy:* Top-level managers' commitment to tolerate failure, provide decision-making latitude and freedom from excessive oversight and to delegate authority and responsibility to managers.
3. *Rewards/reinforcement:* Developing and using systems that reward employees based on performance, highlight significant achievements, and encourage the pursuit of challenging work.
4. *Resource availability:* Evaluating workloads to ensure that individuals and groups have the time needed to pursue innovations and that their jobs are structured in ways that support efforts to achieve short- and long-term organizational goals.
5. *Organizational boundaries:* Precise explanations of outcomes expected from organizational work and development of mechanisms for evaluating, selecting, and using innovations.

While the antecedents to entrepreneurship and innovation continue to be identified and tested, their impact on organizational behavior, especially in the development of effective human resource practices and work systems, should also be discussed. Current human resource systems may not foster the desired innovative and entrepreneurial outcomes because they reinforce standardization, rigidity, and inflexibility instead of promoting creativity, empowerment, and intrinsic motivation. The following section describes the HRM practices and HPWS that are necessary for an organization to foster innovation.

Human Resource Management (HRM) and High-Performance Work Systems (HPWS)

The model in Figure 8.1 proposes that the environmental antecedents impact the development and management of human resources in an innovative organization. A firm's human resources are seen as particularly important for providing a sustained competitive advantage and play an essential role in a firm's ability to be entrepreneurial.[9] Human resource practices that impact creativity, innovation, and entrepreneurship can be categorized as part of a high-performance work system (HPWS). Mitchell, Obeidat, and Bray suggested that high-performance human resource practices play a mediating role between strategic human resources and organizational performance.[10] Bohlander and Snell suggest that HPWS is a result of "a specific combination of HR practices, work structures, and processes that maximizes employee knowledge, skill, commitment and flexibility."[11] Nadler, Gerstein, and Shaw define HPWS as: "an organizational architecture that brings together work, people, technology and information in a manner that optimizes the congruence of fit among them in order to produce high performance in terms of the effective response to customer requirements and other environmental demands and opportunities."[12] Nadler et al. identified ten important principles for designing an effective HPWS. Table 8.1 includes a complete list of these principles. They center on the importance of human resource practices design, empowerment, culture, and accountability.

TABLE 8.1 Ten Principles for Design of HPWS

1. Start the design with an outward focus on customer requirements and then work backward to develop appropriate organizational forms and work processes.
2. Design work around self-managed teams responsible for producing complete products or processes.
3. Work must be guided by clear direction, explicit goals, and a full understanding of output requirements and measures of performance.
4. Variances should be detected and controlled at the source.
5. Design the social and technical systems to be closely linked.
6. Ensure continuous flow of information to all areas of the system.
7. Enriched and shared jobs increase the motivation of individuals and enhance flexibility in assigning work and solving problems.
8. Human resource practices must complement and strengthen the empowerment of teams and individuals.
9. The management structure, culture, and processes all must embrace and support the HPWS design.
10. The organization and its work units must have the capacity to reconfigure themselves to meet changing competitive conditions.

Source: Adapted from Nadler, Nadler, & Tushman, 1997, pp. 147–153.[13]

Specifically, they argued that:

> *[The] key to maintaining this flexible architecture is having clear design intent. If the purpose of the original design—to enhance speed, accountability, customer focus, technological innovation, flattened hierarchy, or whatever—is explicitly articulated, then there are clear boundaries for adding, deleting, or rearranging design elements.*[14]

In the case of fostering innovation and entrepreneurship, the key is to strategically foster innovative behavior by designing human resource systems that support and incentivize this type of behavior.

Beugelsdijk studied the impact of changing six human resource practices on incremental and radical innovations. Incremental innovation focuses on smaller process improvements and changes, and radical innovation includes major product or process changes or new product development. In a study of 988 Dutch firms, he found that firms with decentralized organizational structures and a focus on employee empowerment, as reflected in the use of task autonomy and flexible working hours, generated more product innovations. He also found that performance-based pay and training and development were positively associated with incremental innovation, but not with radical innovation.[15]

Four of the key human resource practices that create a HPWS are performance management, knowledge management, compensation and incentives management, and policies and procedures administration. Each of these practices is described below.

Performance Management

The first component of creating an HPWS is the concept of performance management, especially as it relates to the empowerment of employees. Providing an increased opportunity to participate in decisions is critical to creating an entrepreneurial orientation. This process is considered to be one of the key elements of an HPWS because it allows the employee to make decisions that affect their immediate environment, which in turn affect the entire organization. This empowerment leads to more work commitment and better organizational citizenship. According to Hayton and Kelley,[16] corporate entrepreneurship is promoted by the simultaneous presence of competency in the four roles of innovating, brokering, championing, and sponsoring. In order to foster corporate innovative activity, employee development activities focused on developing these competencies should be a central focus of a corporate innovation strategy. Additionally, employee feedback systems should focus on progress in developing or overcoming weaknesses in these competencies.

Knowledge Management

The second component of creating an HPWS is knowledge management. Knowledge management includes attracting, retaining, and developing individuals with the knowledge, skills, and abilities to meet the goals of the organization. Effective selection of individuals who have the ability or inclination to behave innovatively is important. Also, training and development provides employees with the necessary skills to perform their jobs in a more effective manner as well as the opportunity to assume greater responsibility within an organization. Traditional selection and employee development procedures may not always be productive when it comes to hiring and developing innovative employees. Typical procedures tend to identify individuals that adhere to policies and procedures, follow instruction, and work towards fitting into a company profile in their development activities so they can be labeled key talent in the organizational succession chart. Very little empirical research exists to help us better understand the requirements for and the impact of directly seeking creative and innovative employees. However, there is ample discussion in the applied literature on some recommendations to attract, retain, and develop these types of individuals.

Mercer makes several recommendations for hiring creative and innovative employees. He suggests that we should test individuals to assess their motivation to do creative work and their flexibility in following rules and procedures. He utilizes the "Abilities & Behavior Forecaster™ Test" to assess these scores and suggests that creative people will score high on motivation and low on following rules and procedures. Mercer also suggests that you should assess your current successful employees to establish a benchmark for creative need for hiring new employees. Some of the benchmarking results that he found for creative jobs include artists, supply-chain managers, directors, and administrative assistants. Jobs with low creativity scores included accounting, customer service representatives, regional managers, sales representatives, and convenience store managers.

Mercer cautions over generalizing and encourages organizations to determine their own benchmarks for creative need. He warns of mismatching employees by putting creative individuals in noncreative roles (or vice versa) and resulting frustration and retention issues that could result. If you are not going to utilize a pre-employment test, Mercer recommends restructuring interview questions to ask applicants to describe past creative work experiences, especially in relation to actual problem-solving situations. You should especially avoid yes/no questions and let the applicant tell their story.[17]

Buxton suggests that it is critical to consider the role of teams when staffing for innovation. He suggests several rules of thumb that he believes help build effective cross-disciplinary innovation teams:

- You need people who fill in the gaps that you have in your own and other existing team members' skill sets as you build up competence in your specialty.
- Test for both breadth of literacy and deep competence. You do not need "jacks of all trades."
- Identify the core competencies needed for a team. List them on a bunch of Post-it notes, and have each person on the team write the name of the "go-to" person on the team who has the most depth in that area. If you lack depth in any specified core competency, you should work to find people that can fill the gap.
- You need to hire I-shaped individuals who can think both pragmatically and abstractly.

- Hire people who do not require predictability and stability in order to be effective. Individuals who can continually reconfigure will be more effective in innovative environments.
- Hire people with strong interpersonal skills. Communication and conflict resolutions skills are critical in innovation team environments.[18]

(For more insights on hiring innovative talent, see Table 8.2.)

TABLE 8.2 18 Recommendations for Hiring and Retaining Innovative Talent

1. **Make hiring innovators a primary goal.** Set as one of your primary goals and metrics the increased hiring of more innovative individuals.
2. **Realize the current system may be broken.** Your current system probably restricts the hiring of innovators. Look at every phase of the hiring process to see where nontraditional, diverse, and/or innovative individuals are most likely to be screened out, overlooked, or discouraged.
3. **Develop a hiring plan for innovators.** Prioritize your jobs and business units to make sure that your limited resources and time are directed toward those jobs that, when filled with innovators, have the most business impact.
4. **Create your brand recognition.** Don't expect to have any success in hiring innovative people if you don't make an effort to spread the word by writing and speaking about how your firm desires innovators and, more important, provides them with opportunities to continually innovate and take risks.
5. **Encourage external hiring.** If your organization is currently conservative and scores low on the risk taking scale, you might find hiring external innovators a lot easier than transforming current risk-adverse employees.
6. **Position descriptions.** Most position descriptions don't mention the need for innovation at all. If you expect to be successful, the desire for innovation must be part of every relevant job description, and assessing the need for innovation should be part of every job analysis.
7. **Postings.** Innovation must be part of every job announcement, recruitment ad, and recruiting brochure. Clearly differentiate how your jobs allow individuals more freedom to innovate and take risks than other firms.
8. **Referral focus.** Nothing improves the recruiting of any targeted group better than specifically asking your employees to be on the lookout for referrals who have those skills or characteristics.
9. **Initial résumé screening.** The initial screening process for résumés is usually a primary barrier to innovation. Redesign your system so that it includes options for accepting out-of-the-box résumé formats and content. It is a fact that some innovative people refuse to produce standard résumés.
10. **The interview.** After résumé screening, the interview is a second weak link in hiring innovators. The interview, and in fact the entire assessment process, must be redesigned so that it is tolerant and inclusive (i.e., expect some craziness) if you expect to get a single innovative person hired.
11. **Simulations and creativity assessments.** Whether an online prescreening tool or verbal scenario provided during the interview process, simulations are an effective tool that can excite as well as assess potential applicants.
12. **Contests.** Because most interview formats do not assess the candidate's ability to innovate, recruiting needs to consider contests as a supplement to help identify those that offer innovative ideas and approaches to the problems faced by the company.

13. **Improve the candidate experience.** Most hiring processes are just plain ugly when it comes to customer service and providing a great candidate experience. That weakness becomes critical when you're attempting to hire innovative individuals because they are almost always in high demand. Being in high demand means that they have many options and as a result, they're less tolerant of being treated poorly during any hiring process.

14. **The corporate website.** Almost all candidates, innovative or not, will test the validity of what they have heard by visiting your corporate website. If the message they get there differs from what they've heard, you will lose them in an instant.

15. **Target "magnet" hires.** An effective way of attracting innovators is having the recruiting team specifically identify and target well-known individuals who are known for their innovation.

16. **Follow through with orientation.** Even after they accept your offer, the need to reinforce your message is critical. As part of the orientation process, emphasize the importance of innovation in your organization, educate the new hire on how and where to report ideas, and share how innovation is rewarded.

17. **Follow up with retention.** Even though recruiting doesn't control retention, it is in their best interest to work with retention program managers to ensure that new hires don't immediately exit out the back door.

18. **Improve with metrics.** No matter how well your system is designed, it's critical that you track your success and failures in hiring innovative individuals.

Source: Adapted from: ERE.Net 18 "Things Recruiters Can Do To Hire More Innovative People," by Dr. John Sullivan, Oct 16, 2006; www, ere.net/2006/10/16/18-things-recruiters-can-do-to-hire-more-innovative-people.

Recently, Hamilton and Davison[19] suggested the concept of "knowledge stars." These are individuals hired and developed to hold critical knowledge that give the organization distinctive competencies leading to innovative performance. The authors claim that "the recruitment, search, and selection processes used to obtain workers who would develop and deploy that knowledge have not materially changed for many years." They suggest a new selection model that is reciprocal and iterative and requires inputs from internal and external stakeholders. Also, their model suggests the following:

- An HR approach begins with identifying possible knowledge stars at conferences and tradeshows and nurturing a relationship that may make them feel more comfortable about coming to work with your firm. At this point specific job descriptions are not discussed; it is the search for talent that matters.
- Focus on building social capital with current employees. These individuals may become future knowledge stars and/or may be able to link the company to other potential stars.
- Gain input from internal (line managers and co-workers) and external (customers and vendors) stakeholders before drawing up a description of the job.
- Talent leads to job description and not the other way around.
- Once hired, knowledge stars should work in "communities of practice" such that they enhance their own social and knowledge capital and are more inclined to stay with the organization.

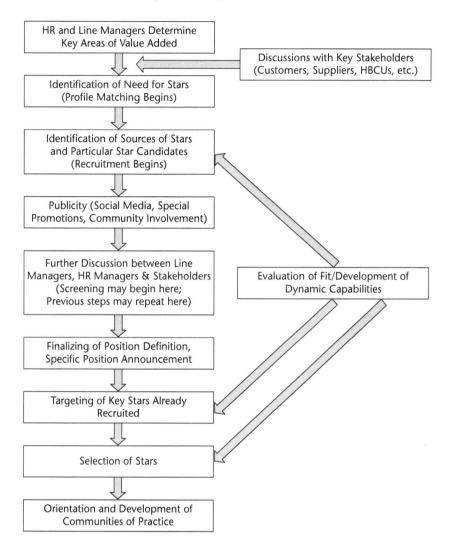

FIGURE 8.2 Innovative Recruiting and Selection Process for Hiring Knowledge Stars.

Compensation and Incentives Management

The third component in creating an HPWS is employee compensation and incentives. The two previous elements help to prepare employees and organizations for successful HPWS implementation and operation, but without effective compensation management, the system will most likely fail. Organizations need to find a way to link pay with performance in order to incentivize an employee to focus "on outcomes that are beneficial to themselves and the organization as a whole."[20] Incentives can take many forms, with some examples being stock options and other equity plans, profit-sharing plans, pay raises, bonuses for meeting performance targets, and other monetary incentives. In addition, incentives can take the form of non-monetary options such as time off, flextime, autonomy, group lunches, and other special employee benefits. In terms of innovation and entrepreneurship, the types of incentives should vary based on the need for incremental or radical innovations. Incremental innovations may be more suited to more traditional incentives including intrinsic rewards (i.e., flextime, autonomy, etc.) and extrinsic rewards (i.e., bonuses, merit increases, profit-sharing, etc.) However, more radical innovations may require more substantial forms of incentives that are often more difficult to administer and tend to foster apprehension from top management. These incentives include organizational equity in the form of stock, stock options, or even large equity stakes in venture spinoffs. Sjoerd Beugelsdijk affirmed this in a study of Dutch firms and found that incremental innovations are relatively easier to motivate with traditional HR practices but the ability to motivate radical innovations is much more limited because more sophisticated reward systems are not available.

Since many innovation and CE endeavors are conducted in team-based situations, the use of compensation and incentive programs become more complex given the team dynamics. The organization is faced with many tough decisions. First, do you compensate at the team level or individual level? More specifically, is your firm up to the challenge of team-based compensation? If so, how do you measure performance and are you prepared for the internal team dynamics that result from shared accountability? Second, what behavior are you trying to reinforce with the team-based compensation? Third, how do you measure team performance? Finally, what incentives do you utilize in the compensation program?

In a study of CE in Israeli defense firms, Lerner, Azulay, and Tishler confirmed the importance of building effective entrepreneurship-oriented compensation programs. The findings of their research suggest that management should not only call for compensation for entrepreneurs, but should also make sure that the system they choose is important and acceptable to the entrepreneurs. Their results show that there is a large gap between the perception of the desired compensation incentives by corporate entrepreneurs and the ones actually practiced by the enterprise. They also found that even when more desirable compensation programs were utilized, many of the corporate entrepreneur respondents were not aware of it.[21]

Whether you utilize individual or team-based compensation programs for incentivizing innovative and entrepreneurial behavior, the design of the program should include the following elements:

- Top management must make entrepreneurship and innovation a strategic initiative for the organization and be willing to alter its traditional culture.
- Top management must provide support for the compensation program so that employees trust the behavior–reward linkage.
- The psychological and behavioral consequences of the incentive structure need to be tailored to the workforce and not haphazardly adopted from external sources.
- Employee feedback should be systematically built into the assessment of the incentive compensation program.

Policies and Procedures Administration

The administration of organizational policies and procedures also impacts the creation of a high-performance work system. Organizations who focus on policies that create boundaries and overly regulate behavior will limit innovative and entrepreneurial behavior. Traditional human resource practices such as creating job descriptions, policy manuals, safety manuals, and operating standards can inhibit desired behavior. Also, a manager's rigid enforcement of policies can have unwanted effects on employee behavior. While some of these are necessary and important to the operation of the organization (especially those legally required), these traditional practices may also inhibit the creativity and innovation behavior desired when implementing a corporate innovative strategy. Hayton[22] suggests that human resource management (HRM) practices fall into two categories: traditional HR practices and discretionary HRM. The traditional practices focus upon "clearly defining jobs in terms of their tasks, duties, and responsibilities; carefully structuring equitable rewards for those jobs; and monitoring individual performance." He hypothesizes that these practices are incongruent with the creativity, innovation, and risk taking required for innovation and entrepreneurship.

Discretionary HRM practices, on the other hand, focus on the discretionary performance of employees by offering incentives and mechanisms for exchanging knowledge and encouraging organizational learning. In a study of 99 small to medium enterprises, Hayton found that discretionary HR practices, specifically discretionary behavior, knowledge-sharing, and organizational learning were positively associated with innovative performance and activity. He also found that strategic human capital management enhanced the relationship, and that the positive relationship was strongest in high technology industries.

Entrepreneurial Orientation (EO)

According to Figure 8.1 cited earlier, organizational entrepreneurial orientation (EO) is the result of effective organizational practices related to attending to the antecedents necessary to implement a CE strategy and practicing relevant HRM for innovation. EO is an organizational state or quality that's defined in terms of several behavioral dimensions. Based on the pioneering work of Miller,[23] Covin and Slevin defined EO as implying the presence of organizational behavior reflecting risk taking, innovativeness, and proactiveness.[24] The three main EO attributes are defined below.

Innovation

According to Lumpkin and Dess, entrepreneurial innovation can be defined as the "willingness to support creativity and experimentation in introducing new products/ services."[25] Covin and Miles suggested that innovation was the single factor most critical in defining CE. They argued that after considering "the various dimensions of firm-level entrepreneurial orientation identified in the literature . . . innovation, broadly defined, is the single common theme underlying all forms of corporate entrepreneurship."[26] All the other dimensions were simply correlates of innovation. Covin and Miles concluded that "without innovation there is no corporate entrepreneurship regardless of the presence of these other dimensions."[27]

Risk Taking

Risk taking has long been conceptually associated with entrepreneurship. Many definitions of entrepreneurship focus on the willingness of entrepreneurs to engage in calculated risks. Interestingly, entrepreneurs may not view themselves as risk takers. Busenitz argued that entrepreneurs tend to view situations more favorably than non-entrepreneurs, even when they are more risky.[28]

Proactiveness

The concept of proactiveness has received less attention from entrepreneurial scholars.[29] It has been defined as "an opportunity-seeking, forward-looking perspective characterized by the introduction of new products and services ahead of the competition and acting in anticipation of future demand."[30]

At least three models suggested by Covin and Slevin,[31] Lumpkin and Dess,[32] and Ireland, Covin, and Kuratko[33] incorporate the antecedents and/or consequences of the organizational-level phenomenon of EO. The Ireland, Covin, and Kuratko model of a corporate entrepreneurship (CE) strategy differs in four ways: (1) by conceptualizing EO as an organizational state; (2) by specifying organizational locations from which innovative behavior may emerge; (3) by specifying a "philosophical" component of a CE strategy; and (4) by specifying that organizations can pursue innovation as a separate and identifiable strategy.

More recently, Anderson, Kreiser, Kuratko, Hornsby, and Eshima[34] suggested a reconceptualization of the EO construct focusing on two components: entrepreneurial behaviors (including the historical innovativeness and proactiveness) and managerial attitude toward risk. The authors conclude that this broader reconceptualization yields a better assessment of the organization and ultimately improved prescriptions for organizational change activities.

It is our contention that human resource practices, as described earlier, play a major role in the execution of an innovative strategy that can lead to EO. The human resource practices that create an HPWS facilitate the execution of such a strategy. Many studies confirm the positive correlation between EO and organizational performance. Rauch et al. observed that the Covin and Slevin EO scale possesses a positive, and moderately large, correlation with performance ($r = 0.235$). Rauch and colleagues equate the strength of the EO–performance relationship to that of taking a "sleeping pill and having a better night's sleep."[35] Some of the areas of performance often linked to EO include financial indicators such as growth, sales, and profit. Nonfinancial measures include the number of ideas implemented and satisfaction.

Organizational-Level Issues

It is well documented in the conceptual literature that managers at all structural levels have critical strategic roles to fulfill for the organization to be successful.[36] According to Floyd and Lane, senior, middle, and first-level managers have distinct responsibilities with respect to each sub-process. *Senior-level managers* have ratifying, recognizing, and directing roles which in turn are associated with particular managerial actions.[37] In examining the role of middle-level managers, Kuratko, Ireland, Covin, and Hornsby contend that *middle-level managers* endorse, refine, and shepherd entrepreneurial opportunities and identify, acquire, and deploy resources needed to pursue those opportunities. Whereas *first-level managers* have experimenting roles corresponding to the competence definition sub-process, adjusting roles corresponding to the competence modification sub-process, and conforming roles corresponding to the competence deployment sub-process.[38] Thus, organizations pursuing corporate innovative strategies likely exhibit a cascading yet integrated set of innovative actions at the senior, middle, and first levels of management. At the senior level, managers act in concert with others throughout the firm to identify effective means through which new businesses can be created or existing ones reconfigured.

Corporate innovation is pursued in light of environmental opportunities and threats, with the purpose of creating a more effective alignment between the company and conditions in its external environment. The innovative actions expected of middle-level managers are framed around the need for this group to propose and interpret innovative opportunities that might create new business for the firm or increase the firm's competitiveness in current business domains. First-line managers exhibit the "experimenting" role as they surface the operational ideas for innovative improvements. An important interpretation of Burgelman's work has been the belief that managers would surface ideas for innovative actions from every level of management, especially the first-line and middle levels. Therefore, managers across levels are jointly responsible for their organization's innovative actions.[39] Based on the different roles of the different levels of management highlighted above, it can be contended that managers at different levels have different perceptions of the feasibility and/or desirability of these organizational factors for promoting innovative action.

Top management support refers to the extent to which one perceives that top managers support, facilitate, and promote innovative behavior, including the championing of innovative ideas and providing the resources people require to take innovative actions. Recent research suggests that top management support has been found to have a positive relationship with an organization's innovative outcomes.[40] Managers differ in their structural ability to use top management support as a resource for innovative action. The more senior a manager is, the closer they are to top management. This closeness enables greater awareness of the nature of that support.[41] For example, more senior managers are likely to better know the bounds of top management support and thereby can utilize them by pushing it to the fullest. While first-line managers may be aware of top management support, they do not have the structural "proximity" to have a fine-grained knowledge of the nature of that support.[42] First-line managers are likely to be more cautious in how they choose to use top management support for their innovative activities.

Work discretion refers to the extent to which one perceives that the organization tolerates failure, provides decision-making latitude and freedom from excessive oversight, and delegates authority and responsibility to lower-level managers and workers.[43] Often innovative outcomes arise from those that have work discretion for innovative experimentation.[44] Managers likely use their work discretion to enhance performance on salient tasks, and task salience differs across managerial level. First-line managers are focused on managing and instructing others to more efficiently perform their tasks, middle-level managers are focused on how to link groups, and senior managers are focused on scanning the environment for opportunities and threats. Innovative actions are more likely to arise from scanning the external and internal environments than focusing attention more narrowly on efficiency.[45] Therefore, more senior managers are more likely to use work discretion to generate innovative outcomes.

Rewards and reinforcement refers to the extent to which one perceives that the organization uses systems that reward based on innovative activity and success.[46] Rewards have been found to be positively related to entrepreneurial behavior.[47] However, unlike the signals of top management support for which senior managers can more fully appreciate, these signals from rewards and reinforcement are typically less ambiguous. Such rewards and reinforcement are likely to have a more positive influence on lower-level managers because, as Hayton argued, these lower-level managers are more risk averse and such rewards likely help overcome that aversion.[48]

Time availability for managers has also been found to be an important resource for generating innovative outcomes.[49] Similar to work discretion, managers are expected to invest "slack" time on those tasks most salient given their roles and responsibilities. The most salient tasks for first-line managers are narrower in scope and center more on adjusting and conforming activities (and often focused on efficiency), whereas the more salient tasks of senior managers are broader, allowing them to scan more broadly the organization and the external.[50] These broader scanning activities are more likely to generate innovative ideas by scanning the environment and recognizing opportunities.[51] Therefore, more senior managers are better able to use time as a resource to generate innovative activities than are first-line managers.

Finally, flexible organizational boundaries are useful in promoting innovative activity because they enhance the flow of information between the external environment and the organization and between departments/divisions within the organization.[52] More senior managers are better structurally positioned to access and use this information given their attention is already broadly allocated across the organization and the external environment. First-line managers also benefit from these permeable boundaries but, given the structural position, they interact across fewer boundaries because of their narrow job focus and therefore benefit less from boundary permeability.[53]

In a recent study on organizational-level effects on corporate innovative behavior, Hornsby, Kuratko, Shepherd, and Bott found support for many of the relationships suggested earlier. They found that managerial level moderated the relationship between top management support and the number of ideas implemented, and moderated the relationship between work discretion and the number of ideas implemented. Managers at higher levels were better able to make the most of top management support and of work discretion. These findings have important implications for innovation and CE. First, under high levels of perceived managerial support, senior and middle managers, by virtue of their higher ranking positions, were more likely to implement innovative ideas. First-level managers, however, were relatively unlikely to see their ideas implemented or make unofficial improvements, regardless of the level of managerial support.[54]

Second, the nature of the interaction indicates that there was a positive relationship between work discretion and number of ideas implemented for senior and middle-level managers; however, for first-level managers, this relationship was negative. These results indicate that work discretion only results in increased innovative actions (in the form of number of ideas implemented) for senior and middle-level managers, or those individuals with the experience and personal discipline likely necessary to support autonomy and discretion. An explanation for this finding may be that these lower-level managers, even though they perceived an environment of work discretion, did not see the link between it and their own activities. Garvin and Levesque refer to this as the "two cultures problem," where organizations traditionally focus on incremental improvement through a focus on stability and efficiency.[55] Corporate innovation requires a "melding" of cultures. If the CE strategy has not been integrated down into lower levels of management, an increased focus on traditional practices could result when a lower manager has more discretion and autonomy. Also, specific control systems that exist in the organization, especially managerial flexibility, may lead lower-level managers to perceive the need to spend more time on standard procedures and activities and not engage in more innovative behavior.[56]

Conclusion

Human resource practices, especially the organizational architecture that creates a high-performance work system, are a critical mediating factor between innovative environments and strategy and actual entrepreneurial and innovative behavior. The relationships between the elements of Figure 8.1 are complex and their linkages are in need of much more research.[57] The more we understand the organizational architecture for an innovative strategy, the more successful firms will be with future corporate innovation efforts. Research also suggests that issues such as management level can moderate the relationships. It seems clear that senior or top management plays a major strategic role in fostering corporate entrepreneurship and innovation. Furthermore, middle and front-line managers also need to facilitate and encourage innovative activity. Table 8.3 summarizes some of the major activities that managers should initiate if they want an entrepreneurial or innovative organization.

TABLE 8.3 Tips for Fostering Innovation

1. Have leaders and managers explicitly discuss their definition of innovation, give examples and explain why innovation is important to the organization's survival.
2. Treat innovation as a key source of economic growth, much like machinery, capital, labor force size, and skills—as an investment, not an expense.
3. Write a "Declaration of Innovation" and have top managers sign it.
4. Partner with leaders to determine barriers to innovation; identify systems to foster an exchange of ideas and information.
5. Have managers verbally solicit ideas and critique each other in a non-threatening way.
6. Make innovation fun.
7. Publicize implemented ideas: how they save money, make the company more efficient, or lead to new products.
8. Establish rewards and recognize that innovation can happen. Plan for and celebrate failure. Praise all suggestions to develop an atmosphere in which employees feel safe to voice ideas.
9. Get cross-functional involvement to gain buy-in from various departments.

Source: Adapted from: Gurchiek, Kathy (2009). Motivating Innovation, *HR Magazine*, 54: 30–35.

Innovation-in-Action

How Netflix Changed Its HR Practices to Manage Growth and Innovativeness

> *Over the years we learned that if we asked people to rely on logic and common sense instead of on formal policies, most of the time we would get better results, and at lower cost. If you're careful to hire people who will put the company's interests first, who understand and support the desire for a high-performance workplace, 97% of your employees will do the right thing. Most companies spend endless time and money writing and enforcing HR policies to deal with problems the other 3% might cause. Instead, we tried really hard to not hire those people, and we let them go if it turned out we'd made a hiring mistake.*
>
> *~Patty McCord, Netflix*

Netflix had grown tremendously from its early roots to a complex company in a very dynamic business environment by 2012. Patty McCord, who served as the Chief Talent Officer at Netflix, identified two critical reasons for innovating Netflix's HR practices. First, only hire "A Players" to work with other "A Players." Talented and effective employees are often discouraged and frustrated by employees who underperform. Second, you need to let go employees if their skills no longer meet the needs of the organization. In a dynamic environment, required skills and competencies change at a rapid pace and employees who fall behind will hinder organizational performance. Based on learning this important lesson, McCord and her team developed HR practices with the following goals:

1. *Tell the truth about performance:* Netflix eliminated formal reviews and asked managers to make discussions about work performance an "organic" part of their work.
2. *Managers own the job of creating great teams:* Team membership in a dynamic environment requires honest communication between manager and team members regarding their ability to keep up with the team. If a team member no longer fits with the team, they should be moved to other roles where their skills and experiences may be more useful. They also used market-based pay to retain the performing members of the team.
3. *Leaders own the job of creating the company culture:* McCord sees three issues to be addressed. First, leaders need to make sure their message is consistent with their employee accountability. Second, team members need to understand the "drivers" of the business. Third, leaders need to be aware of current subcultures that exists before they attempt to change the culture.
4. *Good talent managers think like businesspeople and innovators first, and like HR people last:* HR teams need to be innovated in the same ways other teams do. They need to investigate different ways to develop practices, policies, and procedures that support the business needs and culture that leadership is trying to create.

(Adapted from: https://hbr.org/2014/01/how-netflix-reinvented-hr, accessed April 22, 2018. A version of this article appeared in *Harvard Business Review*, January–February 2014.)

Key Terms

compensation and incentives

corporate entrepreneurship

entrepreneurial orientation

environmental antecedents

high-performance work systems

incremental innovation

knowledge management

knowledge stars

management level and roles in corporate entrepreneurship

organizational boundaries

organizational policies

performance management

radical innovation

rewards and reinforcement

time availability

top management support

work discretion

Discussion Questions

1. What are the antecedents to corporate entrepreneurship and innovation?
2. Why is top management support so important to the implementation of corporate entrepreneurship?
3. How can you create a high-performance work system (HPWS)?
4. What are the important human resource elements of a high-performance work system?
5. What alternative models to employee recruitment, selection, and retention can be utilized to foster innovation behaviors?
6. What are the critical elements of an organizational entrepreneurial orientation?
7. Describe the role of senior, middle-level, and front-line managers in the corporate entrepreneurship process.
8. What role should managers play in the creation of high-performance work systems?

Notes

1 Robinson, K. 2009. *The Element: How Finding Your Passion Changes Everything*, New York: Penguin Books.
2 Hamel, G. 2000. *Leading the Revolution*, Boston: Harvard Business School Press, p. 15.
3 Zahra, S.A., Kuratko, D.F. & Jennings, D.F. 1999. Entrepreneurship and the acquisition of dynamic organizational capabilities. *Entrepreneurship Theory and Practice*, 24: 5–10.
4 Dess, G.G., Lumpkin, G.T. & McGee, J.E. 1999. Linking corporate entrepreneurship to strategy, structure, and process: suggested research directions. *Entrepreneurship Theory & Practice*, 23: 85–102.
5 Ibid, p. 85.
6 Covin, J.G. & Miles, M.P. 1999. Corporate entrepreneurship and the pursuit of competitive advantage. *Entrepreneurship: Theory and Practice*, 23: 47–63.
7 Morris, M.H., Kuratko, D.F. & Covin, J.G. 2011. *Corporate Entrepreneurship and Innovation: Entrepreneurial Development within Organizations*, Mason, OH: Cengage/Southwestern.
8 Hornsby, J.S., Kuratko, D.F. & Zahra, S.A. 2002. Middle managers' perception of the internal environment for corporate entrepreneurship: assessing a measurement scale. *Journal of Business Venturing*, 17: 253–273.
9 Wiklund, J. & Shepherd, D. 2003. Knowledge-based resources, entrepreneurial orientation, and the performance of small and medium-sized businesses. *Strategic Management Journal*, 24: 1307–1319.
10 Mitchell, R., Obeidat, S. & Bray, M. 2013. The effect of strategic human resource management on organizational performance: the mediating role of high-performance human resource practices. *Human Resource Management*, 52: 899–921.

11 Bohlander, G. & Snell, S. 2004. *Managing Human Resources*, Cincinnati: South-Western, p. 690.

12 Nadler, D., Gerstein, S. & Shaw, R. 1992. *Organizational Architecture: Designs for Changing Organizations*, San Francisco: Josey-Bass, p. 118.

13 Nadler, D.A., Nadler, M.B. & Tushman, M.L. 1997. *Competing by Design: The Power of Organizational Architecture*, New York: Oxford University Press.

14 Ibid, p. 121.

15 Beugelsdijk, S. 2008. Strategic human resource practices and product innovation. *Organization Studies*, 29: 821–827.

16 Hayton, J. & Kelley, D. 2006. A competency-based framework for promoting corporate entrepreneurship. *Human Resource Management*, 45: 407–427.

17 Mercer, M. *Hiring Creative Employees: Using Benchmark Testing*. www.sideroad.com/Management/hiring-creative-employees.html (accessed September 29, 2010).

18 Buxton, B. 2009. *BusinessWeek Online*, July 14, p. 9, www.businessweek.com/innovate/content/jul2009/id20090713%5f33.

19 Hamilton, R.H. & Davison, K. 2018. The search for skills: knowledge stars and innovation in the hiring process. *Business Horizons*, 61, May–June: 409–419.

20 Bohlander, G. & Snell, S. 2004. *Managing Human Resources*, Cincinnati: South-Western, p. 698.

21 Lerner, M., Azulay, I. & Tishler, A. 2009. The role of compensation methods in corporate entrepreneurship. *International Studies of Management and Organization*, 39: 53–81.

22 Hayton, J. 2003. Strategic human capital management in SMEs: an empirical study of entrepreneurial performance. *Human Resource Management*, 42: 375–391.

23 Miller, D. 1983. The correlates of entrepreneurship in three types of firms. *Management Science*, 297: 770–791.

24 Covin, J.G. & Slevin, D.P. 1989. Strategic management of small firms in hostile and benign environments. *Strategic Management Journal*, 10: 75–87.

25 Lumpkin, G.T. & Dess, G.G. 2001. Linking two dimensions of entrepreneurial orientation to firm performance: the moderating role of environment and industry life cycle. *Journal of Business Venturing*, 16: 431.

26 Covin, J.G. & Miles, M.P. 1999. Corporate entrepreneurship and the pursuit of competitive advantage. *Entrepreneurship: Theory and Practice*, 23: 47.

27 Ibid, p. 49.

28 Busenitz, L.W. 1999. Entrepreneurial risk and strategic decision making: it's a matter of perspective. *Journal of Applied Behavioral Science*, 35: 325–340.

29 Marino, L., Strandholm, K., Steensma, H.K. & Weaver, K.M. 2002. Assessing the psychometric properties of the entrepreneurial orientation scale: a multi-country analysis. *Entrepreneurship Theory and Practice*, 26: 71–94; and Weaver, K.M, Dickson, M.P., Gibson, B. & Turner, A. 2002. Being uncertain: the relationship between entrepreneurial orientation and environmental uncertainty: a multi-country SME analysis. *Journal of Enterprising Culture*, 10: 87–105.

30 Rauch, A., Wiklund, J., Lumpkin, G.T. & Frese, M. 2009. Entrepreneurial orientation and business performance: an assessment of past research and suggestions for the future. *Entrepreneurship: Theory and Practice*, 3: 761–787.

31 Covin, J.G. & Slevin, D.P. 1991. A conceptual model of entrepreneurship as firm behavior. *Entrepreneurship Theory and Practice*, 16: 7–25.

32 Lumpkin, G.T. & Dess, G.G. 1996. Clarifying the entrepreneurial orientation construct and linking it to performance. *Academy of Management Review*, 211: 135–172.

33 Ireland, R.D., Covin, J.G. & Kuratko, D.F. 2009. Conceptualizing corporate entrepreneurship strategy. *Entrepreneurship Theory and Practice*, 331: 19–46.

34 Anderson, B.S., Kreiser, P.M, Kuratko, D.F., Hornsby, J.S. & Eshima, Y. 2014. Reconceptualizing entrepreneurial orientation. *Strategic Management Journal*, 36: 1579–1596.

35 Rauch, A., Wiklund, J., Lumpkin, G.T. & Frese, M. 2009. Entrepreneurial orientation and business performance: an assessment of past research and suggestions for the future. *Entrepreneurship Theory and Practice*, 33: 761–787.

36 Ireland, R.D., Hitt, M.A. & Vaidyanath, D. 2002. Strategic alliances as a pathway to competitive success. *Journal of Management*, 28: 413–446.

37 Floyd, S. & Lane, P. 2000. Strategizing throughout the organization: managing role conflict in strategic renewal. *Academy of Management Review*, 25: 154–177.

38 Kuratko, D.F., Ireland, R.D., Covin, J.G. & Hornsby, J.S. 2005. A model of middle-level managers' entrepreneurial behavior. *Entrepreneurship Theory and Practice*, 29: 699–716.

39 Burgelman, R.A. 1983. Corporate entrepreneurship and strategic management: insights from a process study. *Management Science*, 23: 1349–1363; and Burgelman, R.A. 1984. Designs for corporate entrepreneurship in established firms. *California Management Review*, 26: 154–166.

40 Antonic, B. & Hisrich, R.D. 2001. Intrapreneurship: constructive refinement and cross-cultural validation. *Journal of Business Venturing*, 16: 495–527; Hornsby, J.S., Kuratko, D.F. & Zahra, S.A. 2002. Middle managers' perception of the internal environment for corporate entrepreneurship: assessing a measurement scale. *Journal of Business Venturing*, 17: 49–63; Kuratko, D.F, Ireland, R.D. & Hornsby, J.S. 2001. Improving firm performance through entrepreneurial actions: Acordia's corporate entrepreneurship strategy. *Academy of Management Executive*, 15: 60–71; Lyon, D.W., Lumpkin, G.T. & Dess, G.G. 2000. Enhancing entrepreneurial orientation research: operationalizing and measuring a key strategic decision making process. *Journal of Management*, 26: 1055–1085; and Morris, M.H., Kuratko, D.F. & Covin, J.G. 2011. *Corporate Entrepreneurship and Innovation*, Mason, OH: Cengage/Southwestern Publishing.

41 Floyd, S. & Lane, P. 2000. Strategizing throughout the organization: managing role conflict in strategic renewal. *Academy of Management Review*, 25: 154–177.

42 Hales, C. 2005. Rooted in supervision, branching into management: continuity and change in the role of first-line manager. *Journal of Management Studies*, 42: 471–506.

43 Hornsby, J.S., Kuratko, D.F. & Zahra, S.A. 2002. Middle managers' perception of the internal environment for corporate entrepreneurship: assessing a measurement scale. *Journal of Business Venturing*, 17: 49–63.

44 Kuratko, D.F., Ireland, R.D. & Hornsby, J.S. 2001. Improving firm performance through entrepreneurial actions: Acordia's corporate entrepreneurship strategy. *Academy of Management Executive*, 15: 60–71.

45 James, R., Lang, J., Calantone, R. & Gudmundson, D. 1997. Small firm information seeking as a response to environmental threats and opportunities. *Journal of Small Business Management*, 35: 11–23; and Beal, R. 2000. Competing effectively: environmental scanning, competitive strategy, and organizational performance in small manufacturing firms. *Journal of Small Business Management*, 38: 27–47.

46 Hornsby, J.S., Kuratko, D.F. & Zahra, S.A. 2002. Middle managers' perception of the internal environment for corporate entrepreneurship: assessing a measurement scale. *Journal of Business Venturing*, 17: 49–63.

47 Sathe, V. 1989. Fostering entrepreneurship in large diversified firm. *Organizational Dynamics*, 18: 20–32; Sykes, H.B. 1986. The anatomy of a corporate venturing program. *Journal of Business Venturing*, 1: 275–293; Sykes, H.B. & Block, Z. 1989. Corporate venturing obstacles: sources and solutions. *Journal of Business Venturing*, 4: 159–167; and Block, Z. & Ornati, O.A. 1987. Compensating corporate venture managers. *Journal of Business Venturing*, 2: 41–51.

48 Hayton, J.C. 2005. Promoting corporate entrepreneurship through human resource management practices: a review of empirical research. *Human Resource Management Review*, 15: 21–41.

49 Sykes, H.B. & Block, Z. 1989. Corporate venturing obstacles: sources and solutions. *Journal of Business Venturing*, 4: 159–167; Stopford, J.M. & Baden-Fuller, C.W.F. 1994. Creating corporate entrepreneurship. *Strategic Management Journal*, 15: 521–536; and Das, T.K. & Teng, B.S. 1997. Time and entrepreneurial risk behavior. *Entrepreneurship Theory and Practice*, 22: 69–88.

50 Floyd, S. & Lane, P. 2000. Strategizing throughout the organization: managing role conflict in strategic renewal. *Academy of Management Review*, 25: 154–177.

51 Shepherd, D.A., McMullen, J.S. & Jennings, P.D. 2007. The formation of opportunity beliefs: overcoming ignorance and doubt. *Strategic Entrepreneurship Journal*, 1: 75–95.

52 Miller, D.J., Fern, M.J. & Cardinal, L.B. 2007. The use of knowledge for technological innovation within diversified firms. *Academy of Management Journal*, 50: 307–326.

53 Hales, C. 2005. Rooted in supervision, branching into management: continuity and change in the role of first-line manager. *Journal of Management Studies*, 42: 471–506.

54 Hornsby, J.S., Kuratko, D.F., Shepherd, D.A. & Bott, J.P. 2009. Managers' corporate entrepreneurial actions: examining perception and position. *Journal of Business Venturing*, 24: 236–247.

55 Garvin, D. & Levesque, L. 2006. Meeting the challenge of corporate entrepreneurship. *Harvard Business Review*, October: 1–11.

56 Morris, M.H., Allen, J., Schindehutte, M. & Avila, R. 2006. Balanced management control systems as a mechanism for achieving corporate entrepreneurship. *Journal of Managerial Issues*, 18: 468–493.

57 Rauch, A., Wiklund, J., Lumpkin, G.T. & Frese, M. 2009. Entrepreneurial orientation and business performance: an assessment of past research and suggestions for the future. *Entrepreneurship Theory and Practice*, 33: 761–787.

9

TEAM-BASED INNOVATION

Individual commitment to a group effort—that is what makes a team work, a company work, a society work, a civilization work.

~*Vince Lombardi*[1]

Introduction

Teams are an important component to the success of corporate innovation and entrepreneurship. They are different from groups because they have a common purpose, complementary skills, common goals, and joint accountability.[2] Teams are also an integral part of the management process in successful organizations.[3] Used effectively, teams enhance performance, quality, efficiency, and innovation.[4] However, few research studies exist that investigate critical issues related to corporate innovation team development. Much of the discussion related to innovation team development borrows heavily from the organizational behavior and human resource management areas, where teams have been a popular area of study over the past 30 years. The need to understand the relationship between teams and innovation and entrepreneurship is supported by several research studies that suggest that team-founded new ventures are more successful than individually founded ventures.[5] Also, current research suggests that team membership and the transition of members on and off the team affects team performance. However, it appears that in many cases teams struggle and often fail due to the collaborative requirements of teams, especially cross-functional teams.[6]

While there is a paucity of empirical research relating teams to innovation outcomes, the literature that does exist supports the contention that teams, if developed and managed well, can be a key component in both product and process innovations. Haneda and Ito[7] found that four management practices were associated with innovation success. The use of interdivisional and cooperative teams headed the list with the other three practices including: having board members with an R&D background, human resource assessment based on R&D outcomes, and the creation of R&D centers.

Additionally, Van Knippenberg[8] in his review of teams and innovation suggested teams serve two purposes. First, teams create a social network of individuals with different backgrounds. Second, once diverse teams are formed, they provide an opportunity for knowledge aggregation and integration. He also concluded that if teams are to be effective in increasing innovation outcomes, they need to focus on diversity, information integration, climate, and cooperative goals. While much more empirical support is necessary, these authors cited above emphasize the importance of team formation and management.

Overview of Team Development

The basic tenet of work teams is that jobs and organizations should be designed around processes instead of functions and that the basic production unit should be the team and not the individual. Fully mature work teams set their own work goals and perform all the tasks associated with the work process. Teams are formed for synergy; that is—to accomplish more than individuals can accomplish separately. The focus of teams is to improve quantity and/or quality of outputs.

Most employers feel like they can immediately reap the benefits of synergistic teamwork right after employees have been assigned to teams. In general, this notion is wrong because management fails to consider the type of team being implemented (functional versus cross-functional, project versus developmental, permanent versus temporary, and autonomous versus semi-autonomous), the need for interpersonal development to enhance team skills in communication, decision-making and conflict resolution, and the team learning curve (the amount of time it takes for a team to become fully functional or productive). For example, many researchers claim that it takes an average of three years for a permanent team to reach its full potential as a team. It is not that the team is performing poorly, but it takes time for individuals to feel comfortable in a team-based environment and they need time to improve their interpersonal and technical skills related to the team activities.[9]

The remainder of this chapter will provide an overview of the critical elements related to effective team development. These elements include team structure, stages in team development, person–team fit and interpersonal skills, and management support including reward systems, information resources, and training and development. Figure 9.1 provides an illustration of the integral elements for forming and sustaining effective innovation teams along with the barriers that may impede team performance. Some suggestions for implementing teams in your organization are also provided.

Levels of Work Team Implementation and Types of Teams

Innovations can range from the radical (new products and methods) to the incremental (process improvements). The type of problems involved in the innovation

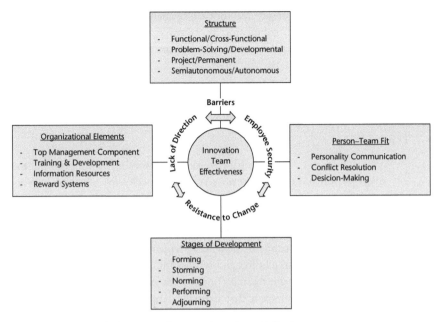

FIGURE 9.1 Critical Elements of Innovation Team Effectiveness.

effort may necessitate a specific team type or structure. There are a variety of team types, each can vary over several dimensions including function, purpose, time duration, and leadership. The choice of team type depends on the nature of the organization, the task to be performed, and workforce expertise. Many different types of teams can exist in the same organization. Team type dimensions include:

- Functionality

    Functional teams: Team members are from the same work unit.
    Cross-functional teams: Cross-functional teams comprise members from different functional units or departments to work on mutual problems. It is also important that these teams have a defined mission. Since these team members are from different functional units, problems related to role conflict can arise since they have to satisfy their line manager as well as team demands.

- Purpose

    Problem-solving teams: Team members are focused on specific issues to develop and implement solutions.
    Developmental teams: Team members concentrate on developing new products or systems.

- Duration

    Project: The team is created for a specific purpose and is dissolved when the task has been completed. They generally are functional in nature and used for problem-solving and root-cause analysis. It is important for these teams to have a defined mission or objective. Once the objective is completed, they should disband to allow team members to focus on their regular tasks.

Permanent: Permanent teams have a long-term focus in order to effectively handle major projects or issues. They are generally cross-functional, especially when related to corporate innovation activities.

- Discretion

  Semi-autonomous: The team has control over enforcing team norms but the manager still has typical human resource authority for selection, performance assessment, and discipline. This is generally a permanent team with some formal authority structure such as a supervisor or facilitator. It can include manufacturing cells, quality/safety teams, and new venture teams. Semi-autonomous teams are generally permanent in nature and autonomy increases as the team matures and reaches full performance.

  Autonomous: The team has full control over its operations and leadership. This is a permanent team that is totally empowered to make decisions concerning group membership, discipline, scheduling, etc. These teams are generally used sparingly and found in professional occupations. Some common areas that utilize self-directed autonomous teams are research and development, engineering, and venture spin-offs.

In relation to corporate innovation, the type of team needed is related to the form of innovation required. Incremental innovations requiring process improvements would tend to be more functionally based to emphasize problem-solving and project orientation since the focus is on more short-term problems. On the other hand, radical innovations focusing on new products and new venture spin-offs would necessitate the need for cross-functionality, developmental emphasis, and a more permanent focus (or at least a long-term focus). However, just as innovation is on a continuum from the incremental to radical, the appropriate team structure should be selected based on the project confronted by the organization.

Researchers Michael Hyung-Jin Park, Jong Won Lim, and Philip Birnbaum-More studied the effect of multi-knowledge (i.e., possessing both marketing and technological knowledge) individuals on performance in cross-functional teams. Their survey of 62 cross-functional teams revealed that the proportion of multi-knowledge individuals has an indirect positive effect through information-sharing on product innovativeness and a direct positive effect on time efficiency of new product development teams.[10] In further support of the importance of using cross-functional teams for effective problem-solving and innovation, researchers Bantel and Jackson investigated the relationship between the social composition (i.e., team size, location, average age, average tenure in the firm, and education level) of top management teams and innovation adoptions in 199 banks. Their results indicate that innovative banks are managed by more educated (based on advanced college degrees) teams who are diverse with respect to their functional areas of expertise.[11]

Another study conducted by Floortje Blindenbach-Driessen and Jan Van Den Ende suggested that we should be cautious in our use of cross-functional teams. A comparison of 135 innovation projects in 96 firms showed that multidisciplinary teams had a lower effect on performance of innovation projects in project-based firms than in other firms. Their explanation for this finding is that collaboration is abundant in project-based firms and that multidisciplinary teams have a limited added effect. However, cross-functional teams enhanced performance in the nonproject-based firms. They further suggest that project-based firms need specialization within their innovation projects instead of collaboration between disciplines and functions.[12]

It is important to realize that an organization should make significant investments in both technical and interpersonal training to help team members maximize their potential as a team and avoid some of the conflicts and pitfalls that hinder team development.

Stages of Team Formation

Borrowing from traditional group behavior research and the formative work conducted by Tuckman,[13] teams appear to go through at least a five-stage process as they mature. This development process occurs for every team, but the pace of progression can vary based on the skill level of the team members, team member experience with teams in the past, and team member interpersonal skills. Initially, Tuckman suggested a four-stage model and then added the fifth stage in the 1972. The following stages need to be recognized by the group so that effective strategies for interpersonal development and leadership can be implemented for team growth. Figure 9.2 presents the stages and the issues facing the team when attempting problem-solving and innovation.

Forming Stage

During the forming stage, team members are on their best behavior. Basic introductions are conducted and team members generally withhold negative opinions about others on the team or the mission of the team. It is important that the team facilitator or manager plays a directing role and initiates formal introductions and encourages each team member to meet each other.

Storming Stage

During this stage, team members search out the power and influence relationships in the team. The formal and informal authority relationships are investigated and each member attempts to assess their own individual place in the group. Obviously, dysfunctional conflicts can erupt during this stage if the individuals do not have the necessary conflict resolution skills and if there is not a strong manager or facilitator that can manage the conflict. The conflict, at least initially, may not be bad, but if left to fester can cause the team to stagnate in the storming stage indefinitely. It is

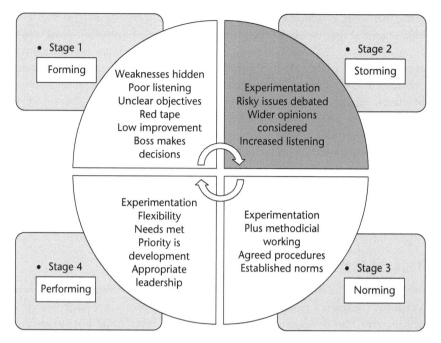

FIGURE 9.2 Tuckman's Model of Team/Group Development.

Source: Adapted from ACCEL Team Development. Accessed September 7, 2010. www.accel-team. com/. . ./02_stages_02.html.

important that the facilitator plays a selling role and fosters group acceptance and develops group decisions, making procedures and other group rules so that the team can successfully complete the storming stage.

Norming Stage

During the norming stage there is an initial integration of team members where there is acceptance by team members of the team's rules of engagement. Each member is relatively satisfied with their place in the group and the leadership structure that is running the group. Group members should avoid an environment of false consensus, where it appears that the individuals agree because they are too afraid to speak out. Since the team may not have reach a desired level of maturity, the facilitator/manager plays a supporting role and may have to intervene and make sure everyone is heard and all alternatives have been discussed.

Performing Stage

During this stage team members become totally integrated and reach full synergy. Team members engage in open, mature communication. Conflicts are dealt with directly and no team member is afraid to speak up. Also, interpersonal and technical skills of each member have developed substantially and start to complement the strengths and overcome the weaknesses of other team members. During this stage, the facilitator/manager should back off in terms of their formal authority role and allow the team to function by consensus as much as possible. The manager becomes more of a liaison between other departments, senior management, and the team.

Adjourning Stage

Some teams are permanent in nature in that they hold a specific place in the organizational chart. These types of teams include manufacturing cells, standing decision-making committees, and research and development teams. However, many other teams are formed for a defined period of time. These taskforces usually have a defined mission to complete. It is important that these teams recognize that once the task has been completed and evaluated, it is time to move on to other projects. Temporary teams, while important for dealing with unexpected problems, cause stress and role confusion to team members since they hold both a formal position in a department (with tasks and responsibilities) along with their obligations to the temporary team mission. The team leader or facilitator plays a delegating role, making sure all team members are invited to lead initiatives and contribute based on their knowledge and experiences.

Given the level of individual and team dynamics at each level of development, team performance generally declines after initial startup but rebounds as the team progresses through the stages of development. Figure 9.3 describes the team learning curve experienced by teams as they advance through the five stages identified earlier.

Key Organizational Elements of Work Teams

Several elements contribute to the successful implementation of the team concept. The following key organizational elements seem to be ones commonly cited by firms that have successfully implemented work teams. These include management

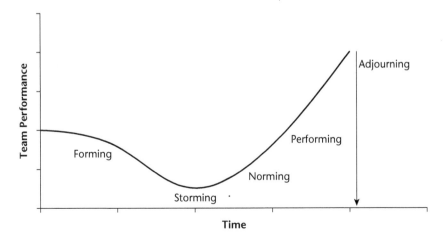

FIGURE 9.3   Team Formation and Performance.

commitment, training and development, information resources, reward systems, conflict resolution, and communication.

Management Commitment

Top management support is critical to team implementation, especially during the forming and storming stages of development. Since it takes time for the synergistic effects of teams to develop, senior management must be patient and willing to expend the resources it takes to develop the team. Results may not be immediately forthcoming. Also, middle managers sometimes thwart team implementations efforts because they feel that their role in the organization will no longer be needed or they are uncomfortable adjusting their role to the new team environment. Top management should work with these managers to develop them and reduce their resistance to change as well.

Training and Development

Whether the team is temporary or permanent, teams should not be constructed and then abandoned. As any other resource, they often need investment. A commitment to both technical and interpersonal training is necessary. Most companies do well at developing technical skills, but the cost-minded CFOs often rebel against expenditures for developing soft skills that they "assume" employees already have.

Information Resources

For teams to perform at their maximum level, they must have access to all pertinent information relevant to their specific tasks. This could include financial/sales data, production data, etc. Teams cannot be spoon-fed information. This is especially problematic for cross-functional teams that require team members to gain an integrated understanding of the problem.[14]

Reward Systems

This is probably the most difficult component. Many organizations and employees are reluctant to provide rewards on a team basis. Most performance measurement/appraisal systems are set up to measure individual performance and would have to be adapted to capture the nature of team performance.[15] Also, individual apprehension by employees exists when there are some team members that may not be as deserving as others.[16]

Person–Team Fit: Personality and Interpersonal Skills

Knowledge of oneself—self-awareness—is essential to one's productive personal and interpersonal functioning and in understanding and empathizing with other people, especially in a team environment. When you are assessing team development issues such as who to include and what type of interpersonal training is required, issues related to individual personality and communication, conflict resolution, and decision-making skills must be examined.

Personality

Personality is a stable set of characteristics and tendencies that determine those commonalties and differences in the psychological behavior (thoughts, feelings, and actions) of people. Perhaps the most common personality assessment instrument is the Myers–Briggs Type Indicator (MBTI). This instrument was based on the early work of Carl Jung and developed by the mother–daughter team of Briggs and Myers. Specifically, they suggest the following four continua of traits:

- Extravert (E) or Introvert (I): Where you prefer to focus and where you get your energy.
- Sensing (S) or Intuiting (N): Type of preferred information.
- Thinking (T) or Feeling (F): How you prefer to make decisions.
- Judging (P) or Perceiving (P): How you prefer to cope with the outside world.

These four traits combine to form 16 possible type or preference combinations. Consulting Psychologists Press (CPP), who currently owns the Myers–Briggs Type Indicator, suggests that there are common traits related to an innovative individual. They suggest the following:

> People with a preference for Sensing are drawn toward details, specifics, and incremental understanding, whereas people with a preference for Intuition are drawn toward the big picture, patterns, and original ideas. The Sensing tendency to build things incrementally based on experience is about seeking to adapt current realities. In contrast, the Intuition tendency to create the big picture from scratch based on hunches and through discerning underlying patterns is about seeking originality. Your *innovation attitude* is determined by your preference for either Sensing or Intuition in combination with your preference for either Judging or Perceiving (the fourth dichotomy, yielding the fourth letter, J or P, of your type code).
>
> ENTPs, unconstrained by boundaries or rules and regulations, constantly seek out opportunities to be creative and think differently about existing problems or processes. At times their insatiable appetite for change and innovation may cause them to spend too much time in the idea generation phase. However, their entrepreneurial disposition and desire to find competitive advantage help ensure that they complete the innovation process.[17]

In general, personality diversity amongst team members is desired to allow for the sharing of different perspectives. However, individuals who are extreme introverts may find working in the social environment of teams overwhelming. While specific types (e.g. ENTP) may lead to more innovative team members, other types may serve a complementary role that enhances overall team performance. The Myers–Briggs Type Indicator can be purchased from the company Consulting Psychologists Press. You can also find many similar assessments by conducting a web search. Some of them have a fee and others are free of charge.

Communication

One of the hardest challenges for individuals when placed in a team-based environment is to effectively communicate with team members. In traditional organizations, many employees are not expected to communicate their opinions or share their ideas. This type of communication is the key to team success. Also, creativity in teams is highly dependent on effective communication.[18] If possible, communication training regarding how to communicate effectively should be conducted prior to team formation and continue on through the team orientation process.

Two major aspects of communication to focus on for development include self-disclosure and receptivity to feedback. Self-disclosure represents your willingness to express your feelings, opinions, and beliefs, while receptivity to feedback represents your openness to receive feedback from others on your behaviors, opinions, and beliefs. In effect, team members must effectively balance the sharing and receiving of information amongst each other. High-performing teams comprise individuals who are high in both self-disclosure and receptivity to feedback. However, this is a struggle for team members, especially in the early stages of development. Individuals struggle to break out of their traditional guarded posture to practice effective open communication.

Conflict Resolution

Conflict is the tension that exists when people or organizations have conflicting and competing goals. An organization's approach to conflict can make it either constructive or destructive. Modern organizations must approach conflict differently. They must realize that conflict in a team-based environment:

- is natural and often inevitable;
- is a possible motivator for change;
- can result from competition over values, power, or resources;
- can be constructive or destructive;
- can contribute to organizational innovation;
- can be managed to minimize losses and maximize gains for all team members.

Most people tend to dislike conflict. We have been taught since early childhood socialization that conflict is bad and should be avoided if possible. However, in many cases, conflict can be a constructive force, especially in an organization that emphasizes innovation and creative problem-solving.[19] In general:

Conflict is destructive if it:

- diverts energy from important tasks and issues;
- produces barriers to cooperation and collaboration;
- decreases productivity;
- deepens differences amongst parties;
- destroys morale;
- produces negative behavior;
- prevents discussion and confrontation of differences.

Conflict is constructive when it:

- opens an issue to cooperative discussion and debate;
- leads to an innovative solution of a problem;
- leads to a higher level of understanding, communication, and trust;
- helps people to grow personally and apply their new knowledge, skill, and understanding to future situations;
- helps individuals realize the importance of communication.

Positive conflict resolution strategies that result in win–win solutions require open communication and a willingness to negotiate on important issues. There appears to be at least five types of conflict management styles:

- *forcing:* assertive and uncooperative behavior where you force your solution on others;
- *compromising:* arriving at a middle ground between the parties;
- *avoiding:* unassertive and uncooperative behavior where the individual runs from the conflict and those engaged in the conflict;
- *accommodating:* cooperative but unassertive behavior characterized by giving in to the other side;
- *collaborating:* cooperative and assertive behavior ending in a win–win solution where both sides get what they really need.

While in the short run, any of the styles may be somewhat effective, most team-based situations require at a minimum compromise and at a maximum collaboration to be a high-performing team. Forcing, avoiding, and accommodating styles often damage relationships and lead to a lack of team integration. Also, while compromising is an easier alternative since you are essentially dividing the "pie" down the middle, teams or individuals in conflict should attempt a collaborative result where each side negotiates the issue until both sides are satisfied that their critical issues are resolved.

Effective management of conflict comes from the following steps:

1. identifying and understanding *root causes* of conflict;
2. recognizing styles of conflict and working towards a collaborative resolution;
3. exploring needs and differences amongst team members; and
4. working toward constructive resolution of the conflict.

What kind of strategies do teams use in situations of conflict and what are the consequences for creativity? Researchers Petra, Goldschmidt, and Meijer analyzed how design teams coped with conflict during idea generation.[20] They found that even in a laboratory environment, design teams encounter a considerable amount of conflict. The high innovation and high functionality groups used a more competing and a more compromising style, whereas groups rated low on the same parameters used a more collaborating style. This result seems counterintuitive and contradicts past research. The authors suggest that creative performance in teams is not achieved mainly by agreement but needs cognitive confrontation. However, this finding makes no suggestion for long-term team survival. One possible explanation of these results is that the design project was viewed as short term and temporary, given its experimental nature, so participants may have engaged in behaviors that could be detrimental to long-term team effectiveness.

Decision-Making

Decisions by teams have many advantages over those made by individuals. Any one individual may be limited by professional expertise, ability to gather information, and ability to integrate information. In a team environment, individuals bring together a broader base of skills, experience, and expertise. Teams also provide a forum for brainstorming and critical evaluation of alternatives. The following guidelines are helpful when deciding who to include in the decision-making process:

- If a high-quality decision is necessary but employee acceptance is not a concern, include those who are experts in the area.
- If acceptance by employees is necessary but quality of the decision is not an issue, include representation by those employees affected by the decision.
- If a high-quality decision and employee acceptance are both important, form a team of experts and employee representatives.
- If both decision-making quality and employee acceptance are not important, make the decision yourself.

When making team-based decisions, at least five steps should be followed. It is important to note that many decision-making processes are suggested in the literature. Critical elements of an effective decision-making process include problem identification, creative brainstorming, action planning, implementation, and evaluation.

Step 1: Identifying/Defining the Problem

The team members must take the time to assess the major issues. You need to make sure you are getting at the root cause of the problem and not merely addressing symptoms. Some specific issues to address at this stage are:

- Was everyone who might have relevant data represented at the team meeting?
- Were those most directly involved in defining the problem encouraged by the leader and other team members to give information?
- Was everyone asked whether they agree with the final problem statement as written?

Step 2: Solution Generation

Activity at this step requires brainstorming possible alternatives. Some specific rules to follow when brainstorming include:

- No evaluation of any kind is permitted as alternatives are being generated. Individual energy is spent on generating ideas, not defending them.
- The wildest possible ideas are encouraged. It is easier to tighten alternatives up than loosen them.
- The quantity of ideas takes precedence over the quality. Emphasizing quality engenders judgment and evaluation.
- Participants should build on or modify the ideas of others. Poor ideas that are added to or altered often become good ideas.

Some issues to be addressed by team members in step 2 include:

- Have all the resources of the team been used to generate ideas?
- Did the leader and other team members take time to encourage those who might be slower at expressing ideas?
- Did the team take time to examine all the ideas and combine them into sets of alternatives?
- Was criticism tactfully discouraged and evaluative comments postponed?

Step 3: Ideas to Action

Once a list of possible solutions has been generated, the team should create an action plan for each of the possible solutions generated. Specifically, the team should assess people, resources (including time), processes, and machinery/equipment involved in the problem. Specific issues to be addressed include:

- Did the team examine the alternatives in terms of human, financial, and other costs associated with each and in terms of new problems that might arise?
- Was the team able to evaluate ideas critically without attacking individuals who proposed or supported those ideas?
- Is the chosen solution related to the problem statement and the goals developed earlier?
- Was final consensus reached on a trial solution? If not, was the extent of agreement among team members clearly established?

Step 4: Implementing the Decision

After the team reaches consensus on the best solution, the action plan (completed in step 3) for that solution must be implemented. Meetings to secure the resources need to be conducted. Also, the team should devise a timeline for full implementation. Issues to be addressed in step 4 include:

- Did the team identify the various forces that might help or hinder the action being planned?
- Were all team members involved in the discussion, particularly in giving information needed to define actions and ensure that essential steps weren't left out?
- Were all the needed resources for taking the action clearly identified?
- Did each person who accepted responsibility for a task make a clear commitment to carry out that responsibility?

Step 5: Team Decision-Making Evaluation

In order to not repeat mistakes made in the first four decision-making steps, the team should evaluate the effectiveness of their decision-making process. In addition, the team should determine the appropriate criteria to evaluate the success of the decision itself. Some final issues to address include:

- Has the team reviewed the desired outcomes and developed measures to indicate the degree of success achieved?
- Were contingency plans outlined for critical steps so that the overall plan could continue with modifications along the way if necessary?

When it comes to innovation project teams, researchers Akgun, Lynn, and Byrne suggest that management should enhance changes in beliefs and routines when facing advances in technological sophistication. They believe that to minimize groupthink, management should break established team mental models and project infrastructures by encouraging new behaviors. They suggest activities such as using a devil's advocate, bringing outsiders into the decision-making process, or training the team on lateral (creative) thinking.[21] Devil's advocates are appointed from within the group to challenge all assumptions and ensure that all possible solutions are considered. Outsiders are experts in the area being addressed who can provide a fresh look to possible alternatives and are not impacted by team conflict or relationships. Lateral or creative thinking involves invoking processes that force team members to continually diverge or brainstorm in an "out of the box" way and not rush to quick problem identification or solutions.

As discussed in this section of the chapter, elements related to person–team fit including personality, communication, conflict resolution, and decision-making styles are positively related to team effectiveness. One other element, the leader–team fit, should also be considered. Researchers Sarin and O'Conner emphasized the impact of team leader characteristics on conflict resolution behavior, collaboration, and communication patterns of cross-functional new product development teams. They surveyed 246 members of 64 new product development teams and found that leader participative management style and initiation of goal structure exerted the strongest influence on internal team dynamics. Both participative management and initiation of goal structure had a positive effect on functional conflict resolution, collaboration, and communication quality within the teams' studies. They also found that dysfunctional conflict resolution and formal communications were reduced.[22]

Commmon Barriers to Implementation

Team implementation, as discussed earlier, is a dynamic process requiring organizational commitment. However, there are several barriers that can inhibit team success. These barriers include resistance to change, lack of proper direction, and threats to employee security.

Resistance to Change

Work teams are not appropriate to all work situations such as highly specialized functions. Approximately 25–30 percent of workers do not want to be "empowered." Some of the most likely contributors to this resistance include previous bad experiences in team environments, introverted personality types, and age of the employees (older workers seem to be more resistant to trying new approaches).

Lack of Proper Direction

Teams are often highly motivated but lack clear direction. Since about 70–75 percent of the workforce is not resistant to teams, initially they feel energized or motivated by the notion of this type of structure and the opportunity to be empowered. However, empowerment does not mean abandonment! While the role of the manager changes to more of a facilitator perspective, it should not go away. Someone has to communicate information to the team and facilitate team discussions and other functions. This "leader" must help secure resources and speak for the team to other organizational units.

Employee Security

Employees need to trust management in that teams are not being used as a mechanism for downsizing, especially when it comes to their own job. Unions often fear teams, unless they are union based, because they also threaten the collective power of the union process. However, many unionized firms have successfully implemented cross-functional teams comprising union and nonunion employees. The key in developing employee teams seems to be a common belief in the team's mission and open communication.

Conclusion: Implementing Effective Teams

In conclusion, team structures should not be implemented without careful study. Remember, one size does not fit all. Consider your mission, the experience level of your employees, top management support, and training resources before you implement such a strategy. These key steps will help with implementing innovation teams:

- Prepare the organization for the change. Effective teamwork requires trust, effective communication, and viable conflict resolution strategies. Also, the right people need to be on the team. The right mix of employee skills and experiences coupled with strong interpersonal skills will increase team effectiveness. Training and development activities may be required to prepare the organization for effective team implementation and utilization.
- Make sure the appropriate team structure is selected to address the problem at hand. Furthermore, understand that there is a team learning curve and it can take many months for a team to reach high performance. A good team leader will recognize the stages of team development and lead the team effectively through those stages.
- Be selective when it comes to team leaders. Besides technical experience, utilize effective selection and training practices to find and develop individuals to be effective motivators and communicators.
- Utilize a process for creative or lateral thinking. Typical problem-solving processes often rush to a solution without diverging deeply on what the problem really is and identifying possible solutions.
- Evaluate team effectiveness on a regular basis and seek ways to continuously improve. Table 9.1 contains important questions to consider when evaluating team effectiveness.

Additionally, Roger Schwarz in the *Harvard Business Review*[23] cited nine key issues that research on team creativity and innovation outcomes have demonstrated to be important. These key issues include:

1. compelling vision;
2. goal interdependence;
3. support for innovation;
4. task orientation;
5. cohesive team;
6. strong internal and external communication;

TABLE 9.1 Ten Questions to Ask about Your Team

Every organizational intervention or change effort should be monitored and evaluated to assess programmatic strengths and weakness. No change effort is flawless, and fine-tuning is often necessary to ensure the continued success of the team implementation effort. Evaluation should take place during implementation as well as when the team effort has been completed and the team is ready to adjourn. The following ten questions are critical to address the success of your firm's efforts in this area.

1. Are the manager/facilitator's expectations clear to everyone?
2. Are members' expectations for each other well communicated? Are individual responsibilities clearly stated?
3. Are you a cohesive and integrated team? Is everyone working toward the same goals?
4. Do members help each other appropriately, giving feedback on how their behavior affects each other's effectiveness? Are members honest with each other?
5. Does the team have all the skills and abilities it needs to do the job?
6. Is each member doing their utmost to help you?
7. Does the team communicate well with others?
8. As a group, do you place a high priority on developing each other?
9. Is each member involved in decision-making?
10. Are you satisfied as a member of this team?

---

7. understanding what part of the problem-solving process you are working in . . . creativity varies depending on the stage;
8. diversity is a benefit but you need to be prepared to manage conflict, build cohesion, and increase empathy;
9. conflict can be good at the right time.

These key elements reflect the need to focus on the team formation guidelines provided in this chapter.

Innovation-in-Action

Creating and Sustaining Hot Spots for Innovation

Hot Spots are the organization phenomena that result from what Linda Gratton refers to as the twin drivers of democratic organizational change. These drivers, democratic organizational change and new technologies, create powerful energy causing innovative forms of business enterprise.

According to the developer of the Hot Spot concept, Linda Gratton, "You always know when you are in a Hot Spot . . . where cooperation flourishes, great energy is created, and innovation, productivity and excitement drive the day." Gratton assesses the necessary ingredients for creating Hot Spot energy and uses the concept of boundaryless cooperation as the fuel for the Hot Spot.

Gratton suggests that Hot Spots' innovation energy comes from people freely combining their insights, wisdom, and intelligence. To create this energy, the following conditions are critical:

1. having a "cooperative mindset";
2. identifying "boundary spanners";
3. sharing "igniting purpose";
4. sustaining sufficient "productive capacity."

Dr. Gratton uses the following formula to suggest how these elements fit together to create Hot Spots.

Hot Spots = (Cooperative Mindset × Boundary Spanning × Igniting Purpose) × Productive Capacity

Five underlying productive practices—appreciating talent, making commitments, resolving conflicts, synchronizing time, and establishing a rhythm—are necessary to create the conditions for Hot Spots. Gratton also argues that the initial step in creating a Hot Spot is to stop doing things. The old language, practices, and processes of competition must be stopped. Since teams of people working together are responsible for most of the modern innovations, we need a new language and practices that promote cooperation.

Gratton makes several suggestions for improving organizational practices to create and maintain Hot Spots:

1. The first thing companies need to do is to stop recruiting people who are very aggressive and could harm or destroy democratic norms established by the organization.
2. Companies need to stop creating reward systems that reinforce competitive behavior. New talent must be identified that focuses on relationships and cooperation.
3. While there is value in benchmarking against other firms who are successful in creating Hot Spots (some examples provided by Gratton include: BP, Ogilvy One, Nokia, and Linux), the real competitive advantage comes from the organization identifying the organization's own "signature processes." These emerge organically and embody a given organization's character. Employee development activities should be focused on identifying collaborative ways of working, cultivating relationships, and motivating people through meaningful purpose, vision, and goals.

(Adapted from: Tavis, A. 2010. Hot spots: why some teams, workplaces, and organizations buzz with energy—and others don't (book review). *Entrepreneur. com*, September. Retrieved September 6, 2010, from: www.entrepreneur.com/ tradejournals/article/166051344.html.)

Key Terms

barriers to team effectiveness:

- employee security
- information resources
- resistance to change

critical elements for effectiveness:

- personality types
- communication style
- conflict resolution style
- decision-making process

stages of team development:

- forming stage
- storming stage
- norming stage
- performing stage
- adjourning stage

team innovation performance/outcomes
types of teams:

- functional teams
- project teams
- cross-functional teams
- developmental teams
- permanent teams
- semi-autonomous teams
- autonomous teams

work teams

Discussion Questions

1. Why are teams so important to the corporate innovation process?
2. Describe the stages of team development. What issues are presented in each stage? How do they relate to innovation?
3. What types of teams would be effective for incremental innovation? Radical innovation?
4. What are the barriers to effective team implementation? How would you overcome these barriers?

5. What are the important steps in a team decision-making or problem-solving process?
6. When is conflict destructive? Constructive?
7. What is the most applicable personality trait for innovation? Why?
8. Why is it important to evaluate team effectiveness? How would you evaluate team effectiveness?
9. What does the research suggest as key issues relating team creativity to increased innovation?

Notes

1 Vince Lombardi, former legendary football coach of the Green Bay Packers, 1959–1967, *Famous quotes by Vince Lombardi*, accessed at: www.vincelombardi.com/quotes.html.
2 Katzenbach, J. & Smith, D. 1993. *The Wisdom of Teams: Creating the High-Performance Organization*, Boston: Harvard Business School Press, p. 45.
3 Griffin, R. & Moorhead, G. 2010. *Organizational Behavior: Managing People and Organizations*, 9th ed., Cincinnati: South-Western/Cengage Learning, p. 253.
4 Wellins, R., Byham, W. & Dixon, G. 1994. *Inside Teams*, San Francisco: Jossey-Bass.
5 Gaylen, N.C., Honig, B. & Wiklund, J. 2004. Antecedents, moderators, and performance consequences of membership change in new venture teams. *Journal of Business Venturing*, 20: 705–725.
6 Jassawalla, A.R. & Sashittal, H.C. 1999. Building collaborative cross-functional new product teams. *Academy of Management Executive*, 13: 50–61.
7 Haneda, S. & Keiko, I. 2018. Organizational and human resource management and innovation: which management practices are linked to product and/or process innovation? *Research Policy*, 47: 194–208.
8 Van Knippenberg, D. 2018. Team innovation. *Annual Review of Organizational Psychology*, 4: 211–233.
9 Griffin, R. & Moorhead, G. 2010. *Organizational Behavior: Managing People and Organizations*, 9th ed., Cincinnati: South-Western/Cengage Learning, p. 253.
10 Hyung-Jin Park, M., Lim, J.W. & Birnbaum-More, P.H. 2009. The effect of multiknowledge individuals on performance in cross-functional new product development teams. *Journal of Product Innovation Management*, 26: 86–96.
11 Bantel, K.A. & Jackson, S.E. 1989. Top management and innovations in banking: does the composition of the top team make a difference? *Strategic Management Journal*, 10: 107–124.
12 Blindenbach-Driessen, F. & Van Den Ende, J. 2010. Innovation practices compared: the example of project-based firms. *Journal of Product Innovation Management*, 27: 705–724.
13 Tuckman, Bruce W. 1965. Developmental sequence in small groups. *Psychological Bulletin*, 63: 384–399; and Tuckman, Bruce W. 1972. *Conducting Educational Research*, 5th ed., New York: Harcourt Brace Jovanovich.
14 Hyatt, D. & Ruddy, T. 1997. An examination of the relationship between work group characteristics and performance: once more into the breech. *Personnel Psychology*, p. 555.
15 Johnson, S. 1993. Work teams: what's ahead in work design and rewards management. *Compensation and Benefits Management Review*, March–April: 35–41.
16 McClurg, L. 2001. Team rewards: how far have we come? *Human Resource Management*, Spring: 73–86.
17 Killen, D. & Williams, G. no date. *Introduction to Type® and Innovation*. Consulting Psychologist Press. Accessed September 8, 2010, at: www.cpp.com/pdfs/6185.pdf.
18 How team communication affects innovation. 2005. *MIT Sloan Management Review*, 45: 7.
19 Carsten, K. 2008. The virtue and vice of workplace conflict: food for (pessimistic) thought. *Journal of Organizational Behavior*, January: 5–18.

20 Petra, B., Goldschmidt, G. & Meijer, M. 2010. How does cognitive conflict in design teams support the development of creative ideas? *Creativity and Innovation Management*, 19: 119–133.

21 Akgun, A., Lynn, G. & Byrne, J. 2005. Antecedents and consequences of unlearning in new product development teams. *Journal of Product Innovation Management*, 23: 73–88.

22 Sarin, S. & O'Connor, G.C. 2009. First among equals: the effect of team leader characteristics on the internal dynamics of cross-functional product development teams. *Journal of Product Innovation Management*, 26: 188–205.

23 Schwarz, R. 2015. What the research tells us about team creativity and innovation. *Harvard Business Review*, December. Accessed April 2, 2018, at: https://hbr.org/2015/12/what-the-research-tells-us-about-team-creativity-and-innovation.

PART 5

Implementation of Innovation (*I-Solution*)

10

INNOVATION TO COMMERCIALIZATION

Persuasion is the centerpiece of business activity. Customers must be convinced to buy your company's products or services, employees and colleagues to go along with a new strategic plan or reorganization, investors to buy (or not to sell) your stock, and partners to sign the next deal. But despite the critical importance of persuasion, most executives struggle to communicate, let alone inspire.

~Robert McKee, screenwriting coach[1]

Introduction

Innovations are not successful without commercial appeal. New products and services, no matter how technologically advanced or sophisticated, will not sell without having an authentic connection with the customer. Richard Maxwell and Robert Dickman capture the essence of this condition with their simple observation that:

There are two things everyone in business does every day. We all sell something—our products, our services, our skills, our ideas, our vision of where our business is going— and we tell stories. We sell things because this is how we as a democratic, capitalist society organize our energy. We tell stories because, as cognitive psychology is continuing to discover, stories are how we as human beings organize our minds. If we want to sell something, we have to persuade someone else to buy it.[2]

In the previous chapters, we discussed how to develop an innovative product or service. In this chapter, we'll provide guidance on how to commercialize your innovation. This chapter opens with a section on how to do market research. Market research will provide the evidence needed to support the potential rewards of your innovation for the company and the customer. This understanding is then used to prepare your selling points. Working with your knowledge of the customer, you'll emphasize the benefits of your product that your stakeholders care most about. You'll then be able to craft a compelling story to tell about your innovation. The chapter concludes with guidance on how to present this story to others.

Market Research

Establishing the viability of an idea is critical when seeking internal or external funding and support. A critical component to establishing viability is market research. The following sections describe the critical steps in identifying your market. Reliable sources of primary and secondary research help identify the market you plan to enter.

Understanding the Real Potential Market

A *market* is a group of (potential) customers who have purchasing power and unsatisfied needs. An innovation will only be successful if a market exists for the new product or service. Marketing research involves gathering and analyzing information about a particular market. The following actions will help you identify a potential customer base for your innovation:

1. Define the Research Purpose and Objectives

You need to construct a concrete and simple description of your product or service. Included in this description is an explanation of the specific product or service, identification of the potential customer base, and an analysis of the issues related to doing business in the market. This market segmentation process identifies a specific set of characteristics that differentiate one group of consumers from the rest. It's the process of identifying your niche in the market. See Appendix A at the end of this chapter for a detailed example of an innovation description.

2. Select Type of Data

Many market identification tools exist, but all research approaches can be categorized as primary or secondary. *Primary data* is information you collect yourself, such as surveys, focus groups, and one-on-one interviews. *Focus groups* are generally utilized for group reactions to a product while surveys and interviews assess widespread interest in the idea. *Surveys* also measure the propensity for others to purchase and/or use the potential product or service. *One-on-one interviews* provide the opportunity to better understand what a target customer *really* thinks about your product without facing the peer pressure present in a group setting. Primary data is time consuming to collect, but it will be current and relevant. *Secondary data* is information that you collect from already published sources such as government reports, chambers of commerce, trade associations, business assistance centers such as the Small Business Development Center (SBDC), and business websites. There are also specific websites that provide important populations statistics. Two of the most popular sites are Google Maps and Trends. These sites provide demographic data based on age, sex, race, location, and household size for stats such as household income. Business information is also available from some of these sources. Hoover's is especially useful for studying your competitors and establishing comparable financial numbers (also known simply as comparables), as it lists company contact information and basic data for each firm. These sites, like many business directories, charge a subscription fee. Cost of Doing Business reports by trade associations are especially helpful for estimating financial numbers. Both primary and secondary data can be good sources for business research.

3. The Survey Process

The participants in your survey will be those individuals or businesses who might potentially buy your product or service. Identify who will make the purchasing decision and ask them to participate in your study.

Next, you need to determine the number of respondents necessary for statistical relevance. Table 10.1 provides some guidelines for identifying the number of surveys needed to represent a specific sized population.

Selecting a survey type is also an important issue. Surveys are usually conducted via in-person interviews, postal mail, email, or on the phone. Response rates vary from 10–30 percent for postal mail and email, and up to 70 percent for in-person and telephone approaches. In general, surveys are more effective when conducted in person near the site of the possible target market. If you must use mail surveys,

TABLE 10.1 Required Samples for Markets of Various Sizes

In the Market	Sample Size
1–55	50
56–63	55
64–70	60
71–77	65
78–87	70
88–99	80
100–115	90
116–138	100
139–153	110
154–180	125
181–238	150
239–308	175
309–398	200
399–650	250
651–1,200	300
1,201–2,700	350
2,701 or more	400

make sure the survey is sent to the appropriate person and try to offer some induce-ment to complete the survey. You could promise a copy of the results, offer a gift certificate or coupon, or have a drawing for a prize for all participants.

4. Construct the Questionnaire

Generally, surveys comprise at least four types of questions. The different types include demographic, factual, attitude, and open-ended questions. Table 10.2 describes each of the different types of questions. Two examples of actual surveys can be found at the end of this chapter in Appendix B.

When constructing a survey, adhere to the following tips.

Tips for Survey Development

- Make sure each question pertains to a specific objective in line with the purpose of the study.
- Keep each question short and simple. Lengthy or wordy questions often cause confusion.
- Avoid double-barreled items. These are items with conjunctions such as "and," "or," and "but." These items confuse the reader, and you won't know which part of the item they're answering.
- Place simple questions first and difficult-to-answer questions later in the questionnaire.
- Avoid leading and biased questions.
- When possible, use scaled questions rather than simple yes/no questions to measure intensity of an attitude or frequency of the experience.

TABLE 10.2 Common Question Formats

Questions	Description
Demographic Questions	These questions assess data that segments your market on variables such as age, gender, race, business, income, education, location, etc. The goal of these questions is to describe your client base. Be sure to only ask necessary questions. Provide ranges of choices for more personal topics such as individual or business income.
Factual Questions	Include questions concerning previous experience or use. Questions focus on yes/no questions for actual use and requests use ranges for amount of usage. It helps to provide ranges instead of asking for exact amounts.
Attitude Questions	Uses rating scale format to assess items like propensity to act, like/dislike, and importance. This is the most important part of the survey. Rating scales are usually 1 to 5, where 1 is not at all likely and 5 is very likely.
Open-ended Questions	These questions are put at the end of the survey.

- Make sure the questions assess what you're trying to measure.
- Keep the survey under two pages if possible. There's an inverse relationship between survey length and quit rate.
- Test face validity on a few people before administering the survey for real. Have others read the survey to ensure it's clear and precise. Test for understanding and measure the time it takes to complete the survey.

5. Analyze Results and Write Report

Typical analyses include averages, frequencies, and cross-tabulations of statistics, and content analysis of open-ended questions. Averages and frequencies are fairly straightforward and provide basic descriptive information about each item. Content analysis is a simple count of the number of times a response was given. Perhaps the most useful analysis is the cross-tabulation. This analysis allows you to cross a demographic item with any other item in the survey. For instance, you may want to know the difference in willingness to purchase your product or service based on sex, income, location, etc. This type of analysis is essential to identify the actual niche of individuals or businesses that would purchase the product or service. You can use this information to estimate percentages of the population who would purchase the product or service and at what price.

Once the analyses are completed, a report should be written summarizing the important findings and interpreting their implications for the viability and feasibility of your idea. This report is often included as part of an innovation plan or feasibility study. Important elements include: a statement of support for the product/service; segmentation of the viable market to determine niche; and projections of sales based on the target customers' likelihood to act and willingness to spend.

A thorough market analysis offers research that supports your idea's potential for success. The following section addresses other considerations required for commercializing your innovation, including business models, values, credibility, legitimacy, location, and strategy.

Preparing for Commercialization

Many managers have interesting and innovative ideas but struggle to move them forward through the ranks of the company. A key source of this frustration is the inability to get other needed constituencies to believe in the concept and vision as the manager does. If a manager can clearly convey the concept, vision, and important details, they're much more likely to gain buy-in from needed stakeholders. Unfortunately, many managers attempting innovation projects have not adequately thought through these concepts or systematically organized them into a compelling narrative.

The following sections of this chapter will assist you in explaining why you want to pursue the innovation and how you'll do it. Once you have answers to the questions in this chapter, you'll be able to better communicate your vision and goals. This preparation will make for better presentations, both formally and informally, to executives, colleagues, customers, and employees. One of the first things you'll be asked about is how your product or service fits the company's business model.

Business Model

A business model answers the question of how your company generates revenue streams. It's a tool that explains what you're selling and to whom, and how products and services are made and sold. A good business model is grounded in logical and well-supported assumptions about your customers, products, and processes.[3] A business model that fits well in a market can support a pipeline of profitable opportunities for a long time. For example, Dell's business model didn't change much for many years since its founding in a dorm room at the University of Texas. Specifically, Dell's business model could be summed up as one focused on providing reliable, low-cost computers to small businesses, educational institutions, and homes through direct selling. It worked quite well while the company scaled its operations to many times its original size. However, with the advent of new platforms, cloud storage, and mobile technologies, Dell had to tweak the business model to reflect the new dynamics of the computer industry. Dell decided to merge with EMC in 2016 to enhance its data storage and analytics business. So far the adjustment to the business model seems to have worked well for Dell, as their revenues increased to $55 billion in 2016.

Straying from a business model though is a risky move for a company, and should be undertaken with caution. A business model that's not well thought out or suitable for market conditions may even cause a company to fail. There are times where it may make sense to pursue revolutionary innovations, but if it doesn't strategically fit well into the company's operations, trouble may follow. The AOL/Time Warner merger is a classic example of an effort to be revolutionary, only to lead to organizational frustration. In 1999, America Online chairman Steve Case was leading a company that was soaring in the stock market. Looking to capitalize on its market value and build the media company of the future, Case pursued content companies that could complement his internet business. He first approached Michael Eisner of Disney with the idea, but Eisner thought the AOL market valuation didn't accurately reflect reality and was reticent to get involved in such a deal. Case then approach Gerald Levine of Time Warner, and a deal was struck that brought the two companies together. It was bad timing for Time Warner, because soon after the deal the internet bubble burst, bringing its value down with the AOL merger.[4]

To make matters worse, AOL and Time Warner struggled in defining a business model that made the arrangement profitable. Originally, AOL was to provide technology support and Time was to offer content for customers, but the business model's underlying assumptions were faulty and caused the new company to struggle.

Had Gerald Levine given more thought to Time Warner's business model, the AOL/Time Warner situation may have been averted.

In considering whether your innovation will gain support from your stakeholders and lead to increased revenues, it's important to consider your company's business model. The first question you must answer in creating a business model is, *"What does your company sell?"* You should be able to describe the general nature of your company's product/service/experience offerings. You should also understand why these commercial offerings are part of the company's strategy. The second important question to answer is, *"Who is your company's customer?"* Provide a profile of the average customer your company sells to. The third question is, *"How does your company make and sell its products/services/experiences?"* You might be asked these follow-up questions too: *Why does your company do it this way? How is your company better than competitors in producing the commercial offering? Why is your company effective in reaching its customers?* Having an answer to these questions will give you better understanding of how your innovation will aid your company in boosting profits. Taking your answers to the above questions, you can now construct your company's business model into one statement:

- Refer to your answers to the questions, "What does your company sell?" "Who is your company's customer?" and "How does your company make and sell its products/services/experiences?" and use them to fill in the blanks in the following statement.
- (fill in your company name) sells/provides/offers (fill in your company's product/service/experience) by/through (fill in how your company produces its offerings) and (fill in how your company sells and distributes it) to (fill in your company's customer).
- Circle the action verbs and prepositions that make the most sense in your statement, i.e., choose the words that help your business model statement to flow better.

Here's an example of what Harley Davidson's business model might be: "Harley Davidson sells performance motorcycles and related accessories and merchandise through mass customization and franchised dealerships to affluent customers." If you were a manager at Harley and wanted to gain support for your innovation, you would be wise to explain how it fits into the company's current business model and strategy.

This statement now allows you to clearly explain how your company makes money and what your company does. With this knowledge, you should now be sure that your innovation fits within that model and be able to explain how it does so to your stakeholders. If your innovation doesn't fit within that model, you better have good reasons for why the company should still pursue it. Does it support the company's overall strategy in some way?[5] Now let's consider how your products create value for the customer.

Value

For a customer to be interested in a new product or service, it must have clear value to them. Value is attained by the customer when they believe the derived benefits from the product or service exceed the costs of purchasing it, as depicted in the formula below:

$$\text{Value} = \text{Perceived Benefits} \div \text{Perceived Costs}$$

If the value of an idea is low, the manager can work on better explaining the benefits of the product or service, or by lowering the costs involved in purchasing and/or using it. For example, the company could lower the price, increase the ease of adoption, and offer incentives for purchasing it. Please refer back to Chapter 9 for more guidance on increasing customer value.

Credibility

One of the most important factors executives and other stakeholders consider when deciding the extent of their involvement with a new project is your credibility. Senior managers often have many choices in their company as to who they'll invest time and resources in and who will gain their chief support. After all, most businesses are not only economic in nature but also political. And in a political climate, you get more approval when your bosses like you. If you can make their job easier or ensure your ideas help them secure more of what matters to them, you'll have their support. It's basic human nature to reciprocate help to those who help you. Senior managers also want reassurance that they're making the right call by supporting you. After all, if they support you, your mistakes become their mistakes once they approve your project. On the other hand, your success becomes their success as well. Explain how your project will improve their numbers and help their part of the business be more successful.

You also get more approval when your bosses trust your competence. Reassure their choice of supporting you by explaining what qualities you bring to the project and why you're able to meet the expectations placed on you. You should also be able to do this for each of your team members. The following questions provide guidance in establishing your credibility with senior managers:

What's your educational background?

What's your employment background?

What experience do you have inside the company?

What experience do you have with new product development or startup situations (either in the past or present)?

How strong are your financial skills?

What's your marketing/sales background?

What experience do you have with research and design?

What experience do you have with production/operations?

What's your technology background and have you worked in customer support before?

What's your relationship with the current target market?

What type of experience do you have in the product domain and content area?

Do you have an effective network inside the company to get the results you desire for the project? If not, who would be helpful in addressing this need?

By collecting profiles on possible teammates and yourself, you'll have information you can use for promoting the capability and strength of your team. Additionally, you'll be able to recognize what your team is lacking and know where to shore up the weaknesses.

Once you've been given the go-ahead to move the project forward, continue to reassure senior managers that they made the right decision in backing your team. One executive friend of ours once advised us that as you move up in an organization, your job becomes exponentially harder. The decisions are bigger and the number of people who rely on them expands. Most executives feel like their day is spent considering requests from people who are seeking favor or approval from them. In other words, most people who want to meet with an executive are doing so because they need something from them. To add to the pressures of an executive's day, a battle of egos often takes place among senior managers. After all, confident people reach the top. If the company culture is especially competitive in a race to reach the CEO job, executives may feel like they're playing a character in a real life *Game of Thrones* . . . and that's within their own ranks. The ranks below them may also include junior executives who are eyeing their position. So how can you continue to reassure your boss that they made the right call greenlighting your project? Try your best to be a source of confidence (and not stress) to your boss through your words *and* your actions. To garner their support in the first place you had to say the right things. That's why the above questions were given as prompts to help you prepare your answers to questions they may ask about your idea and your team's capability to execute. However, now you need to show them everyday that they made the right decision in approving your project. Encourage your team to pursue excellence in everything they do on the project. This is one of your primary responsibilities as leader of the team. Discipline in how you and your teammates interact with others in the company, persistence through the inevitable dips that occur on any project, and relentless problem-solving and attention to details will comfort your bosses and allow them to put their attention to other pressing matters. You don't want to be one of the people they worry about during their day. Always maintain your professionalism even as stress mounts and the long hours wear you down. Creative tension and disagreements may flair up inside the team at times, but keep it inside the group. As leader of the project, it's your job to reach resolution and move the team forward. Don't make the team's problems your boss's problems. Remember, your job is to make your boss's job easier and to make them look good. With limited resources and hard-earned reputations at stake, senior executives want to know that company money is in good hands and on high-return projects.

Now let's flip the situation. Imagine one of your employees has come to you with an idea. What would give you confidence that they're able to make their idea a success? Well, you'll hope to hear them say the right things. After all, their emotional intelligence will be important in how they lead their team and the messages they send throughout the organization. Plus, you'll want to know that they have a track record that evidences their capability to do the job. But how can you tell if they'll *do* the right things once they're working on the project? It's very common for people to enthusiastically present a picture of what they'll accomplish and then not follow through. Are these people lying to you? Usually, no. They actually believe they can do it. When people want approval from you, they'll tell you what they think you want to hear. Once on the job, though, their weaknesses may thwart their efforts. For example, they may not have the work ethic or attention to detail that's required to do innovative work. Maybe they don't manage their team's timeline well. Or, something we see a lot more of these days is that people are often overcommitted to too many projects or distracted by what's going on in their social media world. You want to be sure you support employees who are focused and dedicated to the project. The best leaders support teams that organize and manage their work well and that can problem-solve and rally themselves through their difficult times.

So how can you tell if your well-intended employee will come through on what they promise? What "tells" can reveal how a person will perform on a project? Here's a method we've found very effective in screening requests: Give a little test to evaluate work habits and attitude. Now don't tell them it's a test, because if they know what they're being asked to do is a prerequisite to getting approval, they'll definitely come through on the request. Instead, at the end of the meeting, ask them to do a little task for you as a favor, like the idea is an afterthought. For example, you could say, "Thanks for sharing your idea with me. It's interesting, and I'll consider it. Hey, by the way, can you run this file over to Louise in marketing when you get a chance?" Or you could say, "Hey, when you're not too busy, would you mind sending me the contact information of that engineer you told me about? Thanks." Or maybe, "That was really neat what you told me you read in that *Fast Company* article. Could you send me a copy?" Now wait and see when—or if—they follow through on their promise. If they can't follow through on a small commitment, it's very possible they won't be reliable on the big project. Habits are hard to break, so getting a good read on their discipline and follow-through is important. Once they're on the big project, they'll bring their full selves to the work—the positive and the negative. We've found this little test very effective in screening who will work well with us on big projects and who won't.[6]

And you should also do your due diligence on their work ethic by talking to others who have supervised or worked with them in the past. Chances are they'll be the same when they work for you. Ask your colleague the following questions about your prospective team leader: *Were they reliable? Did they follow through on what they promised? How was their attention to detail? Were they decent to the people around them? Have they ever created something new in the past? How did they do while they worked on that? Did they lead other projects you gave them? Did they meet or exceed expectations? Do they take great pride in their work? Do they aspire toward excellence? Do they get satisfaction from doing quality work? Or were they a "pain-in-the-neck" to work with? Were they reciprocal in their relationships; in other words, did they give as much as they took? Did they talk badly of others behind their backs? Did they maintain confidentiality when requested? Are they "on their game" most of the time, or does chaos seem to be wherever they are? How do they respond to pressure and stressful situations? Would you want them on one of your teams again if the opportunity arose?* It's unlikely you'll find perfection in any employee. Everyone has weaknesses, and some very capable and creative people can be a bit combative or difficult to be around. That doesn't mean you should say "no" to their request because maybe they're exceptional at what they do and they always get the job done. Or maybe their style clicks well with the right people around them. But remember, do your due diligence and make an informed decision before you greenlight a project. Your leadership competence will be judged by the work your employees do.

Customers will also be interested in products developed by a credible team. Some teams are so successful in rolling out innovative products that consumers actually become fans of their work. For example, for almost 30 years Apple fans have been attending the Macworld Expo and WWDC developers conferences. Apple users get sneak peeks at what the company will bring to market that year, and can attend seminars on using the company's products. These venues have helped Apple sell over a billion iPhones over the last ten years. In a very short amount of time, Apple customers adopt the new products that come from these conferences. Apple fans are willing to cross into new product categories whenever the company unleashes its next innovation. Customers trust the innovative reputation of the engineering and management teams at Apple.[7] They look forward to seeing what products the company will roll out next. Imagine your customers asking what's new with your company.

Legitimacy

Another factor that will assist you in successfully launching your idea is to provide a sense of meaning to your project. In *Man's Search for Meaning*, Victor Frankl documents his experiences in a Nazi concentration camp. He discovered that the people who survived under the worst imaginable conditions were those who pursued something meaningful in their lives, whether it was looking forward to seeing family again or finishing a project they had started before their encampment. He later applied this thinking to help people find meaning in the regular world. Frankl discovered that when meaning was present, people performed at their best.[8] The same applies in business. You'll find that your project team will be more committed to your product's development if there's an understood and well-communicated meaning behind it. By sharing this meaning with others, you'll gain legitimacy and generate more interest in your project. Team members will be more motivated to work on it, and others outside the project will be more interested in seeing it be successful if they relate to the purpose and meaning of it. Thus, you should answer the following questions before moving forward on the project:

Why should this project be in existence?

What is the compelling reason for working on this project?

What benefits does this project bring your company?

What benefits does this project bring your customer?

What benefits does this project bring members of the project team?

What benefits does this project bring the world at large (if any)?

Will this project transform your company? If so, how?

Will this project transform your customer? If so, how?

Will this project transform members of the project team? If so, how?

Will this project transform the world at large in some way?

How will this project help prepare future leaders in the company?

How will this project make your company better?

How will this project make your customer better?

How will this project make the world at large a better place (if at all)?

What will we learn from doing the project that we didn't know before?

What new skills and capabilities will be gained by working on the project?

What opportunities may arise in the future from working on this project?

Location

Location, location, location. This often-used expression from marketing carries much wisdom. Where you're located is a major implication on all aspects of the project. Therefore, it's important to consider the locations needed for operations and sales for the product or service. Your supply chain perspective should be able to answer the following questions: *What suppliers will be needed to attain the key resources to build the product or supply the service? Who should you get quotes from in assessing which supplier is best for you? Which suppliers can be backups in case the ones you contract with aren't meeting your expectations? Are you prepared to secure additional supplies if demand for your product exceeds your expectations? How will you provide or sell the product to your customers? Who will help you in getting the product or service to market? What's your backup plan if your chosen distributors don't meet your expectations or can't fulfill their contract? What customer service will you provide, and how will you address customer problems?* Answering these questions will give you more understanding of the complexity and implications of your supply chain network. Once you have these answers, you can then turn to the following questions:

Where will the product be made?

What advantages does this location have with regard to access to supplies?

What disadvantages does this location have with regard to access to supplies?

What advantages does this location have with regard to labor?

What disadvantages does this location have with regard to labor?

What type of facilities will be needed for manufacturing the product?

What advantages does the manufacturing location have with regard to selling the product to customers?

What type of facility will be needed to sell the product/service?

What advantage do we have by using our current suppliers?

What disadvantages do we have by using our current suppliers?

What type of person would be effective selling to this market?

Where's the best location to introduce this product? Why?

Business-Level Strategy

Increasingly, businesses are being managed with a more global outlook, taking the interests of many diverse stakeholders into account. A stakeholder is any group that affects the way a company is run or who is affected by a company's actions. It's believed by many academics and businesspeople that balancing the interests of many stakeholders leads to higher trust in economic and community relations and improves a company's image and reputation. Concurrent with this attitude, the most important factor in business is one's *reputation*; thus, it's essential to manage in a way that develops respect and admiration from both the market and society. If that status is tarnished, it's often very hard to regain a positive reputation. Because of the importance of these issues, answering questions regarding your primary stakeholders, values, principles, mission, and vision are critical.[9] It's important to align your project team's stated goals with your company's expectations, in order to gain the support of your key stakeholders. If your innovation does not fit within the overall mission and values of the company, it will be difficult to gain acceptance among senior management and other stakeholders. Therefore, understanding what your organization focuses on and endorses will help you in crafting your pitch. You'll want your product's story to fit well with your company's narrative. Answer the following questions to gain acceptance for your idea:

Who are your company's key stakeholders?

What do the key stakeholders expect from your company and why do they hold these views?

How does your innovation satisfy the expectations of the key stakeholders?

How does your innovation satisfy the expectations of senior management?

Why will your innovation be accepted by the key stakeholders?

Why will senior management accept your innovation?

What are the values of senior management? What are the values of your key stakeholders?[10]

How does your innovation coincide and support those values?

What will you need to do to gain support of senior management? What will you need to do to gain support of key stakeholders?

What principles will you follow in developing and selling your innovation? What principles do you expect your project team to follow in getting the intended results?[11]

By explaining how your innovation serves the interests of senior management and key stakeholders, alignment of goals will be met for all interested parties. Where there are differences, you'll have a better understanding of how to address the gaps. Without understanding the social nature of innovation, you'll struggle in moving your ideas forward in your company. However, addressing possible criticisms and demonstrating adherence to company principles and values will better your chances of having your innovation accepted.

This section provided the preparatory work needed to provide justification for the commercialization of your innovation. In the following section, we examine how to market the product or service to your customers.

Marketing the Innovation

Many companies make the mistake of going to market with a message that's neither clear nor compelling. A major challenge as a corporate innovator is to present the new product or service in attractive enough form to be interesting to potential customers. The guidelines in this section will help you in delivering a message that resonates with your market.

Taking the information from the previous sections, you can now shape and refine the description of your innovation. After the necessary data and analyses have been compiled, they should be shaped into a compelling narrative for your product or service. After all, large quantities of data are merely facts. To be useful, they must be organized into *meaningful* information. It's at this stage where the project team really begins to take the idea to the next level by giving semantic structure to the underlying concepts of the innovation. Customer mapping is a very effective tool for creating a marketing strategy that will be effective with the customer.

Customer Mapping

Customer mapping summarizes and simplifies information by providing a pictorial representation of how the value proposition, benefits, customer outcomes, and features are in alignment. Features will serve to fulfill the value proposition, and the value proposition will deliver benefits to the customer. The following steps can be performed for virtually any product or service in about 20 minutes. You'll need easel paper or poster board, a marker, index cards, and tape for this exercise.

> *Step 1: Describe the product or service idea you have.* The product description should be very succinct. For example, in a recent workshop, one participant said she worked for a nonprofit that was focused on healthy lifestyles. She said she'd like to open an adult playground where grownups can act like kids again. She was then asked to explain why she came up with this idea. In this particular case, the participant said that for obese people traditional health clubs can be intimidating, and that her idea would make working out more fun. Exercising in a carefree way like kids would change the fundamental nature of the activities. Since burning calories is a key component of fitness, any movement that was done would be more beneficial than staying home and avoiding the gym. Think of this concept as the "anti-CrossFit." CrossFit targets the ultra-exerciser who desires the most punishing and challenging workouts. A CrossFit "box" (also known as a gym to the rest of us) also provides a social setting for these extreme athletes. But the adult playground is for customers who struggle with exercise, so its design would be entirely different from a box.

> *Step 2: What's the value proposition you're offering to the customer with this product or service?* The value proposition succinctly states what the product or service ultimately delivers to the customer. With regard to the adult playground, it provides adults a way to get some exercise, unwind, socialize, and relieve stress during their busy days.

> *Step 3: Who is the target market for this idea?* For the adult playground, it was overweight adults between the ages of 22 and 50.

> *Step 4: Provide a product concept combining the product description, value proposition, and target market.* In this case, the product concept is "a playground that will offer adults between the ages of 22 and 50 an opportunity to play like children again."

Step 5: Put the product concept on an index card and place it in the middle of a large sheet of paper.

Step 6: Answer the following question as many times as possible, "Why would the target market be interested in this product or service?" This question was posed to the workshop participant as, "Why would overweight adults between the ages of 22 and 50 be interested in a playground just for them?" The answers that were given were: "(1) To relieve stress, (2) For a fun place to go on a date, (3) To have a fun way to get exercise, (4) A chance to do something different, and (5) A chance to relive your childhood."

Step 7: Place each answer on separate index cards and place above the first card. Then draw lines up to each card from the original box.

Step 8: Now ask why customers would be interested in the answers to Step 7 and place the new answers to the questions on index cards. So we asked the participant, "Why would these adults be interested in relieving stress, having fun exercise, doing something different, reliving childhood, and having new places for dates?" She responded that, "It would provide a different way for adults to get exercise that's more fun and interesting than the traditional gym experience of weightlifting, running on treadmills, and riding stationary bikes. It would also give you a place to look forward to when you're bored with your usual activities." The cards were then placed on the map and logically linked together with arrows. We then asked her what *customer outcome* these answers would provide: "What outcome would happen if adults had a different way to get exercise that's more fun than a traditional gym?" and "What outcome would happen if you had a workout place that you looked forward to going to?" She replied, "It would increase the number of times I worked out because I'm not intimidated by the surroundings or the people there." It's possible that a participant will have more than one outcome, but in this case workout frequency was the main focus. We then asked why her customers would like this outcome, "Why would adults be interested in getting more workouts in?" She said, "Because it would help people, especially those who struggle with exercise, to become more fit." The map was expanded to the following configuration:

Step 9: Now answer the following question and place the responses on individual index cards: "What features would customers expect this service to have?" or "How could you provide this service to the customer?" The workshop participant stated that there were various ways this could be done, such as building adult versions of traditional playground equipment, providing adult versions of sandboxes where people can gather to socialize, selling adult versions of healthy cafeteria food, and organizing games of dodgeball, flag football, and other childhood games. The cards capturing the service features are then placed below the value proposition. In this step, you provide the ways you'll deliver your value proposition.

Step 10: Now check the logic of your customer map by asking, "If . . . will . . .?" questions. For example, if you offer adult versions of playground equipment, a sandbox, healthy cafeteria food, and playground games, will you be able to provide a playground that will offer adults between the ages of 22 and 50 an opportunity to play like children again? If the answer is yes, the logic of your service is valid and the connections hold. If there are any links that don't make sense, modify or drop that link.

Do this for each layer of the map. For example, if you offer a playground that offers adults between the ages of 22 and 50 an opportunity to play like children again, will this help them to relieve stress, have a fun way to get exercise, give them a chance to do something different, have a chance to relive their childhood, and provide them a fun place to go on a date? If yes, move up to the next layer.

If you help adults between the ages of 22 and 50 relieve stress, have a fun way to get exercise, and give them a chance to do something different, will they have a different way to get exercise that's more fun and interesting than the traditional gym experience of weights, treadmills, and stationary bikes? If the answer is yes, move to the right side and ask the same type of question. If you give adults between the ages of 22 and 50 a chance to relive their childhoods and have a fun place to go on a date, will they have a place to look forward to when they're bored with their usual activities? If the answer is yes, move up another layer.

If you provide a more fun and interesting place to work out that's not boring, will you help increase the number of times adults between the ages of 22 and 50 work out because they're not intimidated by the setting? If the answer is yes, move up to the last layer.

If you help adults between the ages of 22 and 50 increase the number of times they work out, will you help them overcome their struggle to become fit? If yes, you have completed your customer map. If, however, any of the links are questionable, you may need to modify the map or re-examine some of your answers. For example, maybe younger adults are not intimidated by a traditional gym setting. If so, maybe you need to change the target market to adults between the ages of 35 and 50; or maybe one of the features is too expensive or infeasible, in which case you drop it from your plans.

Once you have a map you're satisfied with, draw two lines above and below the value proposition box. Label the middle part *"value proposition,"* the upper layer *"benefits,"* the next layer *"customer outcomes,"* the highest layer *"tagline and customer bliss,"* and the lower part *"service/product features."* The top part of the map provides points you'll emphasize in your branding and selling. This will also be helpful as you develop your marketing campaign. The higher up the map, the more you'll be able to develop taglines and slogans for your company. For example, you could convert "Help people, especially those who struggle with exercise, to become more fit" into "Be a kid again: Smaller and livelier" or "The Adult Playground: The fun way to fitness." You can also start thinking about how you would deliver the features in the bottom of the map as well.

By building a customer map, you'll have a better sense of how to market your idea. You may modify different aspects of the map, such as changing the product, value proposition, or target market as needed. This becomes your road map for crafting your brand and developing a marketing campaign. The customer map is a visual representation of the elements you'll sell to your customers. In the following section, you'll learn how to pull those elements out of the map to craft your innovation story for your customers.

Utilizing the Customer Map

An important marketing concept for any business is branding. In a global marketplace, the number of competitors has grown at an astounding rate. With so many choices available to customers, it's important to gain an identity in your market that others recognize and understand as unique and special. For example, in auto insurance, Geico advertises its advantages of low cost and ease of purchase ("I saved a bundle switching to Geico" and "It's so easy even a caveman can do it") while Allstate advertises its full service approach ("You're in good hands with Allstate"). It's as simple as that, but it does separate the companies from each other. Customers understand the difference. If a company is the same as its competition, its products simply become commodities. In this unfortunate situation, the benefits the product or service provides is seen as easily replaceable. Customer loyalty and emotional attachment to the company is low in this scenario, because in a commoditized market the key source of differentiation is price. While this is sometimes an acceptable strategy, it can be quite risky for an innovative product or service. Ideally, the innovation is offering something never before seen by the target market and is worth paying a higher price for. Therefore, it's wise to create an image and identity that creates a place in the consumer's mind of distinction in quality, utility, and/or service. People will pay more for products and services when expectations are exceeded or if the goods are seen as having a better, distinctive difference from their competitors' offerings. When this condition has been attained, the company has created more value for the customer. The more value created by the company, the more loyalty and attention the customer will confer in return. Utilizing the customer map from the previous section, you can now answer the following questions in building the brand you'll communicate to your customers.

- What's unique about your innovation that will make it attractive to others?
- What's the value proposition you're offering your customer? (The value proposition can be found in the middle of your customer map. You can refine the statements on your customer map to better answer these questions as well.)
- Why will the customer find your value proposition worthy of their purchase?
- What evidence do you have to support the belief that they'll purchase what you offer?

- What evidence do you have to convince the customer that you can deliver the value proposition?
- What benefits does your product or service offer the consumer? (These can be found above the value proposition in your customer map. For the adult playground, the benefits were "(1) To relieve stress, (2) For a fun place to go on a date, (3) To have a fun way to get exercise, (4) A chance to do something different, and (5) A chance to relive your childhood.")
- What's the "ultimate bliss" you offer the customer with this product or service? I.e., what's the tagline for the product or service? (This sentiment will be found at the top of your customer map, and can be modified for the tagline. For example, the workshop participant with the adult playground idea said her tagline would be, "Getting exercise doesn't have to be such a workout anymore.")
- What features will you offer your customers that will make the product or service distinctive? (This can be found on the customer map below the value proposition. For the workshop participant, the features she wanted to include were "building adult versions of traditional playground equipment, providing adult versions of sandboxes where people can gather to socialize, selling adult versions of healthy cafeteria food, and organizing games of dodgeball, flag football, and other childhood games.")
- After developing the customer map and answering the above questions, do you believe you've developed a distinctive brand that separates your product or service from your competition?
- How does the brand fit with your company's current offerings?
- If there's any inconsistency between your innovation's brand and your company's brand, what will you have to do to reconcile the differences?
- What challenges may need to be overcome to develop the features? What could hold you back from developing the features?
- Whose support will you need in overcoming these challenges?

TABLE 10.3 Perceived Characteristics of the Innovation by the Customer

1.	**Relative advantage:** Is the innovation perceived as belter than what existed before it?
2.	**Compatibility:** Is the innovation perceived as being consistent with the existing values, past experiences, and needs of potential adopters?
3.	**Complexity:** Is the innovation perceived as difficult to understand and use by the adopter?
4.	**Trialability:** Can the innovation be tried out on a limited basis by the potential adopter?
5.	**Observability:** Are the benefits of the innovation easily visible to the potential adaptor?

Source: Adapted from Everett M. Rogers, *Diffusions of Innovation*, 4th edition. (New York: The Free Press: 1995), pp. 15–16.

- What evidence can you give these supporters that it's in their best interest to help you overcome these hurdles?
- What can your company learn from meeting these challenges that may be useful in the future?

Table 10.3 provides further considerations you'll need to account for in gaining customer acceptance for your innovation.

Selling Your Innovation Story

Once an innovation is developed and the marketing strategy determined, the next major challenge is presenting the idea to your key stakeholders. A compelling story will sustain the innovation as it passes different trials both inside and outside the company. In the classic business training video *Everyday Creativity*, *National Geographic* photographer Dewitt Jones explains his secret to taking breathtaking photos: He stations himself in unusual spots, remains patient, and opens himself up to photo opportunities as they arise. He's searching for what he calls *"the place of most potential."*[12] It's your chief task as a corporate innovator to explain how your innovation puts your company in the place of most potential. The three key elements that position your company in that place are having the right people (your team) working on the right product or service (your innovation) for the right time and place (your market). Evidence that you've found the place of most potential will be based on the degree of innovativeness, profitability, and scalability your idea has. Simply put, *will it shake up your market, generate large profits, and have the opportunity for further expansion into existing and new markets?*

If you've given serious consideration to all the questions above, you'll be in a good position to communicate your idea to any interested party. The following section provides guidelines for developing a business pitch and a presentation to interested stakeholders. This will help you in winning support for the new idea because you'll now have a well-developed and tested innovation story to tell. The oral presentation—commonly known as an elevator pitch (because of the analogy of riding an elevator and having only two minutes to get your story told to another person in the elevator)—provides the chance to sell the innovation to senior managers. Imagine a key company figure recognizes you and asks if there's anything you're working on that may interest them. Now's your chance to tell your innovation story. The pitch should be organized, well prepared, interesting, and flexible. You should develop an outline of the significant highlights that will capture the senior manager's interest. Although the general outline should be followed, feel free to improvise a bit if needed.

You may get the opportunity to formally pitch your idea to senior management. If so, use the following steps to prepare a more formal boardroom pitch:

1. Know the outline thoroughly.
2. Use keywords in the outline that will help you recall examples, visual aids, or other details.
3. Rehearse the presentation to get a feel for its length.

4. Be familiar with any equipment you may use if your presentation is given in a scheduled meeting—use your own laptop when possible.
5. The day before a scheduled presentation, practice the complete pitch by moving through each slide.[13]

Suggestions for Presentation

Managers are naturally anxious to tell (and sell) their idea. However, if the content is well developed and the delivery practiced, the presentation should go smoothly. In the content of the presentation, it's important to be brief and to the point, to summarize the critical factor or unique "hook" of your innovation up front, and to use no more than 12–15 PowerPoint slides. Consider a prop or story you can use to capture the essence of what your product or service does or to accentuate some feature that sets it apart from its competition. Following are some key suggestions about the actual delivery of the pitch to senior managers and other key stakeholders:

1. Focus on the pain that your innovation solves. Senior management wants to know exactly what problem is being solved by your innovation. Pinpoint the target of your solution.
2. First demonstrate the reachable market. Outline the immediate reachable group of customers that will be targeted. Explain why you've chosen that part of the market as your beachhead. Then extrapolate your numbers to potential markets you could reach in the future.
3. Explain the business model. How does this innovation make money for the company? How does it fit within the company's current financial strategies? What's the breakeven point for the innovation? What percentage of total capacity is the breakeven point? Demonstrating a clear method of getting to market and generating profit and growth will allude to a successful beginning and sustainable future for the new product or service. For example, if you have to operate at near full capacity to make a profit, your idea may be too risky. If, however, you can breakeven at, say, 25 percent of total capacity, your idea has a nice safety net for generating profits. Perfect conditions aren't required to make a profit in the second scenario. Additionally, if your product or service helps reduce organizational slack by better employing underutilized assets in the company, your idea will often be welcomed by senior managers.
4. Tout the project team. Every executive wants to know the skills and abilities of the project team's capacity for delivering and operationalizing the innovation. Emphasize the experienced people on your project team as well as any technical advisors who are on board.
5. Explain your metrics. Rather than using generic assumptions such as the famous "1 percent rule" (when someone says that the company will simply get 1 percent of a huge market with no research to back up the claim), *highlight the metrics that were used to calculate the market size and the revenue projections.* Also provide metrics that can serve to track progress on the project. *What key benchmarks need*

to be reached at each stage of the project? How do you know if you're doing well? What indicators show success? In other words, how do you define success and how do you measure it? What indicators can you use to track improvement? What evidence do you have that your idea is working? What's your proof? What indicators can you track as you sell the product or service? Show your bosses evidence that your project team is doing a good job and that your idea is good for the company.

6. Motivate the audience. The entire purpose of a pitch is to move the audience to the next step: another meeting to discuss everything in more detail. Therefore, you must remember that enthusiasm is hugely important. The senior managers must believe that you're excited before they can be excited.

7. Why *your company* and why *now?* The final point must answer two daunting questions in the minds of every senior manager: *Why is this right for the company, and why is this the right time for it to be launched?* Be confident in yourself, your project team, and your company. Always demonstrate a timeline to show the speed with which your project team plans to roll out the product and how quickly your company can capture a significant portion of the market.

What to Expect

The project team should realize that the audience reviewing their innovation and listening to their pitch can be conservative and sometimes critical. Appreciate that your senior management is just doing their due diligence. It's your job to provide information and evidence that eases their concerns. If you've addressed all the questions in this book, you'll build their confidence in you and your idea. Innovations bring much uncertainty with them. After all, a large capital investment on an untested idea brings great risk. Senior managers may apply pressure in the meeting to test your mettle. Thus, the project team must expect and prepare for a critical (and sometimes skeptical) audience of executive decision-makers. When you make your pitch and submit your plan, executives will listen and then glance at it briefly before making any initial comments. No matter how good you think your plan is, an executive is rarely going to look at it and say, "This is the greatest thing I've ever seen!" Don't expect enthusiastic acceptance or even polite praise. It's highly likely that the remarks will be critical, and even if they aren't, they'll seem that way. Don't panic.[14] Even if it seems like an avalanche of objections, bear in mind that some of the best innovations of all time faced the same opposition. Never expect a "thumbs up" in 20 minutes. Even when a pitch goes well, the senior management team may send you back to the drawing board to rework some of the issues they had problems with. Consider this an opportunity, and rework your innovation where possible. You're still in the game. In fact, they may be testing you to see how you address their concerns. Do you have staying power? Or do you give up when faced with adversity? And even if they turn you down on this idea, they may see something they like about you that they'll remember when another project comes along. Be proud of your effort because it may pay off with another opportunity that comes your way in the future. Remember that corporate innovators are more like marathoners than sprinters. The goal is not so much to succeed the *first* time as it is to succeed in the long run.[15]

Summary

This chapter provided a thorough examination of how to turn your ideas into a compelling story that can be told to senior managers and other key stakeholders to attract their interest and support. Market research provides supporting documentation of customer interest in the innovation. Further sources of information for commercializing your innovation were then covered. The customer mapping approach provided a way to build your brand and craft your marketing messages. Guidelines were then given on how to tell your innovation story.

Innovation-in-Action

A Whale of an Idea

Frank Fish, an unassuming biology professor at West Chester University in West Chester, Pennsylvania, was on vacation and enjoying a fine-art sculpture of a humpback whale when the genesis of a business idea was formed.

Fish thought the sculptor had made an error in sculpting bumps along the edges of the whale's flippers. After all, fluid dynamics dictated that the edges should have been smooth. Intrigued, Fish spent decades studying the flippers and how they worked, discovering a few things about fluid dynamics along the way. In 2004, the results of Fish's and his three co-authors' studies were published in *Science*, *Nature*, and several other publications. The scientific community noticed.

In early 2005, a physics aficionado and entrepreneur by the name of Stephen Dewar met with Fish to learn more about fluid dynamics and humpback whales. Dewar and Fish discussed the potential commercial application of Fish and company's discoveries to the design of airplane wings, boat keels, and turbines.

In late 2005, Dewar and Fish filed patents and, backed by private investors, formed WhalePower, a Toronto company. Knowing that the industry would be hesitant to invest in technology that was a radical departure from conventional wisdom, Fish continued to conduct research. During trials, he discovered that airfoils with his design were up to 13 percent more efficient than smooth-edged airfoils.

Seizing upon the technical term for the "flipper bumps," Fish named the concept Tubercle Technology. Today, WhalePower licenses its Tubercle Technology to the industrial fan industry. And, according to Envira-North Systems, the first company to commercially use industrial fans employing Tubercle Technology, the fans are 25 percent more aerodynamically efficient, consume 20 percent less energy, and create significantly less noise than conventional fans.

WhalePower is growing at double-digit rates and is in the process of negotiating licenses with manufacturers of computers, servers, HVAC units, and other appliances. Fish foresees the use of Tubercle Technology in the wind energy and airline industries too.

(Adapted from: http://inventorspot.com/articles/humpback_whale_inspires_ energy_saving_whalepower_tubercle_techno_30079; www.entrepreneur.com/ article/217520 websites accessed January 10, 2011; and updated with www. wired.com/2015/11/whales-wind-turbines/ website accessed July 26, 2017.)

Key Terms

benefits

business-level strategy

business model

credibility

customer mapping

customer outcomes

demographics

features

legitimacy

location

market research

mission

pitch

presentation

primary data

principles

secondary data

stakeholders

surveys

taglines

value

value proposition

values

vision

Discussion Questions

1. What is the importance of market research?
2. Briefly describe the steps of market research.
3. What are the common question formats for surveys, and why are they used?
4. What is a business model? Why is it important to know your company's business model?
5. How can a manager show credibility to senior management?
6. Why is meaning important in innovative pursuits?
7. What are some factors that must be taken into consideration when selecting a location to produce and sell your product or service?
8. How does a customer perceive value? What can a company do to persuade a customer that an innovation holds value for them?
9. Briefly describe how a customer map is created.
10. How do you prepare your innovation pitch for acceptance by key stakeholders?
11. What important steps must be followed to prepare a successful presentation to key decision-makers?
12. What makes for a good innovation presentation?

Appendix A

Example of an Innovation Description

(Reproduced with Permission)

A. General Description of Innovation

Green Fuel Alternatives will be a fuel refinery of soy biodiesel that will be sold in bulk quantities and to fuel distributors and suppliers in the Midwest. The Green Fuel Alternatives refining plant will be built by Renewable Energy Group in the vacant lot of 8101 W. Morris St. in Indianapolis. This location was chosen because of its excellent access to I-465, US Highways 40 and 36, and on-site rail access. This innovation has been named Green Fuel Alternatives so that customers can easily identify what the product is and know that it is beneficial to the environment.

Biofuels have become very popular in the past few years. A growing number of organizations, such as departments of transportation, school corporations, farmers, US state and local governments, and even traditional diesel vehicle drives, are using biodiesel to meet future sulfur emissions standards (2006 EOA mandate) and become more environmentally responsible. The US currently imports 58 percent of its oil, with fuel prices continually trending upwards. This creates a demand to utilize cheaper and more efficient natural resources to help reduce fuel costs and the dependency on foreign oil. Biodiesel has been tested in labs, and has passed all necessary tests required by the EPA. The American Society for Testing and Materials (ASTM) has even given biodiesel a standard (ASTM D6571) to be used as an acceptable diesel fuel alternative.

Several states around the country, from Maine to Washington, have already initiated biodiesel promotion programs. Three examples are the programs in Minnesota, Arkansas, and Texas. The state of Minnesota has mandated the use of B2 (2 percent blend of biodiesel with diesel) in all petroleum diesel consumed in the state by the year 2005 subject to incentive for biodiesel production for the first 5 million gallons up to a period of five years. Texas now provides a net grant of 16.4 cents per gallon to producers of biodiesel for a period of ten years, but the grant is capped at $3.6 million per plant.[16]

Currently, Green Fuel Alternatives is in the conceptual stage of development because if a biodiesel plant were to be built in Indiana, it would be the first in the state, enabling it to reach northern biodiesel users faster than the competition. Any co-op or other fuel distributor that wants to sell biodiesel to its customers must currently transport it from Ralston, Iowa, Cincinnati, Ohio, Kentucky, Minnesota, or further away. Green Fuel Alternatives will require a 15 million gallon per year (gpy) plant in order to provide enough B100 biodiesel for all of the distributors in Indiana, some outside, and some private sales. Once the division is started and the refinery is producing a steady amount of fuel, production will reach peak capacity

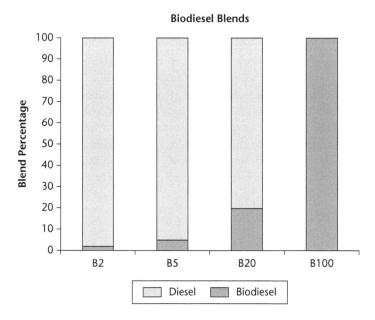

FIGURE 10.1   Example of Diagram for Innovation Description.

and in the future other plants may need to be constructed in order to provide fuel to other areas of the Midwest.

The biodiesel manufactured under the name *Green Fuel Alternatives* is very unique in the fact that it is made from soybean oil only, benefiting local soy biodiesel as well as waste grease and many other types of oils. Green Fuel Alternatives will offer soy biodiesel in an effort to support local farmers and utilize the largest vegetable oil source.

In order to extract the oil from the soybeans, a "cracking" or "crushing" plant is used to heat up the soybeans to a proper temperature in which the soybean oil will come off of the soybeans in a gas form and it will be filtered through a coil to cool it down and revert it to its liquid form. Green Fuel Alternatives will receive its soybean oil from ADM in Frankfort, IN. This oil would then be mixed with methanol to create B100 or "neat" boidiesel. B100 biodiesel is essentially 100 percent biodiesel; other blends such as B5 or B20 contain 5 percent and 20 percent chart with illustrate the most common blends available.

Green Fuel Alternatives will only manufacture and sell B100 to fuel distributors who will mix blends to satisfy each customer.

The business model for Green Fuel Alternatives will be as follows. Green Fuel Alternatives will strive to make soy biodiesel more easily accessible in Indiana and strive for a low-cost alternative. We will provide distributors with a quality refined B100 biodiesel that can be easily blended for any diesel fuel application.

B. Products and Services

Green Fuel Alternatives will provide B100 biodiesel that will be refined by ADM in Frankfort, IN using a "cracking" plant to extract soybean oil feedstock. B100 biodiesel is known as "pure biodiesel" or "neat" because it is 100 percent biodiesel. Some customers prefer B100 because of its increased lubricity and the cleansing characteristics. However, B100 does have trouble in cold weather due to an increased cold flow test and cloud point. Because of this it has become an industry standard when transporting fuel to heat it to avoid gelling in climates below 40 degrees Fahrenheit. The American Society of Testing and Materials has tested biodiesel and uses a standard test for biodiesel called ASTM D 6751.

C. Strategy of Differentiation

Green Fuel Alternatives will have a competitive advantage in Indiana compared with other biodiesel providers because current providers are located hundreds of miles away, out of state. Green Fuel Alternatives will not be a fuel co-op distribution center, but a fuel refinery. Currently there are 40 biodiesel providers or fuel co-ops in Indiana, but they only blend the fuel to make biodiesel and then distribute it to the end user or to a fuel station. Green Fuel Alternatives will provide the B100 (100 percent biodiesel) to customers such as Countrymark, who will blend it with diesel fuel at its terminals to create a biodiesel blend. Countrymark currently has B100 biodiesel transported in from Iowa, Kentucky, and Ohio, and they simply blend the fuel usually using various methods. Some facilities such as the Countrymark Co-op in Jolietville and Peru, Indiana, use a state-of-the-art direct injection method to blend the biodisel proportionately with petroleum diesel. Currently the B100 fuel is received by these terminals (places where co-ops pick up fuel to distribute) to be blended and is then picked up for disbursement. Green Fuel Alternatives can get fuel to these terminals quicker than competitors because of a convenient location in Indianapolis, Indiana. Because of this, the fuel cooperatives will have constant access to biodiesel. Green Fuel Alternatives will attempt to establish a good relationship with Countrymark and other providers in Indiana and eventually elsewhere that distribute biodiesel. This relationship will enable Green Fuel Alternatives to develop long-term contracts with the distributors. These contracts will be a safeguard in case soybean oil prices unexpectedly rise and Green Fuel Alternatives has to keep prices at a high level to maintain profitability.

D. Key Dynamics

There are many keys to why biodiesel makes sense:

1. Biodiesel is 100 percent renewable and can be made in the US, reducing our dependency on foreign oil.
2. Engine life is increased with the use of biodiesel.

3. EPA is requiring the sulfur emissions in 2006 to be reduced from 500 ppm to 15 ppm.
4. Biodiesel has the highest positive energy balance of any renewable fuel to date (3.24 units produced per unit of energy used).
5. Biodiesel can reduce toxic air emissions by as much as 90 percent (B100 compared with petroleum diesel).[17]

Appendix B

Examples of Market Surveys

Example 1: Traffic Reporting App

This survey is being collected to assess the viability of traffic checking apps for phones. Your input is critical to assess the feasibility of this idea and will help determine whether future investment and development is warranted. Thank you in advance for completing the survey!

1. **Gender:** Male _____ Female _____
2. **Age:** _____16–24 _____25–34 _____35–44 _____45–54 _____55–70
3. **Household Income:** _____under 25,000 _____25,001–45,000 _____$45,001–65,000

   _____$65,001–85,000 _____$85,001–105,000 _____$105,001–145,000

   _____$145,001–185,000 _____ Above $185,001

4. **How long, in miles, is your daily commute roundtrip?**

   _____1–15 _____16–20 _____21–25 _____26–30 _____31–40

   _____41–50 _____51–80 _____ over 81

5. **Do you regularly access the internet on your phone?** _____Yes _____No
6. **Do you ever get stuck in heavy traffic?** _____Yes _____No
7. **Is being stuck in heavy traffic, during rush hour or at other times, a problem for you?** _____Yes _____No
8. **How do you check the status of traffic before beginning your commute?** (please check all that apply)

   _____Traffic app _____TV _____Radio _____Internet _____I don't check traffic
   Other (please specify) _____

9. **On a scale of 1 to 5,** 1=not satisfied and 5=completely satisfied, **rate your current traffic monitoring method listed in question #8.**

   Circle one 1 2 3 4 5

   Imagine a service that allows you to check the status of traffic in the Indianapolis area with an app. This service will send you traffic reports according to your commuting route that will alert you of problems **before** you get stuck in traffic. You can choose to have the traffic alerts sent to your email account or sent to your phone as a text message.

10. **Would you subscribe to a traffic alert service that saved you time and frustration on your commute to and from work?** _____Yes _____No

11. **Which of the methods for traffic monitoring would you be most likely to use?** (check all that apply)

    ____App ____Website ____Email ____Phone Messaging

12. **In dollars, what would you expect to pay for an app like this if it was available?**

    ____$1–6 ____$6–12 ____above $12

> Thank you for taking the time to fill out this survey.
> I greatly appreciate all of your help.

Example 2: Business-to-Business Survey for a Vineyard

Demographic Information

Name of Business: _____

Your Name: _____

Your Title at Company: _____ (owner, manager, etc.)

Age of Business: ____1–5 years ____6–10 years ____11–20 years ____21+ years

Number of years you have been with the company _____ Are you the founder? Yes____ No____

Number of employees in the business _____

Company's Annual Sales:

____less than $500,000   ____$500,001–1,000,000 ____$1,000,001–2,000,000
____more than $2,000,000

1. Does the winery use whole grapes in its wine production process? (If no, skip questions 2–4)

    ____ Yes   ____ No

2a. Approximately how many tons of whole grapes does the winery process annually?
2b. Does this amount fill production to capacity? ____ Yes ____ No
2c. If no, what factors are limiting from becoming filled to capacity? (Check all that apply)

    ____ Inadequate space/property

    ____ Lack of agricultural background

    ____ Initial cost of setup

_____ Labor requirements

_____ Time

3a. Do you produce your own grape crop? _____ Yes _____ No

3b. If so, how many acres are involved in grape production?

_____ Less than 25 _____ 25–50 _____ 51–75 _____ 76–100 _____ More than 100

3c. What is your approximate cost per acre?

_____ Less than $2500 _____ $2500–5000 _____ $5001–7500 _____ $7501–10,000

_____ More than $10,000

4. How many suppliers do you currently use to create the desired inventory?
5. What outlets are being used to market the winery's products? (check all that apply)

_____ Retail stores _____ On-site sales _____ Mail order _____Internet _____ Other wineries

6a. How many varieties of grapes does your winery use in its production? _____

6b. Please list those varieties of grapes your winery uses in production:

7. When in the year does the company make most of its buying decisions?

_____ Spring _____ Summer _____ Fall _____ Winter

8. Please rate the following statements on a scale of 1–5, with 1 representing a total disagreement and 5 representing complete agreement.

9a. Approximately how many different products does your company currently offer?

9b. Please list those products.

	Disagree				Agree
a. I am satisfied with the company's current supply chain.	1	2	3	4	5
b. The company could benefit from having a local grape supplier.	1	2	3	4	5
c. I would like to learn more about using organically grown grapes in my operation.	1	2	3	4	5
d. I would like to diversify the number of products the winery offers.	1	2	3	4	5
e. I am satisfied with the current production output of the winery.	1	2	3	4	5
f. It is important to support local agriculture.	1	2	3	4	5
g. Having a quality product is more important than making a large profit.	1	2	3	4	5

10. On average, how many new products does your company introduce every year?
11. Would you like to know the results of this survey?   Yes _____ No _____

Thank you for your cooperation!

Notes

1   McKee, Robert. 2003. Storytelling that moves people. *Harvard Business Review*, 81(6): 51–55.
2   Maxwell, Richard & Dickman, Robert. 2007. *The Elements of Persuasion*, New York: HarperCollins.
3   For more extensive coverage of business models, see Osterwalder, Alexander & Pigneur, Yvez. 2010. *Business Model Generation: A Handbook for Visionaries, Game Changers, and Challengers*, New York: Wiley.
4   Stewart, James B. 2006. *Disney War*, New York: Simon & Schuster.
5   For example, Walt Disney World provides free bus transportation from the Orlando airport to the resort for guests who are staying there on their vacation. The service doesn't generate a profit for the company, and it costs a lot of money to operate. But it serves a strategic purpose for the company because Disney management projected that guests that arrive on a bus instead of driving a rental car are more likely to stay on their property and not leave the park during their stay. Their decision was correct, as the service has been popular with the guests while serving the strategic purpose of keeping them inside the park for more shopping and dining.
6   Sometimes small actions or off-hand comments can reveal a lot about what lies behind a person's public face ... both good and bad. A little gesture might show consideration while another might display selfishness. Listen and watch carefully for these little "tells" when you're interviewing. People often reveal their true selves in the littlest of ways.
7   Campbell, Colin. 2009. Is the iPhone killing RIM? *Maclean's*, 122(22): 30–31.
8   Frankl, Viktor E. 1959. *Man's Search for Meaning*, Boston: Beacon Press.
9   Freeman, R. Edward. 1984. *Strategic Management: A Stakeholder Approach*, New York: Pitman Publishing.
10 *Values* are the ideals that one believes in very strongly and that guide what a person thinks and does.
11 *Principles* are well-developed rules and codes one uses in conducting their daily business.
12 Jones, Dewitt. 2001. *Everyday Creativity*, New York: Star Thrower.
13 Kuratko, Donald F. 2017. *Entrepreneurship: Theory, Process, Practice*, 10th ed., Boston: Cengage.
14 The most painful presentation we ever witnessed was one by a young entrepreneur given to a group of angel investors. When asked ahead of time if he'd worked hard preparing his pitch, he replied he hadn't because he was going to "speak from the heart." The investors shredded his presentation and the Q&A was even more uncomfortable to witness. The young man had no answers to the questions, and eventually broke down in tears before the group. Passion is important, but calm, cool, confident answers grounded in research signal that you're the type of person the company and investors can trust resources with. *You sell during the presentation, you reassure during the Q&A. Confidence comes from good preparation.*
15 Kuratko, Donald F. 2017. *Entrepreneurship: Theory, Process, Practice*, 10th ed., Boston: Cengage.
16 Frazier, Barnes & Associates. 2004. *Mississippi Biodiesel Feasibility Study*.
17 *An Overview of Biodiesel and Petroleum Diesel Life Cycles*, U.S. Department of Energy, National Renewable Energy Laboratory (NREL), and the U.S. Department of Agriculture (USDA). May 1998–March 2004.

11

EFFECTIVE INNOVATION PLANS

Reduce your plan to writing. The moment you complete this, you will have definitely given concrete form to the intangible desire.

~Napoleon Hill, author[1]

As we saw in the last chapter, the realization and then preparation of an innovation for commercialization has specific steps. As you develop your business model, conduct market research and outline your story; each of those elements lays the groundwork for the final innovation plan that you must develop. So the work conducted in the last chapter will now be integrated into the formal elements of an innovation plan.

Planning is essential to the success of any innovative undertaking that you may pursue. Planning is the management key to reducing uncertainty and the risks of change. Although we can never predict the future, planning is a process that allows ventures to stay on track through preparation, expectation, and dedication to the objective. Carefully prepared, these plans are simply the formulation of goals, objectives, and directions for the future of a project. The absence of a plan could mean failure before you even start. In planning, there are critical steps that must not be overlooked. A few of these steps are listed below:

- *Realistic goals must be set.* These goals must be specific, measurable, and set within a timeframe.
- All involved managers, employees, and team members must be *committed to the venture plan.*
- *Milestones* must be set for continual and timely evaluation of progress.
- *Obstacles should be anticipated* with flexible provisions for dealing with a bad turn of events.

Alternative strategies must be devised in the event of unforeseen pitfalls.

The Innovation Plan

Definition

An innovation plan is the written document that details the proposed innovation and its commercial potential as a venture. It must describe current status, expected needs, and projected results of the new concept.[2] Every aspect of the venture needs to be covered: the project, marketing, research and development, manufacturing, management, critical risks, financing, and milestones or a timetable. A description of all of these facets of the proposed venture is necessary to demonstrate a clear picture of what that venture is, where it is projected to go, and how the innovator proposes it will get there. The innovation plan is the roadmap for a successful enterprise.[3]

An effective innovation plan will:

- describe every aspect of a particular innovation;
- include a marketing plan;
- clarify and outline financial needs;
- identify potential obstacles and alternative solutions;
- establish milestones for continuous and timely evaluation; and
- serve as a communication tool for all assessment purposes.

Planning Pitfalls

Pitfalls in planning are abundant—remember, no one says it's easy! The following section outlines planning pitfalls, indicators, and solutions. Read them carefully before embarking on your plan. The comprehensive innovation plan is useful for existing organizations, not just startups. It should be the result of meetings and reflections upon the entire direction of the project. It is the useful tool used today in business to convey the essential components, market feasibility, financial capability, and contingent directions that all interested resource persons in a company wish to see.

Benefits of an Innovation Plan

As we stated in the introduction of this chapter, an innovation plan forces you to plan. All aspects of your innovation idea should be addressed in the plan. You develop and examine operating strategies and expected results. Goals and objectives are quantified, so that you can compare forecasts with actual results. This type of planning can help keep you on track.

Other benefits are derived from an innovation plan for both the innovator (and the I-Team) and the executive team that will read it and evaluate the concept. Specifically for the innovator and the I-Team, the following benefits are gained:

TABLE 11.1 Pitfalls in Entrepreneurial Planning

(Read carefully before assessing your innovation plan.)

Pitfalls	Indicators	Possible Solutions
1. No Realistic Goals	Lack of timeframe to accomplish things Lack of priorities Lack of action steps	*Set up a timetable with specific steps to be accomplished at each elapsed time period.*
2. Failure to Anticipate Issues	No admission of possible road blocks No contingency or alternative plans	*List the possible obstacles you face, flaws or weaknesses, with alternatives written out that state what you "might have to do."*
3. No Commitment or Dedication	Too much procrastination Missed appointments No desire to put up money of your own Project appears to be a hobby or whim for you Appearance of making a fast buck	*Act quickly and be sure to follow up on all professional appointments. Be ready and willing to demonstrate a financial commitment: "Put your money where your mouth is!"*
4. Lack of Demonstrated Experience (Business or Technical)	No experience in the specific area of your venture Lack of understanding of the industry your venture fits into Failure to convey to others a clear picture of what, how, why your venture works, and who will buy it	*Always explain your experience and background for this venture. If you lack specific knowledge or skills, attempt to get help from those who possess the skills. (Demonstrate a "team" concept of those helping you.)*
5. No Market Niche (Segment)	Unsure of who will buy your idea No proof of need or desire for your idea Assuming there will be customers or clients just because you think there will be	*Have an established market segment at which you are specifically aiming your venture. Be able to demonstrate why you chose that market and the steps you are taking to prove that there is a need or desire for your idea.*

- The time, effort, research, and discipline needed to put together a formal innovation plan force the innovator to view the venture critically and objectively.
- The competitive, economic, and financial analyses included in the innovation plan subject the innovator to close scrutiny of their assumptions about the concept's success.
- Since all aspects of the innovative concept as a viable venture must be addressed in the plan, the innovator and the I-Team develop and examine operating strategies and expected results for outside evaluators.

- The innovation plan quantifies objectives, providing measurable benchmarks for comparing forecasts with actual results.
- The completed innovation plan provides the innovator and I-Team with a communication tool for the executive team to analyze as well as an operational tool for guiding the new innovation toward success.

The executive team that reads the plan derives the following benefits from the innovation plan:

- The innovation plan provides for the executive team the details of the market potential and plans for securing a share of that market.
- Through prospective financial statements, the innovation plan illustrates the venture's ability to service debt or provide an adequate return on equity.
- The innovation plan identifies critical risks and crucial events with a discussion of contingency plans that provide opportunity for the venture's success.
- By providing a comprehensive overview of the entire operation, the innovation plan gives executives a clear, concise document that contains the necessary information for a thorough business and financial evaluation.
- For an executive team with no prior knowledge of this type of innovation, the innovation plan provides a useful guide for assessing the innovation team (I-Team) and their planning and managerial ability.

To help you prepare an effective innovation plan, we provide in this chapter an innovation plan section that begins with a complete outline of an innovation plan for you to follow. An evaluation segment is then provided so that you can check your work closely before presenting it to others. Self-assessment of your plan is necessary and worthwhile.

The complete innovation plan assessment provided in Table 11.3 offers entrepreneurs an opportunity to self-evaluate the innovation plan as it is developed. Each section is broken down into questions that examine the information needed in that particular segment of the innovation plan. Then the columns are used to evaluate: (1) whether the information is in the plan, (2) whether the previous answer is clear, and (3) whether the answer is complete. This gives entrepreneurs the benefit of self-evaluating each segment of their plan before presenting it to financial or professional sources.

The Components of an Innovation Plan

Readers of an innovation plan expect it to have two important qualities: It must be organized and it must be complete. Also, the innovator should consider who the intended audience is when the plan is presented for funding. Mason and Stark (2004) suggest that most of the research on innovation plans ignores the needs of the different types of funding sources. Their research suggests that innovation plans should be customized based on the following:

- Bankers stress the financial aspects of the plan and place little emphasis on market, innovator, or other issues.
- Equity investors, capitol fund managers, venture capital fund managers, and business angels emphasize both market and financial components.[4]

With this in mind, the following list describes the ten segments that make up a complete and organized innovation plan.

1. *Executive summary.* A short description of the innovation should be the first information the reader encounters. The executive summary should be written in an interesting way with proper emphasis on the more important aspects of the plan, such as the unique characteristics of the venture, the major marketing points, and the desired end result. Its purpose is to whet the reader's appetite for more information. A good summary will guarantee that the rest of the plan will be read.

2. *Descriptions of the innovation.* This section contains a more comprehensive account of the innovative concept. The description of the innovation should include a brief history of the company where applicable and some information about the overall industry. The product or service should be described in terms of its unique qualities and value to consumers. Finally, goals and milestones should be clarified.

3. *Marketing.* The marketing section is divided into two major parts. The first is research and analysis. The target market must be identified, with emphasis on who will buy the product or service. Market size and trends must be measured, and the market share must be estimated. In addition, the competition should be studied in considerable detail. The second part is the marketing plan. This is perhaps the most important part of the innovation plan. It must discuss market strategy, sales and distribution, pricing, advertising, promotion, and public relations. Some businesses make the mistake of preparing only a marketing plan, but, by itself and outside the structure of an innovation plan, a marketing plan will not meet the needs of a new venture.

4. *Operations segment.* In this segment it is important to describe the mode of this corporate innovation concept (internal, external, or cooperative) and outline its advantages. Operating needs, projected operating costs, and general plans for operations should all be considered in this section. Specific needs should be discussed in terms of the facilities required to handle the new innovation (plant, warehouse storage, and offices) and the equipment that needs to be acquired (special tooling, machinery, computers, and vehicles). Finally, the cost data associated with any of the operation factors should be presented. The financial information used here can be applied later to the financial projections.

5. *Management.* The management team necessarily requires the presence of outstanding individuals to make the venture a success. Methods of compensation such as salaries, employment agreements, stock purchase plans, and ownership levels must be determined. The board of directors, advisors, and consultants also are part of the management team, and their selection should be based on their potential contribution to the enterprise.

6. *Critical risks.* Risks must often be analyzed to uncover potential problems before they materialize. Outside consultants often can be engaged to identify risks and to recommend alternative courses of action. The important concept is that risk can be anticipated and controlled. Doing so will result in a more successful venture.

7. *Financial forecasting.* Accountants can make a major contribution to this section. Obtaining financing always has depended on fair and reasonable budgeting and forecasting. From the sales budget and projected inventory, material and labor requirements can be determined. Variable overhead can be scheduled for various capacity levels, and when these are added to fixed overhead, the budget can be completed. A capital budget then can be prepared; when it is coupled with debt service requirements, cash flow needs can be identified. This information thus developed can be summarized into pro forma financial statements, such as forecasted statements of earnings, financial position, and cash flows. If the work is done well, these projected statements should represent the financial achievements expected from the business. They also provide a standard against which to measure the actual results of operating the enterprise. These financial projections will serve as valuable tools for managing and controlling the business in the first few years.

8. *Harvest strategy.* This segment projects a long-term plan for how the innovator(s) will benefit from the success of the venture. Harvest strategies can include selling the business, going public and offering stock, or merging with another business.

9. *Milestone schedule.* This segment of the innovation plan requires the determination of objectives and the timing of their accomplishment. Milestones and deadlines should be established and then monitored while the venture is in progress. Each milestone is related to all the others, and together they constitute a network of the entire project.

10. *Appendix.* The appendix includes valuable information not contained in other sections. It may include names of references and advisors, as well as drawings, documents, agreements, or other materials that support the plan. If deemed desirable, a bibliography may be presented.[5]

Preparing the Innovation Plan

Constructing an innovation plan is a challenge because of the great amount of work required to put together the ten components just discussed. After the requisite information is compiled, the package must be assembled in good form. Remember that an innovation plan gives investors their first impression of a company. Therefore, the plan should present a professional image. Form, as well as content, is important. The document should be free of spelling, grammatical, or typographical errors. Perfection should be the norm; anything less is unacceptable. Binding and printing should have a professional appearance. The written plan should not exceed 25 pages (20–25 is ideal). The cover page should be attractive, and it should contain the company name and address. A title page should contain the same information as the front cover, as well as the company's telephone number and the month and year the plan is presented.

The first two pages should contain the executive summary, which explains the company's current status, its products or services, the benefits to customers, financial forecast summarized in paragraph form, the venture's objectives in the next few years, the amount of financing needed, and the benefits to investors. This is a lot of information for two pages, but if it is done well, the investor will get a good impression of the venture and will be enticed to read the rest of the plan.

A table of contents should follow the executive summary. Each section of the plan should be listed with the page numbers on which they are found. Obviously, the remaining sections will follow the table of contents. If the last section, the appendix, is too lengthy, it may be necessary to present it is a separate binder in order to keep the plan within the recommended limit of 25 pages. Each of the sections should be written in a simple and straightforward manner. The purpose is to communicate, not dazzle.

An attractive appearance, proper length, an executive summary, a table of contents, and professionalism in grammar, spelling, and typing are important factors in a comprehensive innovation plan. Believe it or not, when reviewed by outside funding sources, these characteristic separate successful plans from failed ones.

TABLE 11.2 Helpful Hints for Developing the Innovation Plan

---

1. Executive Summary

- No more than three pages. This is the most crucial part of your plan because you must capture the reader's interest.
- What, How, Why, Where, etc. must be summarized.
- Complete this part after you have a finished innovation plan.

2. Innovation Description Segment

- Explain your innovation.
- How does it "fit" with the organization?
- The potential of the new innovation should be described clearly.
- Any uniqueness or distinctive features of this innovation should be clearly described.

3. Marketing Segment

- Convince investors that sales projections and competition can be met.
- Use and disclose market studies.
- Identify target market, market position, and market share.
- Evaluate all competition and specifically cover why and how you will be better than your competitors
- Identify all market sources and assistance used for this segment.
- Demonstrate pricing strategy since your price must penetrate and maintain a market share to produce profits. Thus the lowest price is not necessarily the best price.
- Identify your advertising plans with cost estimates to validate proposed strategy.

4. Operations Segment

- Describe the mode of innovation strategy (internal, external, and cooperative).
- Outline the advantages of selecting this mode of innovation.
- Identify operational needs in terms of facilities or equipment.
- Provide estimates for operating costs.
- Provide general operations description.

5. **Management Segment**
   - Supply résumés of all key people in the management of your venture.
   - Carefully describe the legal structure of your venture (sole proprietorship, partnership, or corporation).
   - Cover the added assistance (if any) of advisors, consultants, and directors.
   - Give information on how and how much everyone is to be compensated.

6. **Financial Segment**
   - Give actual estimated statements.
   - Describe the needed sources for your funds and the uses you intend for the money.
   - Develop and present a budget.
   - Create stages of financing for purposes of allowing evaluation by investors at various points.

7. **Critical Risks Segment**
   - Discuss potential risks before investors point them out, e.g.,
     - price cutting by competitors;
     - any potentially unfavorable industry-wide trends;
     - design or manufacturing costs in excess of estimates;
     - sales projections not achieved;
     - product development schedule not met;
     - difficulties or long lead times encountered in the procurement of parts or raw materials;
     - greater than expected innovation and development costs to stay competitive.

   Provide some alternative courses of action.

8. **Harvest Strategy Segment**
   - Outline a plan for the orderly transfer of company assets (ownership).
   - Describe the plan for transition of leadership.

   Mention the preparations (insurance, trusts, etc.) needed for continuity of the business.

9. **Milestone Schedule Segment**

   Develop a timetable or chart to demonstrate when each phase of the venture is to be completed. This shows the relationship of events and provides a deadline for accomplishment.

10. **Appendix or Bibliography**

Table 11.2 presents some helpful hints for developing the innovation plan.[6] Finally, a well-written innovation plan is like a work of art: it's visually pleasing and makes a statement without saying a word. Unfortunately, the two are also alike in that they are worth money only if they're good. Following are ten key questions to consider when you are writing and revising an innovation plan masterpiece.

1. *Is your plan organized so key facts leap out at the reader?* Appearances do count. Your plan is a representation of yourself, so don't expect an unorganized, less than acceptable plan to be your vehicle for obtaining funds.
2. *Is your product/service and business mission clear and simple?* Your mission should state very simply the value that you will be providing to your customers. It shouldn't take more than a paragraph.

3. *Where are you really? Are you focused on the right things?* Determine what phase of the business you are really in, focus on the right tasks, and use your resources appropriately.

4. *Who is your customer?* Does the plan describe the business's ideal customers and how you will reach them? Is your projected share of the market identified, reasonable, and supported?

5. *Why do (or will) your customers buy? How much better is your product/service?* Define the need for your product and provide references and testimonial support to enhance it. Try to be detailed in explaining the customer's benefit in buying your product.

6. *Do you have an unfair advantage over your competitors?* Focus on differences and any unique qualities. Proprietary processes/technology and patentable items/ideals are good things to highlight as competitive strengths.

7. *Do you have a favorable cost structure?* Proper gross margins are key. Does the break-even analysis take into consideration the dynamics of price and variable costs? Identify, if possible, any economics of scale that would be advantageous to the business.

8. *Can the management team build a business?* Take a second look at the management team to see whether they have relevant experience in small business and in the industry. Acknowledge the fact that the team may need to evolve with the business.

9. *How much money do you need?* Financial statements, including the income statement, cash flow statement, and balance sheet, should be provided on a monthly basis for the first year and then quarterly basis for the following two or three years.

10. *How does your investor get a cash return?* Whether it's through a buyout or initial public offering, make sure your plan clearly outlines this important question regarding a harvest strategy.

A Complete Assessment of the Components

There are ten components of an innovation plan. As you develop your plan, you should assess each component. Be honest in your assessment since the main purpose is to improve your innovation plan and increase your chances of success.[7]

Organizing an Action Plan

Why Action Plan?

There is no scarcity of good ideas. There is also no scarcity of good intentions. Why is it then that the shelves of organizational planning departments, university presidents, department heads, community services organizations, and countless other effective innovation people are stacked with plans that were never implemented? More importantly, why is it that so many entrepreneurs never seem to get their innovations off the ground?

TABLE 11.3 Innovation Plan Assessment

Directions: There are ten suggested components of a corporate venture plan. As you develop your plan, you should assess each component. Be honest in your assessment since the main purpose is to improve your innovation plan and increase your chances of success. For instance, if your goal is to obtain internal company financing, you will be asked to submit a complete plan for your venture. The innovation plan will help company executives to more adequately evaluate your business idea. This assessment tool can help you and your I-Team self-evaluate the innovation plan before it is submitted to senior executives. The brief description of each component will help you write that section of your plan. After completing your plan, use the scale provided to assess each component.

5 = Outstanding: thorough and complete in all areas
4 = Very Good: most areas covered but could use improvement in detail
3 = Good: some areas covered in detail but other areas missing
2 = Fair: a few areas covered but very little detail
1 = Poor: No written parts

The Ten Components of an Innovation Plan

---

1. **Executive Summary:** This is the most important section because it has to convince the reader that the innovation will succeed. In no more than three pages, you should summarize the highlights of the rest of the plan. This means that the key elements of the following components should be mentioned.

The executive summary must be able to stand on its own. It is not simply an introduction to the rest of the innovation plan. This section should articulate the new venture concept clearly, describe its uniqueness, formulate the "fit" with the corporate innovation strategy, and demonstrate the future growth potential. Because this section summarizes the plan, it is often best to write this section last.

Rate this component: Outstanding   Very Good   Good   Fair   Poor
                                                 5   4   3   2   1

2. **Description of the Innovation:** This section should provide background information about your industry, a general description of your innovative concept, and the specific mission that you are trying to achieve. Your product or service should be described in terms of its unique qualities and value to the customer. Specific short-term and long-term objectives must be defined. You should clearly state what sales, market share, and profitability objectives you want your business to achieve.

Key Elements	Have you covered this in the plan?	Is the answer clear? (yes or no)	Is the answer complete? (yes or no)
a. What type of innovation will you have?			
b. What products or services will you sell?			
c. Why does it promise to be successful?			
d. What is the growth potential?			
e. How is it unique?			

(continued)

TABLE 11.3 *(continued)*

Rate this component: Outstanding	Very Good	Good	Fair	Poor
5	4	3	2	1

3. **Marketing:** There are two major parts to the marketing section. The first is research and analysis. Here, you should explain who buys the product or service—or, in other words, identify your target market. Measure your market size and trends, and estimate the market share you expect. Be sure to include support for your sales projections. For example, if your figures are based on published marketing research data, be sure to cite the source. Do your best to make realistic and credible projections. Describe your competition in considerable detail, identifying their strengths and weaknesses. Finally, explain how you will be better than your competitors. The second part is your marketing plan. This critical section should include your market strategy, sales and distribution, pricing, advertising, promotion, and public awareness. Demonstrate how your pricing strategy will result in a profit based on the type of corporate venture you are proposing. Make sure to validate your innovation's "fit" with the company's strategy for innovation.

Key Elements	*Have you covered this in the plan?*	*Is the answer clear? (yes or no)*	*Is the answer complete? (yes or no)*
a. Who will be your customers? (Target Market)			
b. How big is the market? (Number of Customers)			
c. Who will be your competitors?			
d. How are their businesses prospering?			
e. How will you promote sales?			
f. What market share will you want?			
g. Do you have a pricing strategy?			
h. What advertising and promotional strategy will you use?			

Rate this component: Outstanding	Very Good	Good	Fair	Poor
5	4	3	2	1

4. **Operations Segment:** In this segment it is important to describe the mode of this corporate innovation concept (internal, external, or cooperative) and outline its advantages. Operating needs, projected operating costs, and general plans for operations should all be considered in this section.

Key Elements	*Have you covered this in the plan?*	*Is the answer clear? (yes or no)*	*Is the answer complete? (yes or no)*
a. What is the mode of this corporate innovation?			
b. Have you outlined the advantages of this type of innovation approach?			

c. Any operational needs
in terms of facilities or
equipment?
d. What estimates do you
have for operating costs?
e. Have you described the
general operations of this
new innovation?

Rate this component: Outstanding Very Good Good Fair Poor
                             5   4   3   2   1

5. **Management:** Start by describing the management team, their unique qualifications, and how you compensate them (including salaries, employment agreements, stock purchase plans, levels of ownership, and other considerations). Discuss how your organization is structured and consider including a diagram illustrating who reports to whom. Also include a discussion of the potential contribution of the board of directors, advisors, or consultants.

Key Elements	Have you covered this in the plan?	Is the answer clear? (yes or no)	Is the answer complete? (yes or no)
a. Who will manage the business?			
b. What qualifications do you have?			
c. How many employees will you have?			
d. What will they do?			
e. How much will you pay your employees and what type of benefits will you offer them?			
f. What consultants or specialists will you use?			
h. What regulations will affect your business?			

Rate this component: Outstanding Very Good Good Fair Poor
                             5   4   3   2   1

6. **Financial:** Determine the stages where your innovation will require financing and identify the expected financing sources (internal venture fund or outside equity sources). Also, clearly show what return on investment these sources will achieve by investing in your business. It is good to develop a budget for the venture. If the work is done well, pro forma financial statements could then be prepared to represent the projected financial achievements expected from your venture plan. They also provide a standard by which to measure the actual results of operating your venture. They are a valuable tool to help you manage and control your business. Two key financial statements must be presented: an income statement (profit and loss), and a cash flow statement (cash inflows and outflows). These statements typically cover a one-year period. Be sure you state any assumptions and projections you made when calculating the figures.

(continued)

TABLE 11.3 *(continued)*

Key Elements	Have you covered this in the plan?	Is the answer clear? (yes or no)	Is the answer complete? (yes or no)
a. Have you staged the funding needs so that executives can gauge the innovations' progression and expected needs?			
b. What is your expected monthly cash flow during the first year?			
c. What is your total expected business income for the first year? Quarterly for the next two years? (Forecast)			
d. What sales volume will you need in order to make a profit during the three years?			
e. What will be the break-even point?			
f. What are your total financial needs?			
g. What are your funding sources?			

Rate this component: Outstanding   Very Good   Good   Fair   Poor

	5	4	3	2	1

7. **Critical Risks:** Discuss potential risks before they happen. Here are some examples: potentially unfavorable industry-wide trends, unexpected innovation, or development costs that could exceed estimates, sales projections that are not achieved. The idea is to recognize risks and identify alternative courses of action. Your main objective is to show that you can anticipate and control (to a reasonable degree) your risks.

Key Elements	Have you covered this in the plan?	Is the answer clear? (yes or no)	Is the answer complete? (yes or no)
a. What potential problems have you identified?			
b. Have you calculated the risks?			
c. What alternative courses of action are there?			

Rate this component: Outstanding   Very Good   Good   Fair   Poor
                              5   4   3   2   1

8. **Harvest Strategy:** Ensuring the survival of an internal venture is hard work. An innovation team's protective feelings for an idea built from scratch make it tough to grapple with such issues as management succession and harvest strategies. With foresight, however, corporate entrepreneurs can keep their dream alive, ensure the vitality of their ventures, and usually strengthen their venture and the company in the process. Thus identifying issues involved with harvesting of the venture as well as management transitions are essential in the early stages (even if they are to change later on in the development of the venture).

Key Elements	Have you covered this in the plan?	Is the answer clear? (yes or no)	Is the answer complete? (yes or no)
a. Have you planned for the orderly transfer of the venture assets if ownership of the business is passed to this corporation?			
b. Is there a strategy for identifying potential harvest opportunities?			

Rate this component: Outstanding   Very Good   Good   Fair   Poor
                              5   4   3   2   1

9. **Milestone Schedule:** This is an important segment of the innovation plan because it requires you to determine what tasks you need to accomplish in order to achieve your objectives. Milestones and deadlines should be established and monitored on an ongoing basis. Each milestone is related to all the others and together they comprise a timely representation of how your objective is to be accomplished.

Key Elements	Have you covered this in the plan?	Is the answer clear? (yes or no)	Is the answer complete? (yes or no)
a. How have you set your objectives?			
b. Have you set deadlines for each stage of your growth?			

Rate this component: Outstanding   Very Good   Good   Fair   Poor
                              5   4   3   2   1

10. **Appendix:** This section includes important background information that was not included in the other sections. This is where you would put such items as: résumés of the management team, names of references and advisors, drawings, documents, licenses, agreements, and any materials that support the plan. You may also wish to add a bibliography of the sources from which you drew information.

(continued)

TABLE 11.3 *(continued)*

Key Elements	Have you covered this in the plan?	Is the answer clear? (yes or no)	Is the answer complete? (yes or no)
a. Have you included any documents, drawings, agreements, or other materials needed to support the plan?			
b. Are there any names of references, advisors, or technical sources you should include?			
c. Are there any other supporting documents?			

Rate this component:	Outstanding	Very Good	Good	Fair	Poor
	5	4	3	2	1

Summary: Your Innovation Plan

Directions: For each of the innovation plan sections that you assessed in the Components section, circle the assigned points on this review sheet and then total the circled points.

Components	Points				
1. Executive Summary	5	4	3	2	1
2. Description of the Innovation	5	4	3	2	1
3. Marketing	5	4	3	2	1
4. Operations	5	4	3	2	1
5. Management	5	4	3	2	1
6. Financial	5	4	3	2	1
7. Critical Risks	5	4	3	2	1
8. Succession Planning	5	4	3	2	1
9. Milestone Schedule	5	4	3	2	1
10. Appendix	5	4	3	2	1
	Total Points:				

Scoring:

50 points	— **Outstanding! The ideal innovation plan. Solid!**
45–49 points	— **Very Good.**
40–44 points	— **Good. The plan is sound with a few areas that need to be polished.**
35–39 points	— **Above Average. The plan has some good areas but needs improvement before presentation.**
30–34 points	— **Average. Some areas are covered in detail yet certain areas show weakness.**
20–29 points	— **Below Average. Most areas need greater detail and improvement.**
Below 20 points	— **Poor. Plan needs to be researched and documented much better.**

The answer is often quite simple. Their innovation plans never actually included the last critical step—action planning. Action planning is the process of taking good ideas and breaking them into manageable steps that can be accomplished and measured. Action planning maximizes success and minimizes failure.

Action planning is often ignored because it is believed that there is "always a market for good ideas" or that the "cream will always rise to the top." Entrepreneurs and innovators are often so in love with their ideas that they can't understand why everyone is not begging to help them put the idea into action.

The reality is that the action planning and implementation phases are often the most difficult. Ironically, developing an action plan often seems to be an exercise in the obvious. That is, everybody surely knows what we have to do to get this idea in place. The action plan is the opportunity to test this assumption. It is the chance to put down in writing exactly how the idea is to be implemented and at the same time make sure that everyone involved knows all the steps.

At the end of this section you will find a set of forms that can be used for constructing your action plan. Please refer to them as you read this section.

The Action Planning Process

Action planning is a clear process with no shortcuts. The steps below demonstrate this process:

- choosing the team;
- naming and describing the specific goal to be accomplished;
- describing the current reality that forms the environment for the project;
- discerning the key actions that need to be performed;
- creating a calendar of actions and assignments for team members.

Each of these outcomes is critical for the success of any project. Without accomplishing each of the above, innovation success is seriously jeopardized.

Naming the Goal

Without specific targets, projects lose focus and flounder. When goals are not clear and specific, the steps to be taken are also not clear. In the space below, write a specific goal statement for your innovation. For example, a goal for a mail order business might be: "To have my first sales catalogue in the mail by June 1."

Write a goal statement for your business in the space below.

Goal Statement:_____

_____

_____

_____

The Current Reality

The next step is to look at the environment of your business. You must be able to identify those aspects of the project that are its strengths and, at the same time, list the benefits that successful achievement of the goal will bring to the organization.

You also must be prepared to face up to its weaknesses and the potential threats that exist to the project. This process is called a force field analysis, where you attempt to identify forces working in favor of success and those working against success. Based on this analysis, you must be able to determine if the balance of forces favors success.

A well-done force field analysis will allow you to align the critical resources necessary for the success of the project. Failure to perform this step may result in unanticipated resistance to a project or lack of an appropriate support base. It is often easier to deal with a problem if it is identified in advance.

Use the current reality worksheet to summarize the success and failure forces confronting your business. Don't be too concerned about the number of factors in each category. What is more important is the relative weight of the factors. A strong success factor may outweigh several irritating failure forces.

Determining Key Actions

The heart of the action plan is the identification of the specific actions to be performed. There is no one best way to accomplish this activity; however, the key is to assure that everyone on your team has an opportunity to provide input. Provided at the end of this section are multiple copies of action identification sheets. Ask each of your team members to take a few minutes and try to identify the action steps that must be taken in order for you to reach your business goal.

Organizing Action Clusters

Once a large group of steps are identified, some editing must take place. Items that are the same can be eliminated as well as those which are not really necessary for project completion. Next, the action steps need to be organized into action clusters.

Action clusters are all actions that relate to one another in some way. For example, there may be several different pieces of financial information that need to be obtained. These can be grouped together in a "financial information" group. The same may be true for acquiring needed equipment. When putting steps into clusters, try to arrange them in the order in which they must be accomplished.

Time for Action

This is a critical element in the process. Once you have organized the steps into clusters, you are ready to make decisions about when each step will be accomplished and by whom. In most cases the steps will be performed by you, but there are several things that may have to be done by your banker, a supplier, or a contractor. By creating a graphic calendar of the action plan, you can make sure everyone knows their assignment and you can keep track of progress. A large chalk or grease board can be used to chart your success.

CALENDAR OF ACTIONS AND ASSIGNMENTS		
(Action Cluster)	(Completion Date)	(Person Responsible)

FIGURE 11.1   Action Planning.

Achieving Success

You now have an action plan that can be used as a tool for achieving the success you desire. You must now put this plan in motion. Everyone has assignments and deadlines. Your job is to build and maintain momentum for your plan.

You must:

- Keep everyone informed and motivated.
- Use milestones with specific dates.
- Update the plan when needed.
- Acknowledge successes, even small ones.

Innovation Action Planning

Choose a Team

In most cases you will need the help of others to bring about meaningful change in your organization. The first step is to identify a group who also has an interest in improving your workgroup. These people can be technical experts, a banker, a lawyer, etc. The real key is that they want you to succeed and are willing to work.

List below potential team members:

1. _____
2. _____
3. _____
4. _____
5. _____
6. _____
7. _____
8. _____
9. _____
10. _____

Deciding the Goal

Name the goal:_____

_____

a. Strengths in your situation that lead toward the goal: _____

_____

_____

_____

b. Weaknesses that threaten the accomplishment:_____

_____

_____

_____

c. Potential benefits of pursuing this course of action:_____

_____

_____

_____

Current Reality Worksheet

Success Forces	Failure Forces
Strengths	**Weaknesses**
_____	_____
_____	_____
_____	_____
_____	_____
_____	_____
_____	_____
_____	_____
_____	_____
Opportunities	**Threats**
_____	_____
_____	_____
_____	_____
_____	_____
_____	_____
_____	_____
_____	_____

Action Steps

Individually list the tasks that will move the project toward the goal (big and small actions).

_____

_____

_____

_____

_____

_____

_____

_____

_____

_____

_____
_____
_____
_____
_____
_____
_____
_____
_____
_____
_____
_____
_____
_____
_____
_____
_____
_____
_____
_____
_____
_____
_____
_____
_____
_____
_____
_____
_____
_____
_____
_____
_____
_____
_____

Action Steps

Individually list the tasks that will move the project toward the goal (big and small actions).

_____
_____

Organize

Group the actions into several clusters of similar activity.

Cluster

*1*_____

*Actions:*_____

_____

_____

_____

_____

_____

Cluster

*2*_____

*Actions:*_____

_____

_____

_____

_____

_____

Cluster

*3*_____

*Actions:*_____

_____

_____

_____

_____

_____

Cluster

*4*_____

*Actions:*_____

_____

_____

_____

_____

_____

Cluster

*5*_____

*Actions:*_____

_____

_____

_____

_____

_____

Summary

This chapter has provided the "road map" for developing an effective innovation plan. Beginning with the important benefits of an innovation plan for the innovator and I-Team as well as for the executive team that evaluates it, we then outlined each segment of an innovation plan. We also provided a complete assessment tool for self-evaluation of the plan. The chapter then described the importance of the action planning process and offered a tool for developing your own action plan. It is hoped that you will be able to utilize these tools in developing an innovation plan and an action plan for your organization.

Innovation-in-Action

Innovation Strategy at Koch Industries

Executives have increasingly embraced corporate entrepreneurship as a strategy for revitalizing their organizations. Koch Industries is an excellent example of an organization that effectively employs a strategy for innovation focusing on three core principles: creating a more supportive environment for innovation, enhancing the creative potential in each employee, and shaping and reinforcing the behaviors required to generate new products, processes, and businesses. Based in Wichita, Kansas, Koch Industries is one of the largest privately owned corporations in the United States, with $100 billion in revenue and more than 70,000 employees. The firm utilizes a self-developed concept called market based management (MBM). According to CFO Steve Feilmeier, the MBM philosophy is:

> based on allowing the freemarket to create long-term value . . . executed by fostering internal entrepreneurialism. Koch Industries is much more interested in hiring people with the right values and beliefs than those with the right skills and knowledge, although [it is necessary that an employee develop] both dimensions (Calabro, 2008).

Specifically, Koch Industries employs the MBM strategy and lives a philosophy with five integral parts: vision, decision rights, knowledge processes, virtue and talents, and incentives (Koch, 2007).

First, Koch focuses on vision and decision rights to create an environment that sets the stage for effective entrepreneurial strategy implementation. According to CEO Charles Koch, vision "begins and ends" with creating value and then implementing strategies that maximize the value for the long term. This value-added perspective is supposed to guide all activities. The firm operationalizes this vision by directing its priorities in two areas: those actions required for staying in business and being legally compliant, and "gap analyses" whereby the risk-adjusted present value of an opportunity is compared with the resources consumed. This quantitative gap analysis process ensures adherence to the vision of creating value.

Koch Industries' employees live this vision by focusing on innovation, operations, trading, transaction excellence, and service to the public sector. An important aspect of the entrepreneurial environment at Koch, decision rights ensure that the proper individuals are in the proper roles, that they have the authority necessary to do their jobs, and that they are held accountable for creating long-term value. Decision rights are viewed as similar to the notion of property rights. Roles are clearly defined, and expectations and standards for behavior are provided. Koch believes that employees with the best "comparative advantage" should make the decision. According to Charles Koch, an individual gains a comparative advantage when they are able to perform an activity more effectively with lower opportunity costs. Company belief holds that everyone is unique, and should look for opportunities where they have the comparative advantage.

Second, Koch Industries emphasizes knowledge processes and virtue and talents. According to Koch, knowledge processes focus on creating, acquiring, sharing, and applying relevant knowledge, and developing systems for measuring and tracking profitability. As stated by CEO Charles Koch, "Knowledge fuels prosperity by signaling and guiding resources to higher-valued uses" (Koch, 2007, p. 101). Activities such as benchmarking, dialogue with specialists, and developing technology and business networks are hallmarks of identifying and creating knowledge resources in the company. Furthermore, employees are sought who have the specific knowledge to successfully perform their roles, and who are willing to share that knowledge with others. Finally, it is believed that knowledge also comes from assessing results. Developing quantitative profit and loss measures and better understanding the drivers of each is the keystone to this assessment. Focusing on virtue and talents ensures that people with the right values, skills, and capabilities are hired, retained, and developed to carry out the vision.

Lastly, Koch understands the importance of incentives to reinforce and shape desired organizational behavior. Company philosophy centers on rewarding people according to the value they create for the organization, not based on job title or tenure. According to Koch Industries, profit is a powerful incentive for entrepreneurs to take risks and satisfy consumer needs. Incentives are utilized to align employee interests with the interests of the company and society. Employees are paid a portion of the value they create. Furthermore, Koch Industries tailors each employee's compensation package to achieve maximum motivation. Employee needs, ability to create value, and time preference for compensation are considered when determining the compensation package.

Koch Industries' adherence to these five core principles has led it to be a global leader in the following sectors: refining and chemicals; process and pollution control equipment and technologies; minerals and fertilizers; fibers and polymers (including Stainmaster and Lycra Spandex); commodity and financial trading and services; and forest and consumer products. The company's business interests originated in refinery machines and evolved into Koch Pipeline, Koch Alaskan Pipeline, INVISTA, and Georgia-Pacific. Koch Industries provides an illustration of how organizations can create a competitive advantage by implementing innovation and corporate entrepreneurship strategies. These strategies necessitate a top–down bottom–up approach, whereby senior management must set the entrepreneurial strategy and provide a supportive organizational environment structure to motivate the deliberate practices of innovation and entrepreneurship by employees at all levels of the organization.

References

Calabro, L. 2008. Koch Industries' Steve Feilmeier: The CFO of the United States' largest private company explains what it's like to not worry about earnings. *CFO Magazine.* Retrieved from www.cfo.com/article.cfm/10317304?f=search.

Koch, C.G. 2007. *The Science of Success: How Market Based Management Built the World's Largest Private Company*, Hoboken, NJ: Wiley.

(Adapted from: Hornsby, J. & Goldsby, M. 2009. Corporate entrepreneurial performance at Koch Industries: a social cognitive framework. *Business Horizons*, 52: 413–419.)

Key Terms

action plan

critical risks

executive summary

financial forecast

harvest strategy

innovation plan

market niche

marketing segment

milestone schedule

planning pitfall

Discussion Questions

1. Describe each of the five planning pitfalls entrepreneurs often encounter.
2. Identify the benefits of an innovation plan (a) for an innovator and (b) for executive-level sources.
3. What are the three major viewpoints to be considered when developing an innovation plan?
4. What are some components to consider in the proper packaging of a plan?
5. Identify five of the ten guidelines to be used for preparing an innovation plan.
6. Briefly describe each of the major segments to be covered in an innovation plan.
7. Why is the summary segment of an innovation plan written last?

8. Why are milestones important to an innovation plan?
9. Describe the "action planning" process.
10. What is innovation action planning?

Notes

1 Hill, Napoleon. 1937. *Think and Grow Rich*, Meridian, CT: The Ralston Society.
2 For additional information on writing effective plans see: Timmons, Jeffrey A., Zacharakis, Andrew & Spinelli, Stephen. 2004. *Business Plans that Work*, New York: McGraw-Hill.
3 Barringer, Bruce R. 2008. *Effective Business Plans*, New York: Prentice Hall.
4 Mason, Colin & Stark, Matthew. 2004. What do investors look for in a business plan? *International Small Business Journal*: 227–248.
5 Kuratko, Donald F. 2017. *Entrepreneurship: Theory, Process and Practice*, 10th ed., Mason, OH: Cengage/Southwestern.
6 Ibid.
7 Kuratko, Donald F. 2015. *The Complete Entrepreneurial Planning Guide*, Bloomington, IN: Kelley School of Business, Indiana University.

12

SCALING MOMENTUM FOR DISRUPTION

Sequencing markets correctly is underrated, and it takes discipline to expand gradually. The most successful companies make the core progression—to first dominate a specific niche and then scale to adjacent markets—a part of their founding narrative.

~Peter Thiel[1]

Introduction

A final challenge confronting senior-level managers is how to scale any innovative momentum that is developed. More importantly, they need to accelerate that momentum so the innovative pace continues. There are two major aspects of this challenge: the role of managers and the role of the organization.

The Role of Managers

As we discussed in Chapter 8, there are critical strategic roles that managers have in the innovation process.[2] Senior, middle, and first-level managers have distinct responsibilities with respect to each sub-process. Thus, organizations pursuing corporate entrepreneurship strategies likely exhibit a cascading yet integrated set of entrepreneurial actions at the senior, middle, and first levels of management.[3] At the senior level, managers act in concert with others throughout the firm to identify effective means through which new businesses can be created or existing ones reconfigured. Corporate entrepreneurship is pursued in light of environmental opportunities and threats, with the purpose of creating a more effective alignment between the company and conditions in its external environment. The entrepreneurial actions expected of middle-level managers are framed around the need for this group to propose and interpret entrepreneurial opportunities that might create new business for the firm or increase the firm's competitiveness in current business domains. First-line managers exhibit the "experimenting" role as they surface the operational ideas for innovative improvements. An important interpretation of previous research has been the belief that managers would surface ideas for entrepreneurial actions from every level of management, especially the first line and middle levels. Therefore, managers across levels are jointly responsible for their organization's entrepreneurial actions.

In order to maintain this "entrepreneurial mindset," managers must assume certain ongoing responsibilities.[4] The first responsibility involves *framing the challenge*. In other words, there needs to be a clear definition of the specified challenges that everyone involved with innovative projects should address. It is important to think in terms of, and regularly reiterate, the challenge. Second, leaders have the responsibility to *absorb the uncertainty* that is perceived by team members. Entrepreneurial leaders make uncertainty less daunting. The idea is to create the self-confidence that lets others act on opportunities without seeking managerial permission. Employees must not be overwhelmed by the complexity inherent in many innovative situations. A third responsibility is to *define gravity*— that is, what must be accepted and what cannot be accepted. The term *gravity* is used to capture limiting conditions. For example, there is gravity on Earth, but that does not mean it must limit our lives. If freed from the psychological cage of believing that gravity makes flying impossible, creativity can permit us to invent an airplane or spaceship. This is what the entrepreneurial mindset is all about— seeing opportunities where others see barriers and limits. A fourth responsibility of entrepreneurial leadership involves *clearing obstacles* that arise as a result of internal competition for resources. This can be a problem especially when the entrepreneurial innovation is beginning to undergo significant growth. A growing venture will often find itself pitted squarely against other (often established) aspects of the firm in a fierce internal competition for funds and staff. Creative tactics, political skills, and an ability to regroup, reorganize, and attack from another angle become invaluable. A final responsibility for entrepreneurial leaders is to keep their finger on the pulse of the project. This involves constructive monitoring and control of the developing opportunity.

An organization's sustained effort in corporate entrepreneurship is contingent upon individual members continuing to undertake innovative activities and upon positive perceptions of the activity by the organization's executive management, which will in turn support the further allocation of necessary organizational antecedents.[5]

The Role of the Organization

The dynamic entrepreneurial organizations of this twenty-first century will be ones that are capable of merging strategic action with entrepreneurial action on an ongoing basis.[6] This type of entrepreneurial organization could be conceptualized in the "new thinking" that is needed by today's leaders. A comparison of philosophies in traditional leadership versus the philosophies in entrepreneurial leadership is shown in Table 12.1. As has been shown in much of the recent literature, the strategic mindset must lean towards the more innovative concepts in leading organizations today. It is important to recognize a critical factor that researchers Jeffrey Covin and Dennis Slevin[7] point out. The "hardware" side of organizations (strategy, structure, systems, and procedures) is the contextual framework within which individuals take their behavioral cues. The "software" side of organizations (culture and climate), while more subtle and informal, is the locus for the acceptance or rejection of true entrepreneurial activity. Leaders cannot simply send an edict to the organizational members that entrepreneurial activity and innovations are to take place. Rather they must focus on the development of an entrepreneurial climate to facilitate the entrepreneurial actions of organizational members.

To establish an entrepreneurial mindset, organizations need to provide the freedom and encouragement required for employees to develop their ideas. This is often a problem in enterprises because many top managers do not believe entrepreneurial ideas can be nurtured and developed in their environment. They also find it difficult to implement policies that encourage freedom and unstructured activity. But managers need to develop policies that will help innovative people reach their full potential. Five important steps for establishing this new thinking follow:

- Set *explicit innovation goals*. These goals need to be mutually agreed by the employee and management so that specific steps can be achieved.
- Create a system of *feedback* and *positive reinforcement*. This is necessary for potential innovators or creators of ideas to realize that acceptance and reward exist.
- Emphasize *individual responsibility*. Confidence, trust, and accountability are key features in the success of any innovative program.
- Provide *rewards* for innovative ideas. Reward systems should enhance and encourage others to risk and to achieve.
- *Do not punish failures*. Real learning takes place when failed projects are examined closely for what can be learned by individuals. In addition, individuals must feel free to experiment without fear of punishment.[8]

Asking the Key Questions

What can a corporation do to re-engineer its thinking to foster the innovative process? The organization needs to examine and revise its management philosophy. Many enterprises have obsolete ideas about cooperative cultures, management techniques, and the values of managers and employees. Unfortunately, doing old tasks more efficiently is not the answer to new challenges; a new culture with new values has to be developed. Although each enterprise must develop a philosophy most appropriate for its own entrepreneurial process, a number of key questions can assist in establishing the type of process an organization has. Organizations can use the following questions to assess their enterprise. Applying these questions helps them feed back to the planning process for a proper approach.

- *Does your company encourage innovative thinking?* Will individuals receive the corporation's blessing for their self-appointed idea creations? Some corporations foolishly try to appoint people to carry out an innovation when in fact the ideas must surface.

- *Does your company provide ways for innovators to stay with their ideas?* When the innovation process involves switching the people working on an idea—that is, handing off a developing business or product from a committed innovator to whoever is next in line—that person is often not as committed as the originator of a project.

- *Are people in your company permitted to do the job in their own way, or are they constantly stopping to explain their actions and ask for permission?* Some organizations push decisions up through a multilevel approval process so that the doers and the deciders never even meet.

- *Has your company evolved quick and informal ways to access the resources to try new ideas?* Innovators usually need discretionary resources to explore and develop new ideas. Some companies give employees the freedom to use a percentage of their time on projects of their own choosing and set aside funds to explore new ideas when they occur. Others control resources so tightly that nothing is available for the new and unexpected. The result is nothing new.

- *Has your company developed ways to manage many small and experimental innovations?* Today's corporate cultures favor a few well-studied, well-planned attempts to hit a home run. In fact, nobody bats 1,000, and it is better to try more times with less careful and expensive preparation for each.

- *Is your system set up to encourage risk taking and to tolerate mistakes?* Innovation cannot be achieved without risk and mistakes. Even successful innovation generally begins with blunders and false starts.

- *Are people in your company more concerned with new ideas or with defending their turf?* Because new ideas almost always cross the boundaries of existing patterns of organization, a jealous tendency to "turf protection" blocks innovation.

- *How easy is it to form functionally complete, autonomous teams in your corporate environment?* Small teams with full responsibility for developing an innovation solve many of the basic problems, yet, some companies resist their formation.

Developing a corporate innovative philosophy provides a number of advantages. One is that this type of atmosphere often leads to the development of new products and services and helps the organization expand and grow. A second is it creates a workforce that can help the enterprise maintain its competitive posture. A third is it promotes a climate conducive to high achievers and helps the enterprise motivate and keep its best people.

This new millennium has been characterized as an age of instant information, ever-increasing development and application of technology, experimental change, revolutionary processes, and global competition. It is now an age filled with turbulence and paradox. The words used to describe the new innovation regime of the twenty-first century are: *Dream, Create, Explore, Invent, Pioneer,* and *Imagine*! As scholars and researchers dedicated to the field of entrepreneurship and corporate innovation, we believe this is a point in time when the gap between what can be imagined and what can be accomplished has never been smaller. It is a time requiring innovative vision, courage, calculated risk-taking, and strong leadership. It is simply *"the innovative imperative of the 21st Century."*[9]

Innovation-in-Action

Haier's Process of Consumer-Based Innovation

Corporate innovation is a continuously evolving process for any organization. Today there are many successful companies using consumer feedback to spawn "design innovation." One such company is Haier, a Chinese major home appliance manufacturing company. Haier was founded in 1984, and for over seven years produced one single refrigerator model. In the early 1990s, they adopted a diversification strategy rather than rely on this single product strategy. Since then Haier has grown rapidly to become the fourth-ranked white appliance manufacturer in the world. Haier is the world market share leader in two of the largest major home appliance industries, and they manufacture appliances in over 96 unique product categories worldwide. Haier's culture of innovation has also led to more than 7,000 patents.

One of the major reasons for Haier's success has been an ability to design innovations based on consumer feedback. Starting in 1999, Haier has developed into a horizontally-structured organization. One of the goals of this structural change was to reduce the distance from the company's engineers and managers to the customers and end-users. Reducing this distance was crucial to obtaining the information flow of customers' individualized demands.

This information flow from the consumer to Haier's managers and engineers has led to many customer-oriented design innovations. When the Chinese government distributed over $2 billion in subsidies to rural consumers for buying home appliances, Haier took advantage. Based on extremely unique consumer feedback from these rural consumers, Haier invented several new appliances. Many rural consumers were complaining that excess dirt was clogging up their washing machines. Many of these consumers were farmers and these farmers were washing potatoes and vegetables in their new washing machines, which was indeed the cause of the clogging. The customers thought that these washing machines should be able to wash other items beyond normal laundry. Instead of telling the customers to stop this behavior, Haier instead asked their engineers to modify their existing products. New washing machines were designed with wider pipes that would not clog with dirt or vegetable peels. New products were designed and manufactured that could wash laundry, potatoes, and vegetables. Haier even took these iterations a step further. They began designing washing machines that could wash and peel potatoes, and they developed a washing machine that could make cheese from goats' milk.

On the refrigerator side of new products, Haier launched a "design the ice-box yourself" campaign. This campaign invited both existing users and potential users to participate as co-innovators and has since resulted in more than 1 million customized orders per year.

Hundreds of similar design innovations helped Haier win the market leadership in China's rural provinces, and this led to billions of dollars of new revenue. Although several other factors have contributed to their success, the ability to increase the acceptability of its products among rural Chinese was a significant cornerstone to Haier's success.

(Adapted from: www.plm.automation.siemens.com/CaseStudyWeb/dispatch/viewResource.html?resourceId=11003; www.jamieandersononline.com/uploads/Serving_the_World_s_Poor.pdf; www.springerlink.com/content/x0h57107671l7r4/fulltext.pdf; www.haier.com/images/pdf/backgrounder.pdf; http://blogs.forbes.com/china/2010/06/17/haier-a-chinese-company-that-innovates/ websites accessed January 8, 2011.)

Key Terms

absorb the uncertainty

clearing obstacles

framing the challenge

gravity

"hardware" side of organizations

innovation goals

innovative imperative

"software" side of organizations

Discussion Questions

1. Briefly describe the roles of managers in the innovation strategy.
2. Describe how senior, middle, and first-line managers impact entrepreneurial actions.
3. Identify the four responsibilities of managers in maintaining the "entrepreneurial mindset."
4. Explain "gravity" in terms of an entrepreneurial mindset.
5. Describe the "hardware side" of organizations.
6. Describe the "software side" of organizations.
7. What five important steps help an organization establish innovative thinking?
8. Identify some of the key questions that need to be asked in order to assist in the planning of any innovative activity.

Notes

1 Thiel, Peter. 2014. *Zero to One*, New York: Crown Business Books, p. 56.
2 Floyd, S. & Lane, P. 2000. Strategizing throughout the organization: managing role conflict in strategic renewal. *Academy of Management Review*, 25: 154–177; and Kuratko, D.F., Covin, J.G. & Hornsby, J.S. 2014. Why implementing corporate innovation is so difficult. *Business Horizons*, 57(5): 647–655.
3 Kuratko, D.F., Ireland, R.D., Covin, J.G. & Hornsby, J.S. 2005. A model of middle level managers' entrepreneurial behavior. *Entrepreneurship Theory and Practice*, 29(6): 699–716.
4 McGrath, R.G. & MacMillan, I. 2000. *The Entrepreneurial Mindset*, Boston: Harvard Business Press.
5 Morris, M.H., Kuratko, D.F. & Covin, J.G. 2011. *Corporate Entrepreneurship and Innovation*, Mason, OH: Cengage/SouthWestern Publishers.
6 Ireland, R.D., Hitt, M., Camp, S.M. & Sexton, D.L. 2001. Integrating entrepreneurship and strategic management actions to create firm wealth. *Academy of Management Executive*, 15(1): 49–63.
7 Covin, J.G. & Slevin, D.P. 2002. The entrepreneurial imperatives of strategic leadership, in Hitt, M., Ireland, R.D., Camp, M. & Sexton, D. (eds.), *Strategic Entrepreneurship: Creating a New Mindset*, Oxford: Blackwell Publishers.
8 Kuratko, D.F. 2017. *Entrepreneurship: Theory, Process, and Practice*, 10th ed., Mason, OH: Cengage/South-Western Publishing.
9 Kuratko, D.F. 2009. The entrepreneurial imperative of the 21st century. *Business Horizons*, 52(5): 421–428.

APPENDIX

An Innovation Plan for GlaxoSmithKline (GSK) in Africa: The Aquafresh Teacher Academy

Company and Project Background

GlaxoSmithKline (GSK) was a global pharmaceutical and healthcare company based in the United Kingdom with $76 billion in assets, $41 billion in annual revenue, and $3 billion in annual profit. The company's purpose was to "to help people do more, feel better and live longer" supported by a goal "to be one of the world's most innovative, best performing and trusted healthcare companies." The business of the company divided itself between pharmaceuticals, vaccines, and consumer healthcare. Although consumer healthcare was half as profitable as pharmaceuticals and vaccines and only a fourth of company revenue, it was a more nimble product category because of less government regulation and quicker inventory turnover enjoyed by over-the-counter (OTC) medical products.[1]

Although global growth was strong, there were disproportionate growth opportunities in developed and emerging economies. Markets in slow-growing developed countries were saturated with competitors. Success required expensive marketing and carefully positioned differentiation. In contrast, markets in emerging economies offered expansive opportunity. Although incomes were lower, markets grew quickly and new middle class households could now afford branded consumer healthcare products.

South Africa offered GSK opportunity for unique growth in an emerging economy. GSK products were in South Africa as early as 1902. The company built manufacturing facilities in the 1950s and made South Africa a base for consumer healthcare production and sales that served the Middle East and the rest of Africa. Total OTC medical purchases in South Africa were $1.4 billion and grew 9 percent per year (compared with 5 percent in the United States). Purchase of all GSK products gave the company an 8 percent market share.[2] Grand-Pa Headache Powder was GSK's most popular product with a 15 percent share of the analgesics (pain relief) market, up from 12 percent just ten years earlier. Grand-Pa was the South African brand leader in the analgesics category.[3] While growth was steady, GSK's South African subsidiary felt that innovation could drive a stronger market presence.

Grand-Pa Headache Powder was a long-established local product sold only in South Africa and surrounding countries. One dose consisted of white powder packaged in a white paper sachet that customers unfolded to mix with water. Aspirin, acetaminophen, and caffeine combined to form the powder. A new tablet version of Grand-Pa sold in limited quantities. South Africans visually associated the brand with the blue-and-white picture of a comforted young girl seated in the lap of an older bearded grandfather figure to read a book together. Grand-Pa competed most closely with Panado and Disprin. The market perceived Disprin as a quick-acting source of targeted pain relief. In contrast, consumers received Panado as a less-intense, slower-acting family product. Grand-Pa also delivered quick relief, but customers enjoyed it at a much lower price than Disprin and Panado. For a long time, Grand-Pa was the only product available in single doses (one sachet) at retail shops. Affordability and access gave Grand-Pa high market share in less affluent communities, especially within the townships where black South Africans were forced to live under Apartheid racial segregation laws that ended in 1994. GSK did not want to take its strong market position in townships for granted. Competitors aggressively targeted the fast-growing township economies. GSK sought innovation that strengthened Grand-Pa's brand proposition in the townships beyond existing strength in price and packaging.[4]

Townships offered companies access to large numbers of customers in densely-populated settlements deliberately engineered to achieve racial segregation. Apartheid land planning located townships close to mines and industrial districts to ensure supplies of cheap labor but far from Caucasian residential and business communities. After Apartheid, township populations grew as they absorbed migrants from rural South Africa and other countries in Africa. Although poor, townships offered a high concentration of customers who spent money, especially on fast moving consumer goods (FMCG) such as beverages, toiletries, and OTC medical products. Brand development for a global company like GSK was difficult in a township. After decades of racial oppression, residents did not trust outsiders, especially if there was a legacy of alignment with Apartheid. Through marketing and engagement, a company new to townships had to show residents in a culturally-relevant way its commitment to a permanent community presence that generated social good. Additionally, a company had to distribute its products through a fragmented system of social networks. Economic activity in townships was informal. Roads did not accommodate large delivery trucks, high-volume national retailers had no presence, and township businesses and consumers rarely exchanged money through the banking system. Companies had to rely on word-of-mouth instead of mass advertising to build brand awareness. Even though Grand-Pa was already a market leader, GSK needed to re-engineer marketing and distribution to gain new customers and win more market share in the townships.[5]

Spaza shops were an important point-of-sale for Grand-Pa Headache Powder in the townships. They populated every township corner and were the main source of groceries and household products for township residents. In these establishments, a shopper asked the attendant through a gated service window for the products she wished to purchase. The attendant then gathered the desired items from behind the partition and processed the sale. Spazas were born out of informal economic activity. They had little access to water and electricity and faced constant threat from robbery. Spaza owners often had limited literacy, recorded few if any transactions, possessed no bank account, and enjoyed no access to credit. The few spaza shops that were profitable had no feasible way to scale. A harsh business environment kept the income of most spaza owners at a subsistence level.[6]

Although spaza shops were a strong channel of retail entry into township markets, their nature of business seeded several specific challenges for aggressive growth of Grand-Pa sales. High fixed costs created by a small scale of operation kept prices higher than in larger more formal retail shops. Because placement on shop shelves did not drive sales in a spaza shop (shoppers instead requested products at the service window), the ability to leverage package visuals to attract customers was limited. GSK typically relied upon customer-solicited consultation with pharmacists to drive sales within stores. Government regulations prohibited free samples or company-sponsored promotion. The limited education of spaza shop owners, though, constrained their ability to guide buying choices. GSK as a global pharmaceutical company was also an impediment. Township residents distrusted large corporations because of historical association with institutional structures under Apartheid. Altogether, these challenges associated with spaza shops generated barriers that innovation at GSK needed to overcome.

Since they were the anchor of Grand-Pa's presence in the township market, GSK made spaza shops the focus of corporate innovation efforts. GSK collaborated with the Gordon Institute of Business Science at the University of Pretoria to launch as a pilot the "Grand-Pa Spaza Academy" to upskill shop owners and improve their capacity to manage business. To an inaugural class of 63 spaza shop owners, the program delivered 13 business acumen modules over three months focused upon topics such as inventory control, marketing, business finance, and human resource management. Instruction included coaching and mentoring. Outcomes suggested success. Among program graduates, four in five reported an increase in weekly sales and one in five grew enough to hire additional employees.[7]

The "Grand-Pa Spaza Academy" as a fully credentialed new venture within GSK could theoretically strengthen township supply chains and generate returns for stockholders. Shop owners with new knowledge would better price and market their products and sustain inventories that are more consistent. Profits from heightened success could fund new business growth and employment. Investment in the success of shop owners might win favor among township residents who would begin to accept GSK as a positive business citizen within their communities. An imbedded township presence would deepen GSK's knowledge of customers and enable product portfolio expansion beyond Grand-Pa. Success of the Academy as an enterprise would not dramatically increase net income for GSK South Africa in the short run. While social goodwill from the project would generate good press and incrementally strengthen Grand-Pa's brand equity in the townships, ultimate returns for GSK were more long term as the Academy worked to strengthen the business environments that drove Grand-Pa sales.

The Academy enabled a different type of innovation at GSK. Innovation at GSK typically focused on product chemistry improvements that required several years to commercialize. The Academy instead changed the business model around the product by improving value for the customer in the "last mile" of the supply chain. The "last mile" for traditional fast moving consumer goods (FCMG) companies in informal markets such as townships was difficult to navigate. Data on inventories, location of shops, and consumer behavior was difficult if not impossible to access. A long-term partnership with spaza shops through the Academy provided GSK a unique presence in this "last mile." This was an opportunity not shared by competitors to learn and gather market insight. Knowledge gained could be a source of advantage not only for Grand-Pa, but also for other consumer health products offered by GSK. Enjoyment of exclusive information about South Africa's fastest growing consumer market emphasized the long-term nature of the returns from this investment in innovation.[8]

With the Academy pilot now a success, GSK needed an innovation plan to broaden and scale the concept and win internal funding. The pilot touched less than a hundred spaza shops. Market transformation for GSK ultimately meant impact upon tens of thousands of spaza shops. Success required growth of sales in Grand-Pa and other GSK consumer health products. Success also meant opportunity for GSK to better customize products for township communities based on knowledge it gained from engagement through the Academy. GSK needed an innovation plan that convinced senior executives of bold value creation for stakeholders and stockholders. The following presents a potential innovation plan that fulfills this need and illustrates application of previously offered concepts and templates.

Innovation Plan: Aquafresh Teacher Academy

Executive Summary

This five-year project expands the Grand-Pa Spaza Academy to serve 10,000 spaza shop owners. A Teacher Academy is launched to train 7,000 teachers to deliver personal and oral hygiene instruction to students. Teachers distribute coupons to students for free Aquafresh toothpaste samples (another GSK product). Through use of technology, student families receive promotions that drive business at spaza shops registered with the Spaza Academy. The combined impact of the Spaza Academy and the Teacher Academy is a 20 percent increase in annual GSK sales at participating spaza shops. GSK revenue increases R11.5 million (R denotes units of South

African currency, the rand, which typically trades at R13 for US$1) by the end of year five and the project generates an internal rate of return of 18 percent. The project is supported by five new salaried staff with experience in inclusive markets. Implementation includes expanded partnership with the University of Pretoria and construction of a new technology platform that connects GSK with spaza shops, customers, and teachers. Market data from township business transactions allows GSK to understand supply chain dynamics within the "last mile" of product delivery within South Africa's poorer communities. The company is able to expand sales while also enhancing perception of good corporate citizenship.

Innovation Description

The Grand-Pa Spaza Academy scales to graduate 10,000 spaza shop owners over four years in Johannesburg, Cape Town, and Durban. GSK also launches the Aquafresh Teacher Academy to train 7,000 teachers over four years on personal and dental hygiene instruction for children. Each teacher receives a booklet with 100 coupons redeemable for a toothbrush and free tube of Aquafresh at a GSK-registered spaza shop. GSK-registered shops are Spaza Academy graduates or future enrollees. Coupons are distributed to students for their family members to redeem. When the coupon is redeemed, the shopkeeper asks for the cell phone number of the customer so that the customer can receive text message promotions and discounts directly from GSK for purchases at the same spaza shop. Each coupon is coded so that GSK can trace redemption back to an individual teacher who completed the Teacher Academy. For six months after completion of the Teacher Academy, the teacher receives her own text message promotions and discounts on GSK products proportional to the volume of purchases traced to cell phone numbers associated with coupons she distributed to her students.

Scaling the Spaza Academy and launching the Teacher Academy fits well with GSK's desired market presence in the townships. The Spaza Academy spurs income creation for spaza shop owners and the Teacher Academy furthers public health goals with free access to a toothbrush and toothpaste. These positive outcomes strengthen perception of GSK as a productive corporate citizen in township communities. The trade of cell phone numbers for free toothbrushes and toothpaste allows GSK to link a spaza shop with an individual customer who is connected to a Teacher Academy graduate. The six-month reward period that follows the Teacher Academy incentivizes educators to reinforce hygiene instruction and motivate students to encourage good habits and behavior at home. This along with promotions and discounts sent by GSK directly to student households increase sales of GSK products at individual spaza shops. Loyalty of a spaza shop owner to GSK is reinforced not only by connection to the Spaza Academy but also by customers driven to the owner's shop by GSK. An ability to directly connect with customers and spaza shops and, furthermore, to link customers with individual spaza shops provides newly-enabled data on the "last mile" of GSK products within the townships that is otherwise impractical to collect.

Marketing Segment

Project success depends upon delivery of results by both academies. GSK must yield 10,000 Spaza Academy graduates that implement best practices that they are taught. The Teacher Academy must touch 7,000 teachers who distribute coupons and motivate enthusiasm among students to change hygiene behavior for themselves and within their families. Success of the pilot offers solid proof of concept for the Spaza Academy. Sales increased among four in five participants and one in five grew enough to hire additional employees. Half of participants implemented formal accounting and inventory systems after graduation. Good instruction adapted lessons to business decisions within the context of township environments. Not only did participants retain and apply concepts, but they felt pride in completion of a formal university-sponsored program (and reception of a certificate to validate it), especially when many had not completed formal secondary schooling. Success in collaboration with the University of Pretoria on the Spaza Academy spurs expansion of the partnership for the Teacher Academy. The School of Dentistry leverages undergraduate students in delivery of dental hygiene education and oral health services within community schools. This complements the goals of the government's Integrated School Health Policy that is a collaboration between the National Department of Health and the National Department of Basic Education to implement programs that promote development of lifetime healthy behaviors among young students.[9] Existing public health promotion efforts and broad health education research on how to motivate hygienic behavior informs a progressive and effective curriculum for the Teacher Academy.

While the Teacher Academy generates public health benefits, it only benefits GSK if the program translates to higher sales. Each teacher distributes 100 coupons to students for families to redeem at specifically-listed spaza shops (shops affiliated with the Spaza Academy) located within close radius of the school. Aquafresh (13 percent market share) is the second most popular toothpaste on the market behind Colgate (22 percent market share).[10] Priced at just over R10 for a 100 milliliter tube, branded FMCG products like Aquafresh have high attraction among township residents, so the willingness to redeem the coupons is strong. Smartphone penetration among even the poorest township residents is very high. They afford social and commercial connections that significantly improve the quality of life. Transactions of money to complete purchases are often done between cell phones instead of through exchange of cash. Individuals who redeem their coupons for free Aquafresh and a toothbrush are thus accustomed to providing their cell phone number for the purpose of receiving discounts and promotions. Because the discounts and promotions will be specific to the spaza shop where the coupon is redeemed, spaza shop owners have an incentive to ensure customers are directly connected with GSK via their cell phone. The plan budgets funds for discounts up to R100 over six months for a teacher that continues to motivate purchase of GSK products (especially Aquafresh) after the original coupon disbursement. GSK adds to this a competition among Teacher Academy graduates with monetary prizes that further motivate advocacy.

Operations Segment

The first step of implementation is to assemble the salaried staff. Once the team is in place, effort shifts to mapping and choice of township neighborhoods in Johannesburg, Cape Town, and Durban to target for the Spaza Academy and Teacher Academy. Spaza shops and schools should be within the same vicinity. Once specific geographical zones are identified, work begins on curriculum design with partner faculty and staff at the University of Pretoria. Construction of the technology platform also begins to ensure it is ready for launch before the start of year two. The last set of tasks before the pilot cohorts are launched are the recruitment and training of instructors and the start of registration for participating spaza shops and teachers. The last quarter of the fourth cohort sees five pilot cohorts of 50 spaza shop owners for the Spaza Academy and four pilot cohorts of 50 teachers for the Teacher Academy. This increases to eight and five cohorts in the first quarter of year one. Implementation reaches a steady state in the second quarter with 13 Spaza Academy cohorts and nine Teacher Academy cohorts each quarter. This implies instruction of 650 spaza shop owners and 450 teachers each quarter. Soon after the cohorts begin, a program of support for Spaza Academy graduates goes operational. The intended timing of these steps and tasks are summarized in the following Gantt Chart.

Management Segment

The project is led by a director who has led inclusive market business enterprises in South Africa, Brazil, and Mozambique. Two coordinators report to the director. The outreach coordinator held previous positions both within marketing and human resource training at GSK South Africa. The operations coordinator came to GSK from Standard Bank where she recruited and trained township residents to be agents who opened and serviced new bank accounts via cell phones. Two support staff also report to the director. They assist the coordinators with implementation tasks.

Financial Segment

Current annual consumer health sales in South Africa for GSK are R1.8 billion (R denotes units of South African currency, the rand, which typically trades at R13 for US$1) and have grown at 8 percent per year for the last five years.[11] There are 134,000 spaza shops in South Africa that earn R46 billion in total sales, or R343,284 per store. A third of all consumer goods package sales occur through spaza shops, which implies spaza shop revenue of R600 million for GSK or R4,478 per store.[12] The incremental revenue from scaling the Spaza Academy and launching the Teacher Academy will be the expansion of sales in GSK products at spaza shops that graduate from the program and draw business from the same neighborhoods targeted by the Teacher Academy. Program preparation requires one year before enrollment can begin. The project thus does not incur incremental revenue until year two.

EXHIBIT A.1 Project Implementation

	Year 1				Year 2				Year 3				Year 4				Year 5			
	Q1	Q2	Q3	Q4	Q1	Q2	Q3	Q4	Q1	Q2	Q3	Q4	Q1	Q2	Q3	Q4	Q1	Q2	Q3	Q4
Hire Salaried Staff																				
Determine Target Neighborhoods and Map Spaza Shops and Schools																				
Design Curricula with University of Pretoria																				
Build and Test Technology Platform																				
Hire and Train Instructors																				
Recruit and Register Spaza Shops and Teachers																				
Spaza Academy Pilot Cohorts (5 cohorts of 50 in 1st qtr, 8 cohorts in 2nd qtr)																				
Teacher Academy Pilot Cohorts (4 cohorts of 50 in 1st qtr, 5 cohorts in 2nd qtr)																				
Spaza Academy (13 cohorts of 50 each qtr)																				
Teacher Academy (9 cohorts of 50 each qtr)																				
Support Program for Spaza Academy Graduates																				

EXHIBIT A.2 Project Financials

GSK Sales per Spaza Shop = R4,478
Project Impact = 20.0%
Inflation Rate = 6.5%
Weighted Average Cost of Capital = 13.7%

Year	0	1	2	3	4	5
Spaza Academy Graduates	0	0	2500	5000	7500	10000
Teacher Academy Graduates	0	0	1750	3500	5250	7000
Baseline Sales Per Shop (without Project)		R4,478	R4,769	R5,079	R5,409	R5,761
Incremental Revenue per Shop from Project		R896	R954	R1,016	R1,082	R1,152
Total Incremental Revenue from Project		R0	R2,384,535	R5,079,060	R8,113,798	R11,521,593
Spaza Academy Delivery Cost per Enrollee		R1,200	R1,278	R1,361	R1,450	R1,544
Spaza Academy Enrollees		0	2500	2500	2500	2500
Total Spaza Academy Delivery Expense		R0	R3,195,000	R3,402,675	R3,623,849	R3,859,399
Teacher Academy Delivery Cost per Enrollee (including free samples and discounts)		R700	R746	R794	R846	R901
Teacher Academy Enrollees		0	1750	1750	1750	1750
Total Spaza Academy Delivery Expense		R0	R1,304,625	R1,389,426	R1,479,738	R1,575,921
Salary Expense - Project Director		R250,000	R266,250	R283,556	R301,987	R321,617
Salary Expense - Outreach Coordinator		R150,000	R159,750	R170,134	R181,192	R192,970
Salary Expense - Operations Coordinator		R150,000	R159,750	R170,134	R181,192	R192,970
Salary Expense - 2 Support Staff Members		R175,000	R186,375	R198,489	R211,391	R225,132
Total Salary Expense		R725,000	R772,125	R822,313	R875,763	R932,688
University of Pretoria Consulting Expense	R100,000					
Technology Expense	R175,000	R50,000	R50,000	R50,000	R50,000	R50,000
Total Incremental Expense from Project	R175,000	R775,000	R5,321,750	R5,664,414	R6,029,351	R6,418,008
Total Incremental Income from Project	−R175,000	−R775,000	−R2,937,215	−R585,354	R2,084,447	R5,103,584
Net Present Value (after 5 years) =	R406,147					
Internal Rate of Return (after 5 years) =	18.1%					
Payback Period (Years) =	4.5					

The South African consumer price index has increased at an average annual rate of 6.5 percent the past five years. This is the assumed inflation rate for the analysis. Any cash flow assumed in year one will annually inflate itself at this rate for purposes of estimation in future years of the project.

The fixed costs of the project are the management team salaries and expenses to deploy and maintain new technology. New technology is needed to support the promotion and discount program and the exchange of data between GSK and the spaza shops. Based upon current annual market salaries, GSK should budget in year one R250,000 for the director, R150,000 for each of the two coordinators, and R175,000 for each of the two support staff. Add to these a consulting expense of R100,000 payable to University of Pretoria faculty and staff for their assistance in curriculum design and program implementation. The new information technology system is expected to cost R175,000 to construct and install and R50,000 per year to maintain.

Adapting costs of the pilot to delivery of courses on a large scale, GSK estimates a delivery expense in year one of R1,200 per Spaza Academy enrollee and R700 per Teacher Academy enrollee. This covers materials, facilities rent, meals, the instructor stipend, and discounts and promotions extended to teachers and enrollees for GSK products. This also anticipates the expense of free Aquafresh samples for the students of Teacher Academy participants. Operations are adapted for program delivery to 2,500 Spaza Academy enrollees and 1,750 Teacher Academy enrollees per year over four years of implementation.

Based on the positive impact on performance for Spaza Academy graduates in the pilot and the anticipated impact from the Teacher Academy on demand, the analysis assumes an average 20 percent increase in sales of GSK products (that would not otherwise occur) for a spaza owner that completes the program. This equals an average increase of sales of R896 per store in year one (20 percent of baseline sales of R4,478 per shop). Sales increases for GSK are not realized until year two because of a one-year delay to prepare and scale the Academy programs.

An analysis of South African government bond rates and GSK financials suggests a weighted average cost of capital of 13.7 percent. At this discount rate, the net present value for a five-year horizon is positive and the internal rate of return is 18.1 percent. The project is thus expected to generate economic profit. This result does not count any incremental revenue earned beyond year five or any sales increases beyond Spaza Academy graduates tied to the public relations value of national publicity from the project. Inclusion of these benefits would increase the NPV and IRR calculations.

Launch requires a total outlay from corporate funds of R5 million: R1 million now, R3 million after one year, and R1 million after two years. The project is expected to be cash flow positive in year three and to achieve full payback by the end of year five. Funds from within the South African subsidiary are the default source of capital. The Global Health Unit within GSK corporate is a possible source of funds. A proposal would need to outline how the Spaza Academy and Teacher Academy concepts can be replicated within other emerging economy GSK subsidiaries (e.g., Kenya, India, Brazil). Successful integration of the Teacher Academy with government programs could generate some public subsidy of delivery expenses.

Critical Risks Segment

GSK faces the following risks with this project but choices exist for mitigation.

Risk: Spaza shop owners do not share accurate inventory and business performance data with GSK in a sustained and ongoing manner.

Mitigation: Data input is easy and convenient via the technology interface. Shop support after Spaza Academy graduation is consistent and high value and the traffic of customers with shop-specific discounts and promotions from GSK is heavy.

Risk: GSK competitors benefit from the Teacher Academy health campaign and heightened awareness of the value of consumer health and hygiene products.

Mitigation: Promotions and discounts are strong enough to preserve consumer loyalty and ensure GSK sales growth even if competitor sales expand.

Risk: Motivation of students by teachers does not translate to increased purchases by family members.

Mitigation: Design of the Teacher Academy curriculum leverages the newest research on how children become agents of health behavior change within a family unit.

Risk: Average impact on spaza shop performance diminishes with volume of Spaza Academy graduates.

Mitigation: Maintain the ratio of spaza shops to instructors at 50 or less. Consistently monitor performance of graduates and provide interventional support when needed. Continuously tweak content and delivery of the Spaza Academy curriculum to insure high-level impact.

Risk: A high percent of Spaza Academy graduates exit their spaza shops to pursue other economic opportunities.

Mitigation: The Spaza Academy curriculum motivates shop owners to transfer management skills and knowledge to employees and plan for enterprise-ownership succession. GSK maintains its business and data connection with a spaza shop even if the original Spaza Academy graduate leaves. New owners become priority candidates for the Spaza Academy.

Harvest Strategy Segment

The project begins as an internal venture with a director that reports directly to the General Manager of GlaxoSmithKline South Africa (Pty) Limited. At the end of year five, a decision is made to permanently integrate the project into market outreach activities. This occurs if the total incremental revenue produced generates margins high enough to justify continued incurrence of staff salary and program delivery expenses. Technology represents the only fixed assets associated with the project. Permanent integration will shift management of the program to the portfolio of the GSK South Africa Marketing Manager. In the event of discontinuation, the marketing department will assume ownership of the technology assets and redeploy them to other market outreach activities.

Milestone Schedule Segment

The project has a planned life of five years. At the end of five years, the economic value of the project is evaluated. If the economic value meets internal thresholds, the Spaza Academy and Teacher Academy become permanent fixtures within the GSK South Africa marketing division. If thresholds are not met, the program is discontinued and any technology assets are absorbed by the marketing division for alternative corporate purposes. Preparation consumes the first three quarters of year one. Pilot cohorts for spaza shop owners and teachers run the last quarter of year one and the first quarter of year two. These two quarters provide opportunity for assessment and adjustment before delivery runs at full pace in the second quarter of year two.

(**NOTE:** This case background and innovation plan was developed by Philip Powell, associate dean and economics professor at the Indiana University Kelley School of Business, and Tashmia Ismail, CEO of Youth Employment Service (YES) in Johannesburg and instructor at the Gordon Institute of Business Science at the University of Pretoria. Some elements of the case background were adapted from their co-authored book chapter "GSK in Africa: An inclusive strategy case study for low-income market segments" in *Inclusive Innovation for Sustainable Development: Theory and Practice* published in 2016 by Macmillan Publishers. The innovation plan was inspired by a solution to the case presented in 2015 by Kelley School of Business MBA students Hany Farag, Suchit Patel, Mark Rees, and Matthew Roby as part of a course exercise.)

Notes

1 GSK. 2018. *Annual Report 2017*. Retrieved June 3, 2018. www.gsk.com/media/4751/annual-report.pdf.
2 Euromonitor International. 2017. *Consumer Health Care in South Africa*. Passport GMID Country Report, October.
3 Euromonitor International. 2017. *Analgesics in South Africa*. Passport GMID Country Report, October.
4 Ismail, T. & Powell, P. 2016. GSK in Africa: an inclusive strategy case study for low-income market segments, in Agola, N. & Hunter, A. (eds.), *Inclusive Innovation for Sustainable Development: Theory and Practice*, London: Macmillan Publishers Ltd., pp. 129–148.
5 Ibid.
6 Ismail, T. 2013. *The Reinvention of the Spaza: Foreign Ownership and Inclusive Business*. Inclusive Markets Programme, Gordon Institute of Business Science, University of Pretoria.
7 Ibid, Ismail & Powell.
8 Ibid.
9 National Department of Health & National Department of Basic Education. 2012. *Integrated School Health Policy*. Pretoria, South Africa. Retrieved June 8, 2018. www.health-e.org.za/wp-content/uploads/2013/10/Integrated_School_Health_Policy.pdf.
10 Euromonitor International. 2017. *Oral Care in South Africa*. Passport GMID Country Report, July.
11 Ibid, Euromonitor International, 2017, *Consumer Health Care in South Africa*.
12 The Nielsen Company. 2016. *South Africa's Not So Traditional, Traditional Trade*. Retrieved June 7, 2018. www.nielsen.com/content/dam/corporate/us/en/reports-downloads/2016-reports/south-africa-traditional-trade-report-jan-2016.pdf.

INDEX